The Making of a Railway Artist

BRIAN WILSON

recounts the artistic development of his late brother's life

LAWRENCE ROY WILSON

who was fascinated by railways

ROY WILSON – FOREWORD

by Dr Paul Atterbury

"As an artist, the task is to press new and personal insights. If you fail to do this, if you treat yourself as only a camera, you are at best a craftsman."
Roy Wilson

"Reality is only one part of art, the artist's feeling completes it... if you have really been moved by a subject, you will transmit your emotion to it"
Eugene Delacroix (quoted by Roy)

I first met Roy in 2015, the year his long role as President of the Guild of Railway Artists finally ended. At that point I was a relative newcomer to the varied, occasionally challenging but always interesting world of the GRA. In the busy surroundings of the Guild's annual exhibition, Roy was a calming figure, widely respected, friendly, modest, welcoming, easy to talk to and, to my eyes, an exceptional railway artist. When we met again a year later, nothing changed that first impression and it was an honour and a privilege for me to open his final exhibition.

The story of railway painting in Britain is a long and well-documented one, stretching from Turner and David Cox to Eric Ravilious, Terence Cuneo, David Shepherd and other more modern figures, and the diversity of railway artists working today reflects that long historical tradition. In recent decades there has been a shift from the depiction of trains as they are to the detailed recreation of historical scenes, a process that can result in a certain loss of originality and artistic integrity at the expense of nostalgia. Through his long life Roy painted past and present with equal enthusiasm and facility but his work stands out because he was, first and foremost, a fully trained and professional artist for whom command of technique and hard work were merely the means to an end. Roy was many things, engineer, draughtsman, designer, observer of people and nature, transport enthusiast, but the thing that marked his long career was a passion for drawing. He was taught to draw at art schools in the 1940s, a time when drawing was still seen as the necessary foundation for any kind of artistic creativity. This vital foundation helped to define his work through his long career, from sketchbook to finished picture. The other thing that set his work apart was his chosen medium of pastel. Roy was a master of pastel, whose total command of a difficult process brought together a sense of modernism with the traditional techniques of the 18th and 19th centuries. Roy drew light, colour, movement, emotion and structure with a freedom that goes beyond the subject matter, and that gave his work an enduring freshness and appeal that took it well beyond the conventions of railway art.

There is no doubt that Roy Wilson was an exceptional person, and his essential character, and his qualities as an artist have been memorably expressed by the author, his brother Brian. Beyond being an evocative and colourful record of Roy's work as an artist, this book is many things: it places Roy firmly in the pantheon of great modern railway artists, it defines the nature of art as a mixture of observation, technique, originality of ideas, emotion, commitment and hard work, it reveals his painstaking working methods, it offers a valuable insight into Roy's family background and how that shaped his life and it is, above all, a powerful statement of brotherly love.

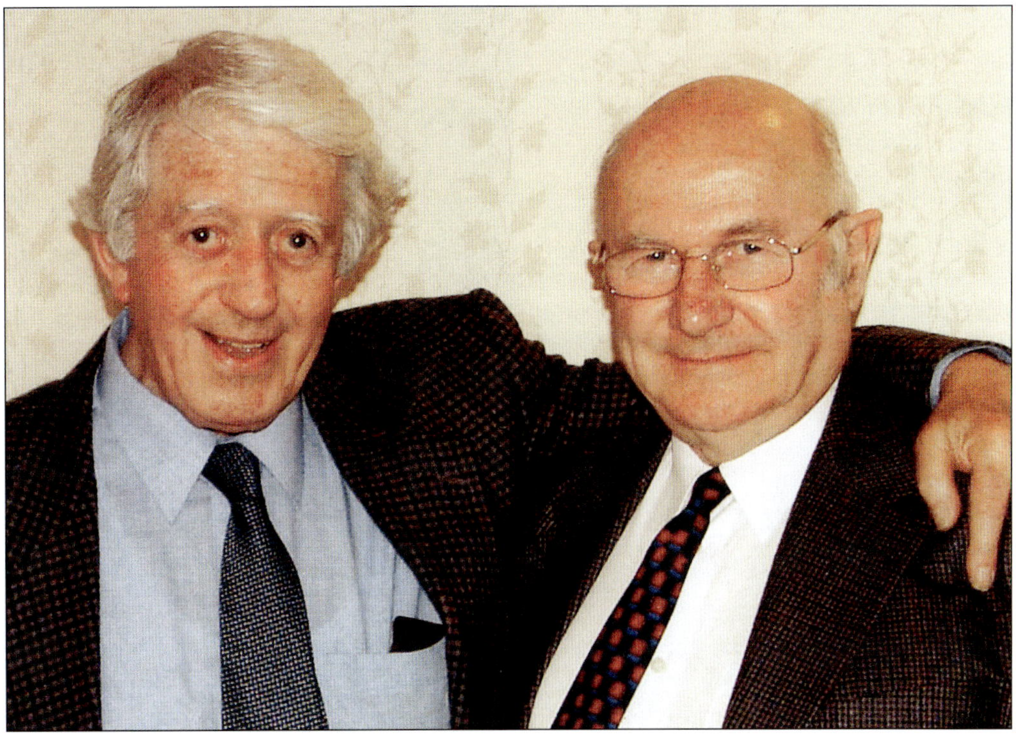

Brothers Lawrence Roy and Brian Wilson, who have always been known as "The two Puddin-eds." (With deference to Mark Twain's book entitled 'Pudd'n Head Wilson'!)

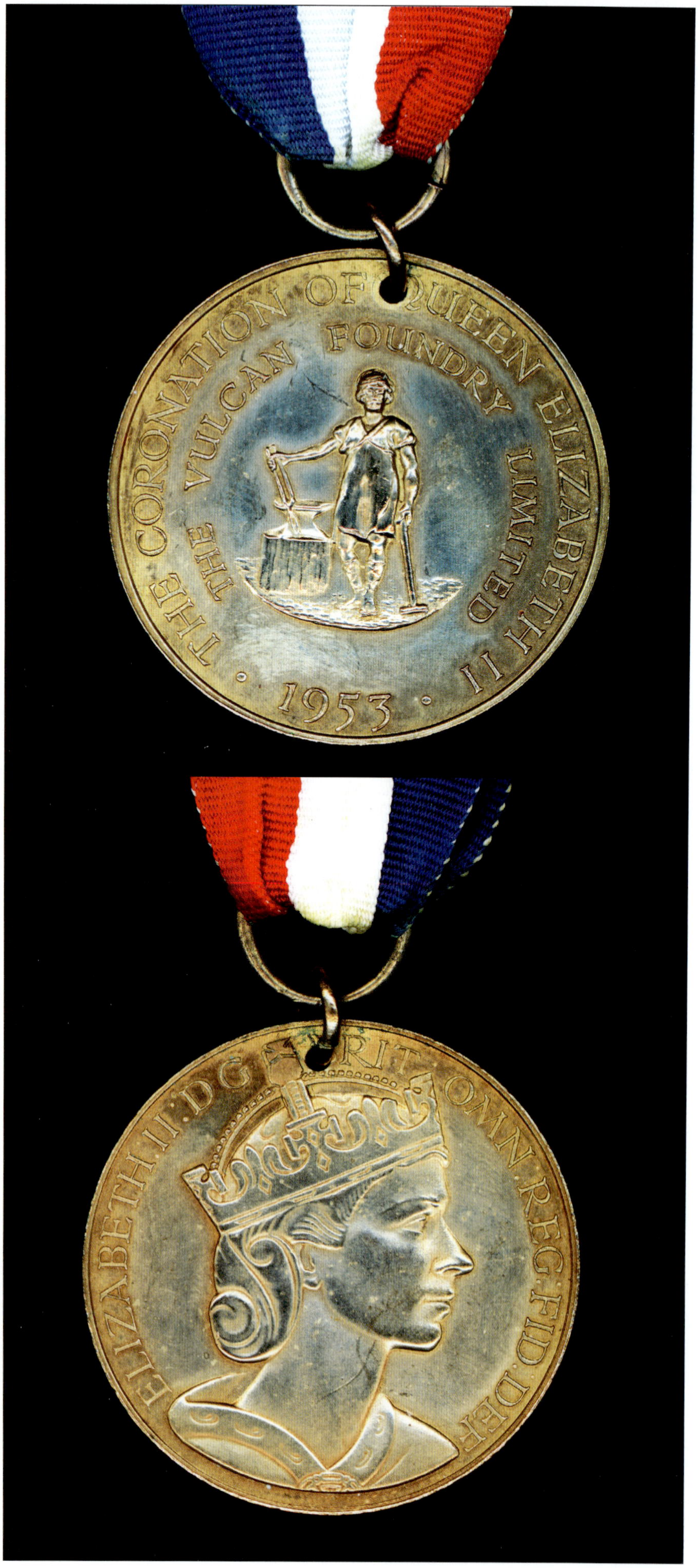

Commemorative medal, issued by the Vulcan Foundry, to celebrate the Coronation of Queen Elizabeth II. This was during Roy's first appointment as a draughtsman at the Vulcan.

Published in 2020 by Barrai Books,
Barrow in Furness
ISBN 978-0-9569709-3-0

Printed by Henry Ling Ltd,
The Dorset Press, Dorchester DT1 1HD.
Design and production by
Trevor Preece: trevor@trpub.net

CONTENTS

INTRODUCTION

Lawrence Roy Wilson came into this world on 17th June 1926. Lawrence is Mother's family name and he has always been known as Roy. He ceased to be an artist around 2016. This date marked an exhibition of some of his work at the Carnforth Heritage Centre, which we arranged to celebrate his 90th Birthday.

For a number of years Roy suffered from Vascular Dementia and no longer knew that he was an excellent artist. He had two of his paintings on the wall in his room, but he did not remember that he painted them. However he thought that they were quite good. This was his comment when I last showed them to him. He died on 4th February, 2019.

However, back to the beginning and the continuation of the introduction to this book. I was not around to witness the arrival of Roy onto the scene. It occurred in a small railway town called Wolverton, in Buckinghamshire. I appeared some seven years later, being born on 28th April 1933. I arrived in another small railway town, called Earlestown, in Lancashire. This marked the start of our lives together and the future events that I recall from our shared experiences.

We have always been very close, as brothers, although throughout our lives we have frequently been very distant geographically. This will emerge during the telling of his story but, first of all, why am I telling this story?

Roy has never sought public recognition of his work. He has never been driven by the commercial opportunities provided by his artistic ability. His satisfaction came from the fact that people liked his work. He was very self-critical, but once he was satisfied with a painting, the fact that other observers liked it was sufficient reward. Later in life he became a member of the Guild of Railway Artists and served as its president. Through this association his work was exhibited and, of course, some paintings were sold. He also acquired some commissions, but this was incidental.

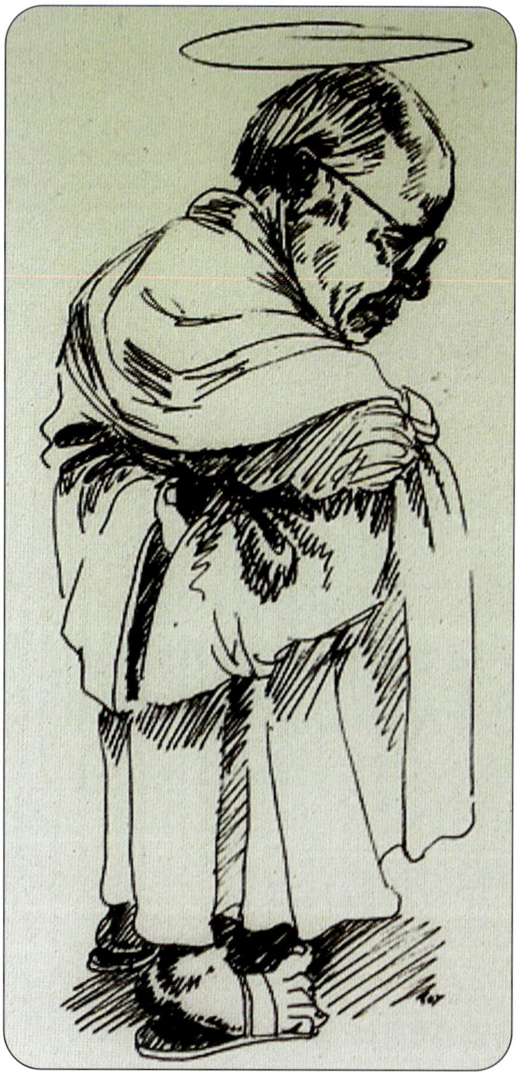

Brother Brian
Courtesy of Lawrence Roy Wilson

It is my desire to rectify that situation and to make his work available in the public domain. It is also my wish to display the development activity that he pursued at art school and college, in order to attain such a high level of artistic ability. In my view, being a competent artist requires more than an inbuilt skill with colour and form which is with one from birth. It also requires some degree of hard work to be competent at displaying that ability.

He spent some time observing life around him. He would sit in one of the arcades in Leeds (while his wife did the shopping) equipped with his sketch book and, over a cup of coffee, he would record people, their dress, attitudes and gestures. These would be included in some of his paintings.

He would also record the planning activity he went through before committing the ideas to canvas and these thoughts are available through log books in which his initial layouts are available.

I have also included material from these log books to illustrate the total effort that went into the production of some of his later paintings. In my view he was a real artist of (you might say) the old school. Good work requires both skill and effort. Roy had both of these in abundance and this is reflected in the standard of his final works.

Finally, the story is being told from my memory. Dates are unimportant although he did sometimes apply dates to his work. I believe that I have got the facts and sequence of events right, but any errors are entirely mine and I apologise if I have mis-represented any aspects of the story. *Brian Wilson*

CHAPTER ONE

The Formative Years

Roy left Patterson Street School in nearby Earlestown at around 16, and went directly to The Technical College, also in Earlestown. Here he took engineering drawing, and other engineering-oriented subjects, to train as a draughtsman. This led to his first job in the drawing office at the Vulcan Foundry.

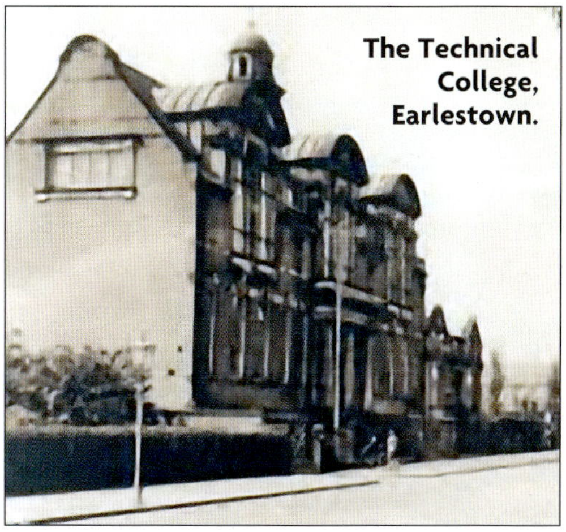

The Technical College, Earlestown.

The Vulcan had been established in 1832 by Charles Tayleur and Robert Stephenson to provide locomotives and other railway equipment for the newly-opened Liverpool to Manchester Railway. Newton-le-Willows (and Earlestown) are about halfway between the two termini – much closer than the works in Newcastle.

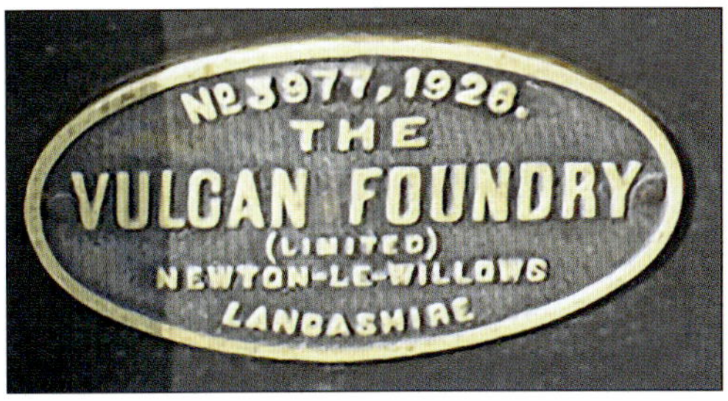

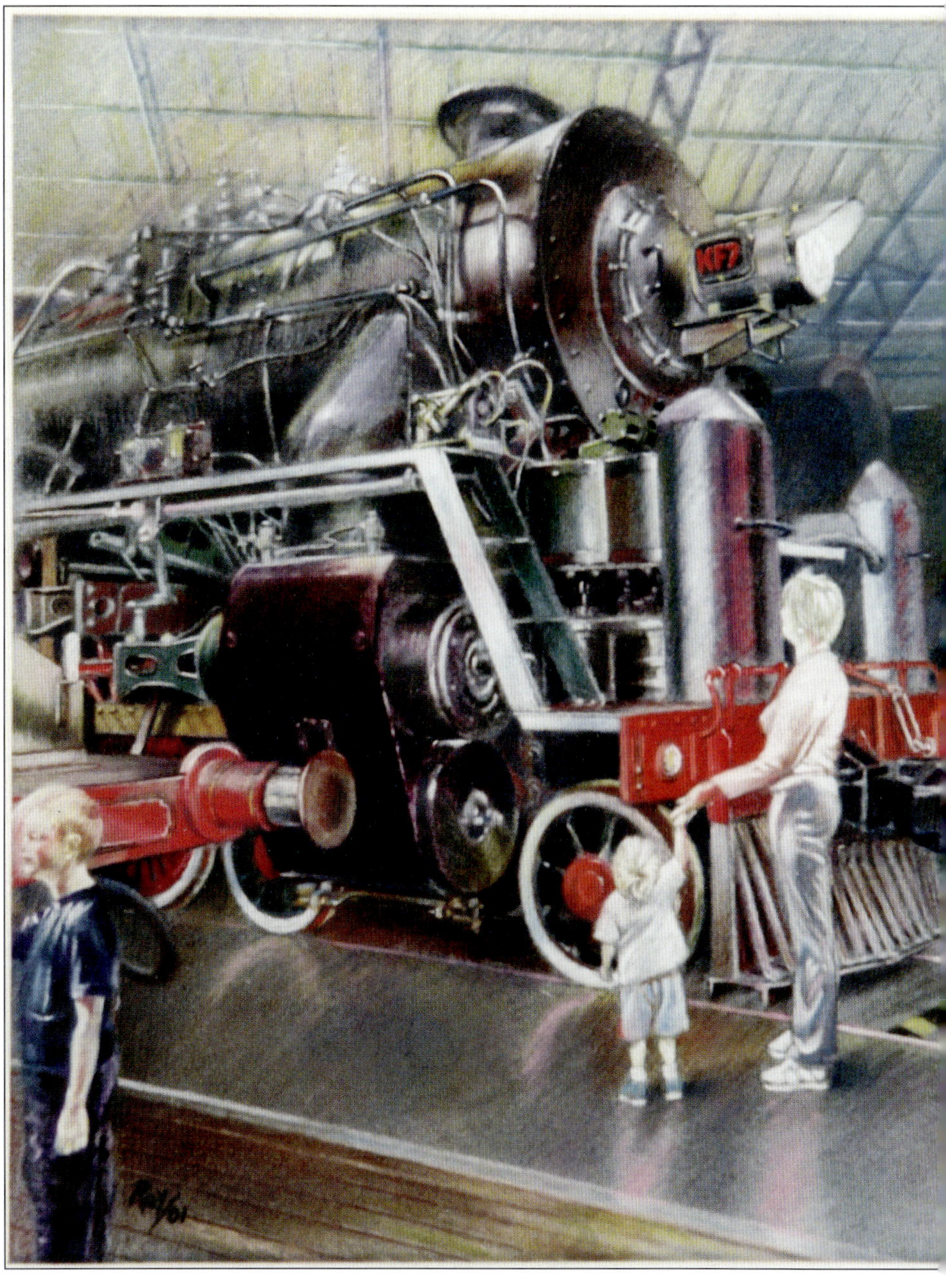

The locomotive side of the business had developed significantly since the early years and, at the time of Roy's employment, manufactured massive steam locomotives for the Tata railways of India and the Chinese State railways in particular. There is an example of the latter in the National Railway Museum at York. This was the subject of one of Roy's later paintings.

It was an exciting time, as I remember from my own schooldays, to see one of the massive steam locomotives, produced later for the Tata Railways, being transported to Liverpool docks. They would pass close to where we lived and we would assemble to watch them pass under the Liverpool to Manchester Railway. The road dipped towards the bridge and rose away from it. The clearance was only 15 feet and as much of the superstructure, that could be removed, had to be removed from the locomotive to allow it to pass under the bridge. It could take it a couple of hours to complete the manoeuvre and would frequently remove some of the road surface in the process.

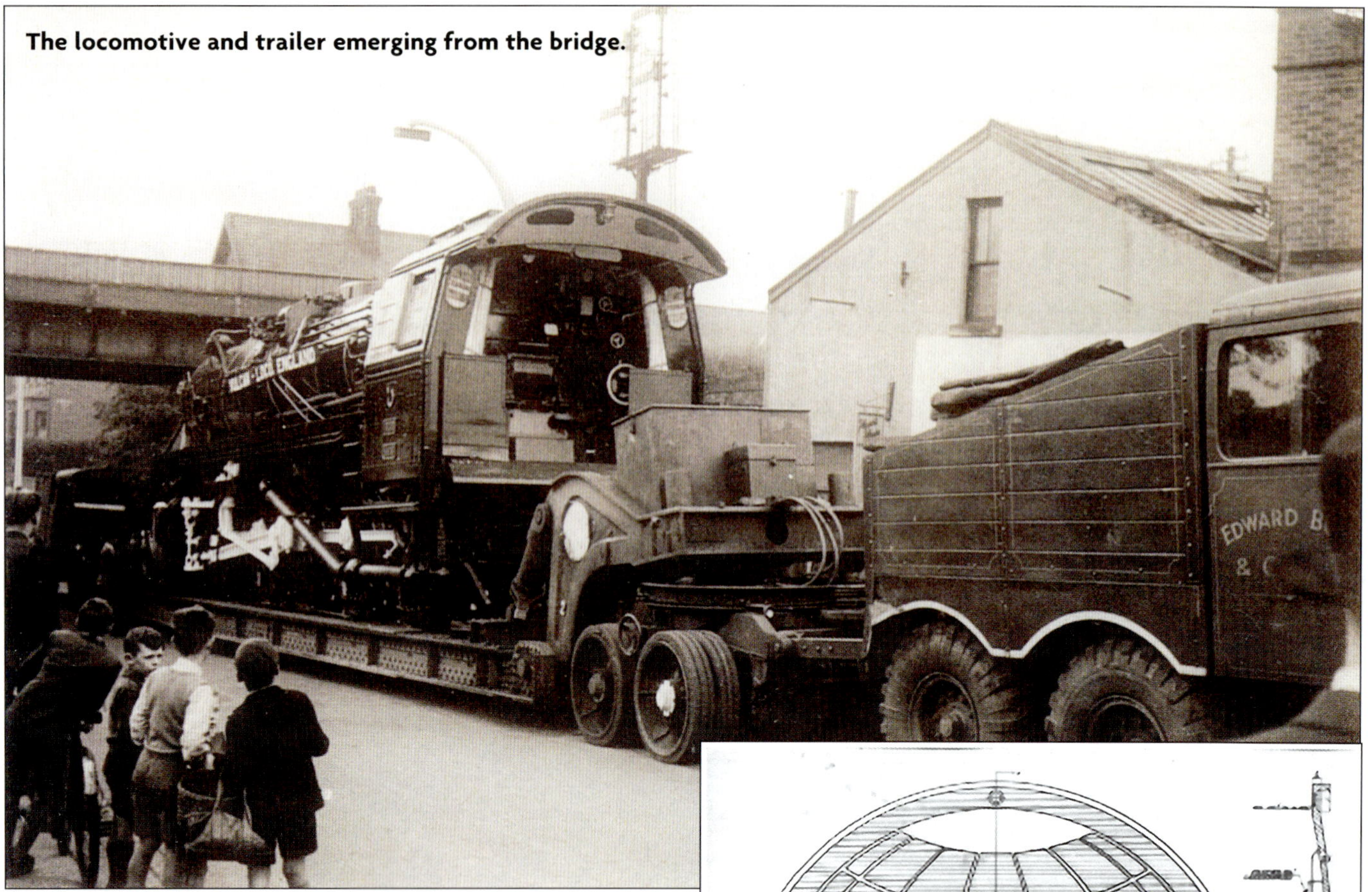
The locomotive and trailer emerging from the bridge.

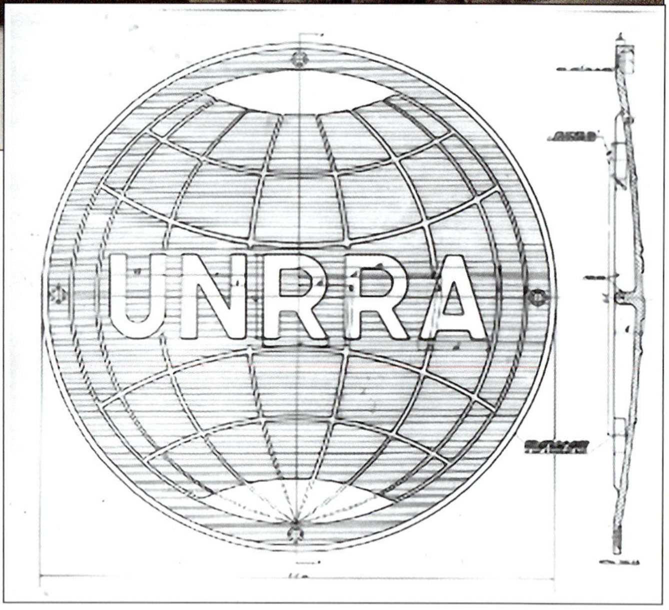

Roy's occupation as a draughtsman at the Vulcan Foundry continued both during and after the Second World War. From 1939 to 1945 the works switched from producing steam locomotives to producing tanks and, for Roy, this was a reserved occupation. Post 1945 they returned to producing steam locomotives and their immediate product was "The Liberation" locomotive.

The Liberation Class was a class of 2-8-0 steam locomotives designed for heavy freight work in post-Second World War Europe. The Vulcan produced 120 of them in 1946.

During this period of time (i.e. before Computer Aided Design) the sectioned drawings of the locomotives were produced by the draughtsmen (in the Drawing Office) and these were copied (in the Tracing Office) by a team of young ladies. There would need to be some collaboration during the production of the tracings and the opportunities for other relationships were also provided (of course under the strict supervision of the head tracer). Dorothy (who was to become Roy's wife) was a tracer.

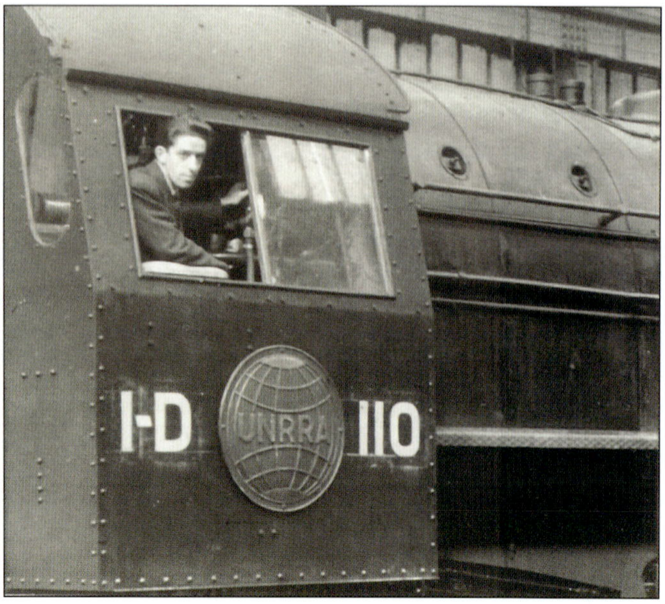

The "Liberation" locomotive was produced under the auspices of "The United Nations Relief and Rehabilitation Administration" or UNRRA and this was indicated below the cab. This was Roy's design and is illustrated with Roy in the cab.

Both the drawing of a sectioned view and the tracing of it are extremely complex and demand good eyesight and a steady hand. Below is an example of that for a locomotive, destined for the East India Railway, produced by Dorothy following Roy's drawing.

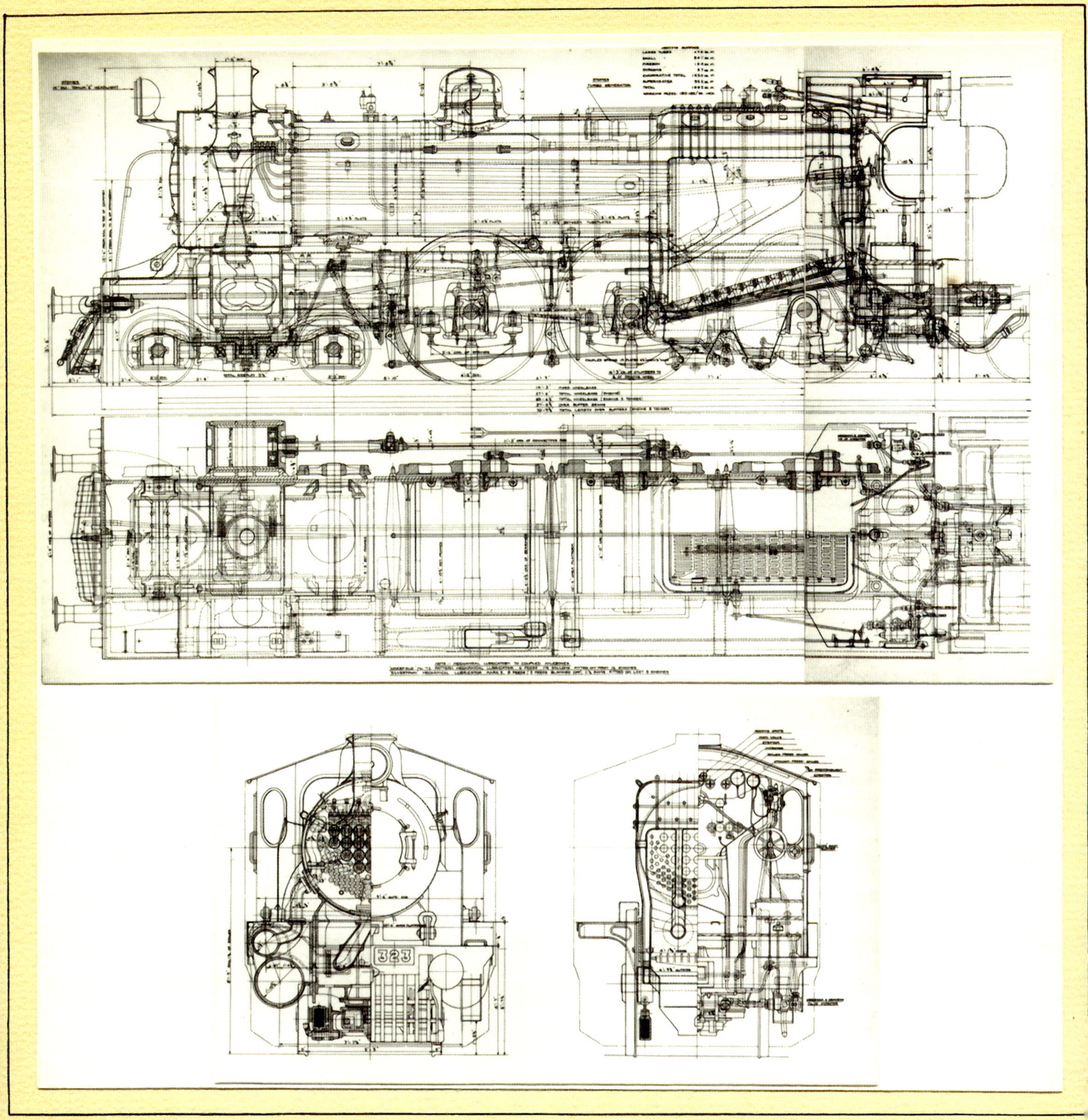

SCALE OF ORIGINAL DRG. 1" TO 1'

EAST INDIAN RAILWAY

4·6·0 (H.P.S.)

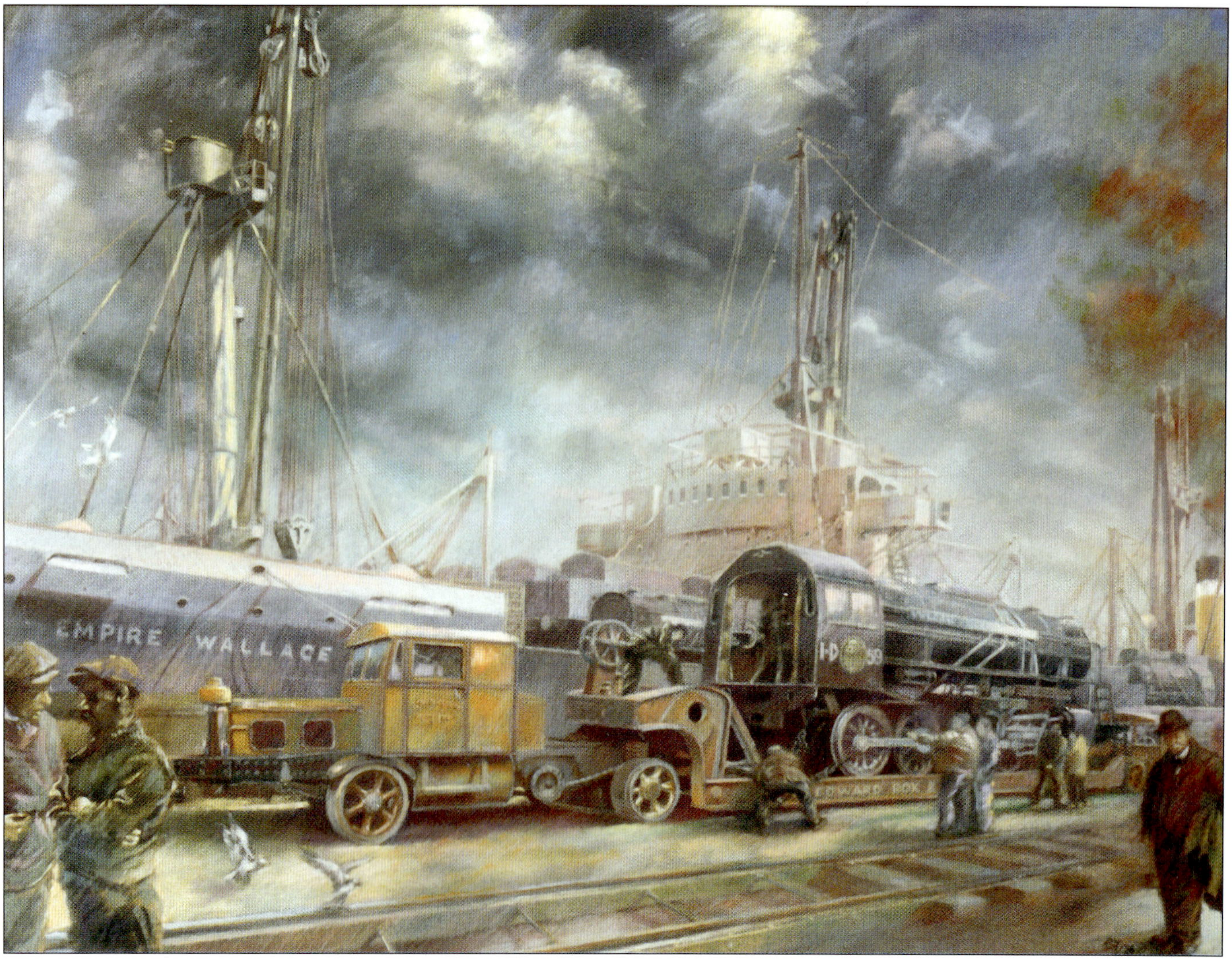

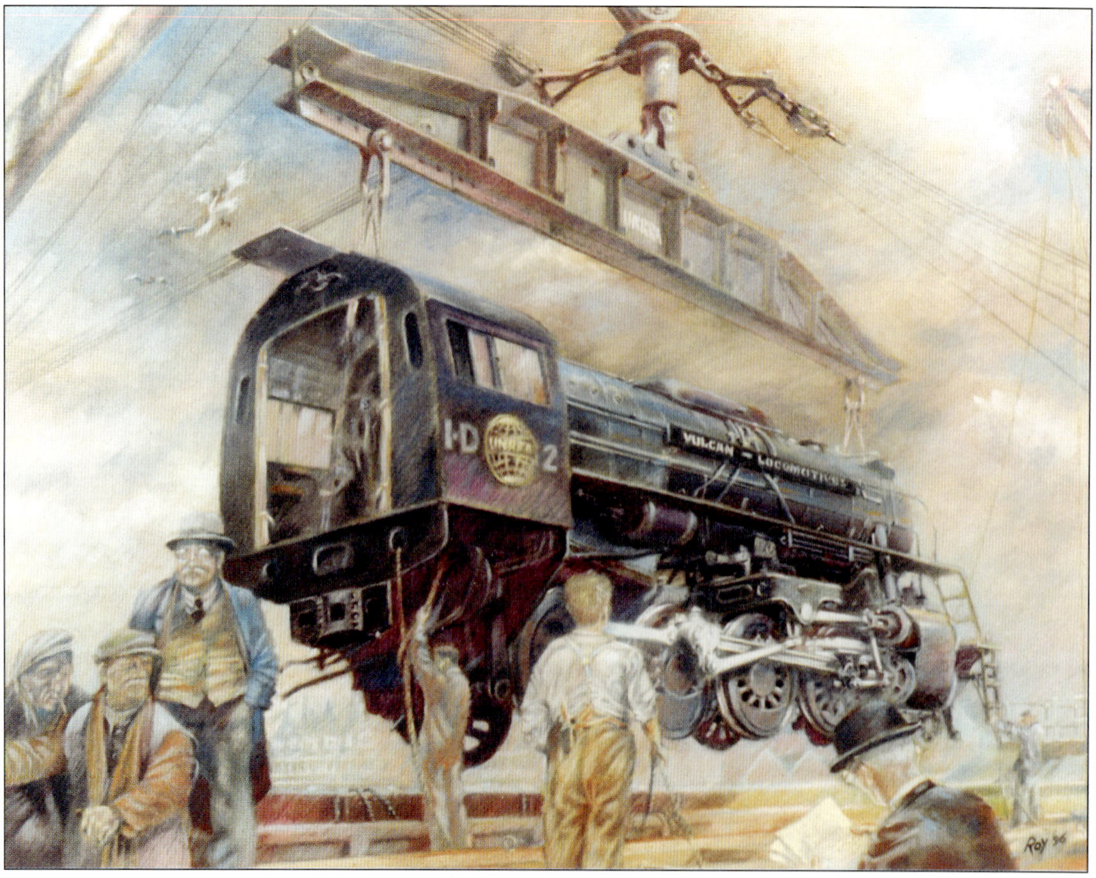

The activity at the Liverpool Docks following the arrival and loading of the Liberation Locomotives is further illustrated by two of Roy's later paintings.

It has already been mentioned that, during the war, the Vulcan was producing tanks for the war effort. It was also being recognized, by the company, that Roy had capabilities beyond being a draughtsman. He had already produced the design for the cab emblem and he was asked to produce publicity material for the company. An example is reproduced below.

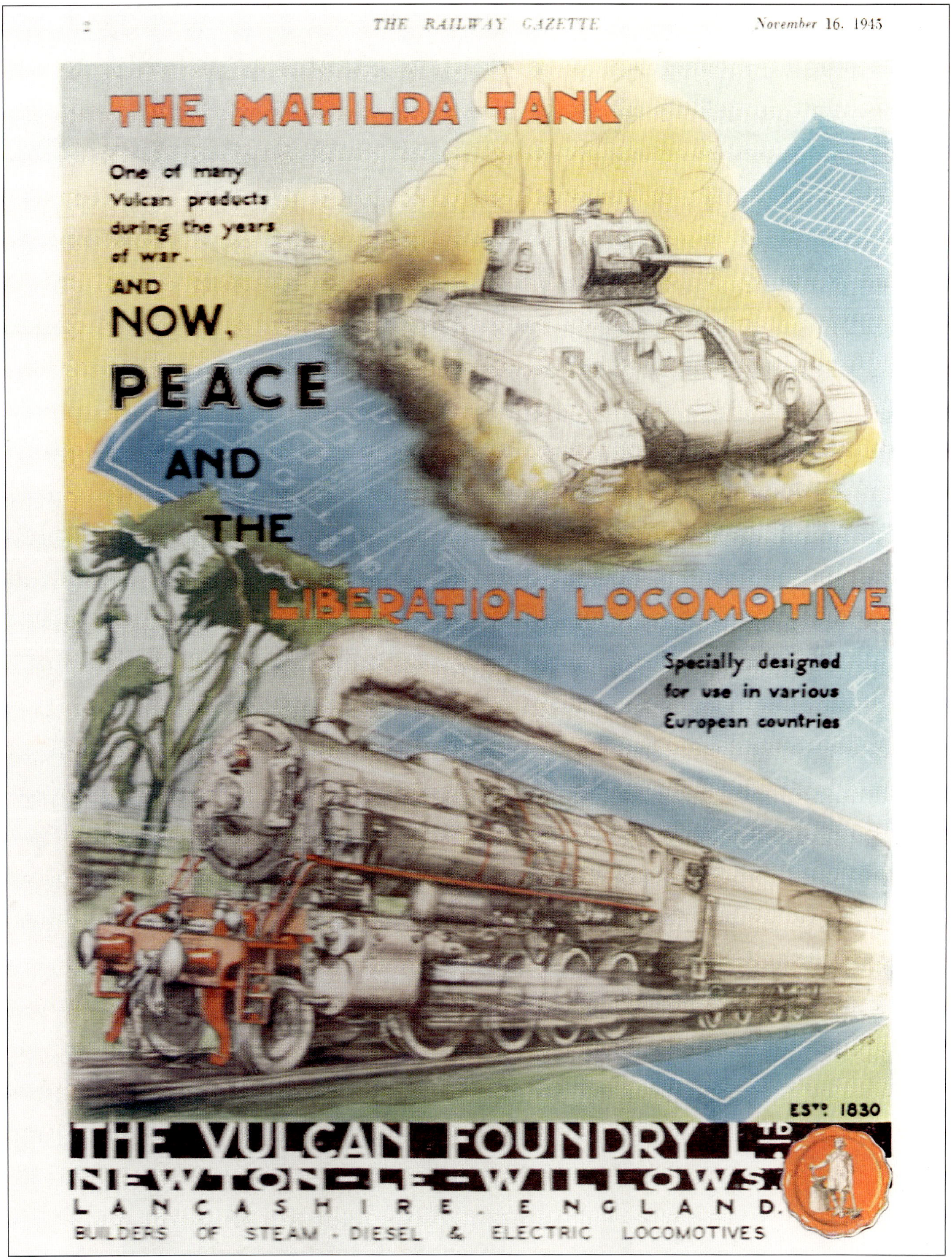

As well as producing art work for the Vulcan, Roy produced some for himself. Being a draughtsman he would make use of a scale ruler. This would help to ensure that a drawing was correct in relation to the ratio of all measurements to the actual locomotive dimensions. Roy had one, made out of Ivory, shown here:

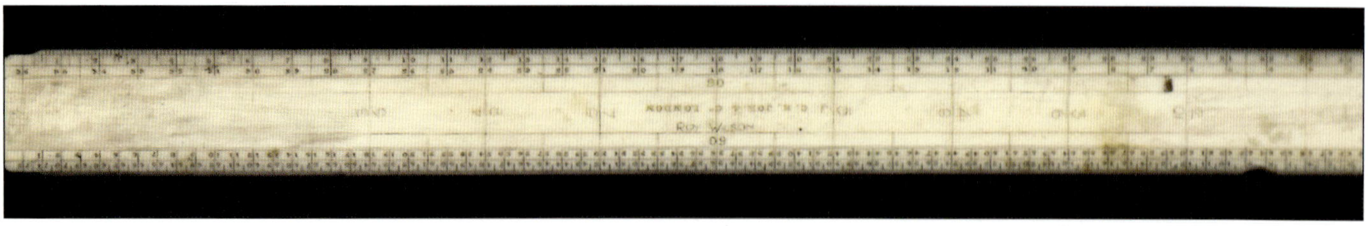

If this is turned over we see the cartoons of all the senior managers in the drawing office. I don't know if they ever saw the cartoons of themselves, but they would no doubt have been amused by them. Roy had produced these by scratching the faces using a compass point and then highlighting them with Indian Ink.

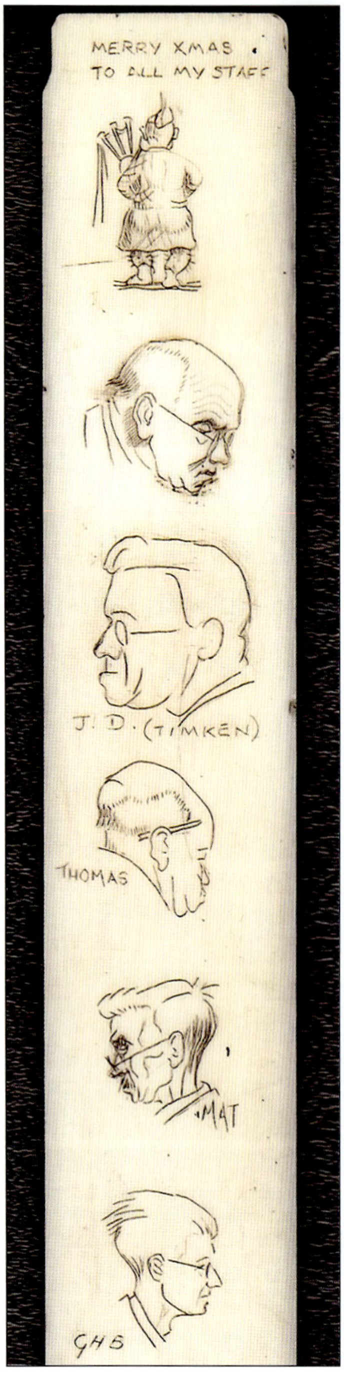

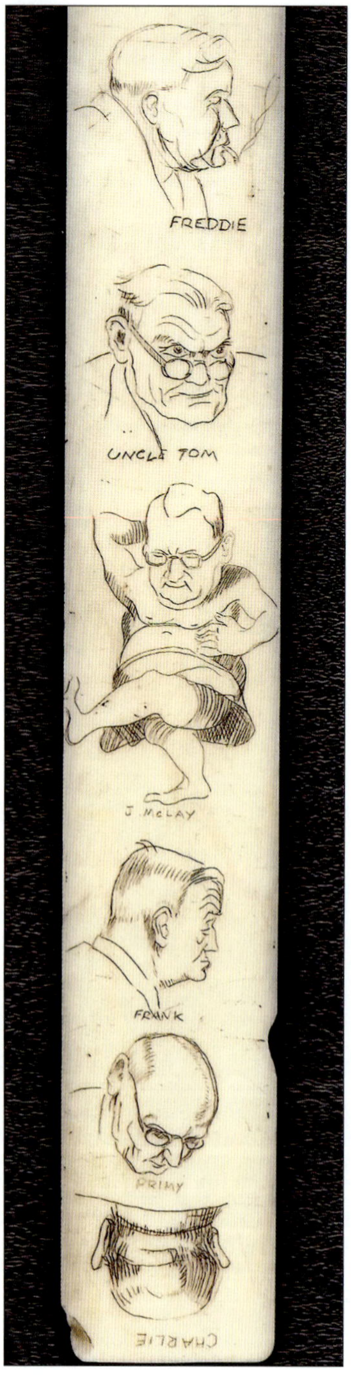

I don't know if Roy applied for day release or whether the Chief Draughtsman arranged for him to be allowed it, but around this time Roy attended the Manchester College of Art and studied to achieve his National Diploma of Design (NDD) as a part-time activity. This required a variety of areas of study involving anatomy (including life drawing), comic strip, sculpture, advertising and elements of architecture. Examples of his work are included below. These illustrate the basic requirements and skills needed to be able to practice as an artist in the 1940's. I don't know how many of today's practitioners can claim such a comprehensive background.

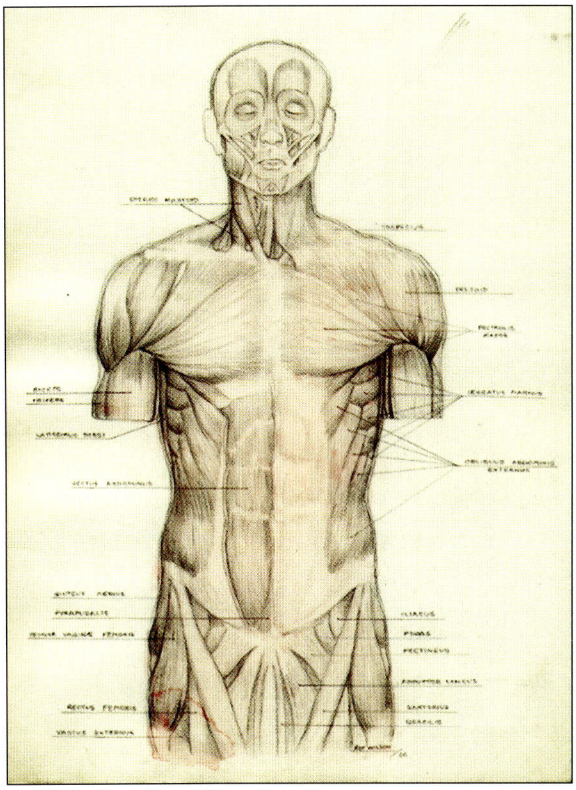

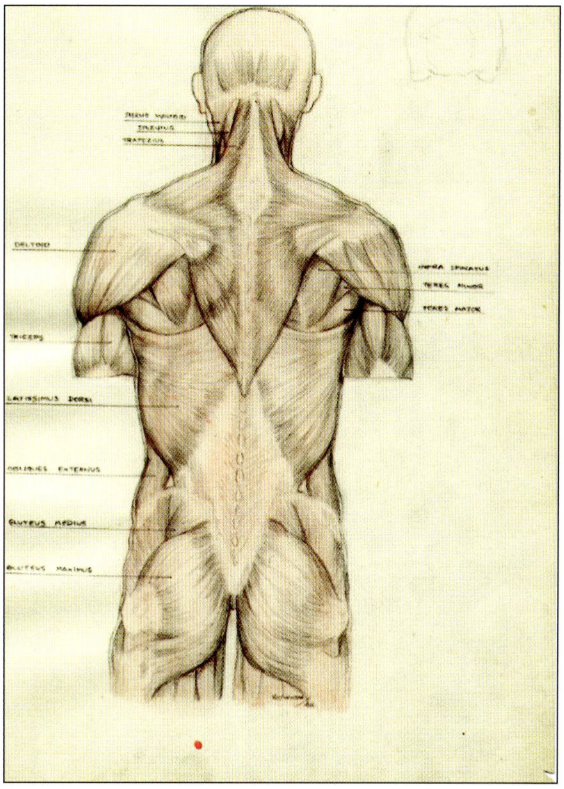

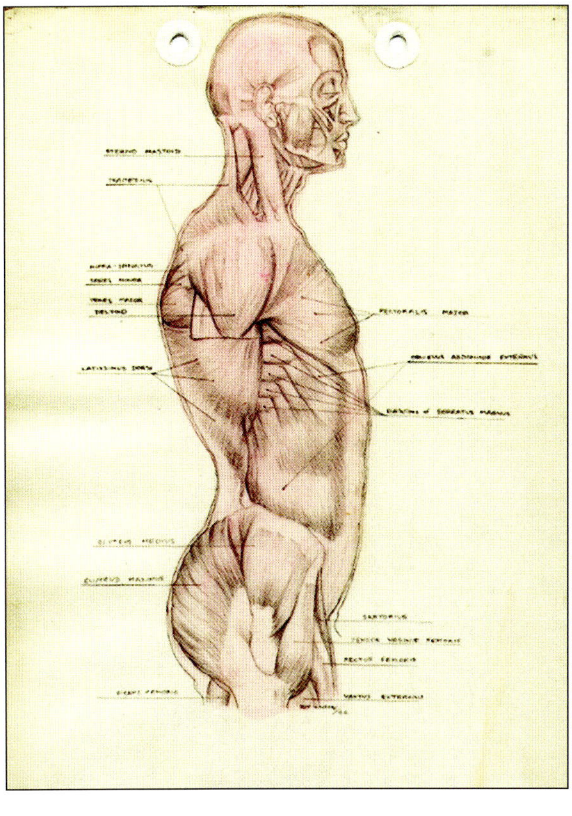

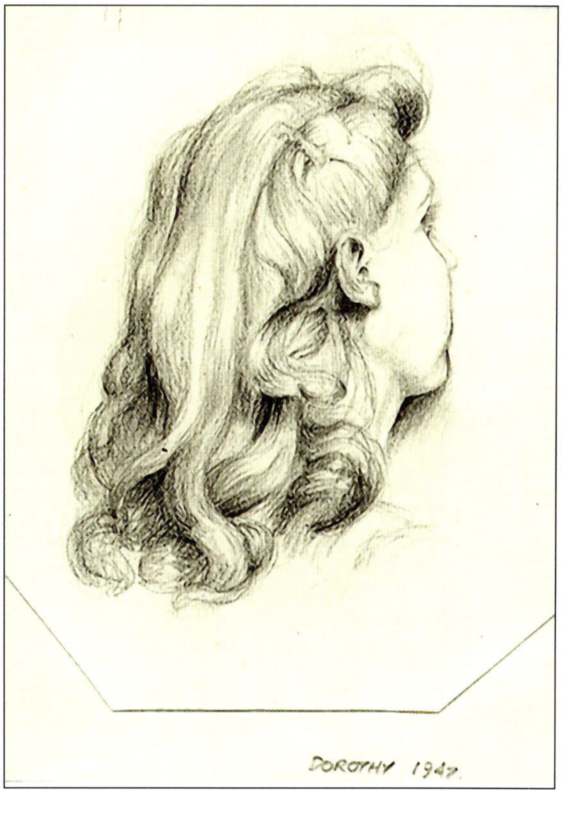

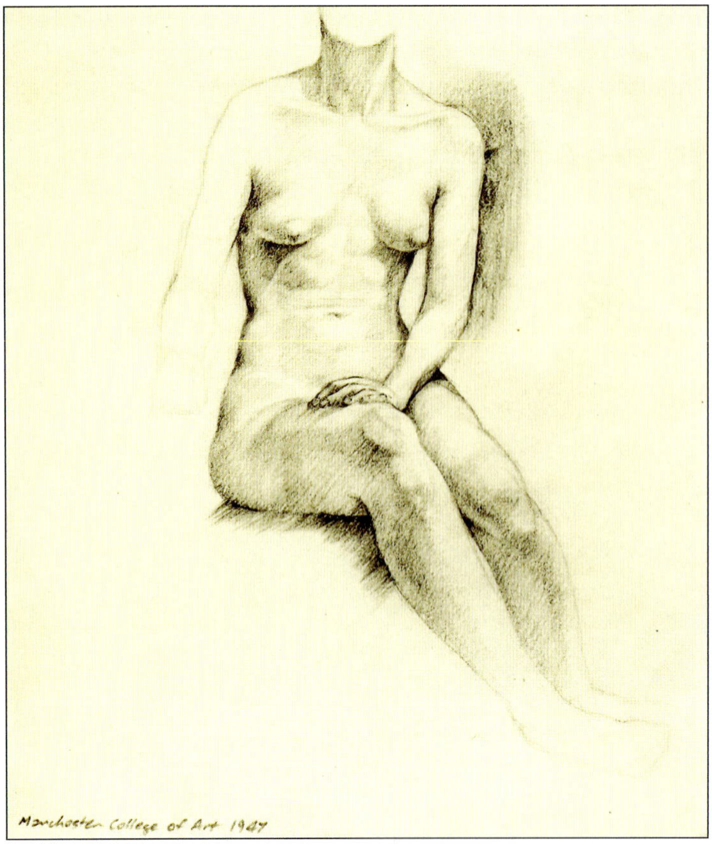

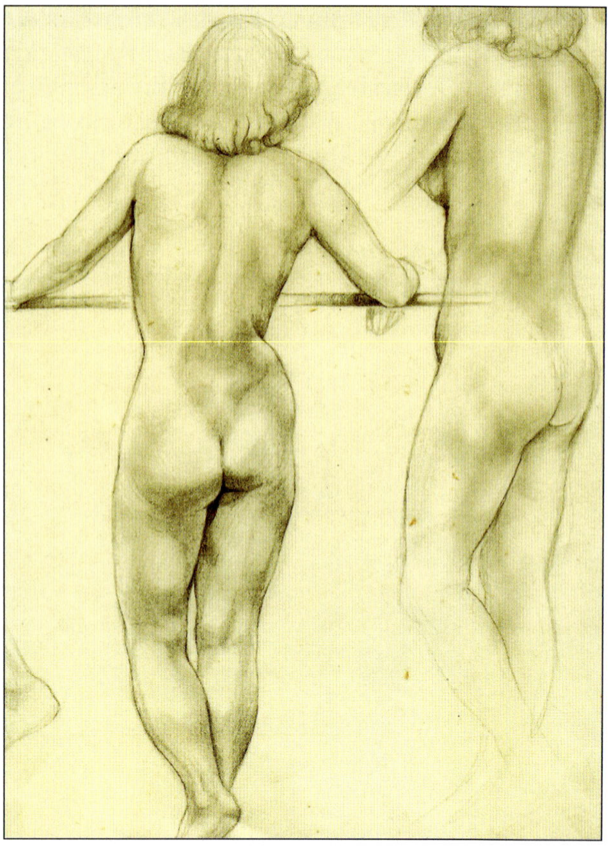

Examples of pencil sketches

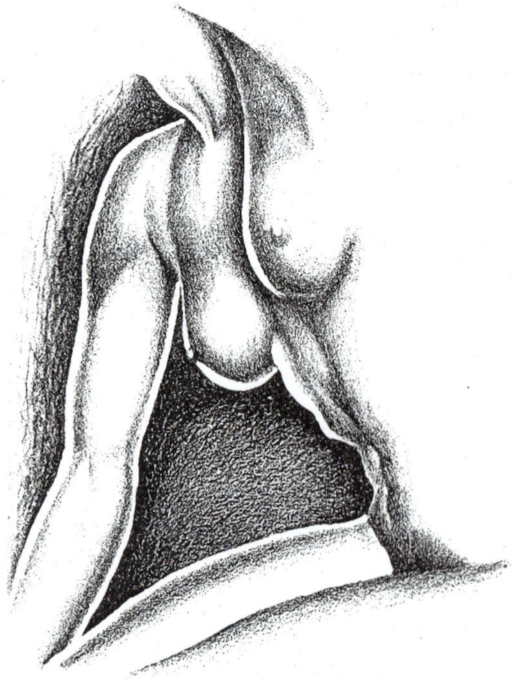

Charcoal Study

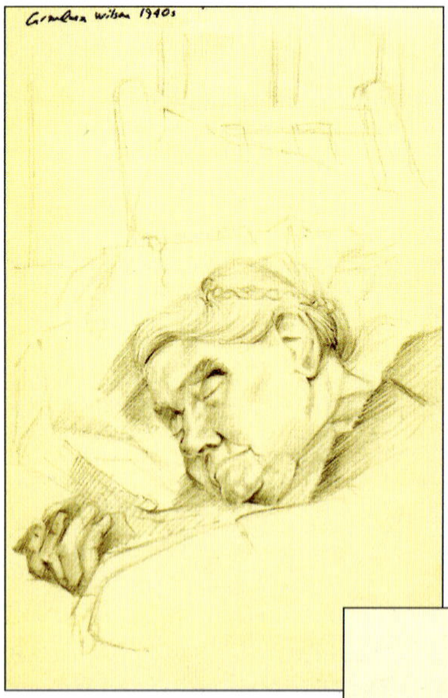

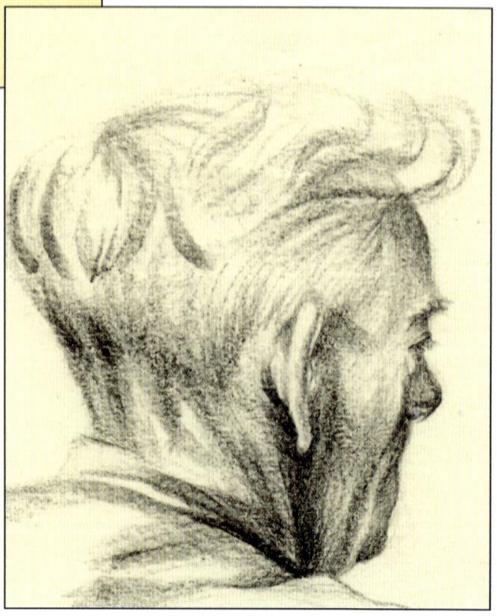

Lithograph - NDD Course
Manchester College of Art

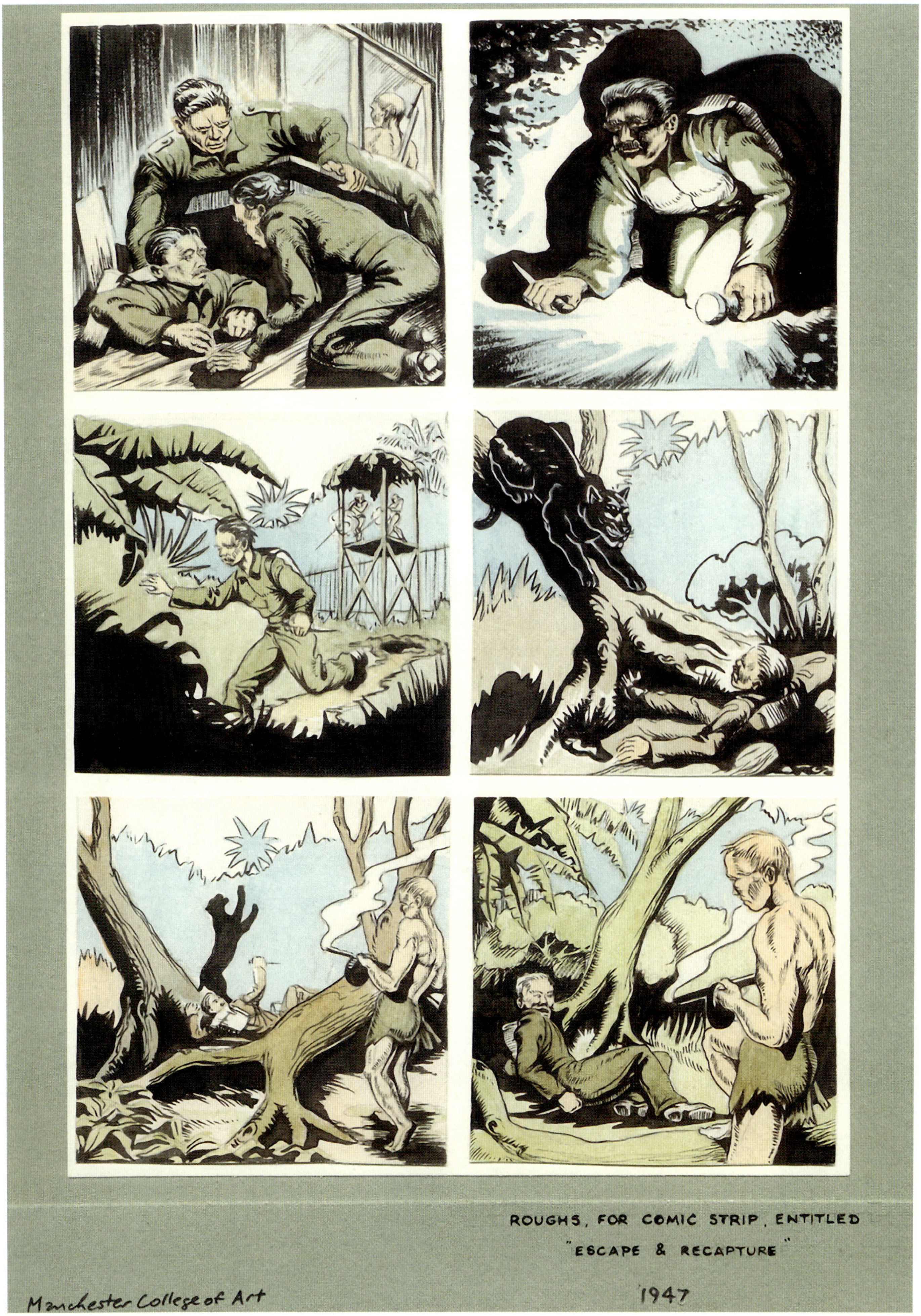
ROUGHS, FOR COMIC STRIP, ENTITLED
"ESCAPE & RECAPTURE"
1947
Manchester College of Art

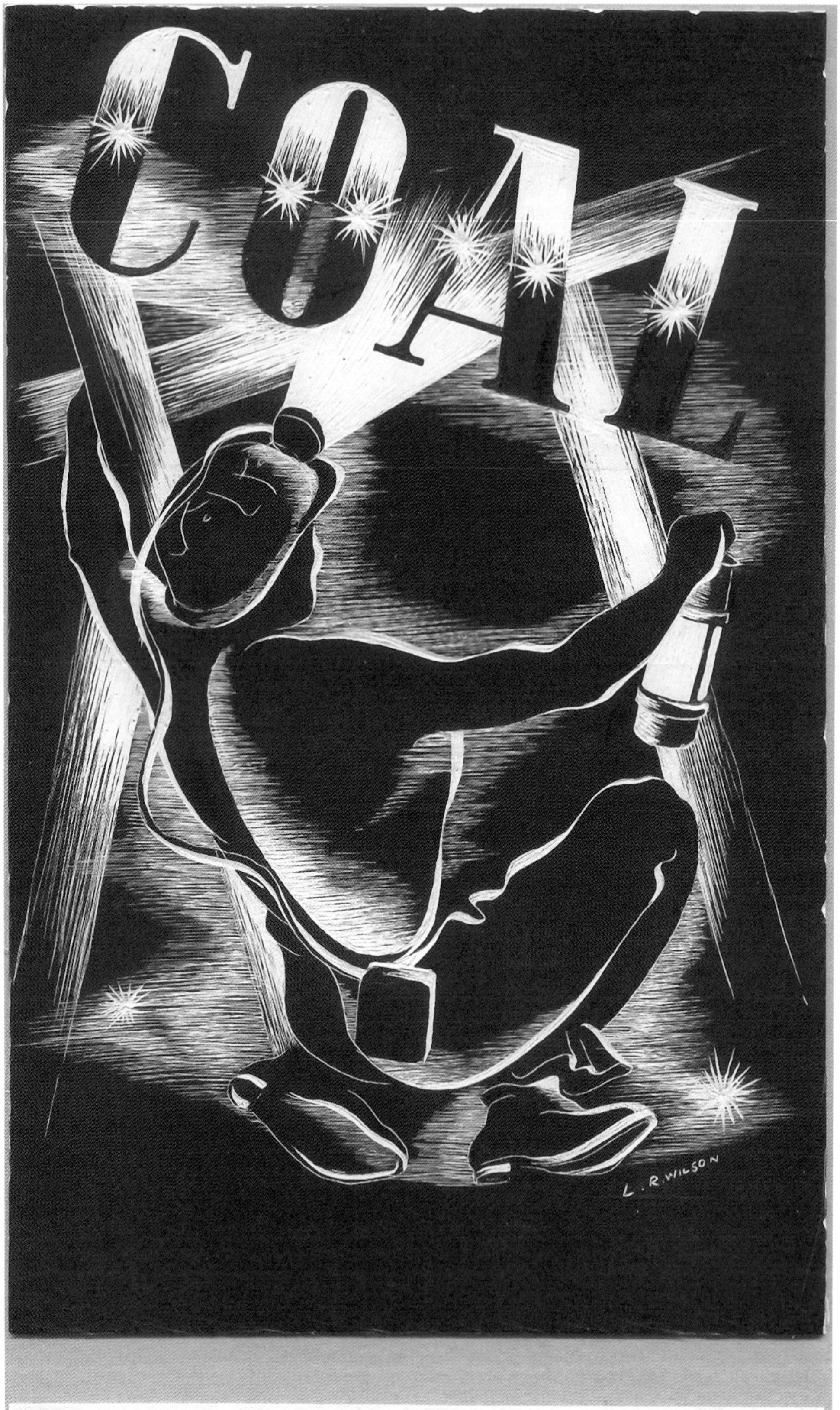

COVER FOR BOOKLET ON COAL - 1948
Manchester College of Art - NDD Course

An illustration for the title: "The Crash"

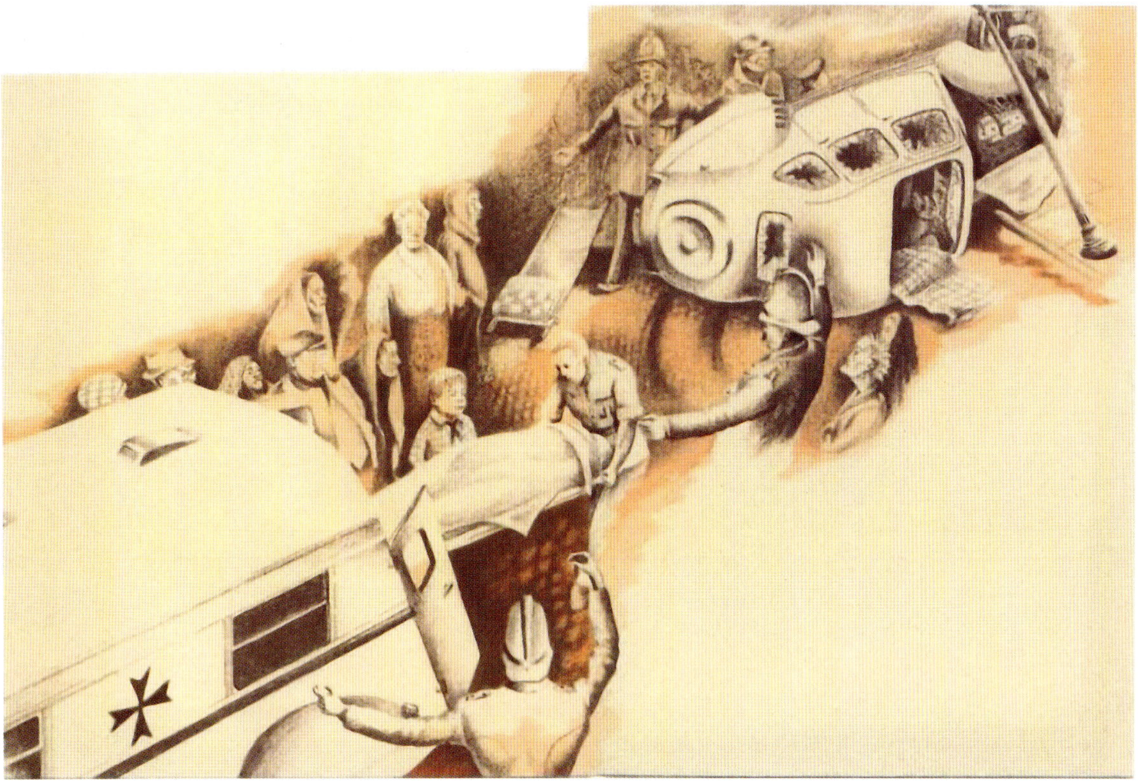

Self Portraits were also required as part of the learning process.

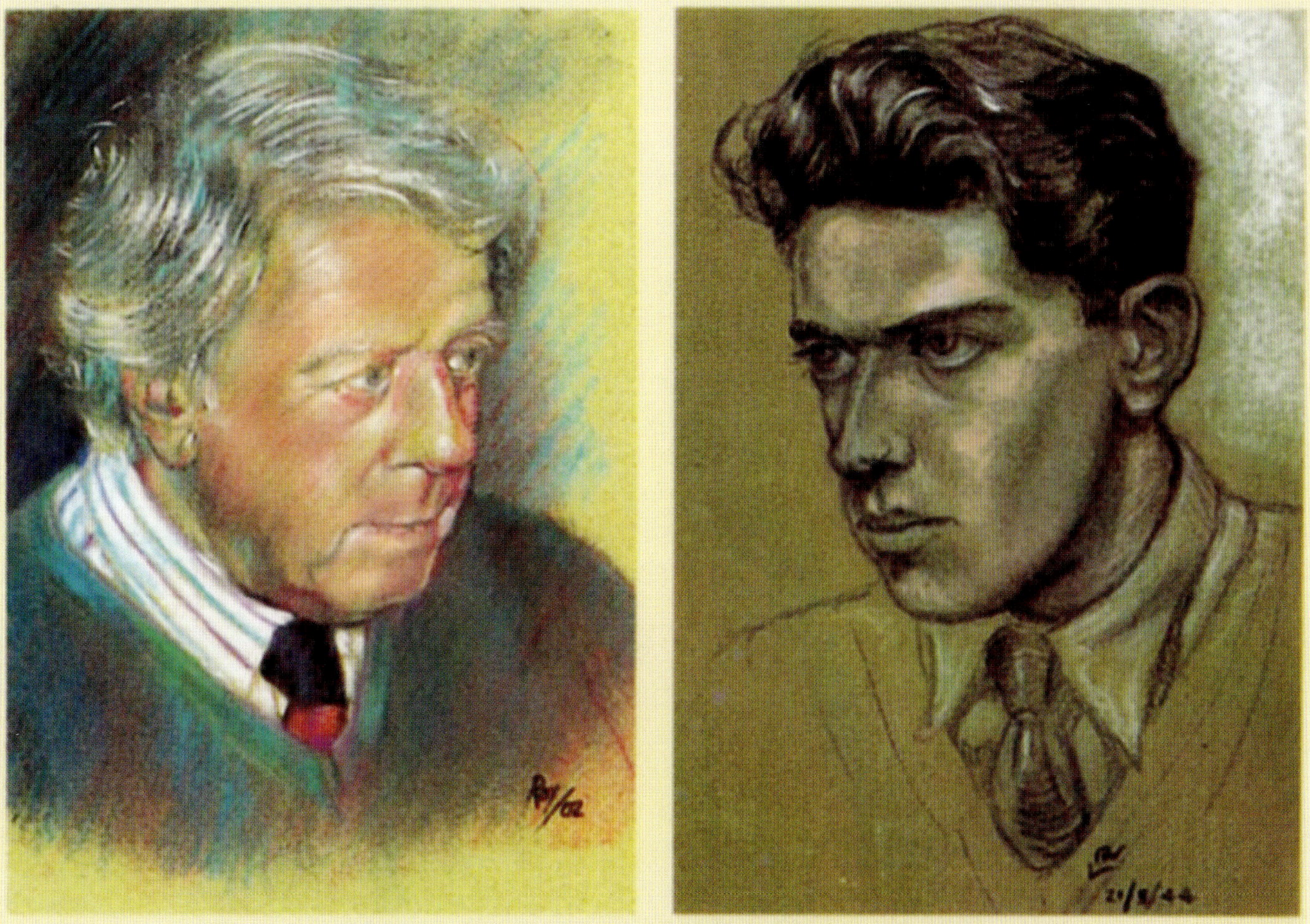

Self portraits by the artist in 2002 and 1944.

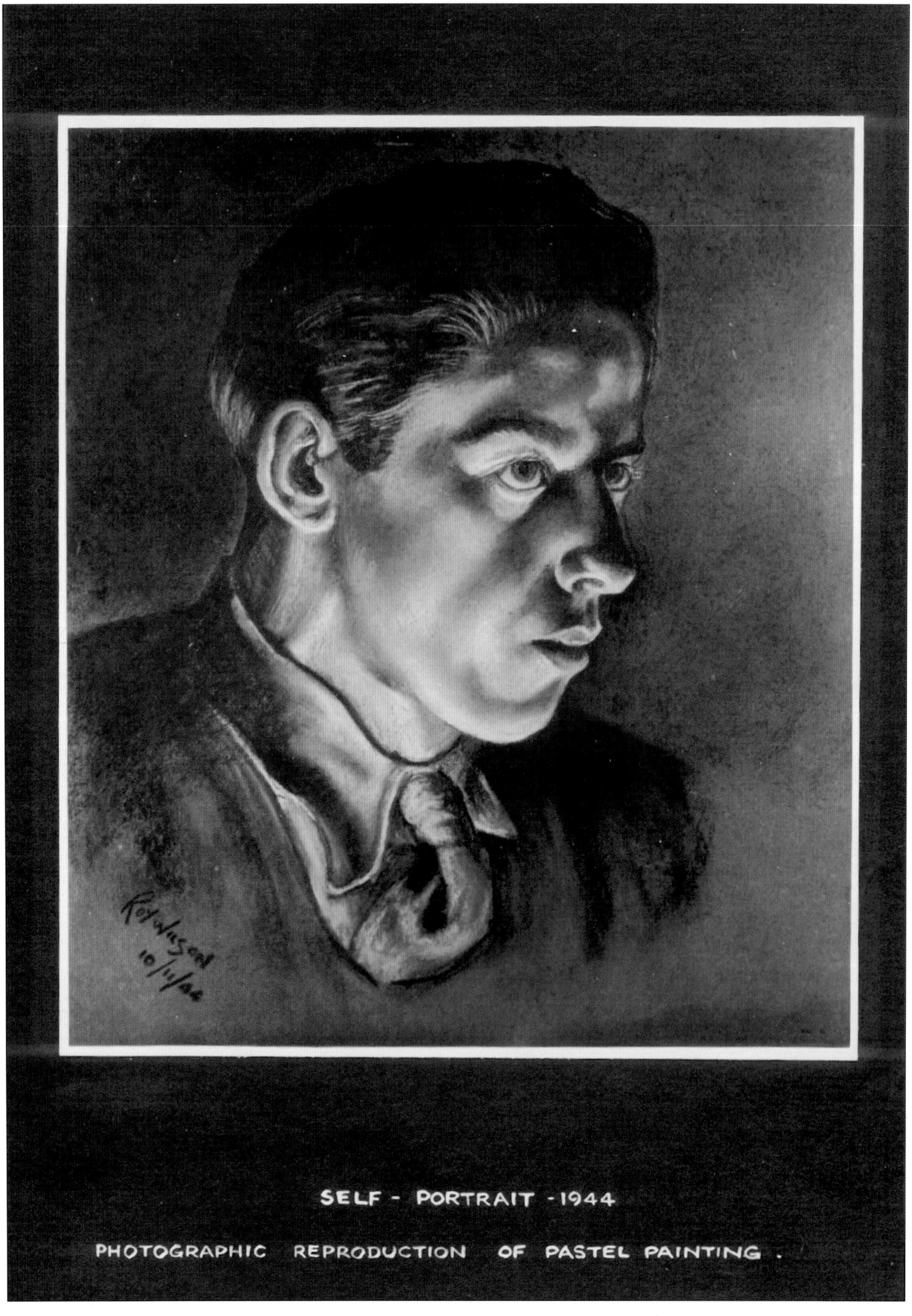

SELF - PORTRAIT - 1944

PHOTOGRAPHIC REPRODUCTION OF PASTEL PAINTING.

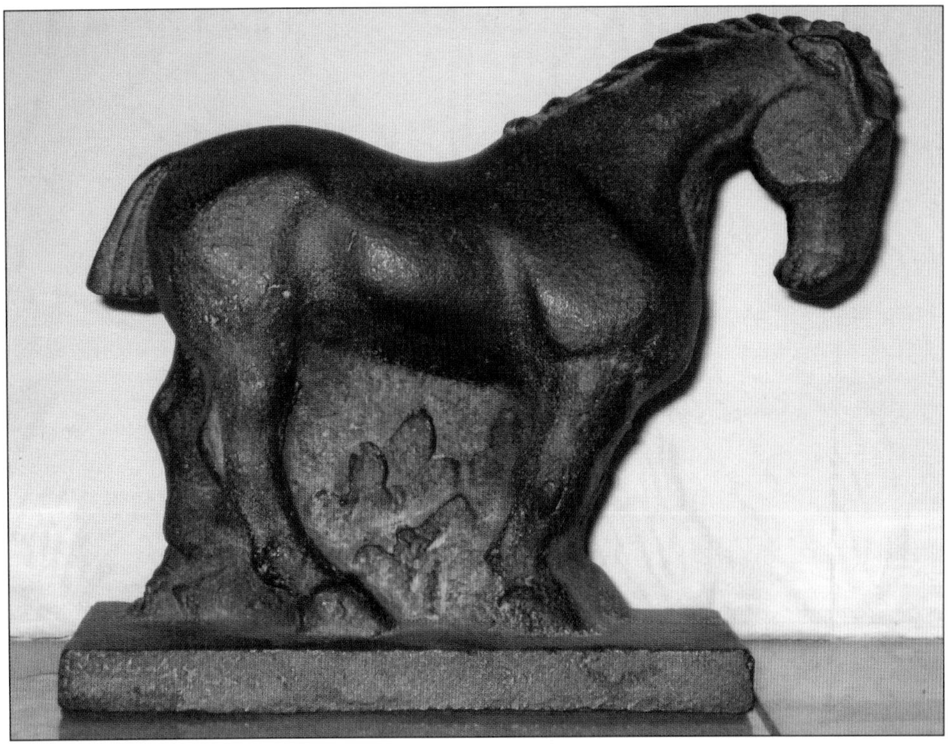

A Bronze sculpture of a horse submitted as part of the NDD course.

Wider approval of his work

There were two occasions during this period of his early life when Roy's artistic ability was recognised by a wider audience.

In 1943 Roy took me to the Curzon cinema in Earlestown to see a film called "Ships with Wings." This was produced by United Artists and released in 1941. Following our visit Roy produced a poster advertising the film and sent it to the manager of the cinema. It appears that he was so impressed by the poster that he sent it to United Artists. The result was correspondence from Michael Balcon (the director of the film), and an invitation to visit the studios. This correspondence is reproduced over page:

The other example was associated with our membership (at that time) of the Brunswick Methodist Church, also in Earlestown. This was Roy's only example (that entered the public domain) of his use of oil paints. At this time Roy was 33 years old, had left the Vulcan and had joined Electro-Hydraulics as their publicity manager. It was a large painting of "The Nativity".

Roy donated this oil painting to the church. A report appeared in the local paper; "The Earlestown Guardian" and is reproduced below.

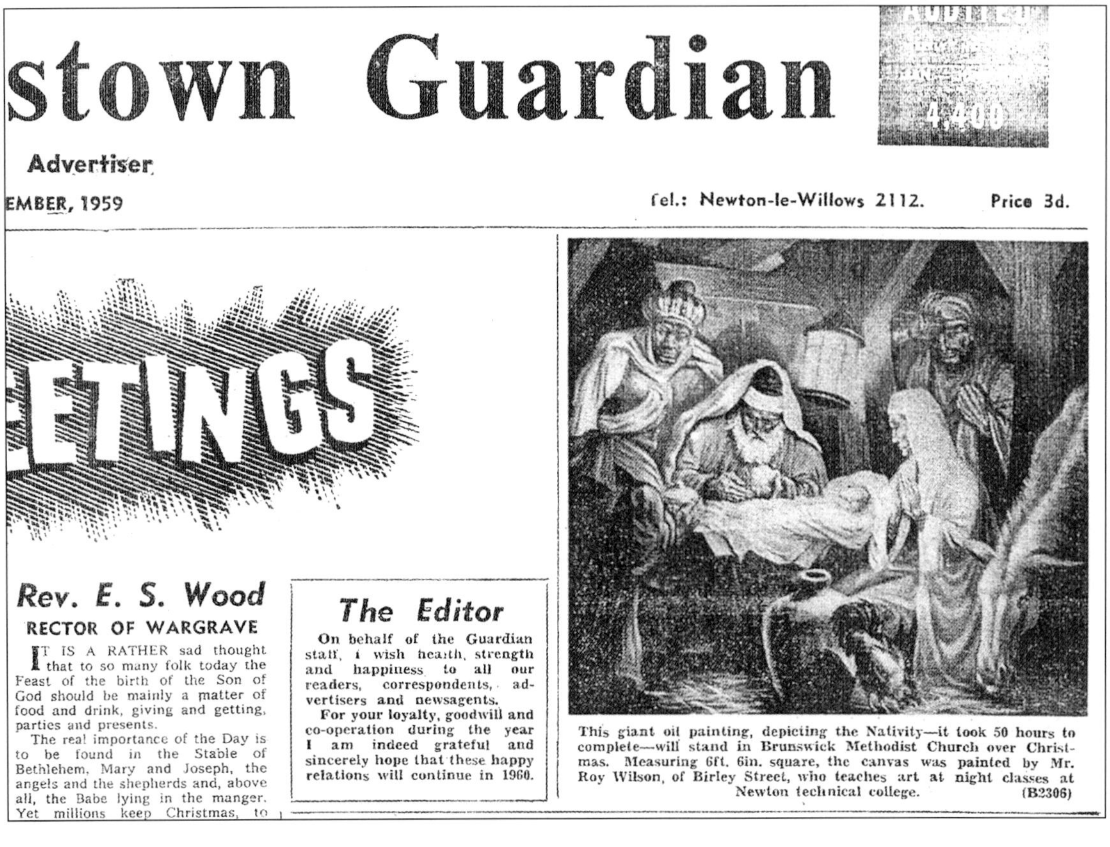

stown Guardian

Advertiser

EMBER, 1959 — Tel.: Newton-le-Willows 2112. — Price 3d.

ETINGS

Rev. E. S. Wood

RECTOR OF WARGRAVE

IT IS A RATHER sad thought that to so many folk today the Feast of the birth of the Son of God should be mainly a matter of food and drink, giving and getting, parties and presents.

The real importance of the Day is to be found in the Stable of Bethlehem, Mary and Joseph, the angels and the shepherds and, above all, the Babe lying in the manger. Yet millions keep Christmas, to

The Editor

On behalf of the Guardian staff, I wish health, strength and happiness to all our readers, correspondents, advertisers and newsagents.

For your loyalty, goodwill and co-operation during the year I am indeed grateful and sincerely hope that these happy relations will continue in 1960.

This giant oil painting, depicting the Nativity—it took 50 hours to complete—will stand in Brunswick Methodist Church over Christmas. Measuring 6ft. 6in. square, the canvas was painted by Mr. Roy Wilson, of Birley Street, who teaches art at night classes at Newton technical college. (B2306)

United Artists Corporation Ltd.,

12, Norton Street,
Liverpool, 3.

ASSOCIATED WITH
The Allied Artists Corporation Ltd.

Chairman:
A.W. KELLY. (British)
(ALTERNATE F.W. SLATTERY)
Managing Director:
E.T. CARR. (Born Russian: naturalised British)
Directors:
MARY PICKFORD. (American)
(ALTERNATE W. J. SMITH)
CHARLES CHAPLIN. (British)
(ALTERNATE C. GORDON ROSS)
ALEXANDER KORDA.
(Born Hungarian: naturalised British)
(ALTERNATE H.G. BOXALL)
DAVID O. SELZNICK. (American)
(ALTERNATE
L. LEWIS, A.C.A. (British)

MARY PICKFORD.
CHARLIE CHAPLIN.
DOUGLAS FAIRBANKS.
SAMUEL GOLDWYN.
ALEXANDER KORDA.

HEAD OFFICE:
FILM HOUSE, WARDOUR STREET,
LONDON, W.1.

TELEGRAMS: UNARTISCO, LIVERPOOL.
TELEPHONE: NORTH 0022/3.

UNITED ARTISTS

OUR REF. SBD/MEH

27th May 1943

F. Harrison Esq.,
Curzon Cinema,
EARLSTOWN, Lancs.

Dear Mr. Harrison,

I received your letter, and the enclosed drawing on "SHIPS WITH WINGS" which I personally think is very good, and I am forwarding this on to Mr. Michael Balcon at Ealing Studios, as I certainly think that this boy's work should be noticed, and no doubt he will be hearing from Mr. Balcon in due course.

Hoping you are well, and with kind regards.

Yours faithfully,
UNITED ARTISTS CORPORATION LTD.

BRANCH MANAGER.

Dear Mr. Harrison,

Mr. Dubow of United Artists sent on to me your letter of the 26th May with a drawing by one of your young patrons, Roy Wilson. As I have not got his address I cannot write to him direct, but I do hope you will show him this letter and say how much we admire his drawing, - the reproduction of some of the faces is quite remarkable and there is no doubt he has considerable talent.

I am returning the drawing for the time being but if Wilson some time would like it autographed by the various players, I am sure they would be only too glad to do this.

Yours faithfully,

Michael Balcon.

ADDENDUM TO
The Making of a Railway Artist

25th September will live in my memory for a long while to come.

It was the date on which the order had been placed with the printers for the book and printing was under way. When writing this book it had been my intention to include the first ever painting by Roy that had received public acclaim. This is referred to on page 17 with the resulting correspondence on page 18. It is his poster for the film 'Ships with Wings'.

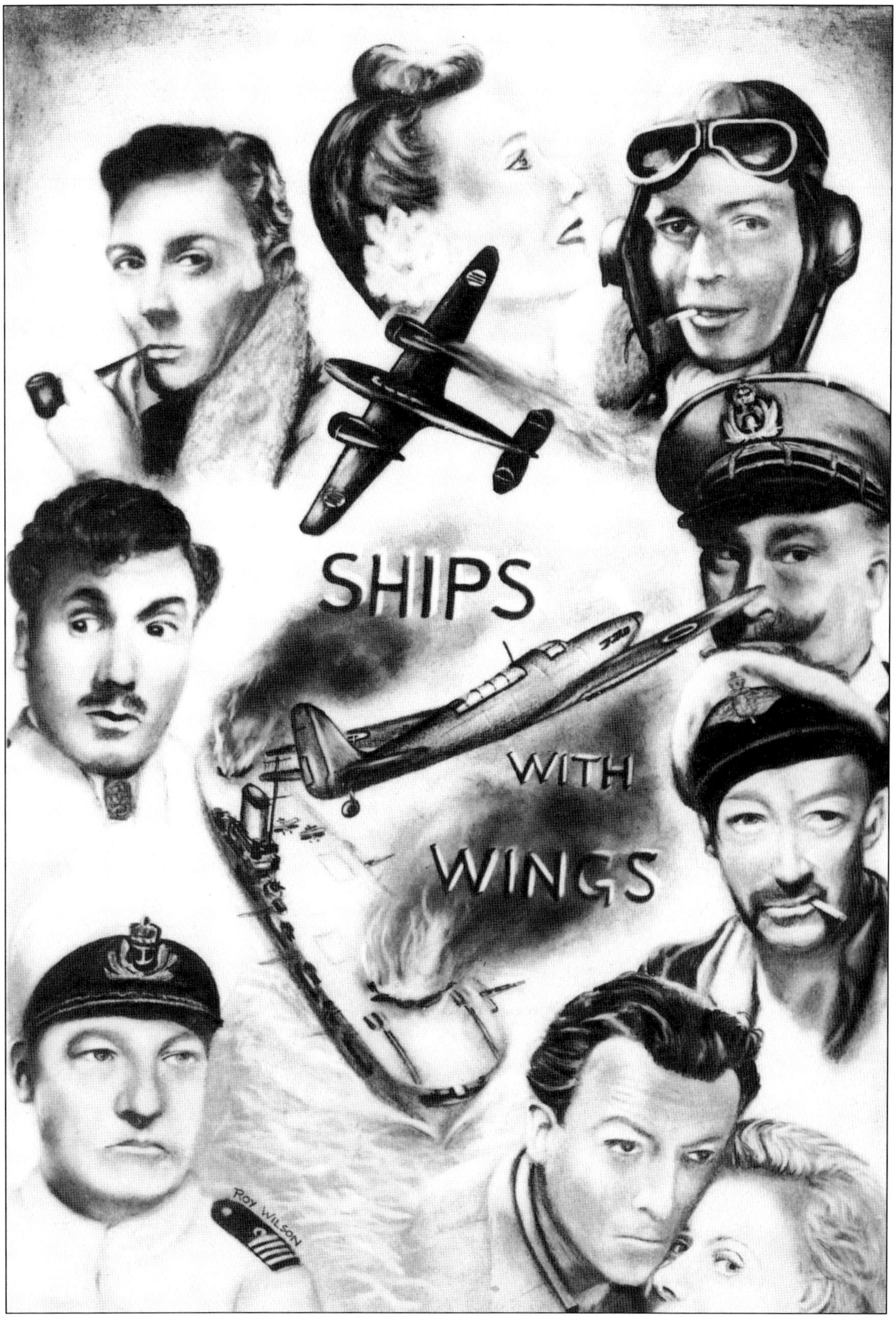

I had searched all of the rooms in his house including several searches of his attic studio and office without success. Thus the book had proceeded without its inclusion.

On 25th September I was in Leeds, clearing Roy's house for sale. Roy's extensive library of books (about 1000 of them) had been taken by a lady, Jennie, who ran a second hand bookshop in Harrogate.

On the morning of 25th September there was a knock on the door and Jennie handed me an autograph book that had been amongst the books. She thought I would like to keep it.

As I took it from her the photograph alongside fell to the floor.

Brian Wilson

CHAPTER TWO

THE BURTONWOOD STORY

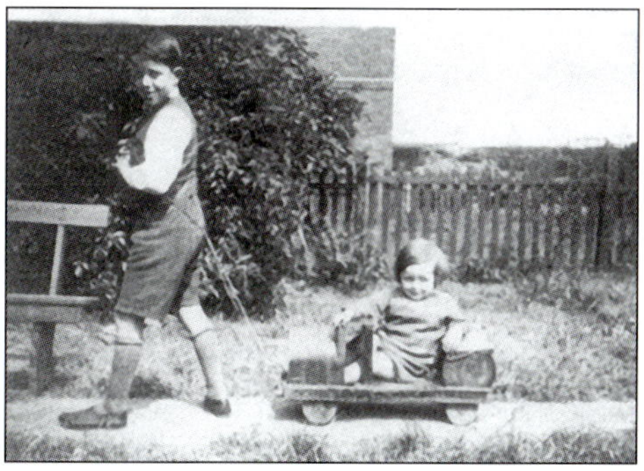

Roy and I have an early association with locomotives. The rather strange looking object in the locomotive is me. The locomotive is by courtesy of Dad and Roy is providing the motive power.

I am now retired but occasionally lecture to various societies, such as historical societies, lecture societies, etc. and, if it is appropriate to the particular lecture, I will introduce myself as having been born in 1933 B.C. The B.C. in this case is Before Computers. I then explain that it makes me wonder what modern kids think about what life must have been like, in the old days, before they could spend their time playing with X-Boxes and peering at mobile phones for large periods of time.

I feel that I was lucky to have been born then, because what we did was spend our leisure time outside; roller skating, rock climbing, cycling etc. What Roy and I did, whenever possible, was watch steam trains. We also did all the other things as well, but our major joint activity was to cycle to a place called Winwick Junction. This was about 5 miles from where we lived and it is where the main West Coast line from London Euston to Scotland branched off and joined the Liverpool to Manchester Railway at Earlestown junction, which is about halfway between the two cities. I was delighted when I found the following photograph taken by J.R. Carter. This shows the salt box that Roy and I sat on to watch the trains.

Winwick Junction. Here's the salt box we used to sit on.

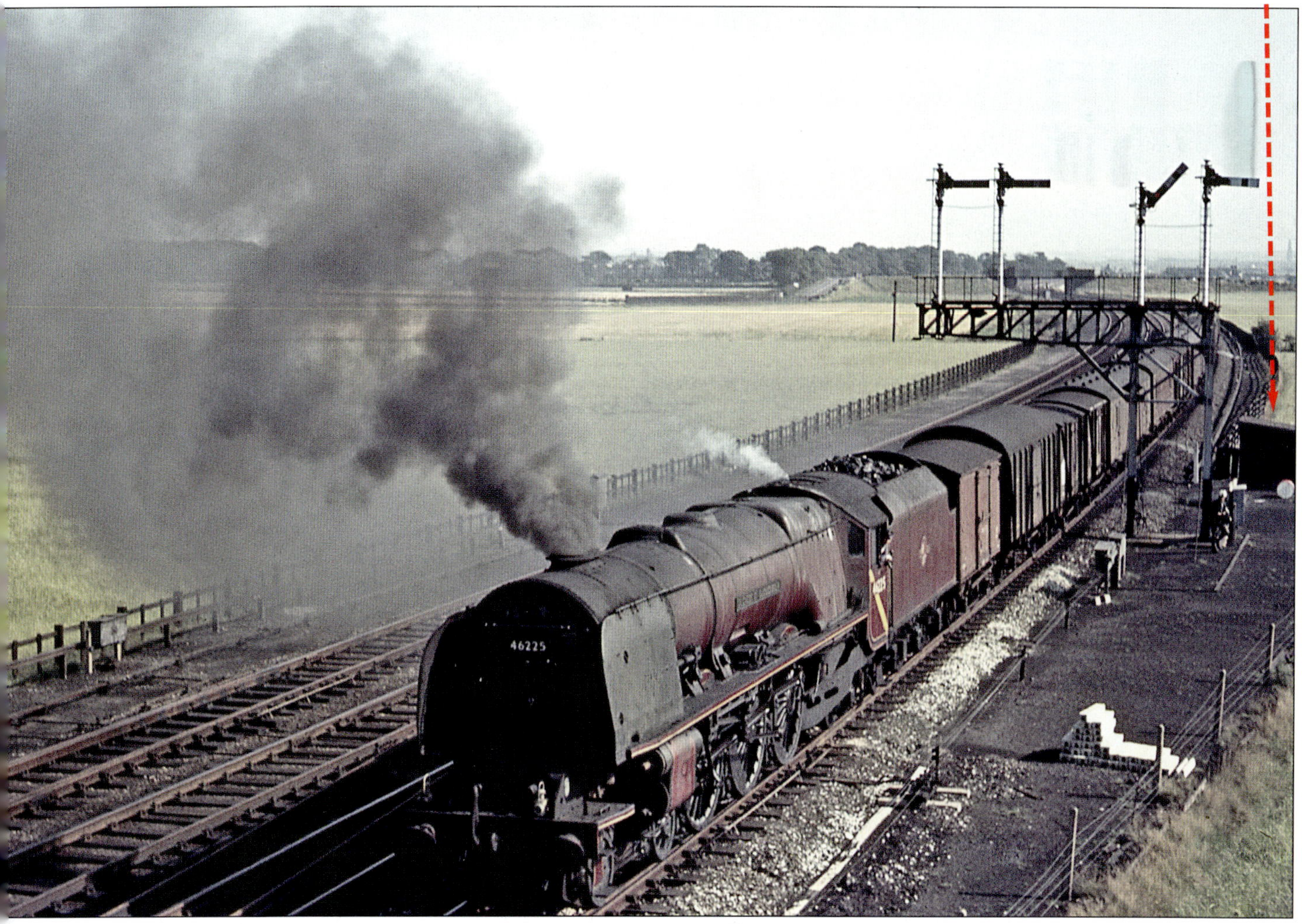

It was possible to see and hear the trains approaching from some way off and we would start to get excited while wondering whether it was just a Black Five or something more exciting such as "Coronation Scot" or one of the other "Duchesses". As it got closer the noise would increase, the ground would start to shake and the characteristic smell of the smoke would permeate our nostrils. Our position was only a couple of yards from the track so if it was one of the London to Glasgow expresses it would be an incredible experience as it hurtled past so close to us. The noise was amazing. We were shaking as well as the ground and we would be enveloped in the steam and smoke. I cannot imagine anything on an X-Box being quite as exciting. This experience was probably the start of both our interests in railways in general and would lead to Roy's commitment to Railway Art and a joint research project related to Monorail History and development.

During the Second World War the USAAF had an airbase which was about 8 miles from our house. This was situated in the small village of 'Burtonwood'. Between this and the council estate on which we lived was the Sankey Valley. This had been the home of the Sankey Sugar Works and a small chemical company. The Sankey Valley is highly significant for two features. First, the Sankey canal was built to carry coal from the Haydock mines down to Warrington to access the river Mersey. This was the first canal to be built in the UK. It was built in 1757 before the Bridgewater canal. Spanning the canal is the Nine Arches. This is a viaduct on Stephenson's Liverpool to Manchester Railway. Thus the Sankey Valley has the first viaduct crossing the first canal.

It was also significant for me since I used to spend quite a large amount of time there. This was mainly cycling in the woods close by and rock climbing on "The Mucky Mountains." This was our name for a dump of chemical waste that had weathered over the years to form an outcrop that resembled a rock face. I notice that the name has been adopted by the local council for a nature park.

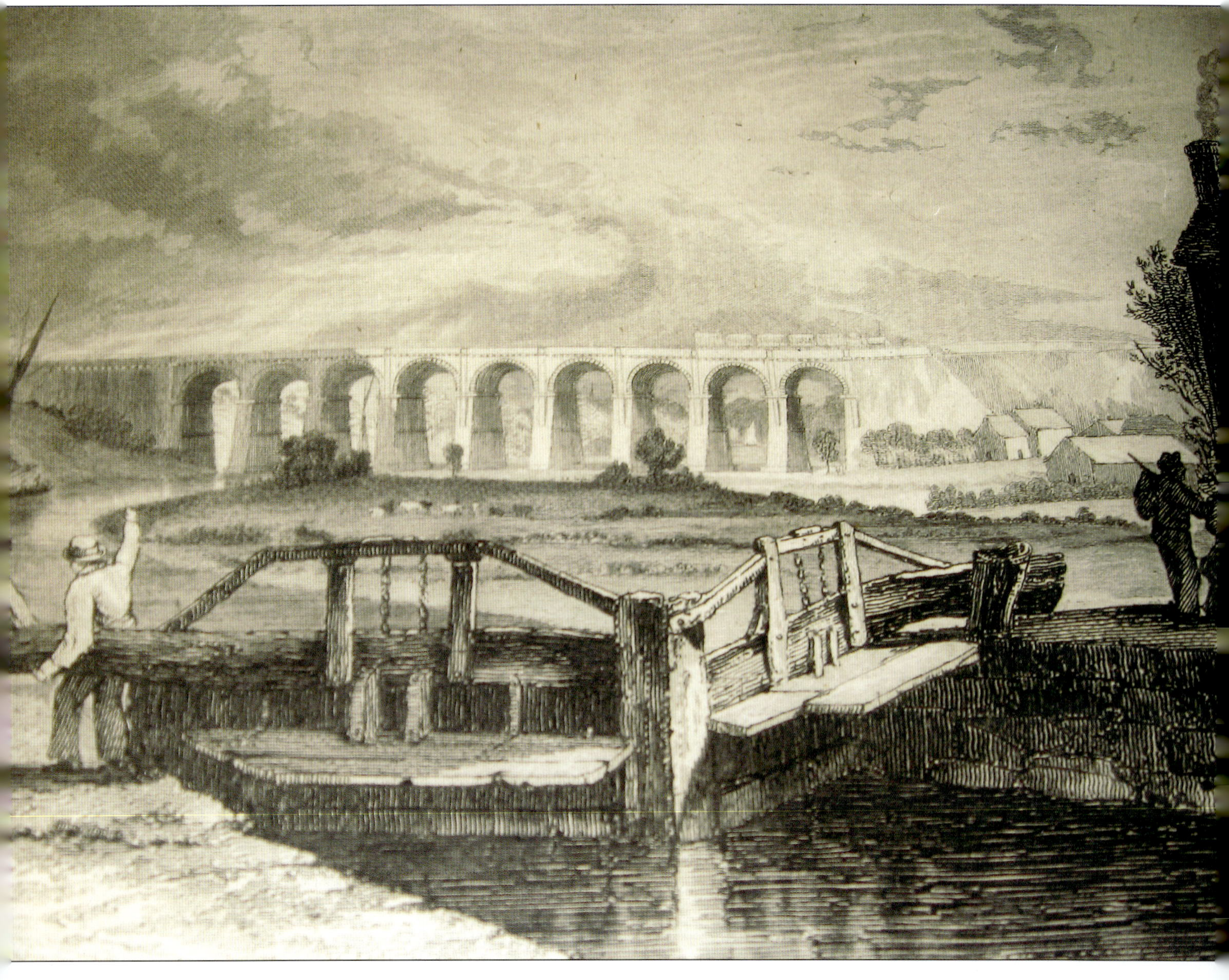

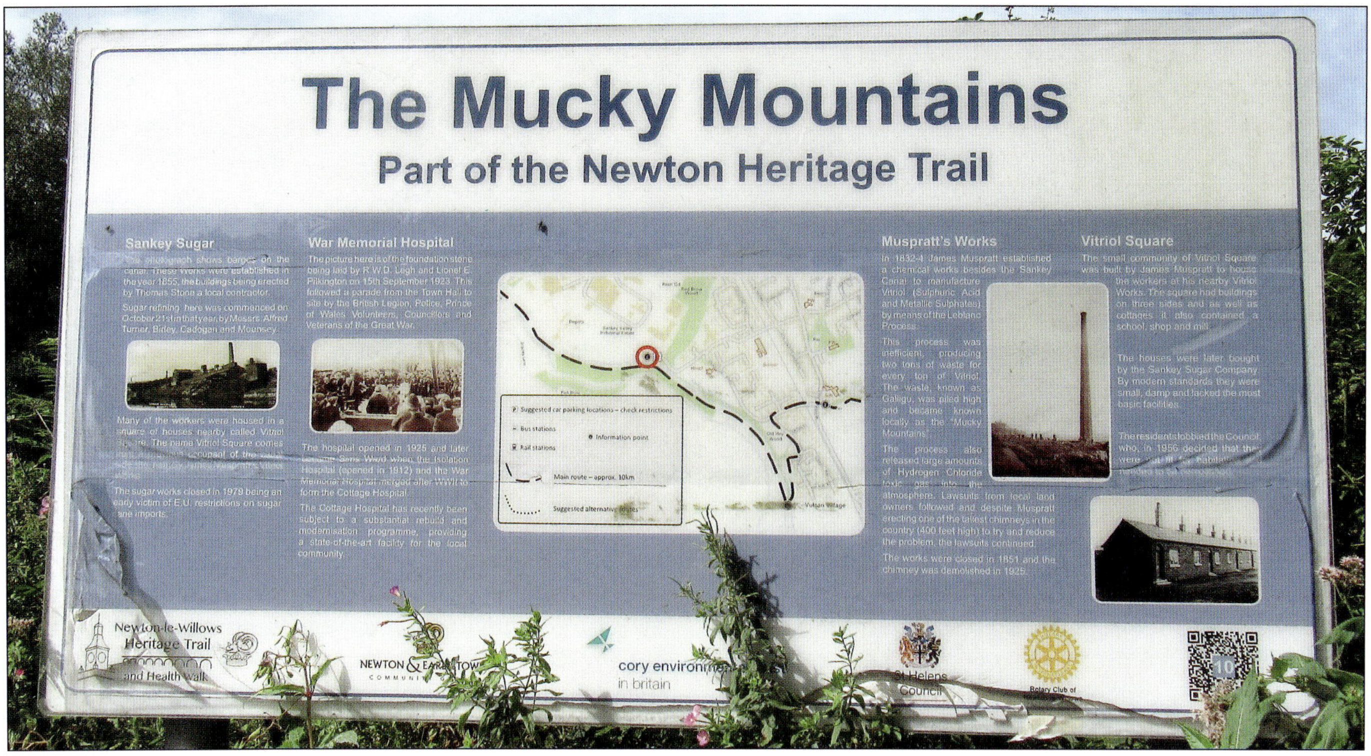

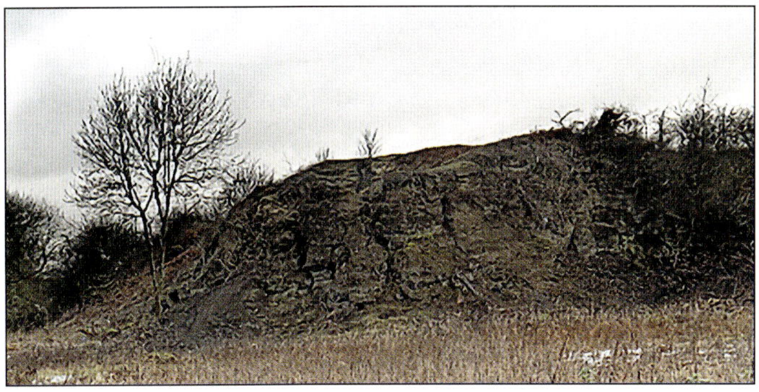

The Mucky Mountains, and left, the outcrop (showing the climbing routes).

During the war, Burtonwood had been a large and significant airbase, with a large squadron of Flying Fortresses (B17s) and Liberators, as the following illustration shows:

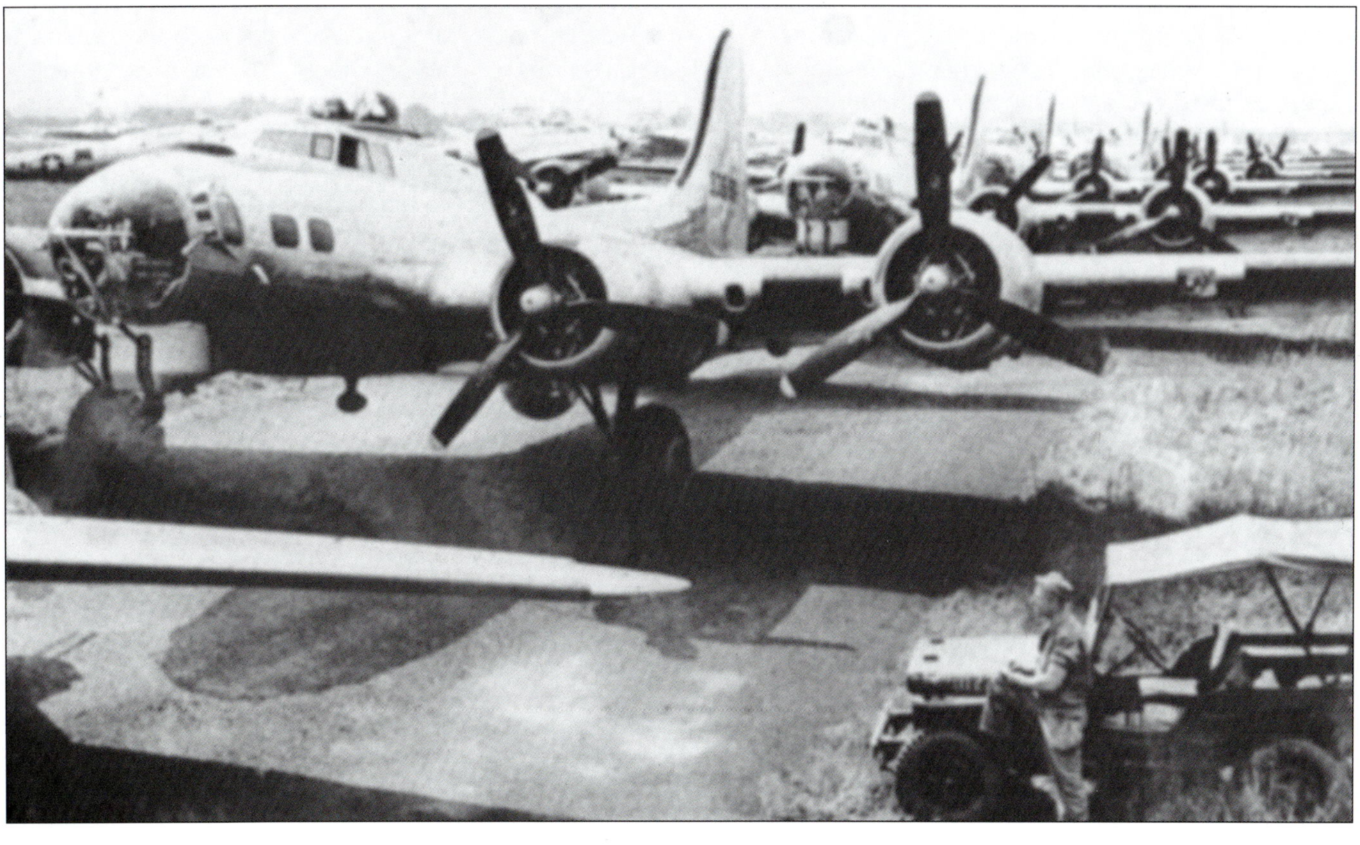

The location of all the above features and their relation to our council estate is illustrated by this annotated map.

Thus to get from our house to the airbase we would cycle there via the Sankey Valley.

It was around the time that Roy was studying at the Manchester College of Art that we had a joint adventure. It was an occasion that could happen only once in a lifetime and then only rarely. I will describe the event as I can remember it. The illustrations are all by courtesy of Roy.

Environs of Newton-le-Willows in 1933

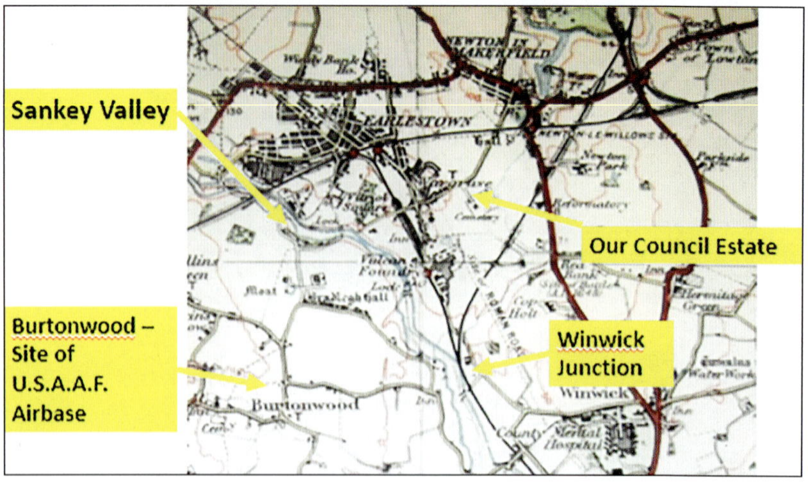

I enjoyed Christmas; I imagine that everyone does at a young age. Putting up the Christmas decorations still gave rise to feelings of excitement and the eager anticipation of the presents to come. The major pre-Christmas event though that really brought home to me that Christmas had at last arrived, was the collection of the chicken. I don't think that we could rise to a turkey or maybe my father preferred to spend the limited money he had available on presents for my brother and I. My father, being the kind of father he was, would probably have thought that the two of us would enjoy presents more than roast fowl of whatever kind. He knew a farmer from Burtonwood and each year Roy cycled over to collect it. On this occasion, however, I was to go with him.

So, wearing wellies, mac and school cap as my attire, we set off on a route that we were to repeat many times over the next eighteen months. Being more expert on the bicycle than I was, and being a bit stronger, my brother was given the haversack to carry that would eventually contain the chicken. There was a slight fall of snow on the ground and, as we left, we were given the usual type of parental good wishes, like don't do anything silly and don't be long.

The first half mile of the journey was within our council estate and then we took the road toward the Mucky Mountains and the stinking brook. This took us into the Sankey Valley and the road was reduced to a track as it descended towards the canal and brook and then skirted the opposite bank towards the Nine Arches, or viaduct, of Stephenson's railway. Before reaching the farm, however we joined a country lane, which bordered fields for a couple of miles until we approached the Air Base. The farm that we were visiting was close to the perimeter fence and as we skirted this along the lane, we were amazed to see one, then another and finally three large mound-like heaps of wrecked aircraft. They were in a field adjacent to the perimeter fence; the nearest being some 50 yards from the road but separated from it by a barbed-wire fence. We stopped and stared and, in excited voices, started to shout out the names of aircraft as we identified them. Flying Fortresses, Liberators, Thunderbolts and Lightenings. There must have been hundreds of them. The number was probably an exaggeration but the variety wasn't. Later we added Bostons, Seafires, Martlets, Corsairs, Beauforts and Barracudas to our initial list of aircraft types. The RAF had added to the list as well.

Christmas was almost forgotten as we surveyed these 'Boot Hill' like graveyards and talked excitedly about our find. We eventually continued on our journey and collected the chicken. Having had to drink a cup of hot Bovril to 'warm us on our way', we set out again; both of us knowing that we were headed for 'the dumps' as they came to be known. We left our bicycles on the grass verge close to the barbed-wire fence and walked a little way down the lane out of sight of the farm house and the farmer; whose fields were believed we were about to trespass upon. We crawled underneath the fence and I dragged the haversack containing the chicken along the ground.

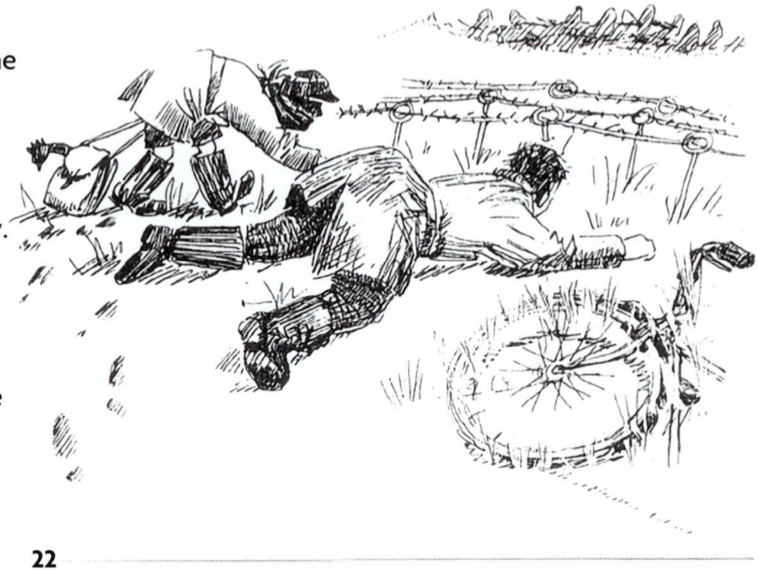

The start of the adventure

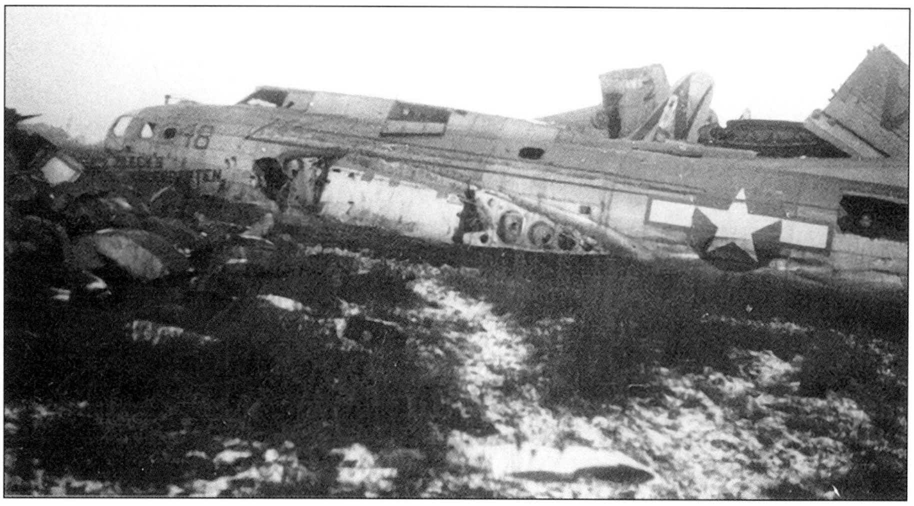

A section of the graveyard

This was a difficult and unpleasant manoeuvre since the lowest strand of barbed wire was close to the ground and, as the fence had been newly erected, the wire was quite taut. Although I managed to crawl through the space created by Roy relatively easily, taking the haversack and chicken with me, his was not such a pain free journey. I could not stretch the wire as far as he could and, since he was also bigger than I was, he was caught by the barbs several times. Apart from the barbed wire, it was also unpleasant because we had to crawl through long grass and, as I have already mentioned there was a slight fall of snow, it was a somewhat damp passage.

Our adrenaline flow rose considerably as we realised that we were now on a mission that could give rise to serious consequences if we were caught. We decided to continue our crawl. It was wet, but we thought it was worth it if it allowed us to escape observation. It did and we made the first of the three dumps without any problem. It was quite an amazing sight. Here were mainly flying Fortresses and Liberators. All the wings and engines were removed, the tails had been severed and the Perspex domes and windows had all been smashed. In the centre of the dump, Fortress had been laid alongside Fortress like so many sardines, body to body but minus their tails. Their aluminium skins and the shattered fragments of Perspex that remained in the mouldings glistened with the dampness provided by the snowfall as the sun's rays were reflected from one corpse to another.

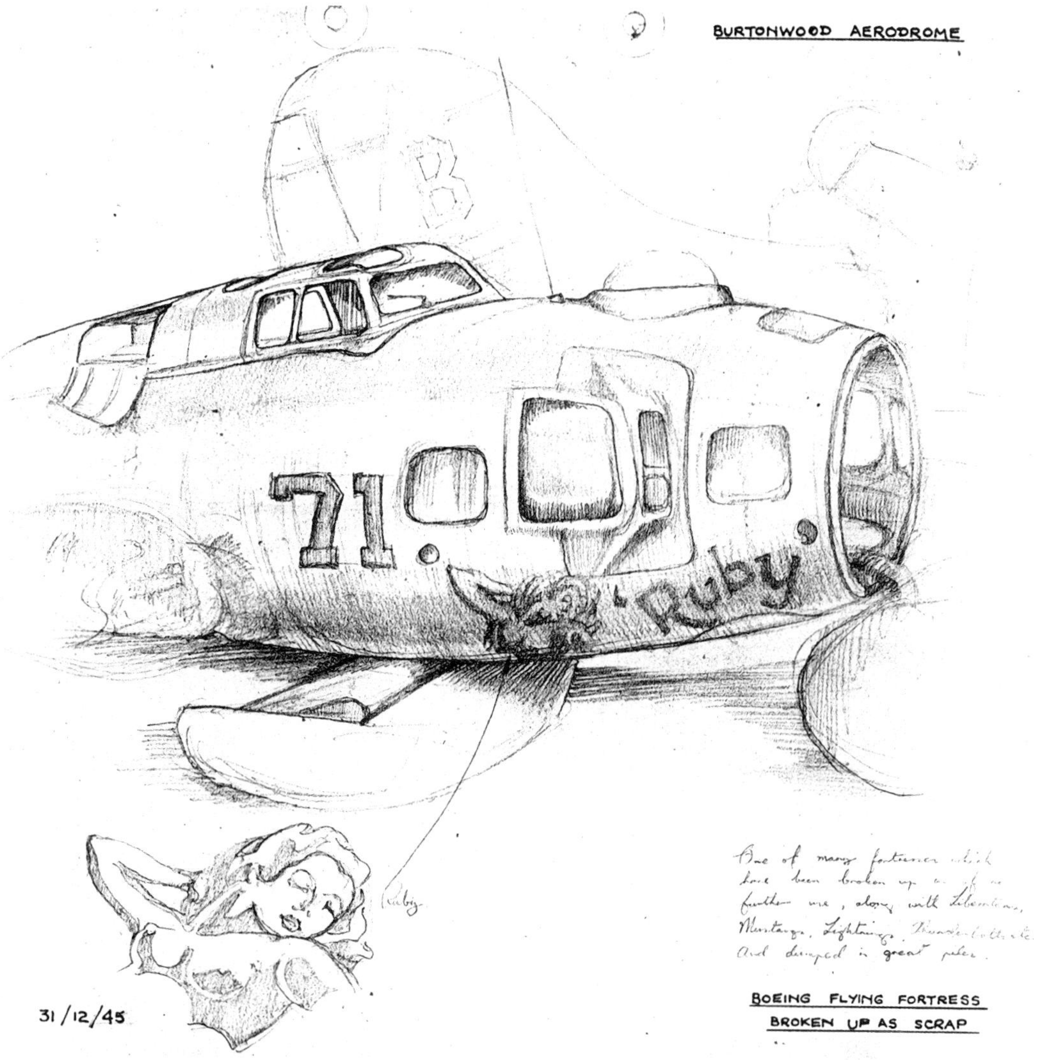

Other bodies were strewn across the lower ones in random fashion and here and there, the tail plane of a Fortress or Liberator rose from the dump; silhouetted against the deep blue of the winter's sky like some enormous headstone marking the spot.
We clambered excitedly over one fuselage to gain higher elevation and jumped from one to another in order to explore the extent of the mound. There must have been around forty to fifty remains in this

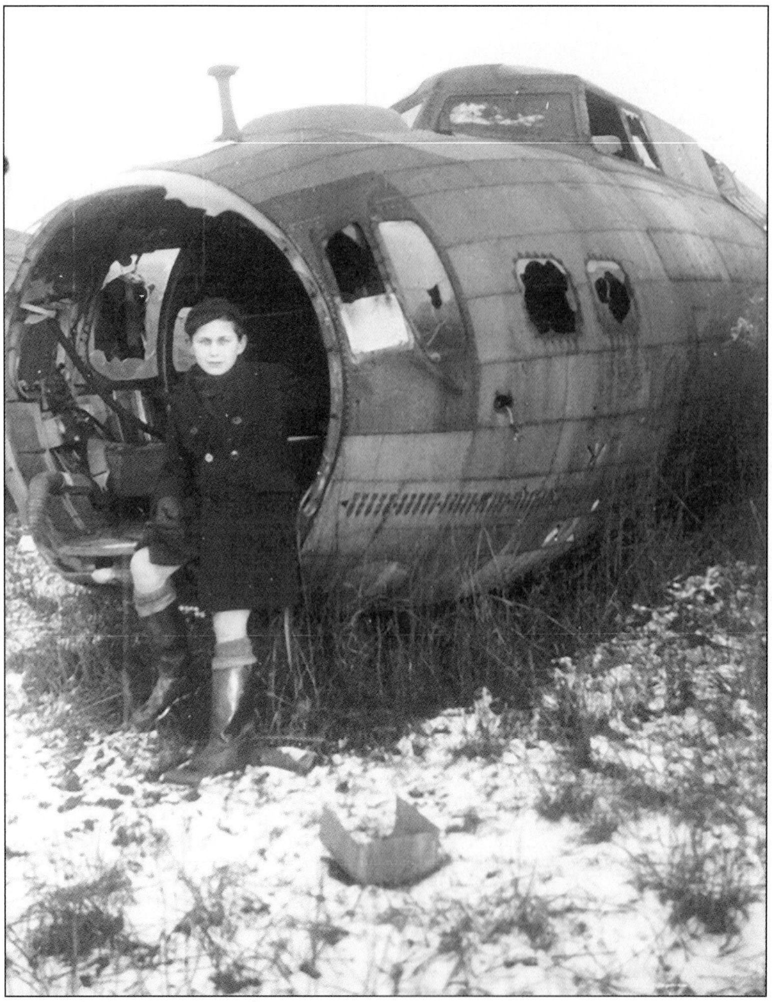
Me and the remains of a B17.

one dump and, as it turned out, this was the smallest of the three.

Having explored the size of our find we turned to a more detailed examination. I just felt excitement then; the sadness of it all only came to me much later as I have reflected upon the experience many times. Some of the B-17s were decorated and named. On the nose of one was an outline of the upper torso of a nude. I guess that she was blonde although in this form her hair, and everything else for that matter, was aluminium colour. One hand was behind her head producing a casual and provocative stance and her name was 'Ruby' (see previous page). Other B-17s were called 'June', 'Stardust', 'Eileen's Kindergarten' and 'Damn Yankees'. These are just a few that appeared on the 'Brownie' photographs that were taken by my brother on a later visit.

Rows of black painted bombs decorated the noses of some of the other aircraft indicating the number of missions successfully completed. Here were the veterans of the daylight raids.

Their usefulness now expended, they were laid to rest; not gracefully as befitted such heroes but disdainfully as if ready for the knackers yard. It seemed to me much later that this was such an ignominious end to these reliable and faithful servants of the aircrews who had all returned safely in them. In 1945 I would have dismissed such romantic thoughts as rubbish, they probably still are, for after all these aircraft were just inanimate objects. With excitement then as our only sensation, we began our disrespectful plunder.

It was quite common in those days, at least among our acquaintances, to fashion costume jewellery from pieces of Perspex. The supply was limited and I never knew where it came from, but my brother had been the one to bring this craft into our house. You could make rings, brooches and bracelets quite easily using a fretsaw, sandpaper and files. Perspex could be shaped by holding it in the steam jet from the spout of a kettle of boiling water. This would soften it and, on cooling, it would retain the new shape. It could be decorated by cutting the surface or by drilling small holes and then injecting paint. Reject dentist drills enabled holes of various shapes to be made quite easily. I don't know where Roy acquired these from either.

Well, here we had an almost unlimited source of Perspex and he began to fill the haversack with various shaped pieces. Being of a somewhat younger age and less interested in artistic endeavours, I collected souvenirs, cannon shells, bits of instrumentation of various unknown purposes, dials etc. All were piled into the haversack as my treasure.

Once the haversack was full Roy announced that we were leaving. He also announced that it was too heavy and ejected a number of my 'finds'. The argument that this caused was only brought to an end by his promise that he would bring me back. What a story we would have to tell our parents. They would also be excited.

They were not. For a start we were very late and secondly we had forgotten about the chicken at the bottom of the haversack. No longer did it look like the elegant bird that would grace our Christmas table. It was a mangled wreck. Once we had been suitably chastised it was, of course, forgotten except that the story entered family legend as one of the many amusing conversation pieces, when describing the 'two lads' to new friends or visitors.

We returned to these dumps many times and on some occasions I merely went to share what I believed might have been some of the experiences. I would sit in the cockpit of a B-17, don a flying helmet

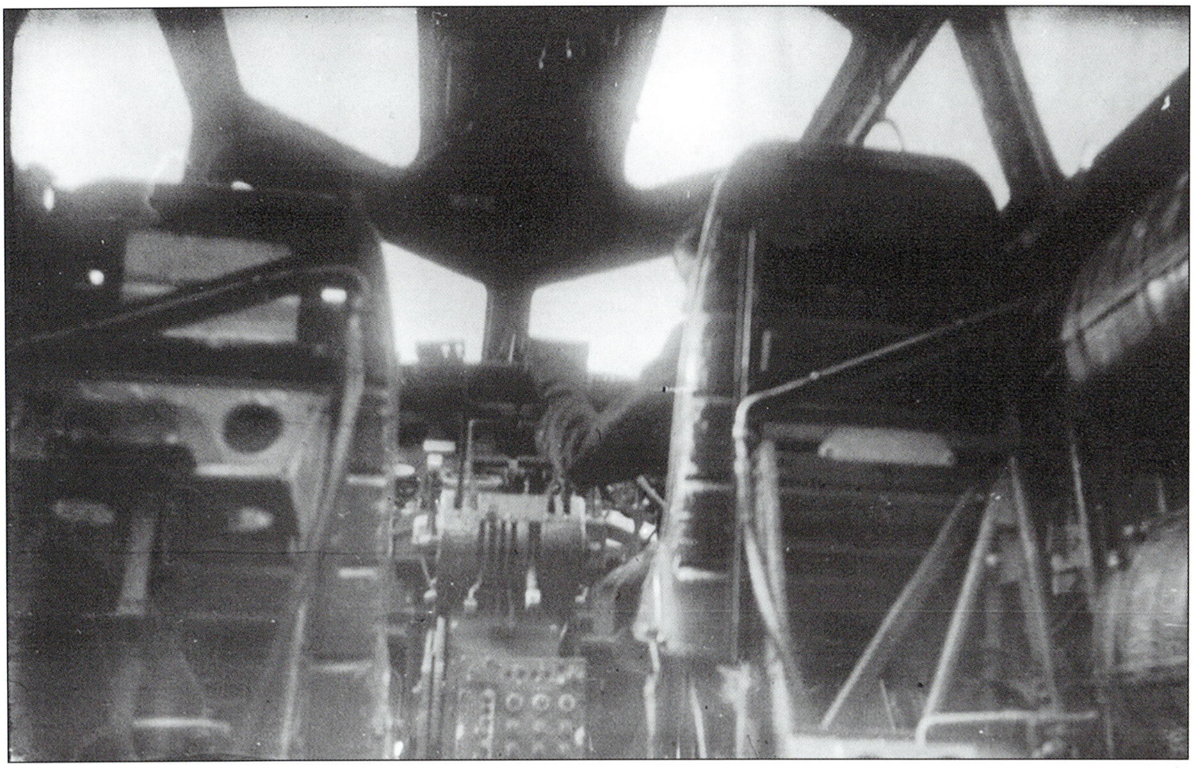

Co-pilot at the controls.

and oxygen mask that I had found on a previous visit and imagine myself setting out on a mission. I usually chose the co-pilot seat not realising then that the pilot occupied the one on the left. Little matter, it did not affect the fantasy. On my left were the four hand throttles and I would gently ease these back as we became airborne. I would accompany the flight with suitable sound effects. The engines would roar and whine as we took evasive action to avoid enemy shells and searchlights. Shells would explode all around us and I would shout instructions to the rest of the crew using a hand microphone or through the throat microphone embedded in the oxygen mask. Eventually we would return to base; a perfect landing every time and congratulations on a successful mission from the base commander.

Further sketches, illustrating various features of the aircraft follow.

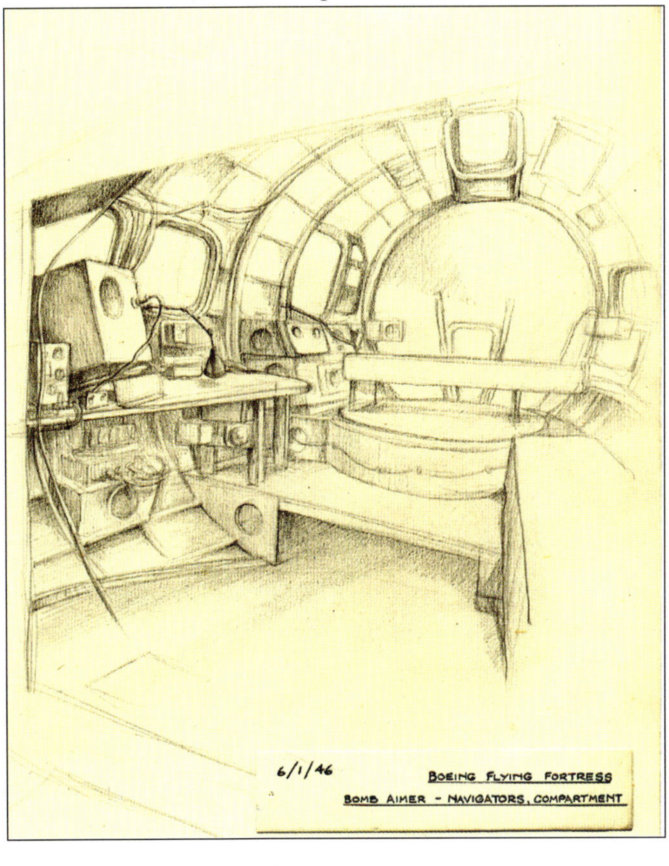

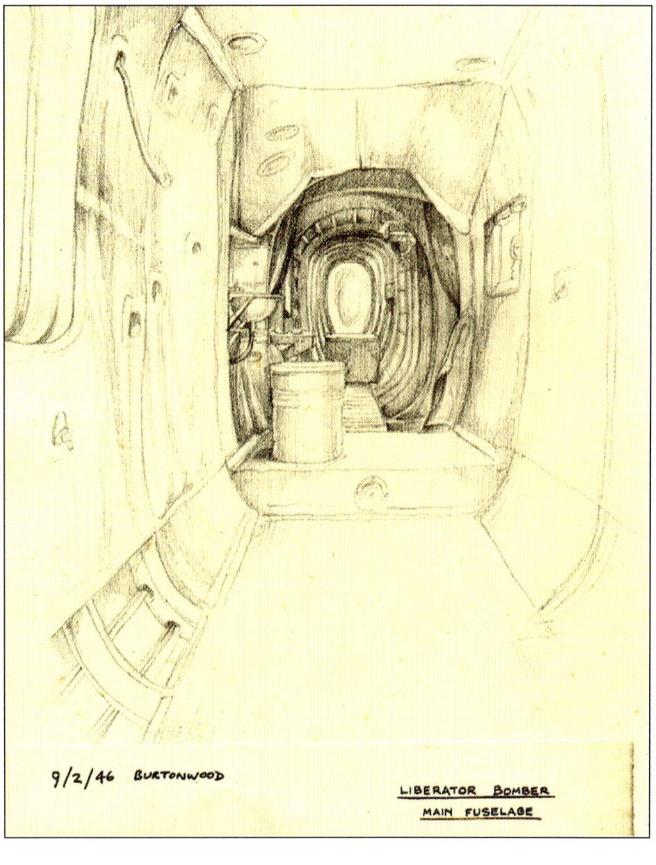

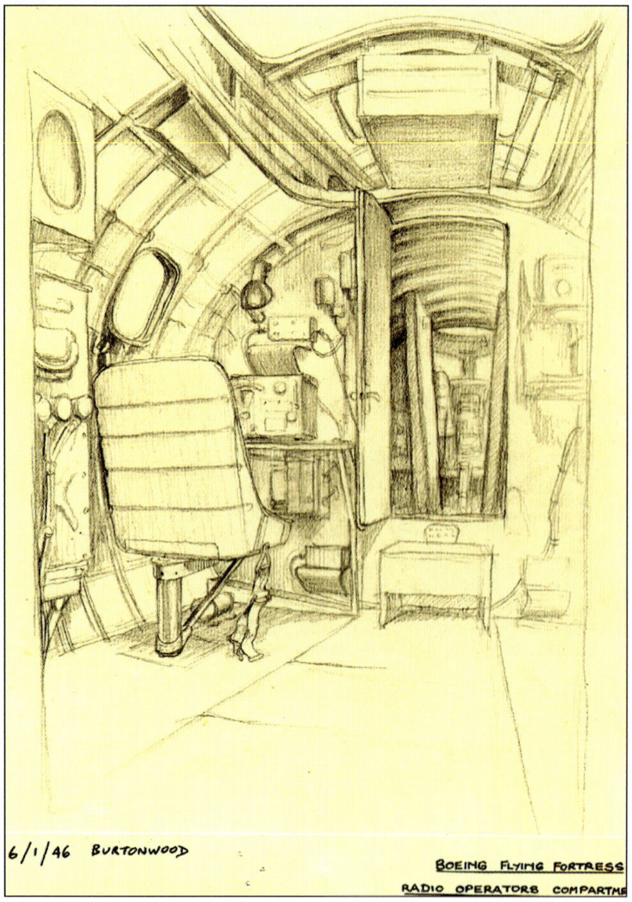

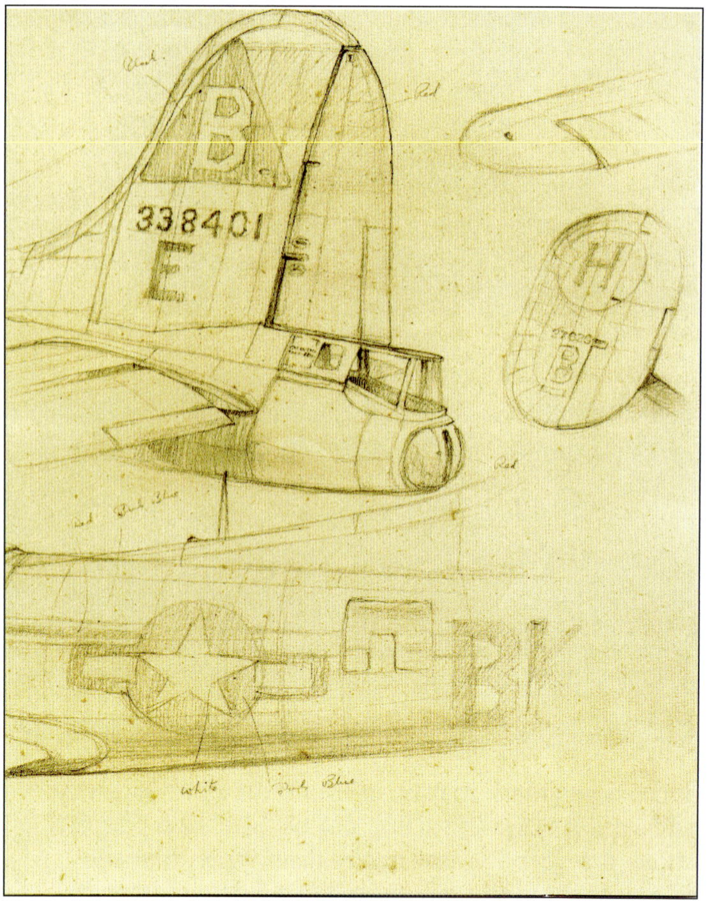

If Roy was with me he would usually tell me to shut up and this would bring me back to earth somewhat quicker. It was the case that the dumps were patrolled and we sometimes had to sit very tight and watch American servicemen pass within yards of the aircraft we were inhabiting. I was less aware of the need for caution as was Roy and on one occasion I found a fire extinguisher with a plastic conical nozzle that ejected 'dry ice' at high speed and volume. It had a pistol grip that fascinated me. Of course I squeezed the trigger and the din that it created inside this closed aluminium body frightened both of us. We remained quiet for a long time after that before daring to venture from the aircraft in case the noise had been heard by a passing patrol. It had probably sounded ten times more ear piercing inside than it did outside but we were not to know that. We were fortunate and we were never caught on this, or on any of our other visits.

Roy's main occupation (being the artist of the family) was to record some of the sights. The illustration (right), showing the cockpit, represents his impression of the B17 that I was pretending to fly. As well as Perspex he also acquired a few souvenirs. Some of the items that we collected were usable such as angle-poise type lamps off navigator's tables, adjustable swivel chairs and cork-handled knives, out of dinghy survival kits.

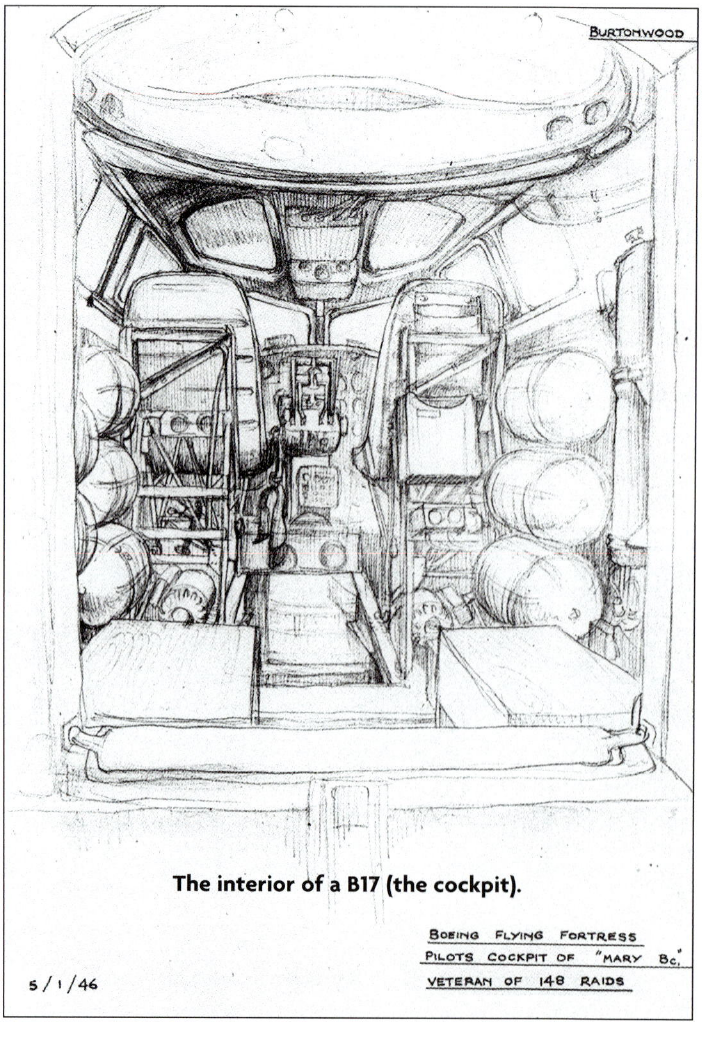

The interior of a B17 (the cockpit).

Most of what I collected however wasn't. It largely comprised bomb-aiming sights, the masks and microphones that I have already mentioned, various cockpit instruments, including a liquid-filled compass that was too bulky to carry around and a variety of cannon shells; a large number of which were live. The best find of all in my view, which of course Roy got, was a Very pistol. This is not a device that has much of an application on a council estate but we did use it to good effect on one bonfire night when we had managed to acquire a cartridge. It caused much consternation to the two little old maiden ladies who lived next door. It was quite spectacular and much more impressive than any rockets that we, or any of our neighbours could afford to buy.

The following illustrations give some idea of the souvenirs that formed my collection.

Trophies

- **Flying Helmet**

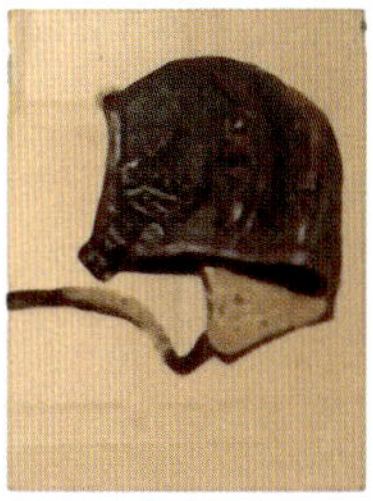

- **Throat Microphone**

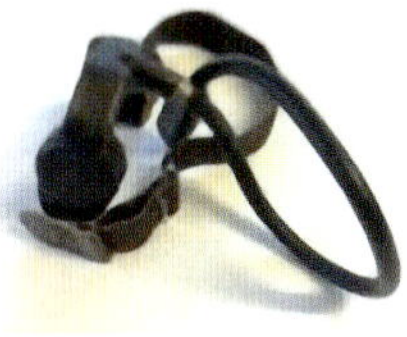

- **Oxygen Mask**

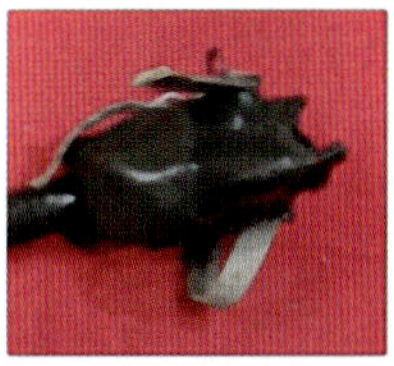

- **Very Pistol**

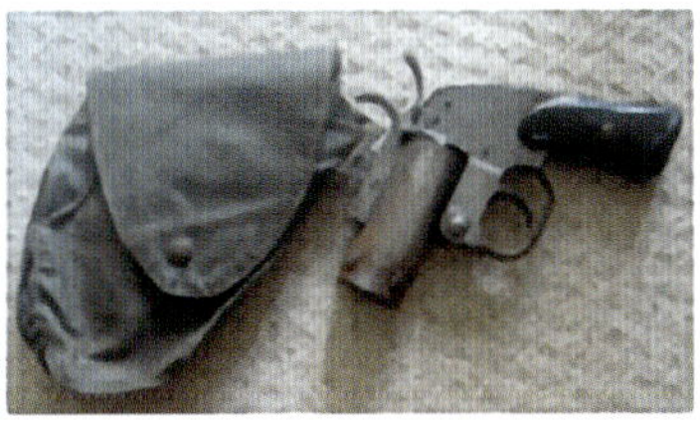

- **Dinghy Knife**

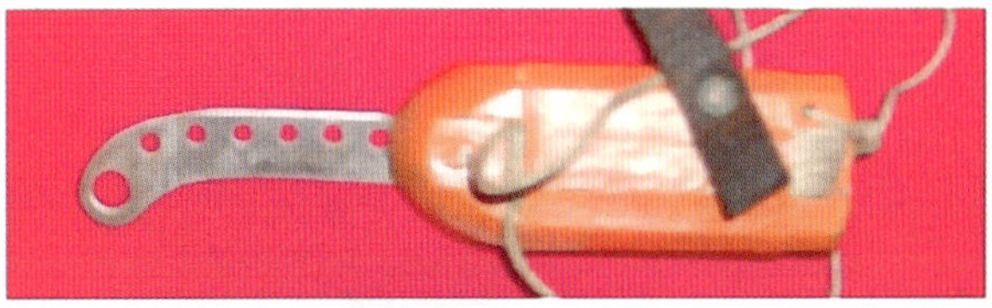

- **Live Cannon shells**

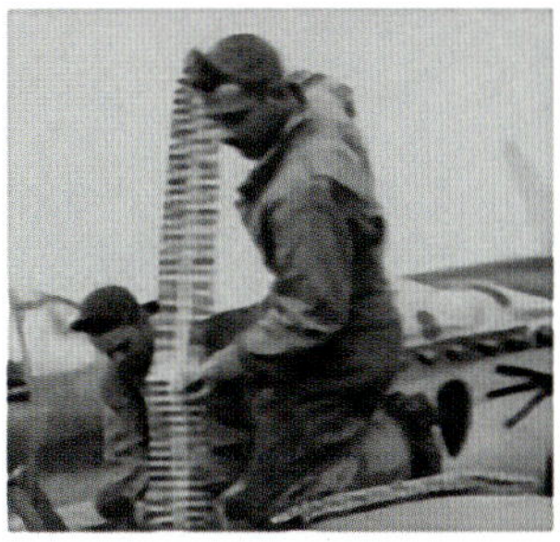

Collecting all this stuff provided one problem and that was what to do with it. Although it was useless it was, along with my bits of shrapnel, my war memorabilia collection.

I found the ideal hiding place. The living room (or kitchen as we called it) in our council house had one of those old-fashioned large steel fireplaces and grates that you had to black-lead. It was situated in a central chimney breast that protruded into the room.

On either side were built-in cupboards and drawers. The left one contained two small drawers at the top alongside each other and two long drawers underneath. The space below the bottom drawer made an ideal store. You had to remove the drawer completely to know that there was anything there. There my collection remained until 1961 when father died and mother moved out of the house. When Roy and I were clearing the house we came across the collection. Shrapnel, gun sights and other such objects could just be thrown away on the local tip but we felt that we couldn't do that with unexploded shells. Our solution was to dig what we thought was a deep hole in the back garden and bury it. It might have been there still if the house had not been occupied by a keen gardener.

This is why a headline 'Bomb disposal experts called to remove unexploded shells from council estate', was of such interest to me. It appeared in a local paper when I was working for the U.K.A.E.A. back in the 1960s and it was brought to my attention by a colleague. Bomb disposal experts indeed! The stuff had been sitting next to our kitchen fire for sixteen years. Unfortunately this was a time when photocopying was uncommon so I do not possess a copy of the article. I have searched newspaper archives, but since I do not remember which paper it appeared in or the date, I have so far been unsuccessful.

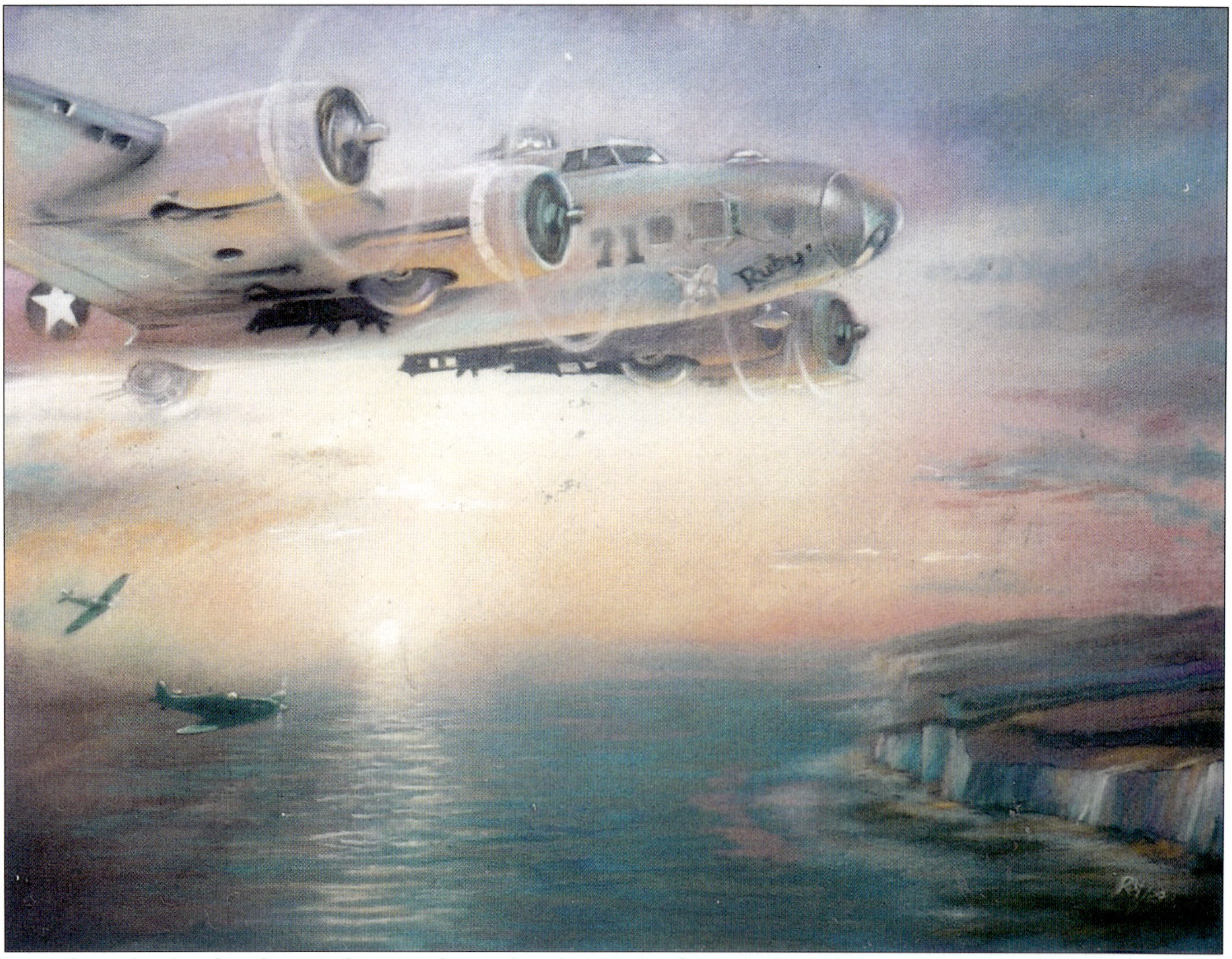

Apart from the sketches done, on location, he produced a painting for one of my Christmas presents some 60 years after the event as a special reminder of the above adventure. This is his only aircraft painting.

CHAPTER THREE

CAREER DEVELOPMENT

For some time Roy was engrossed in developing his career. This involved him in changing employment; doing a considerable amount of travelling and moving house. He had married Dorothy and, initially, had taken up residence in Birley Street in Newton-le-Willows.

Roy's artistic activity became related to commercial business interests and away from a leisure activity.

He left the Vulcan Foundry sometime in the fifties and took a job with a firm called Electro-Hydraulics in Penketh near Warrington. It was a post concerned with advertising and general publicity. They manufactured forklift trucks and hydraulic undercarriages for aircraft. He stayed for a few years and then became publicity manager for the Palace of Variety in Leeds. It is now called Leeds City Variety, but it is best remembered for the TV series called "The Good Old Days" featuring Leonard Sachs.

Here he became friends with "Big Daddy" the professional all-in wrestler and the two of them viewed and Roy bought the house in Alwoodley, Leeds, where Roy and Dorothy have lived for the last sixty-odd years. It was either very brave or reckless of him to buy a house without Dorothy having viewed it first.

A few years later he took a job with a Singapore-based exhibition management company, called Interfama, where he stayed for the remainder of his working life, with the exception of doing the same activity as an individual for the last two years. He basically designed exhibition arrangements for a variety of industries from mining to armaments and acquired the exhibitors. This involved him in extensive world travel, which he enjoyed. It is this period in his life which has provided the motivation for exploring and painting railways in various countries. The last two years were spent arranging exhibitions in Chile for naval and associated industries.

Once he had retired he became engrossed in the kind of art for which he is best known, i.e. Railway Art. He experimented with painting in oils, but decided that he preferred pastel as the most expressive medium.

Roy did not completely ignore railways during the above period of career development and he and I took on a research project related to the history and development of monorails for which he produced the following "Artist's Impressions".

Palmers Monorail 1825.

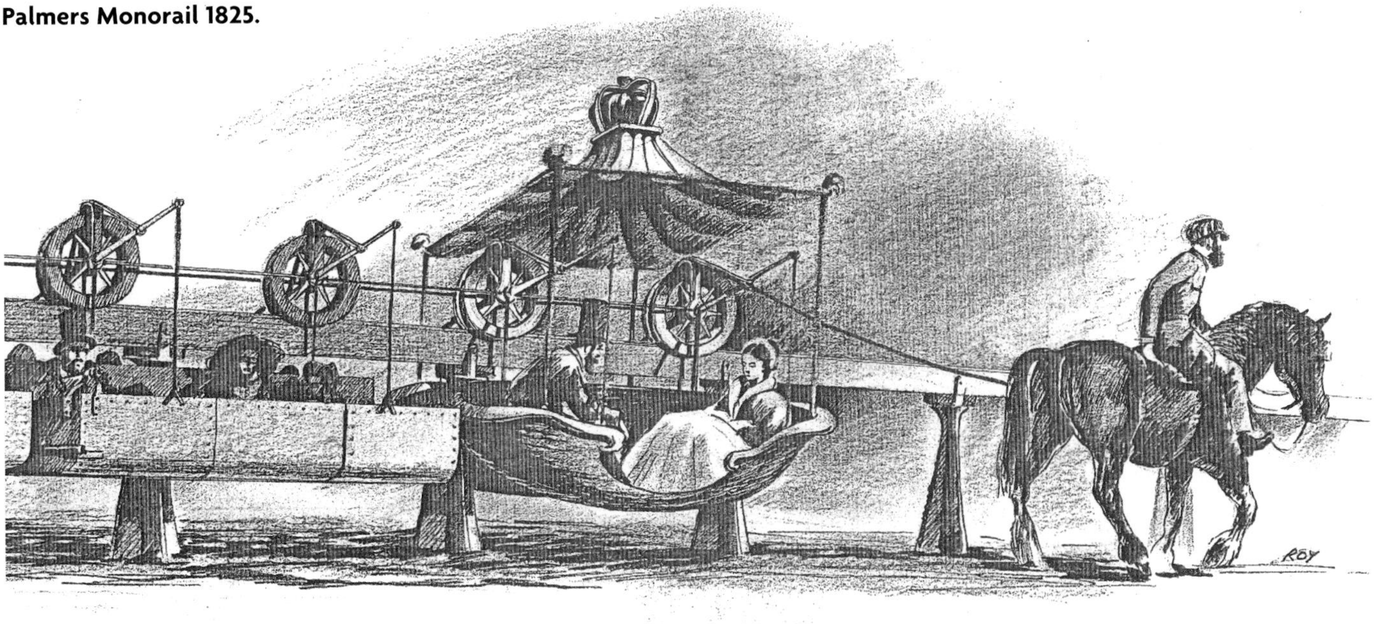

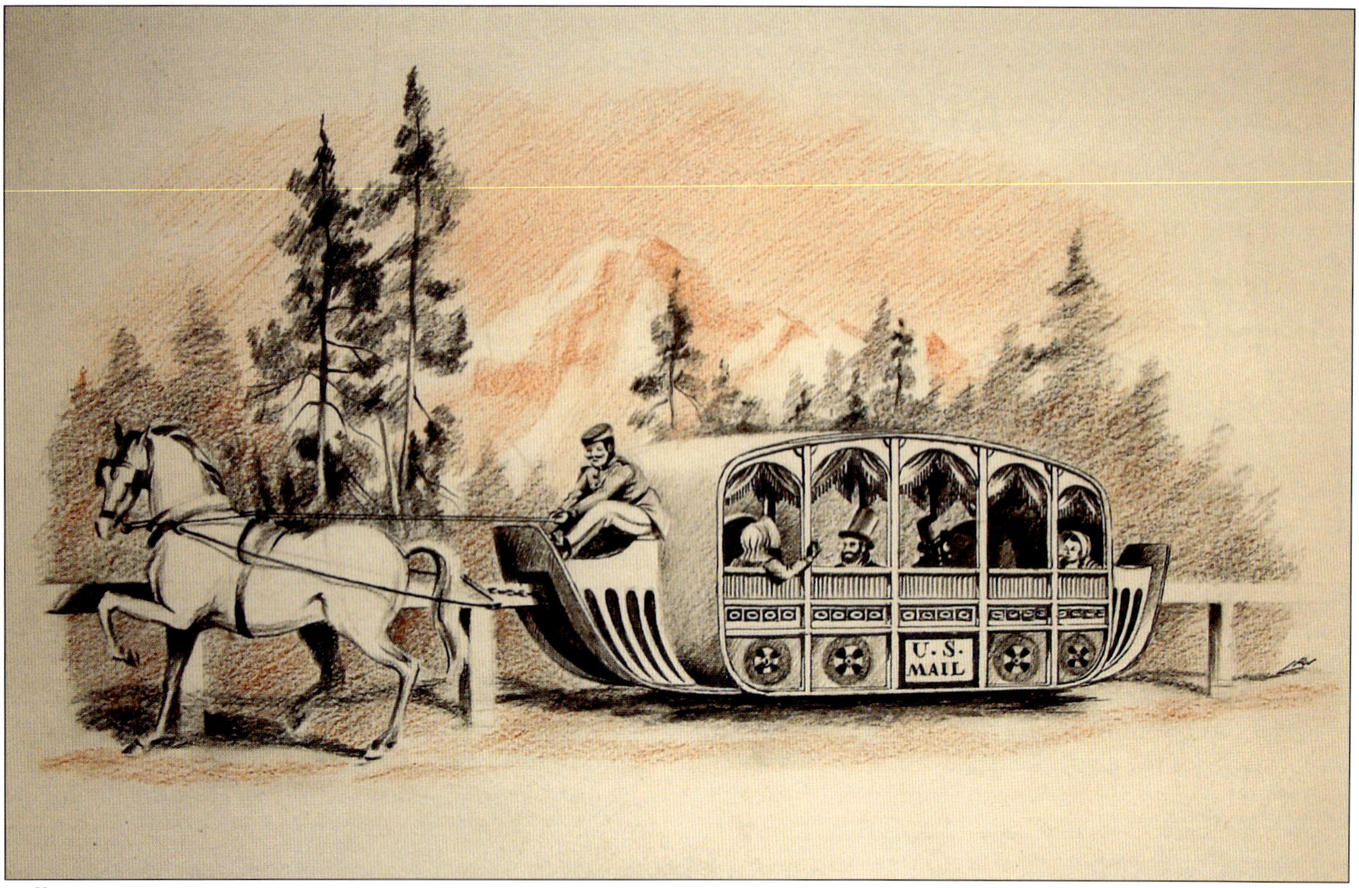

Mills 1824.

William IV Car 1830.

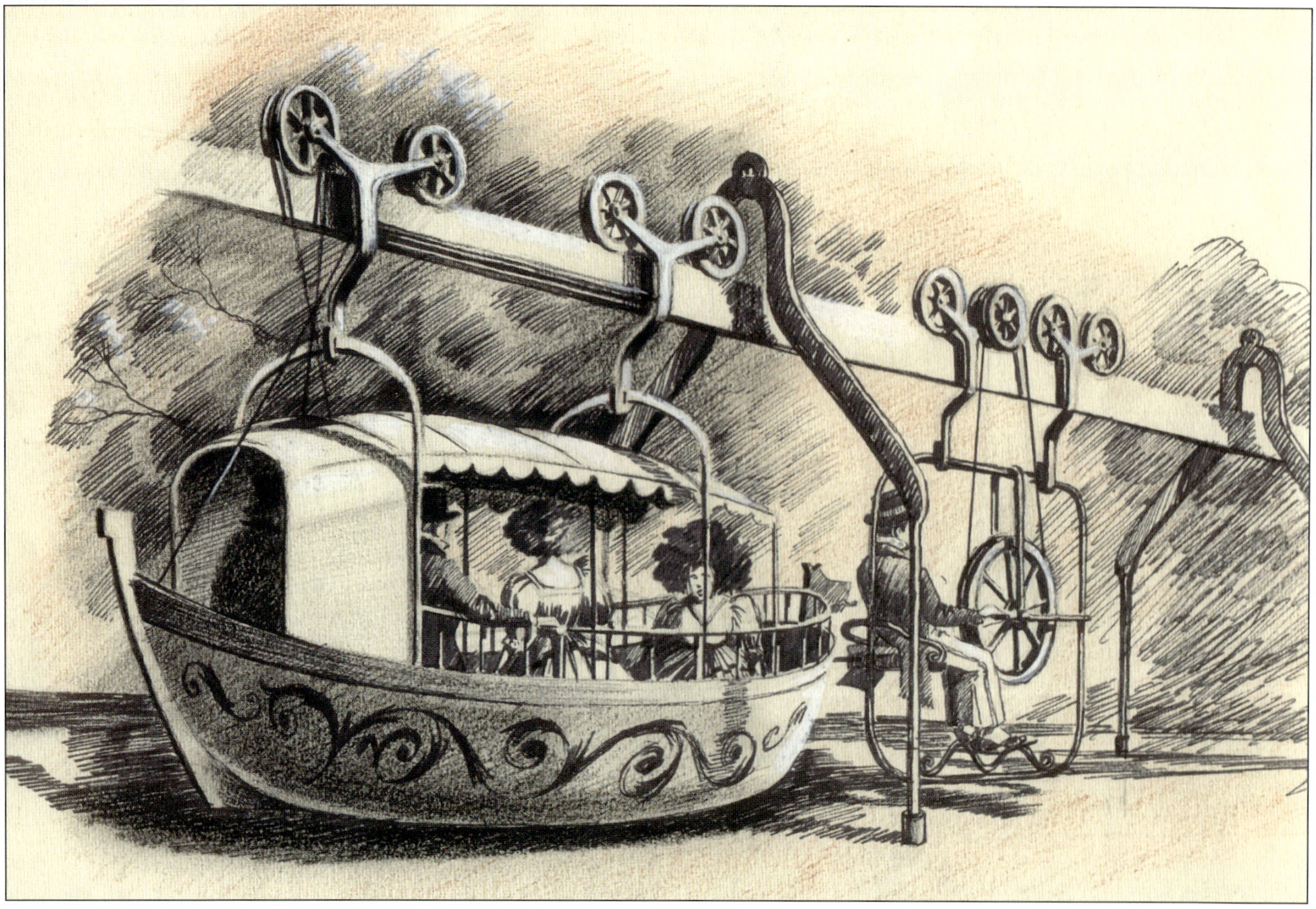

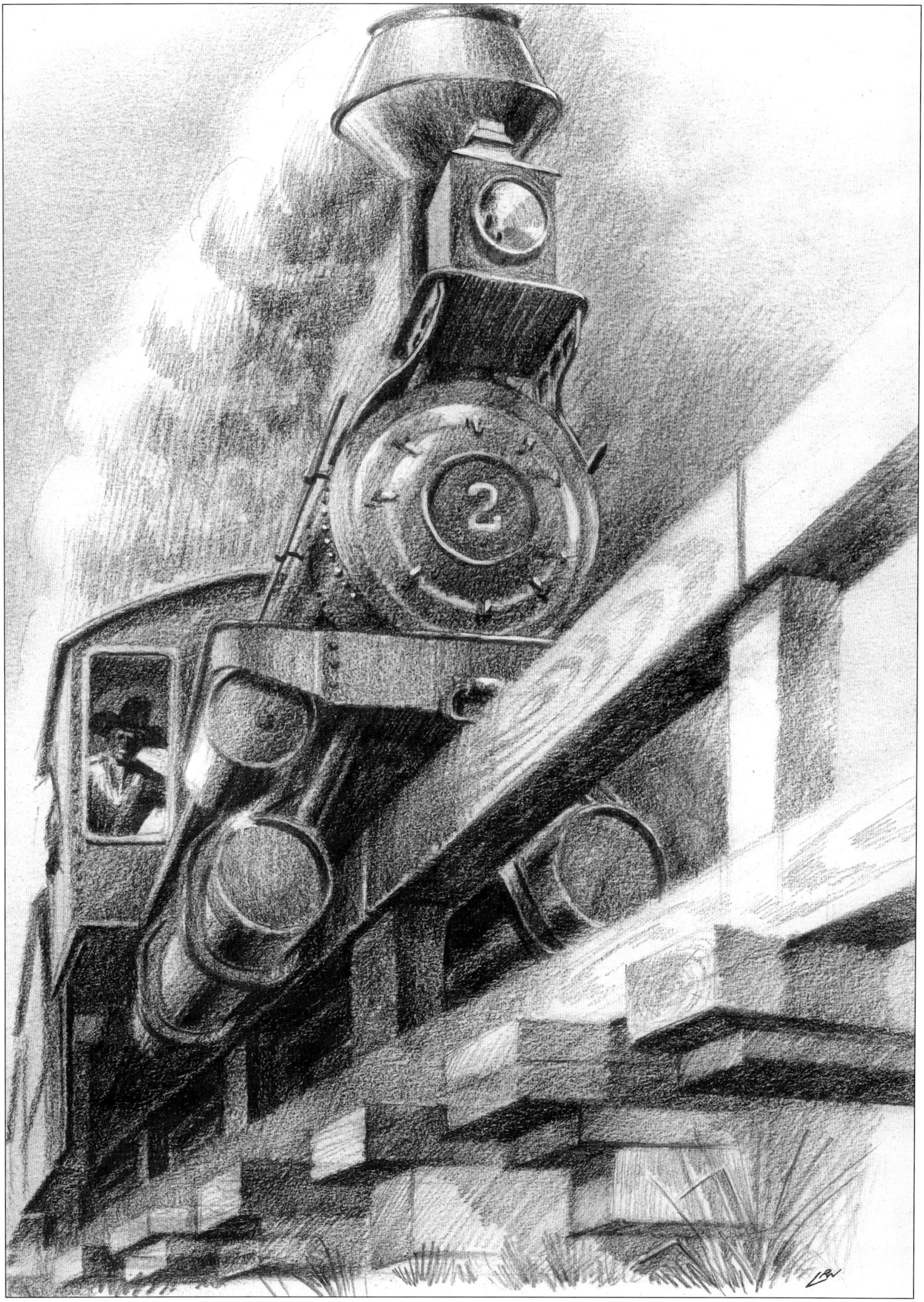

Pegleg (Bradford & Foster Brook Rly. Co.) 1878.

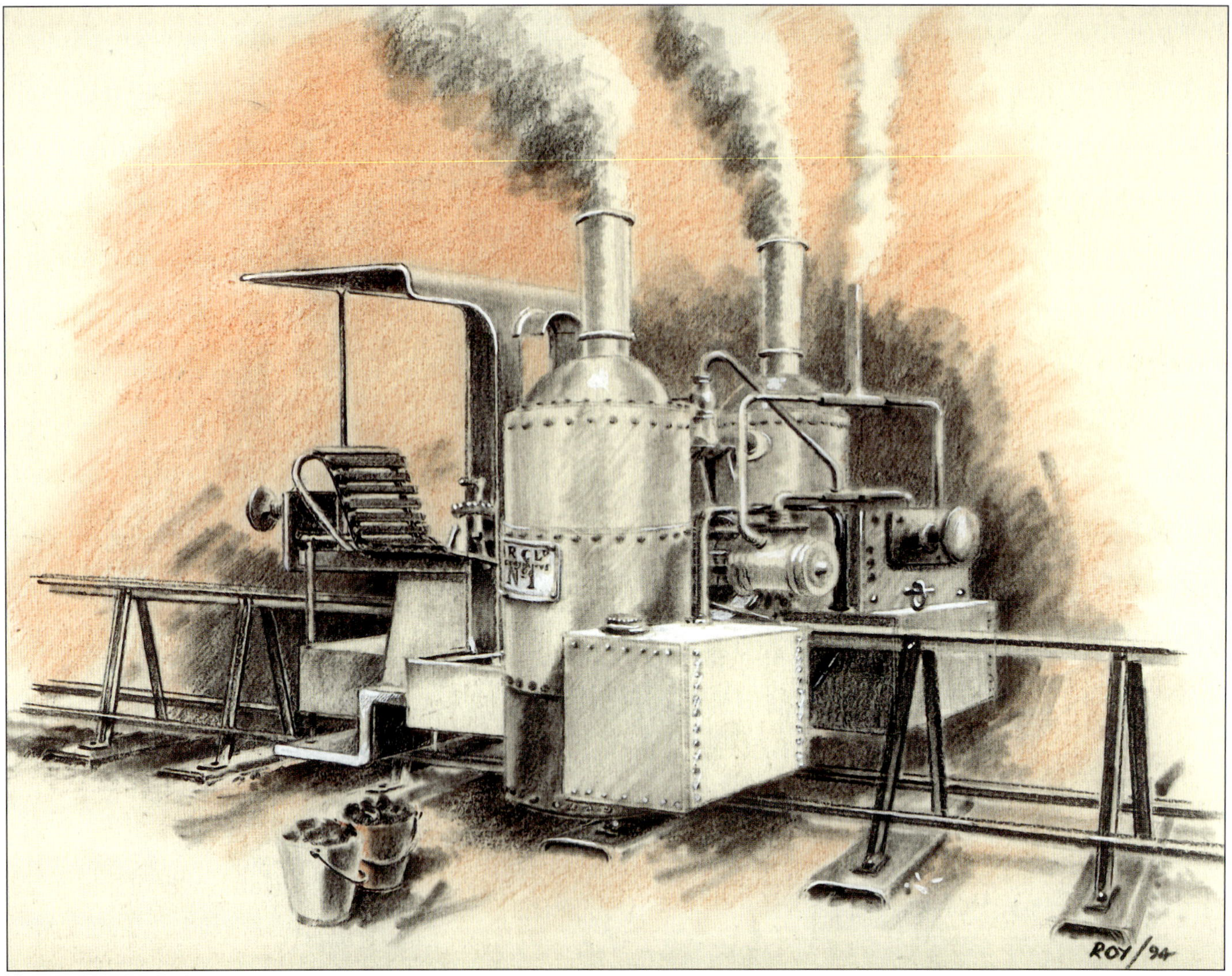

Lartigue 1886.

Listowel & Ballybunion 1888.

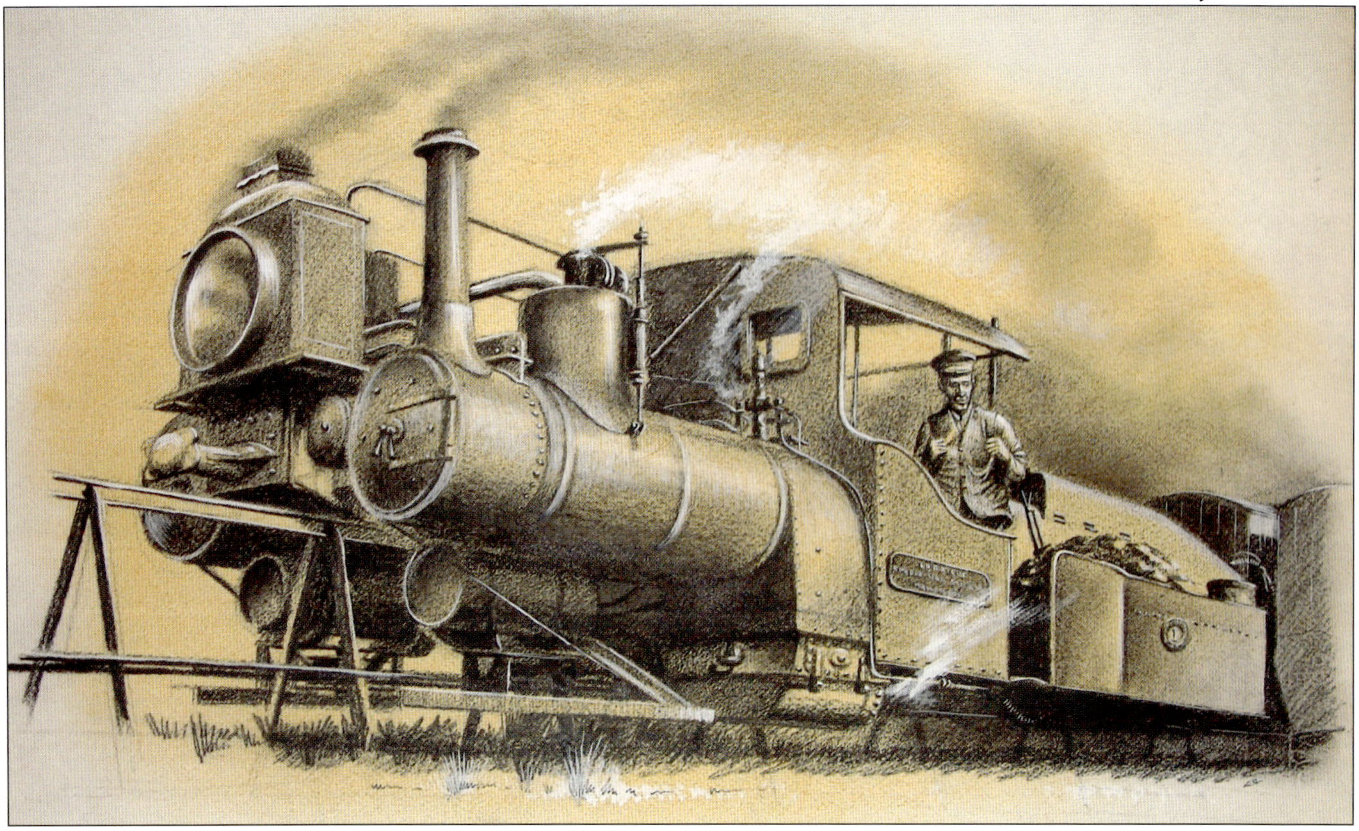

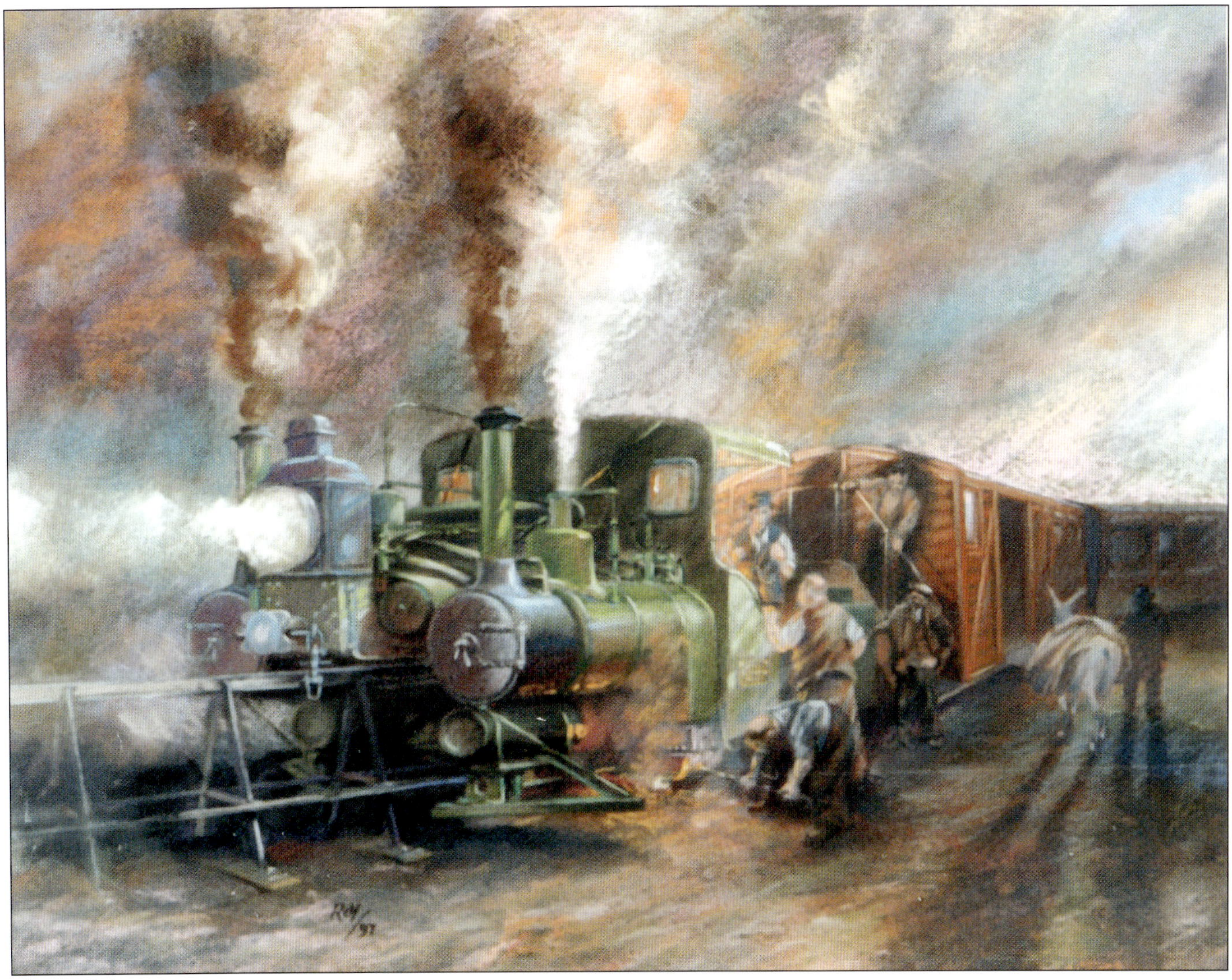

Also Ballybunnion.

Alweg 1952.

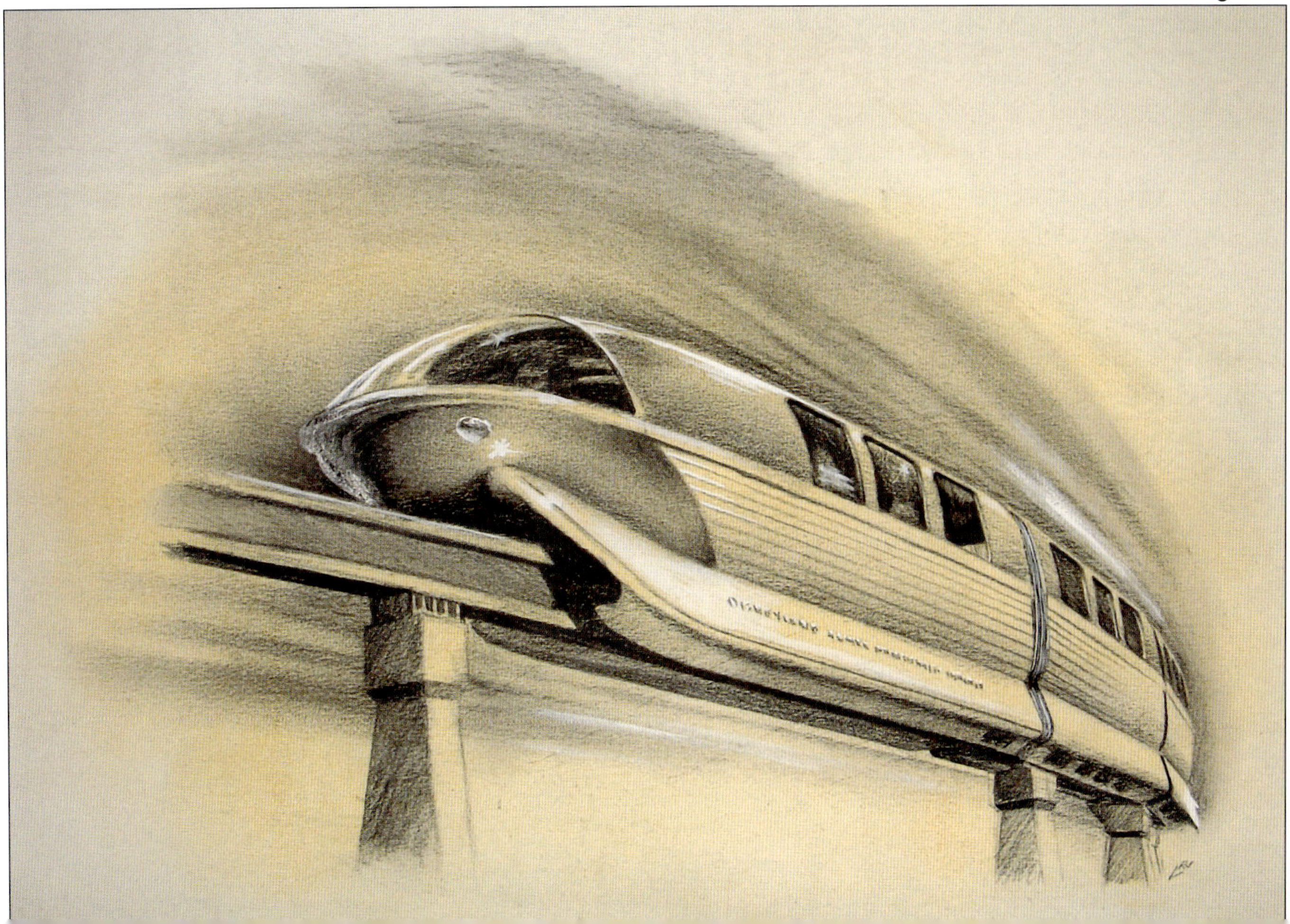

Outcome of the research project

The research must have occupied us, intermittently, for about 50 years and it is still ongoing for me. The outcome of our joint activity was in the form of:

1) A lecture to the Newcomen Society in London. This was given by me.

2) A series of 14 articles in the National Railway Museum Review, produced by Roy.

2) A lecture called "Monorail to Maglev" which forms one of my current lecture series. (Here "Maglev" is not a town on the eastern seaboard of Russia, but is short for "Magnetic Levitation").

During our research into monorail development we came across the following cartoon from an early issue of Punch. I always end this lecture with the cartoon as it illustrates a monorail.

" Quick ! Dismantle It !

Romans are coming ! "

(Reproduced by courtesy of "Punch")

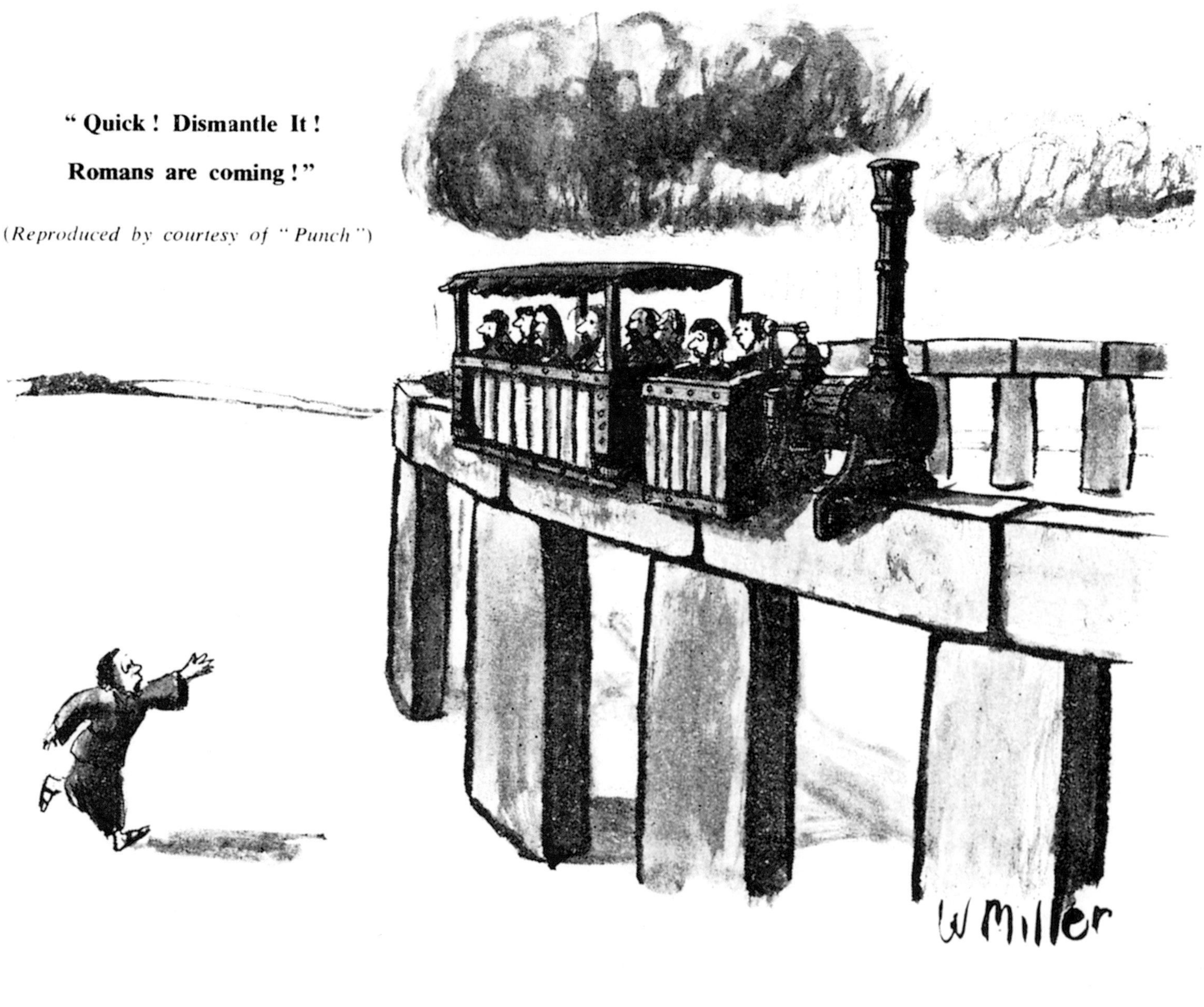

CHAPTER FOUR

EXTRACTS FROM AN ARTIST'S LOG BOOK

There are six log books in all and I have reproduced a selection of contents just to give an impression of the kind of sketches Roy did to record his thinking about the paintings prior to their production. He also included, within the books, sketches of the people he observed displaying their attitudes and gestures. The log books themselves represent an illustration of his artistic abilities. What follows is a record of the dedication and enthusiasm that he retained for the locomotive and the appropriate settings. He never forgot people and these feature in most of his paintings.

Roy was not entirely focused on railways. He produced Christmas cards, though those that he produced for the National Railway Museum were, appropriately, reproductions of some of his railway paintings. He produced a number of paintings for myself and members of my family. The B17 picture is one such example. Some other examples follow:

The illustration below was again a Christmas present for me. It is a picture of the A49 road from Warrington to Wigan as it passes under the Stephenson's Liverpool to Manchester railway at

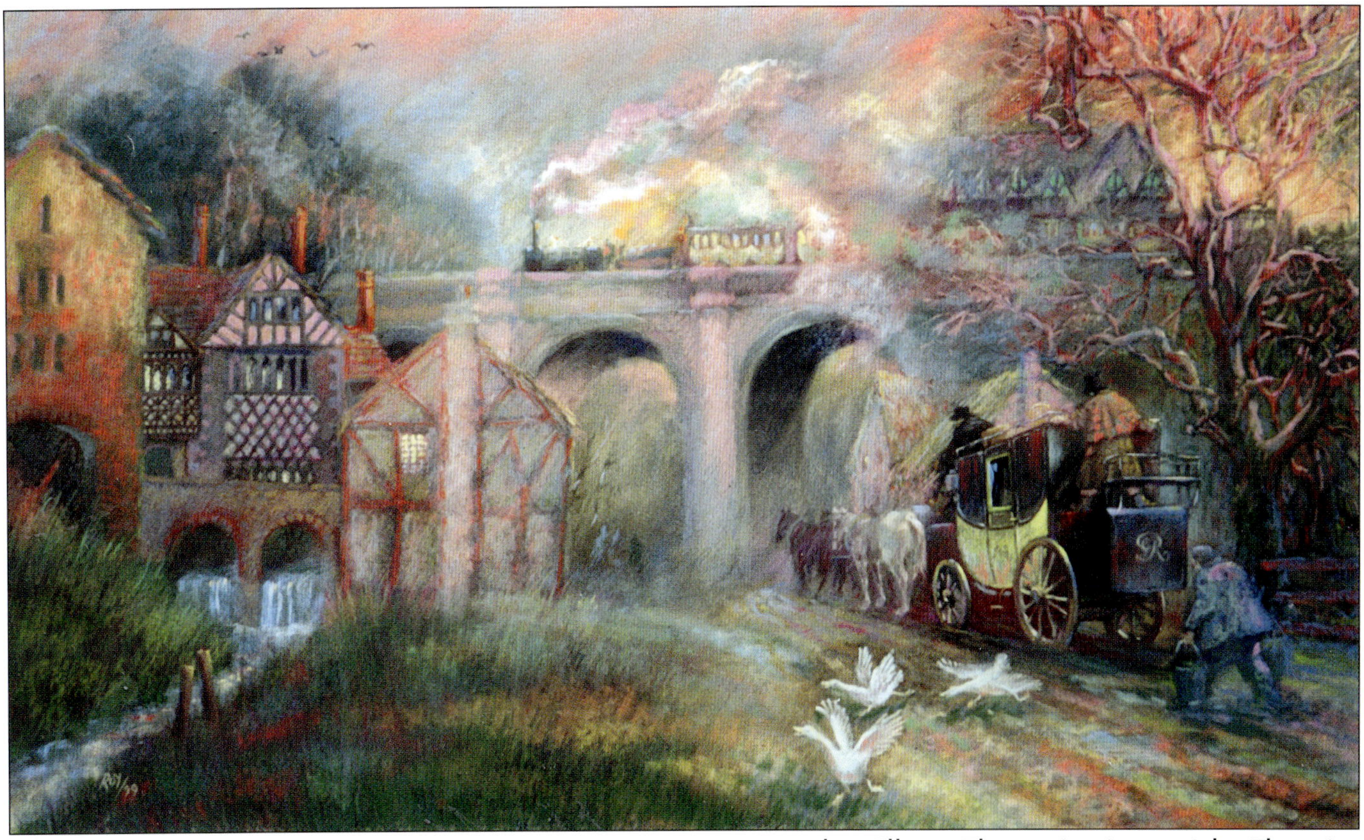

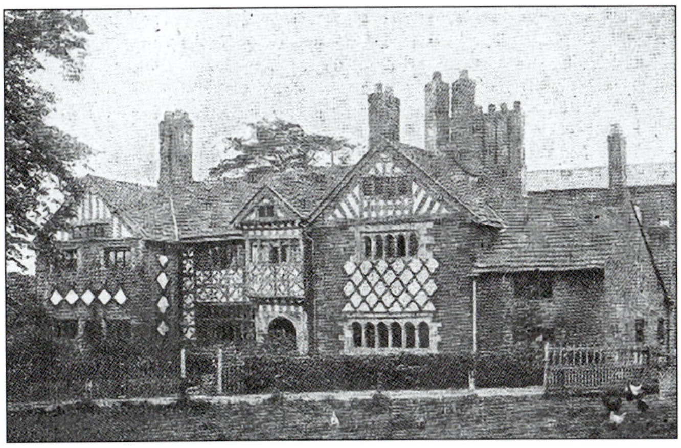

Newton-le-Willows. The station is top right. There is some "artistic licence" in that it shows Newton Hall in the wrong place. However, this Elizabethan hall was demolished in 1965 and my wife and I both remembered it well and regretted that it had gone; hence its inclusion in the painting. An actual photograph is included alongside.

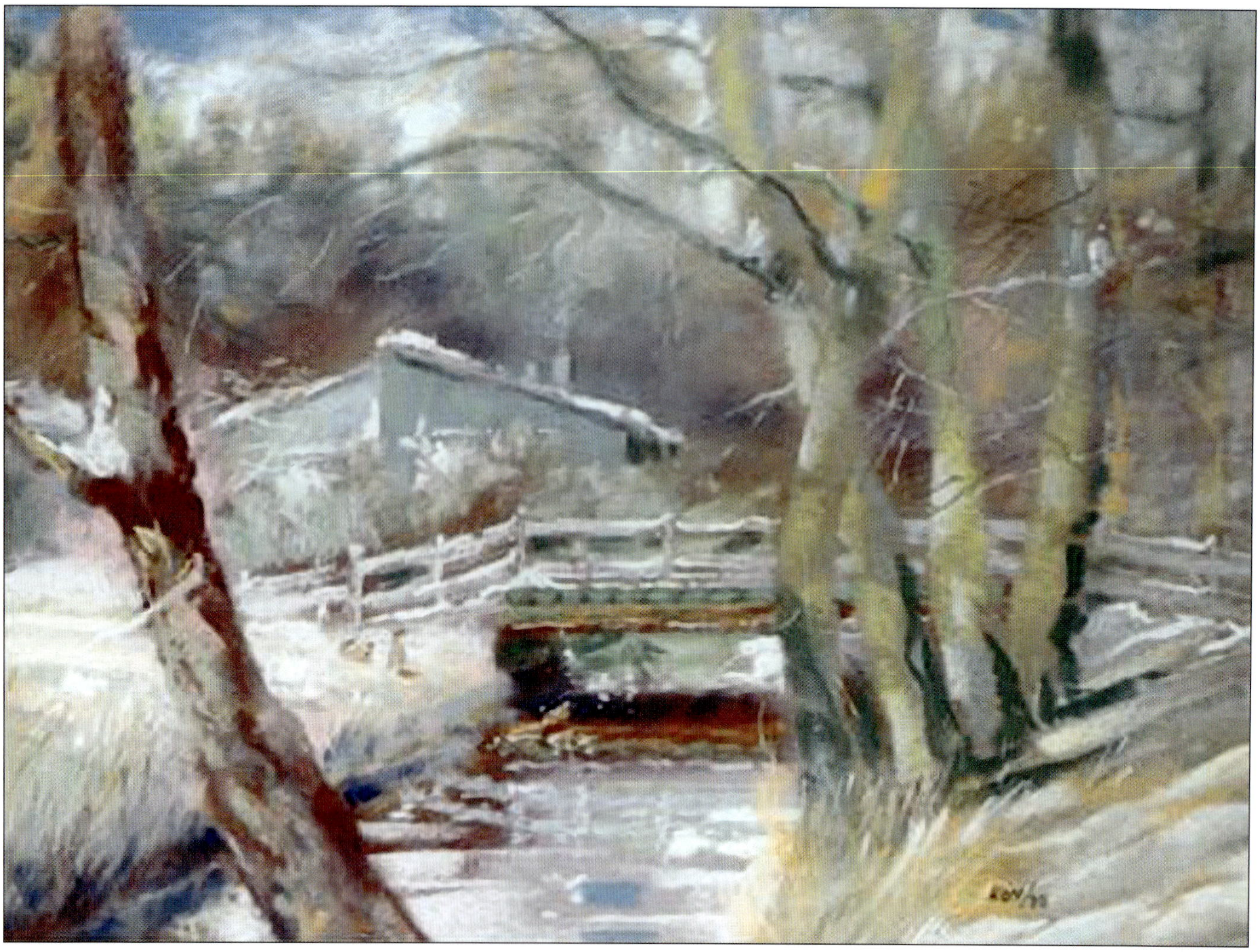

Another of his paintings illustrates the bungalow in which we used to live, as a winter scene.

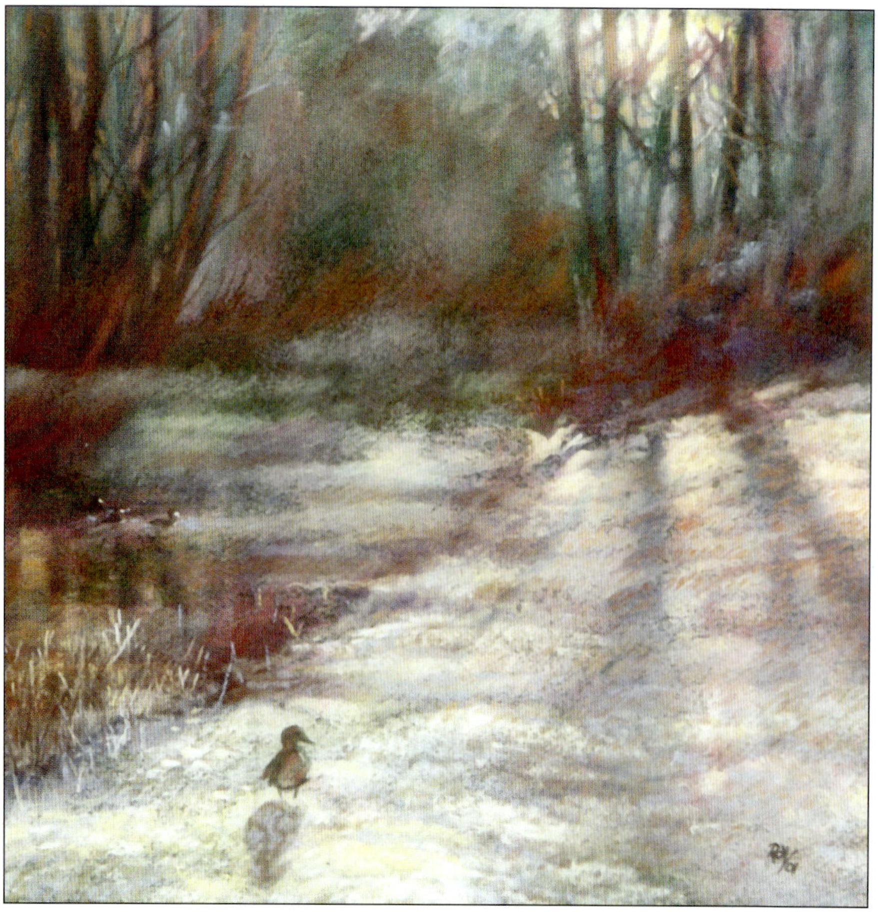

Shortly after we moved in we started to feed the ducks which paddled around on the beck. One had an injured wing and we called this Jemima until we discovered (when she changed her feathers) that he was male. He then became known as Jim. He became very friendly and eventually he would knock on the front door for his bits of bread, which he would take from my hand. He featured on one of Roy's Christmas cards. He eventually disappeared and we never knew why. Since he could not fly he might have been taken by a fox or, maybe, he just went somewhere to die. The painting shows him on the way to our front door.

The remainder of this chapter contains extracts from Roy's log books.

"AS AN ARTIST ..... THE TASK IS TO EXPRESS NEW AND PERSONAL INSIGHTS. IF YOU FAIL TO DO THIS, IF YOU TREAT YOURSELF AS ONLY A CAMERA, YOU ARE AT BEST A CRAFTSMAN"

"THE ULTIMATE CHALLENGE PRESENTED BY NATURE TO THE ARTIST IS TO CAPTURE AND INTERPRET IN HIS OR HER OWN STYLE THE CHARACTER OF A PARTICULAR REGION THROUGH AN UNDERSTANDING OF LIGHT AND ITS EFFECT UPON THE COLOUR."

"ABOUT TWO-THIRDS OF THE EFFORT THAT GOES TOWARDS THE EXECUTION OF A PAINTING CAN BE ATTRIBUTED TO OBSERVATION .... DISCIPLINES OF APPLICATION AND OBSERVATION and eventual development of style. (or technique)"

"Reality is only one part of art, the artist's feeling completes it ... if you have really been moved by an object (a subject), you will transmit your emotion to it" (Eugene Delacroix)

.... appropriate, assimilate, interpret, modify, change or transform reality. ... from his mental archive the artist will create - style. (synthesis)

Any good painting is the product of thought, planning, and thorough knowledge of the medium that comes from practice and experimentation.

Never be discouraged, and never be satisfied, either. Both are killers of progress

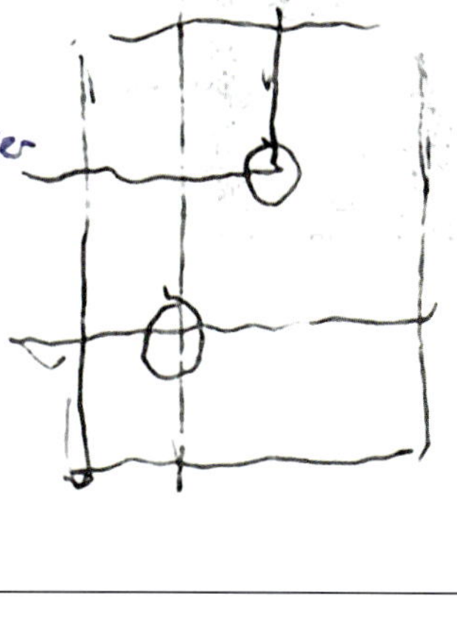

It doesn't take courage to paint what you see. To paint what you think and feel takes guts

The road to art is the way of trial and error

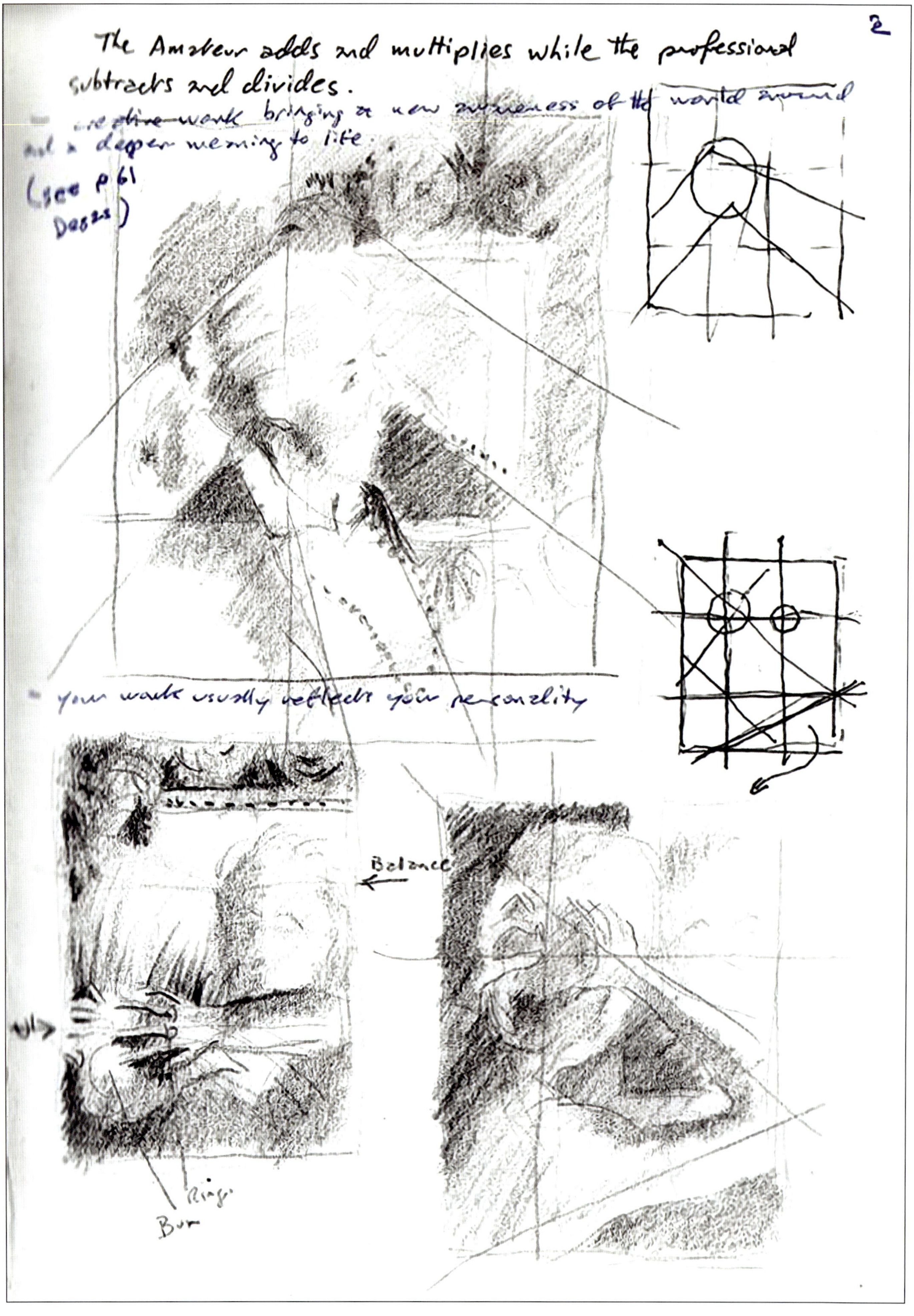
2
The Amateur adds and multiplies while the professional subtracts and divides.
– creative work bringing a new awareness of the world around and a deeper meaning to life.
(see p 61 Degas)
– your work usually reflects your personality
Balance
Rings
Burr

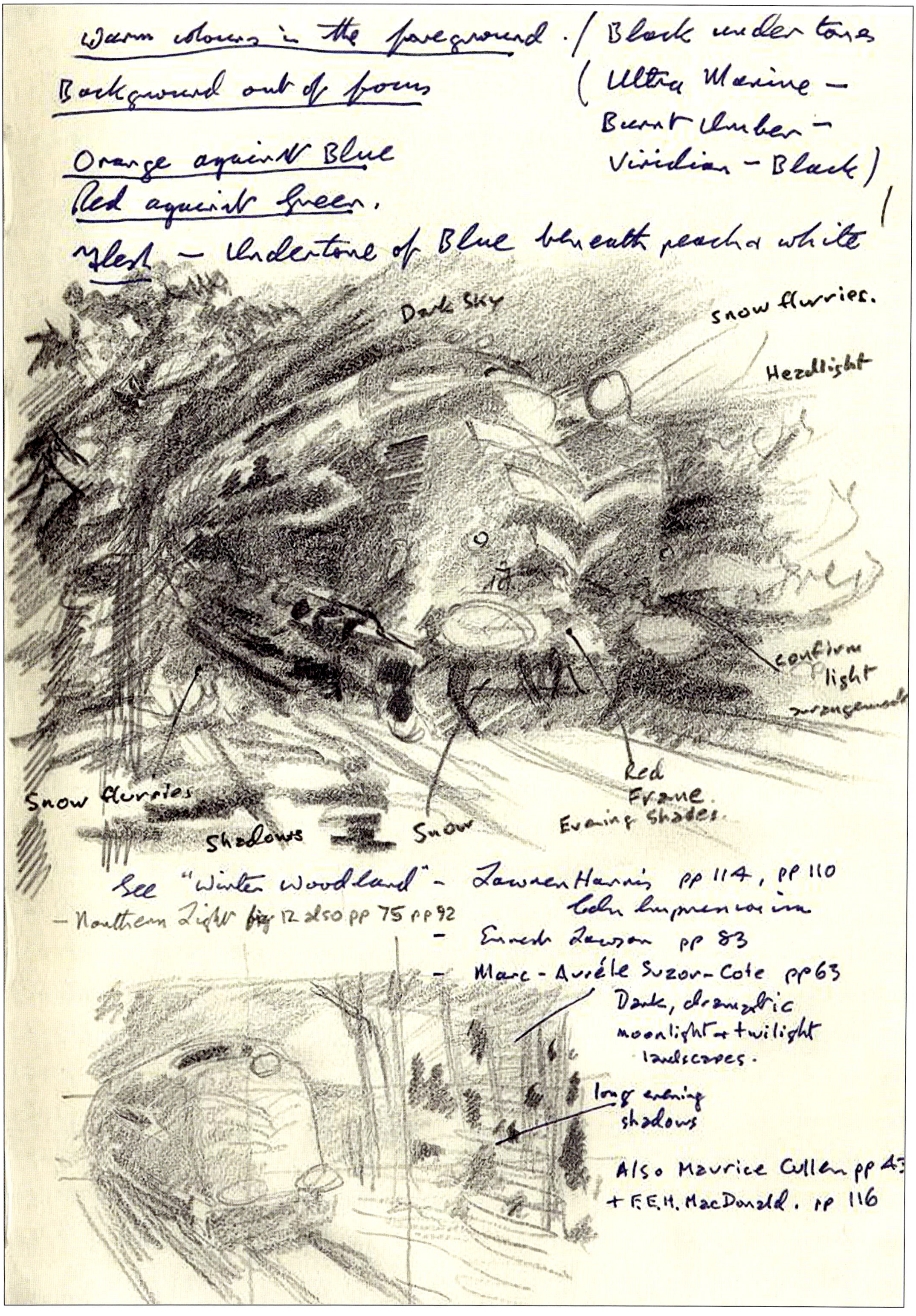
Warm colours in the foreground. / Black under tones
Background out of focus
(Ultra Marine –
Burnt Umber –
Viridian – Black)
Orange against Blue
Red against Green.
– Undertone of Blue beneath peach & white
Dark Sky
Snow flurries.
Headlight
light
Red
Frame.
Evening shades.
Snow flurries
Shadows
Snow
See "Winter Woodland" – Lawren Harris pp 114, pp 110
– Northern Light fig 12 also pp 75 pp 92
– Ernest Lawson pp 83
– Marc-Aurèle Suzor-Coté pp 63
Dark, dramatic
moonlight + twilight
landscapes.
long evening
shadows
Also Maurice Cullen
+ F.E.H. MacDonald. pp 116

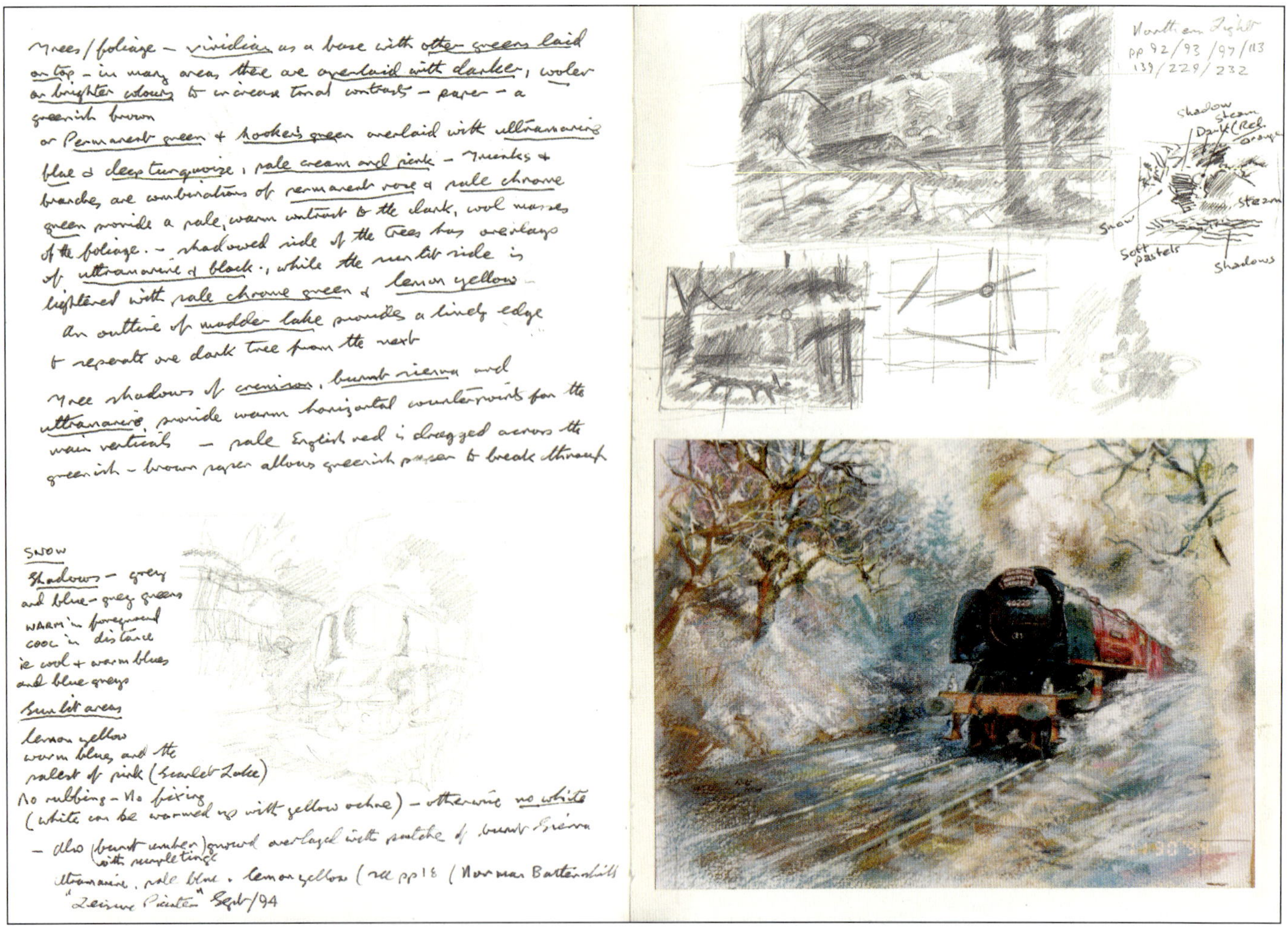
Trees / foliage – viridian as a base with other greens laid on top – in many areas these are overlaid with darker, cooler or brighter colours to increase tonal contrasts – paper – a greenish brown
or Permanent green + hooker's green overlaid with ultramarine blue & deep turquoise, pale cream and pink – Trunks + branches are combinations of permanent rose & pale chrome green provide a pale, warm contrast to the dark, cool masses of the foliage. – shadowed side of the trees has overlays of ultramarine & black., while the sun lit side is lightened with pale chrome green & lemon yellow –
An outline of madder lake provides a lively edge to separate one dark tree from the next
Tree shadows of crimson, burnt sienna and ultramarine provide warm horizontal counterpoints for the main verticals – pale English red is dragged across the greenish – brown paper allows greenish paper to break through
SNOW
Shadows – grey and blue-grey greens
WARM in foreground
COOL in distance
ie cool + warm blues and blue greys
Sun lit areas
lemon yellow
warm blues and the palest of pink (Scarlet Lake)
No rubbing – No fixing
(white can be warmed up with yellow ochre) – otherwise no white
– also (burnt umber) ground overlayed with patches of burnt sienna with purple tinge
ultramarine, pale blue, lemon yellow (see pp18 (Norman Battershill "Leisure Painter" Sept/94
Northern Light
pp 92/93/97/113
139/229/232
Shadow
Steam
Snow
Soft pastels
Steam
Shadows

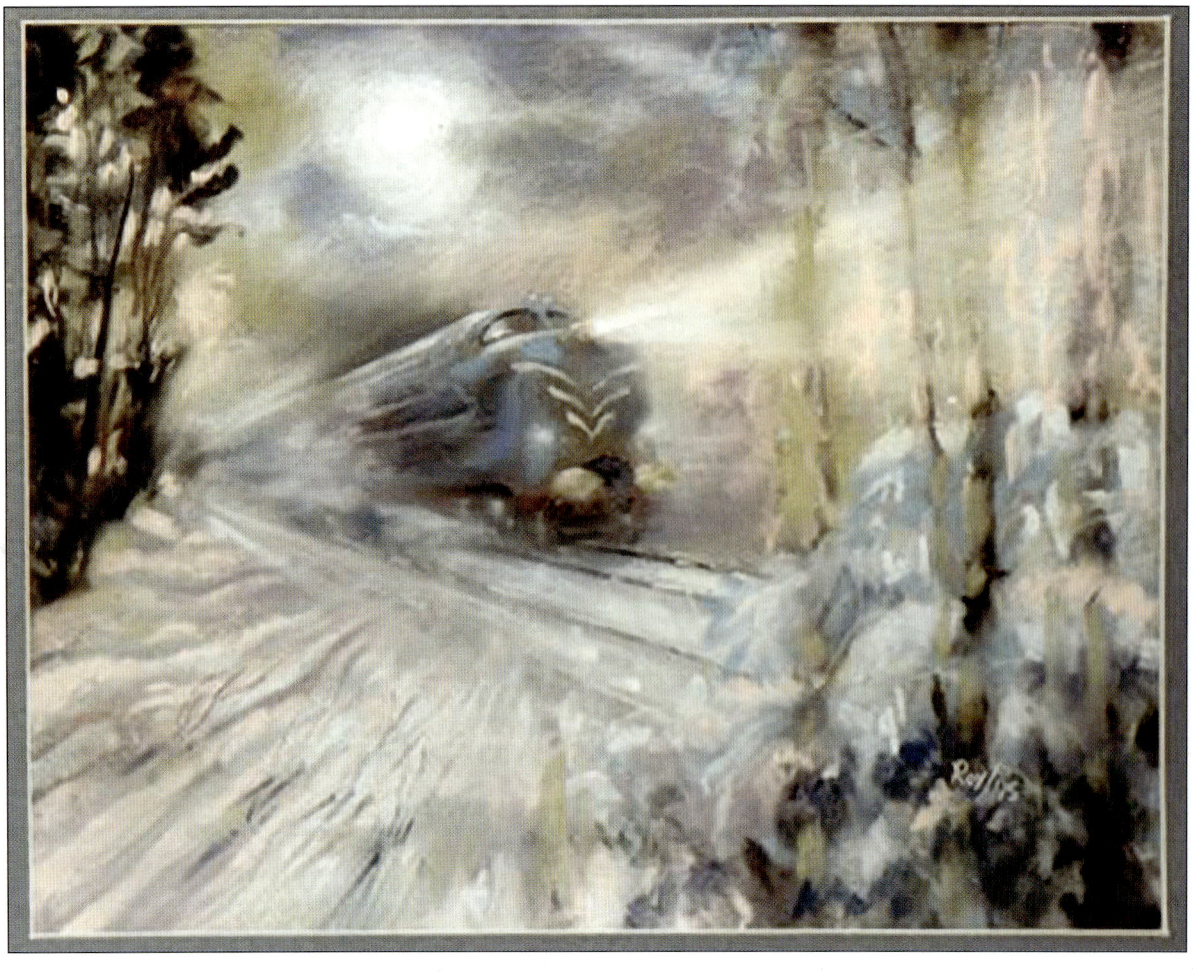

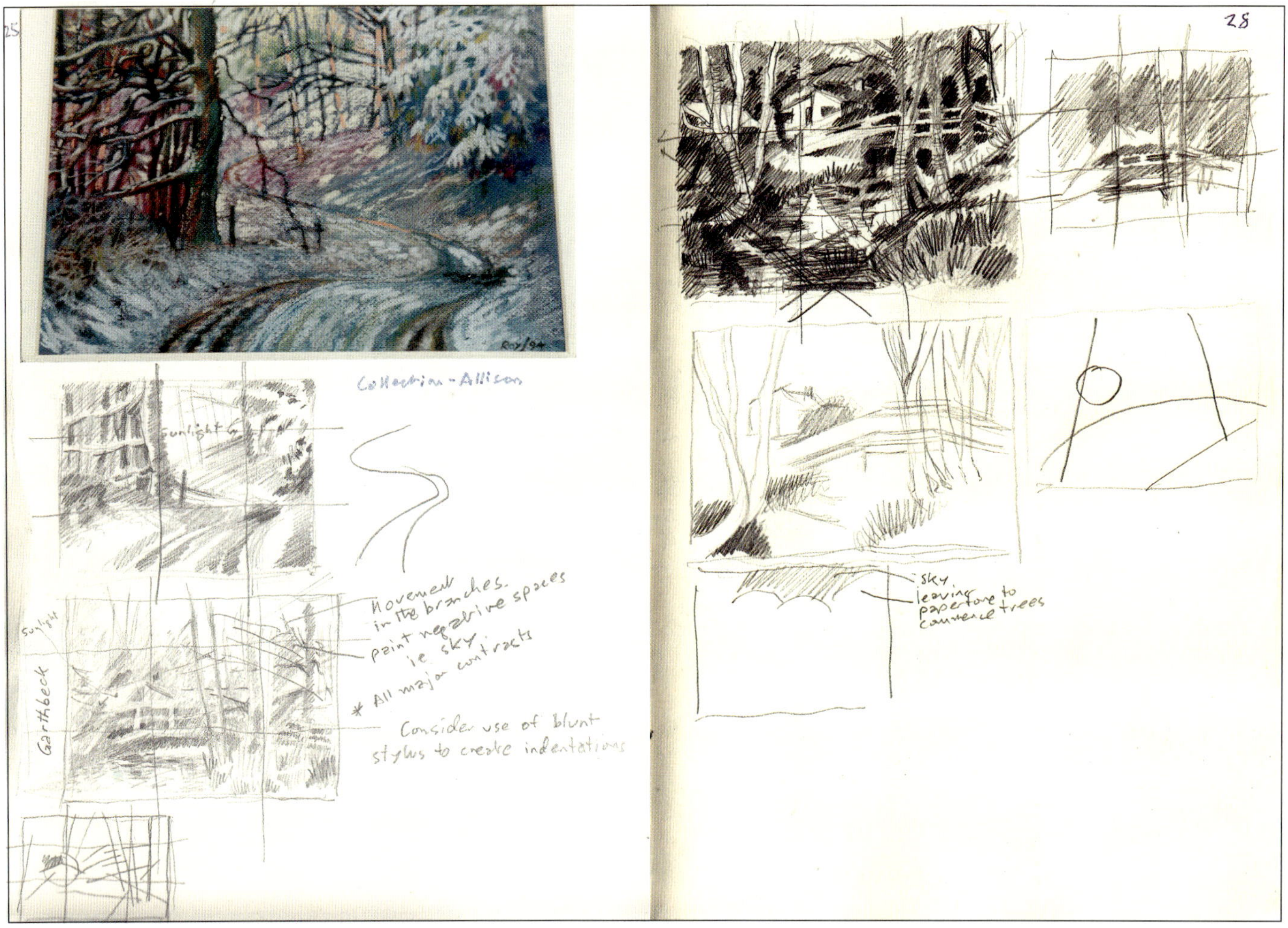
Collection - Allison
Movement in the branches.
paint negative spaces ie sky
* All major contrasts
Consider use of blunt stylus to create indentations
Garthbeck
28

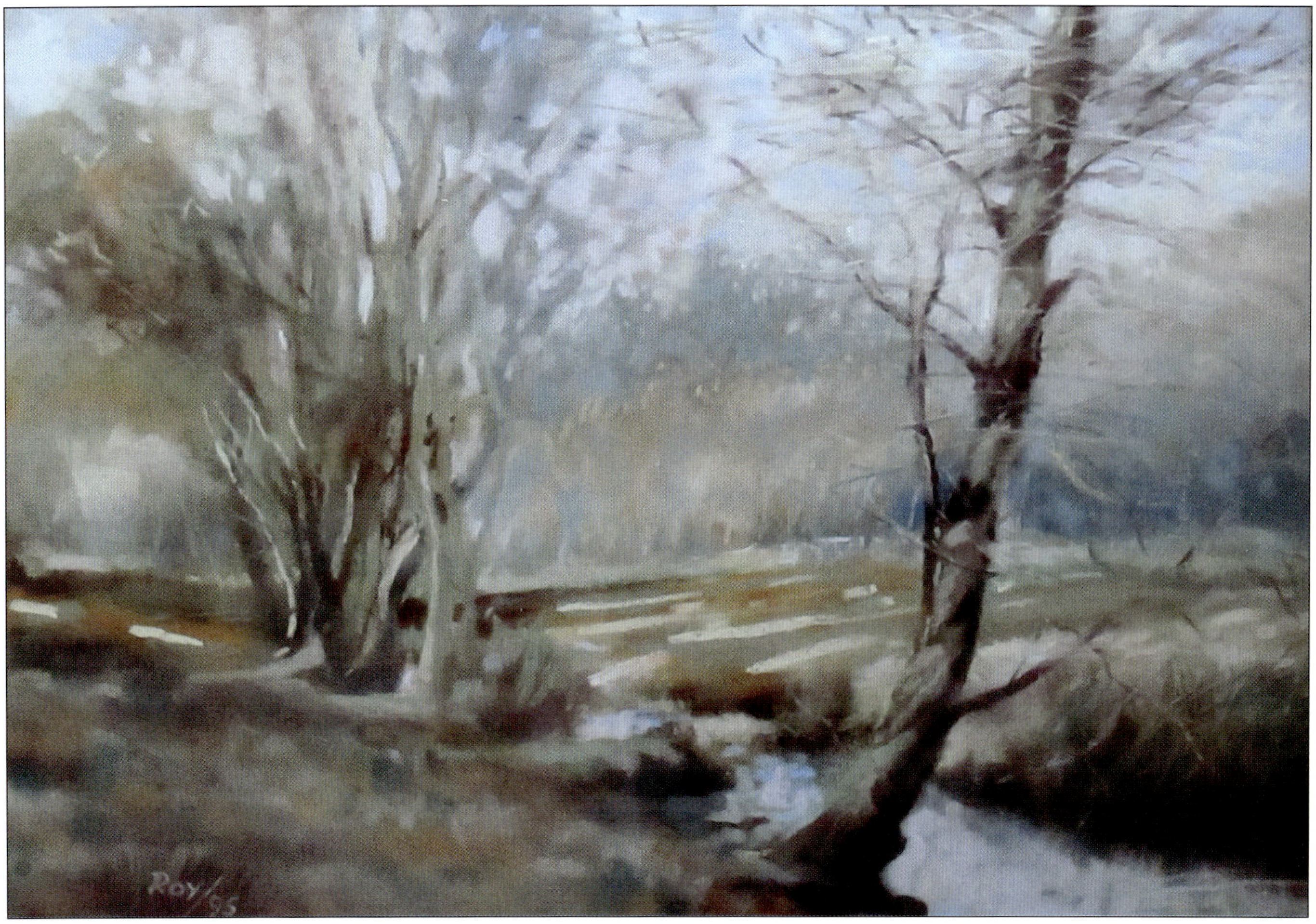

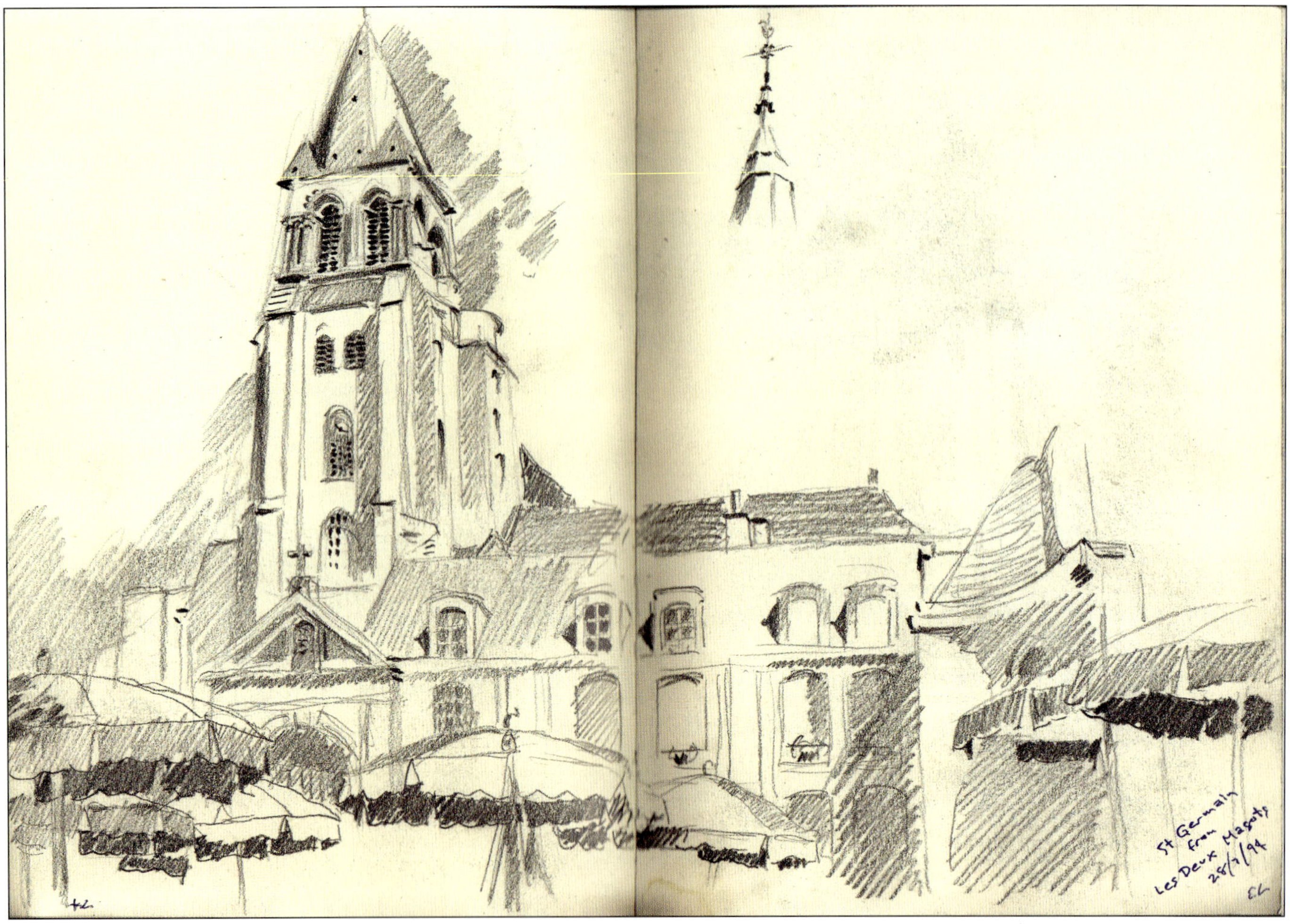
St Germain
from
Les Deux Magots
28/7/94

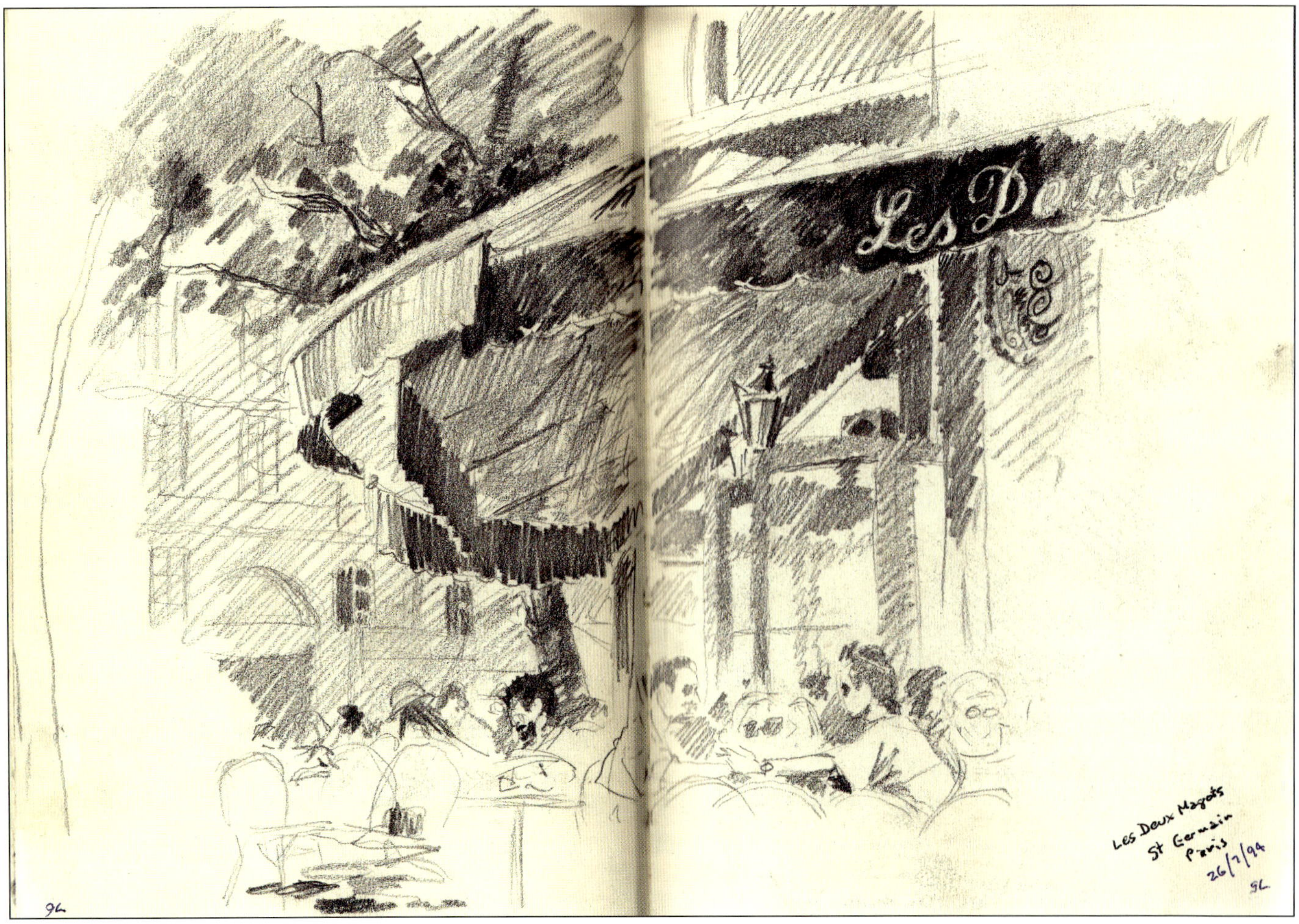
Les D
Les Deux Magots
St Germain
Paris
26/7/94

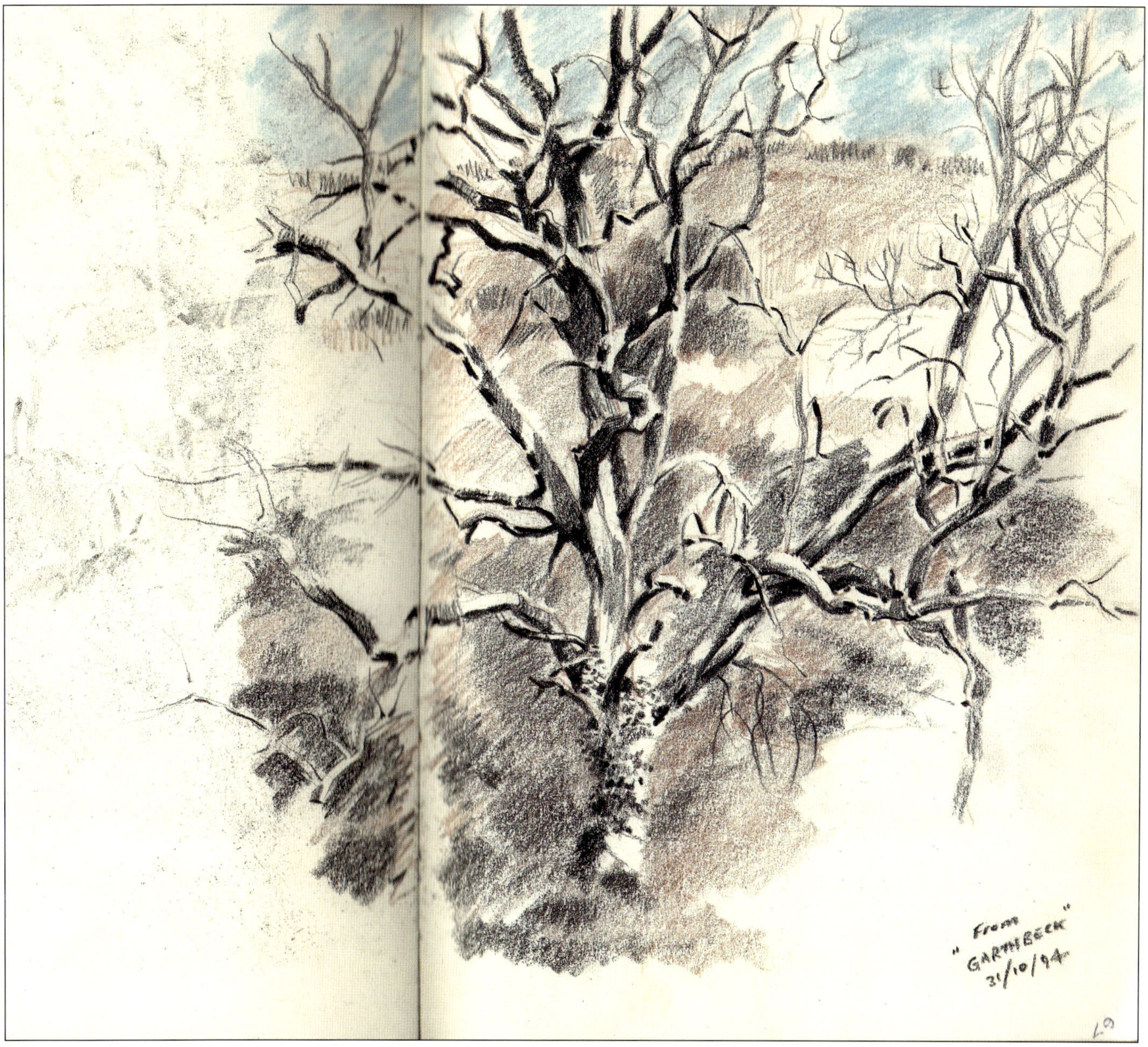
From
"GARTHBECK"
31/10/94

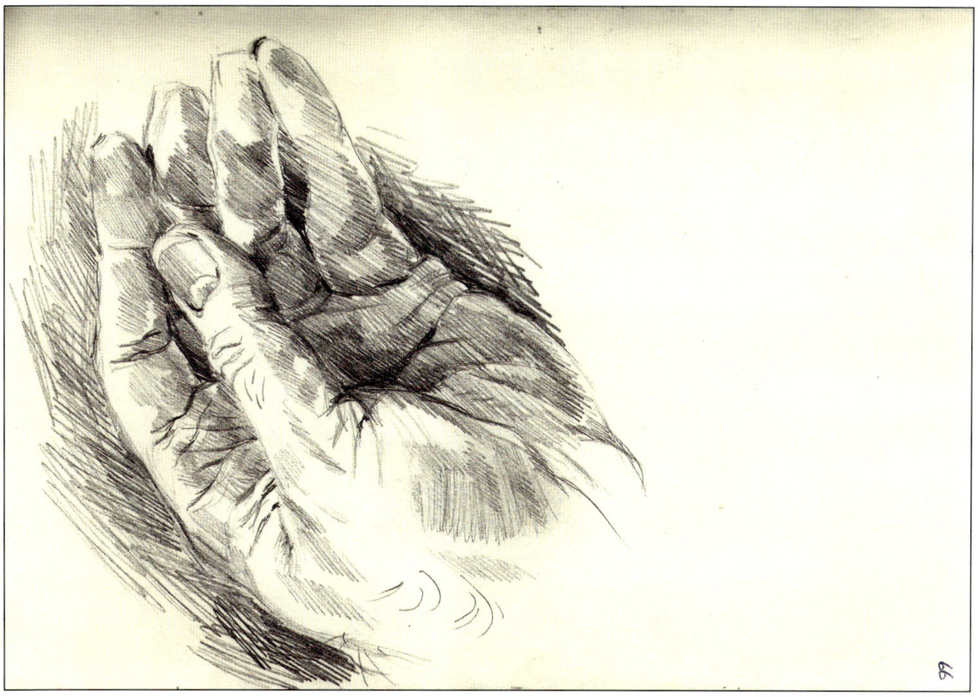

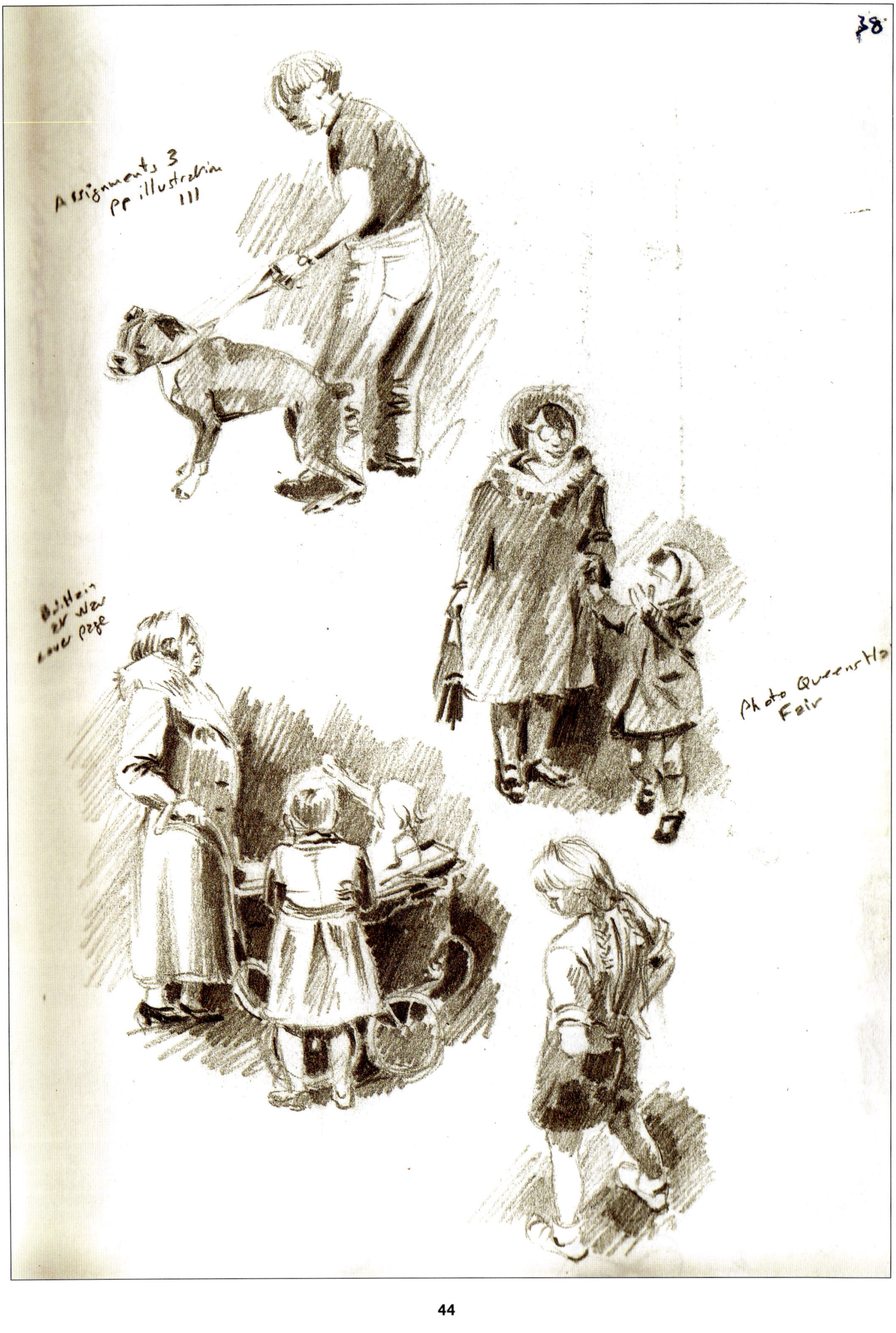
38
Assignments 3
111
Photo Queens Ha
Fair

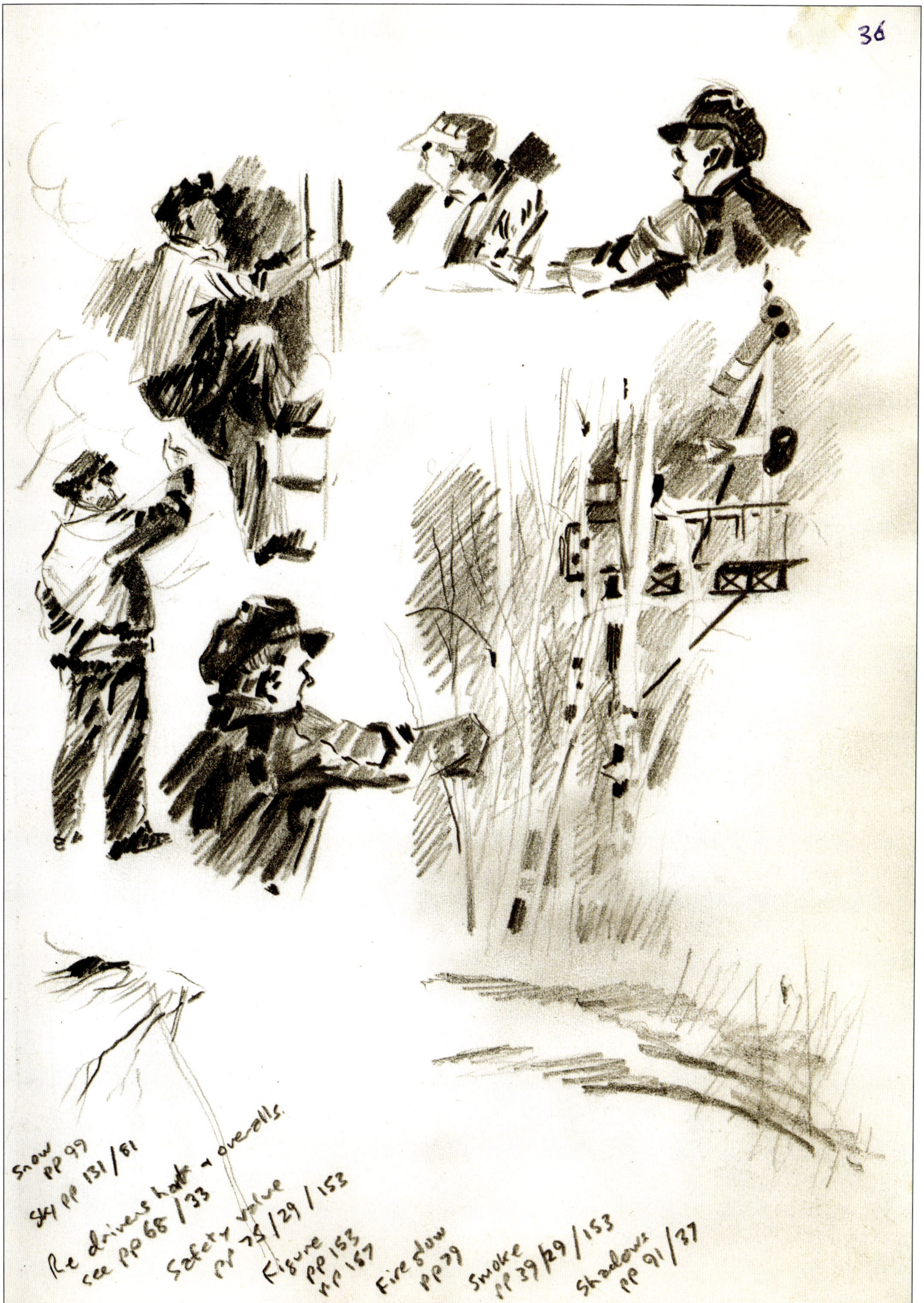
36
Snow pp 99
SH pp 131/81
Re drivers hats + overalls. see pp 68 / 33
Safety valve pp 75/29/153
Figure pp 153 pp 157
Firedow pp 79
Smoke pp 39/29/153
Shadows pp 91/37

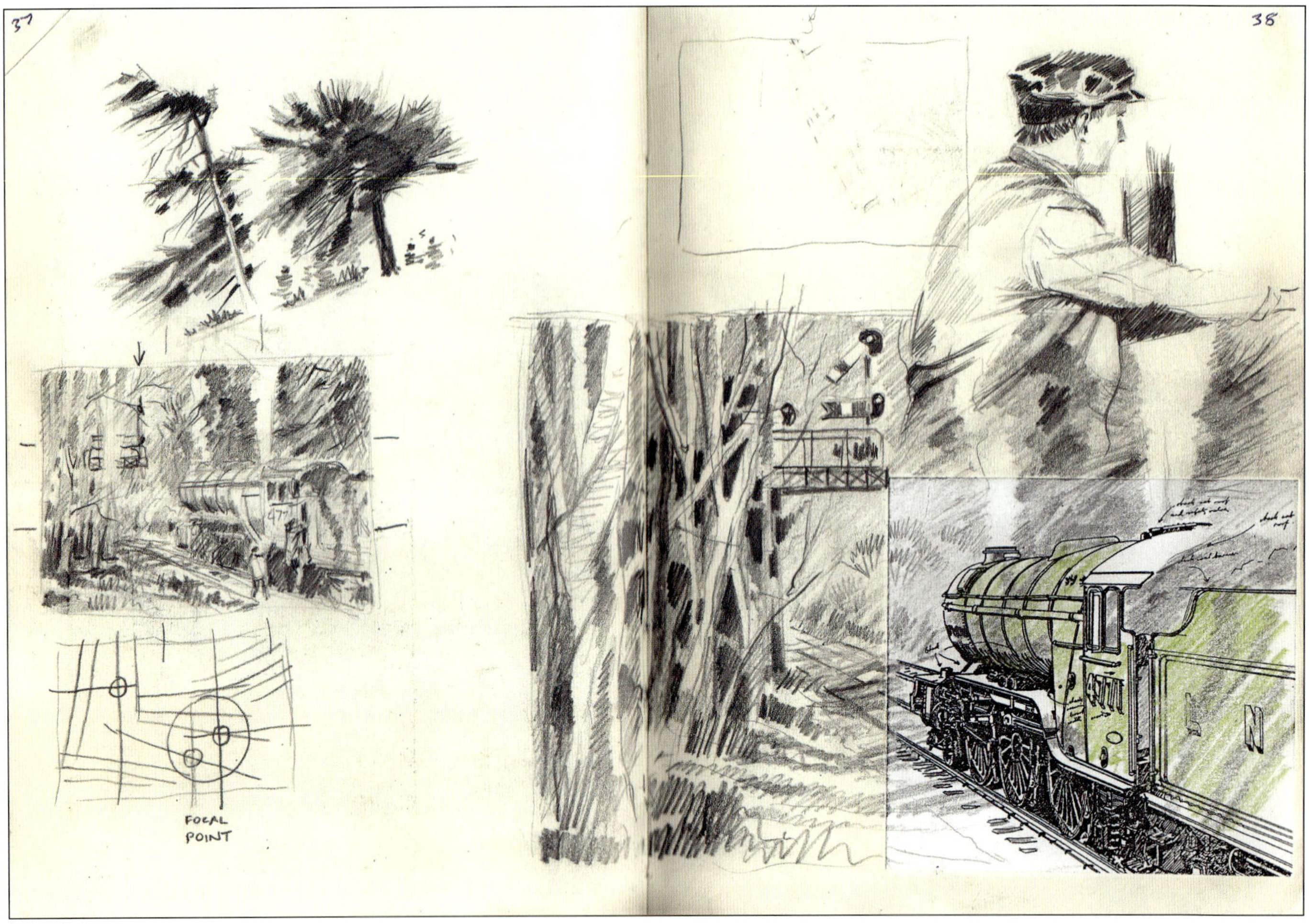
37
38
FOCAL
POINT

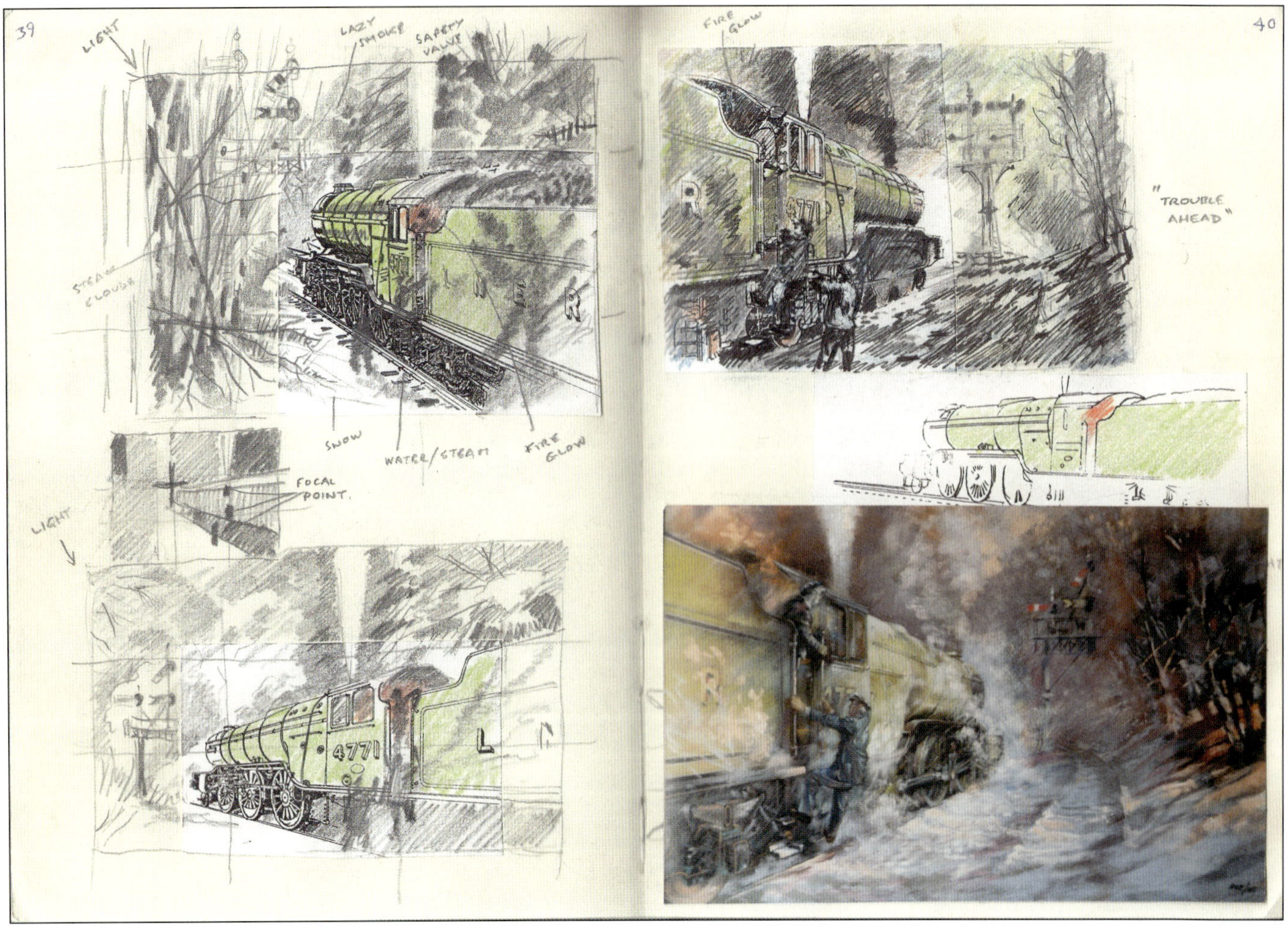
39
40
LIGHT
LAZY
SMOKE
SAFETY
VALVE
STEAM
CLOUDS
SNOW
WATER/STEAM
FIRE
GLOW
FOCAL
POINT.
LIGHT
FIRE
GLOW
"TROUBLE
AHEAD"

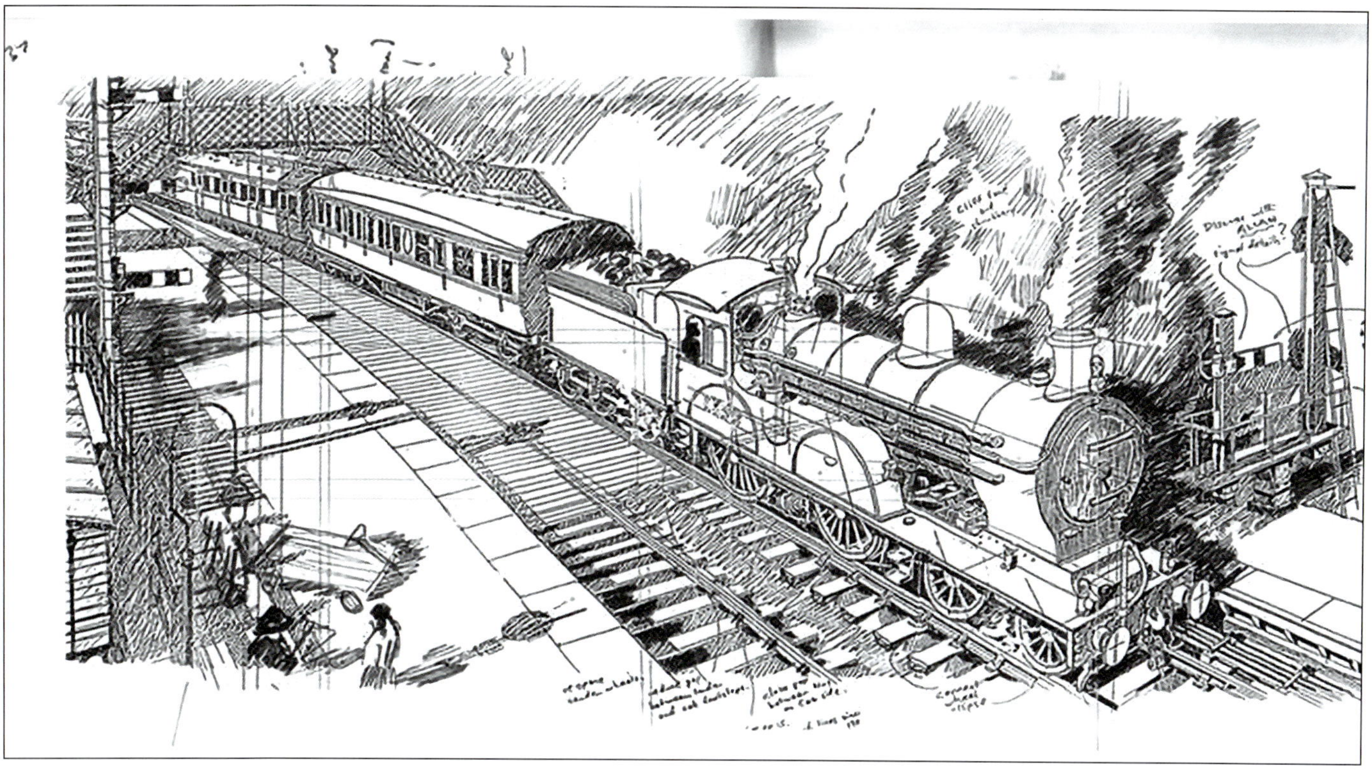

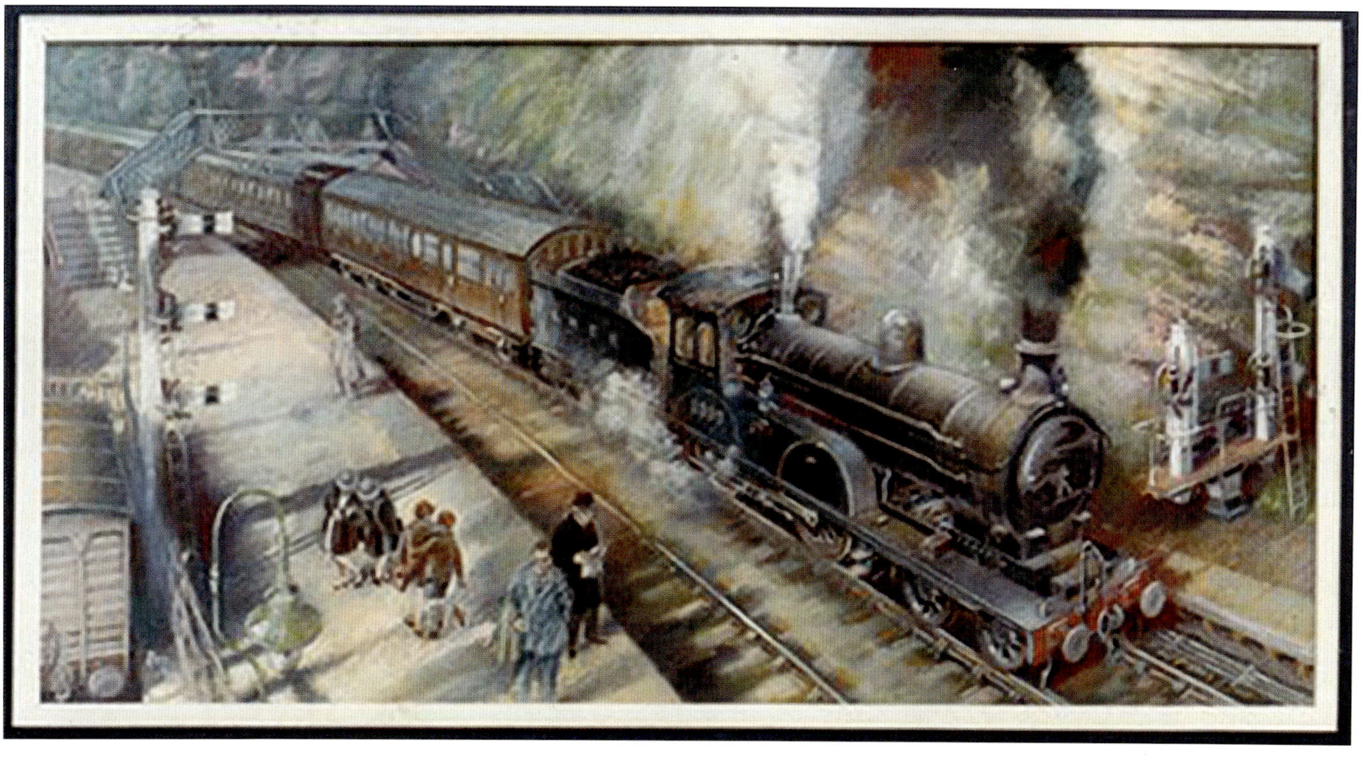

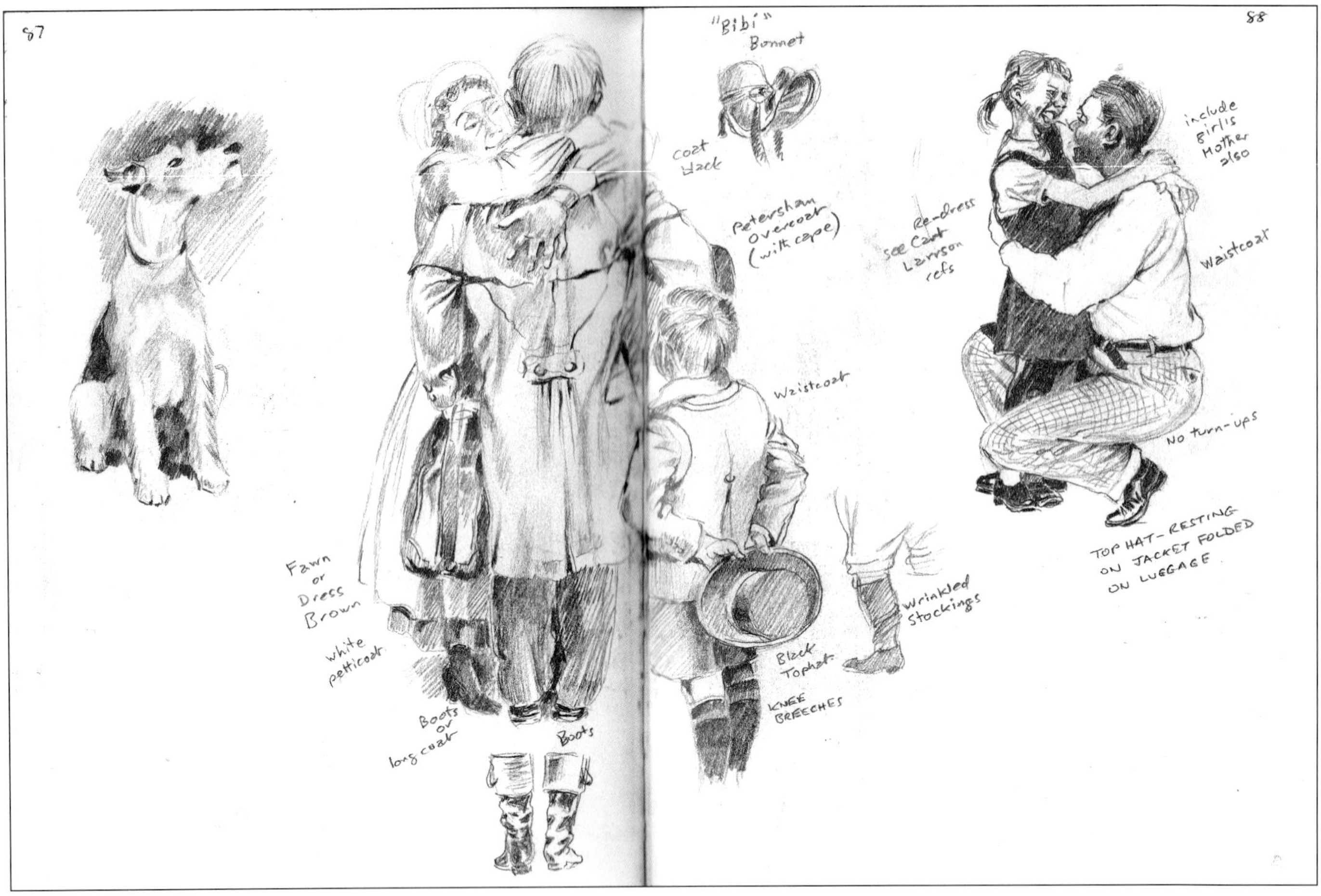
87
88
"Bibi" Bonnet
Coat Back
Petersham Overcoat (with cape)
Re-dress see Carl Larrson refs
include girl's Mother also
Waistcoat
Waistcoat
No turn-ups
TOP HAT - RESTING ON JACKET FOLDED ON LUGGAGE
Fawn or Dress Brown
white petticoat
Boots or long coat
Boots
Black Tophat
Wrinkled Stockings
KNEE BREECHES

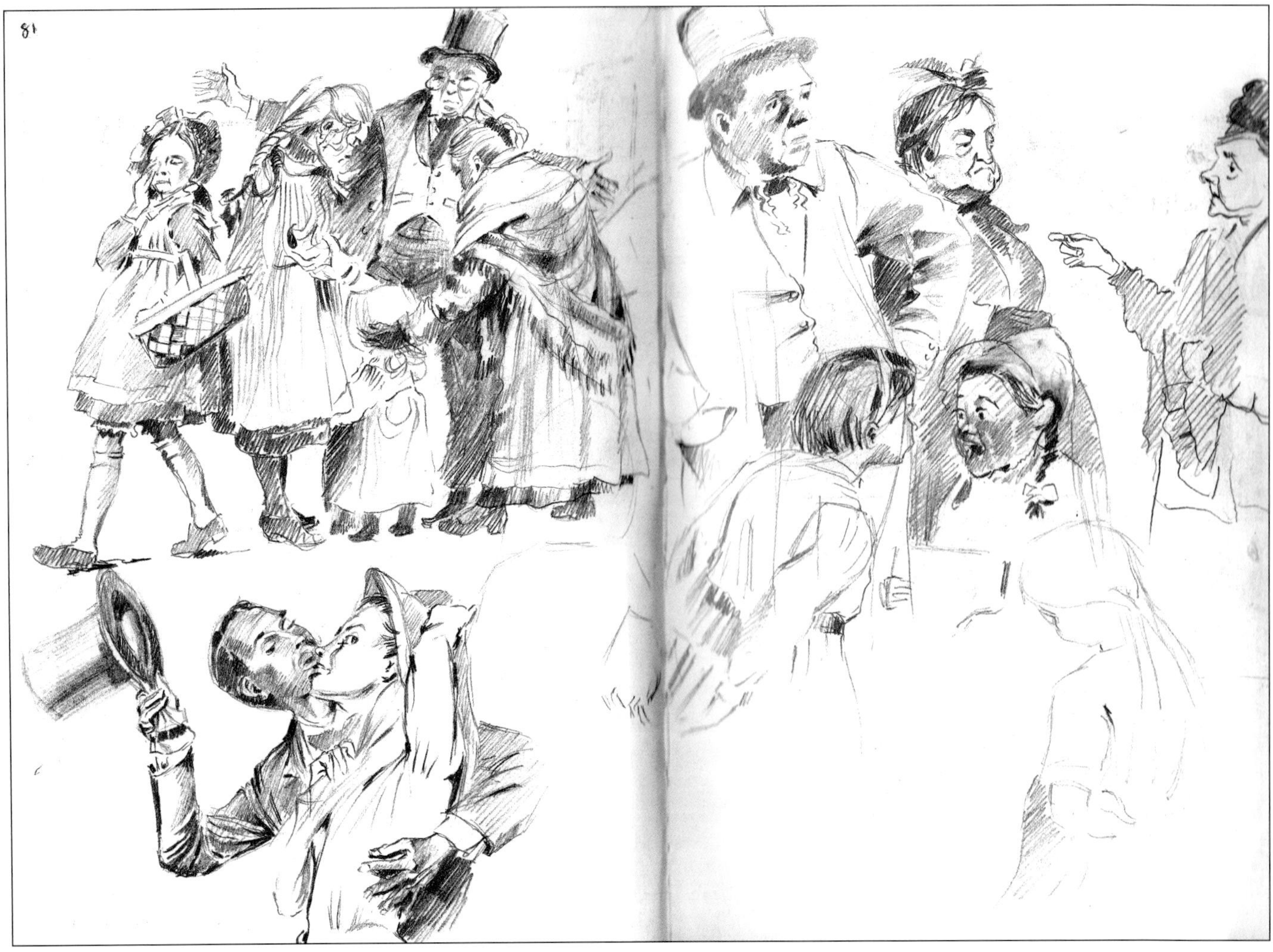
81

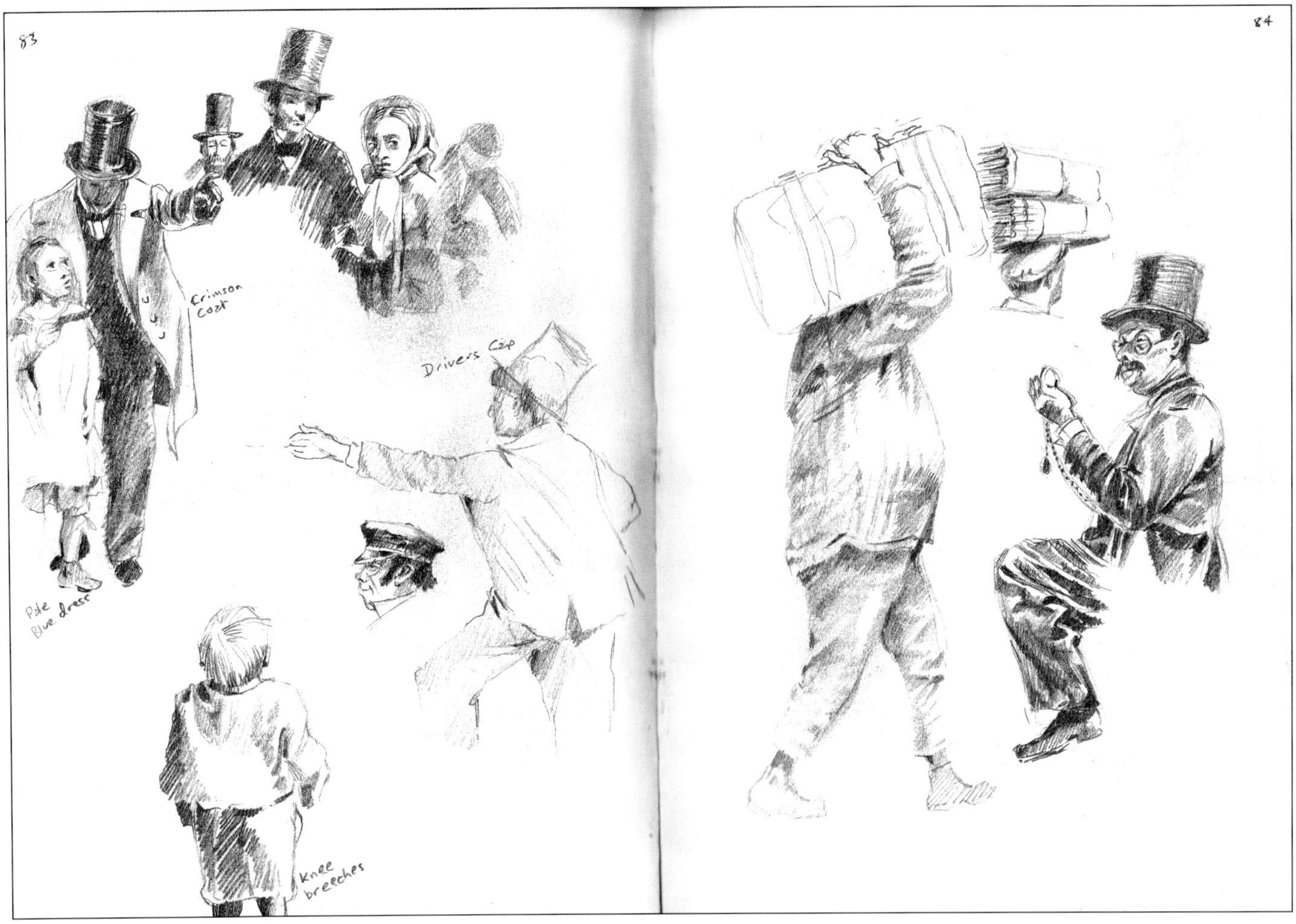
83
84
Crimson Coat
Drivers Cap
Pale Blue dress
Knee breeches

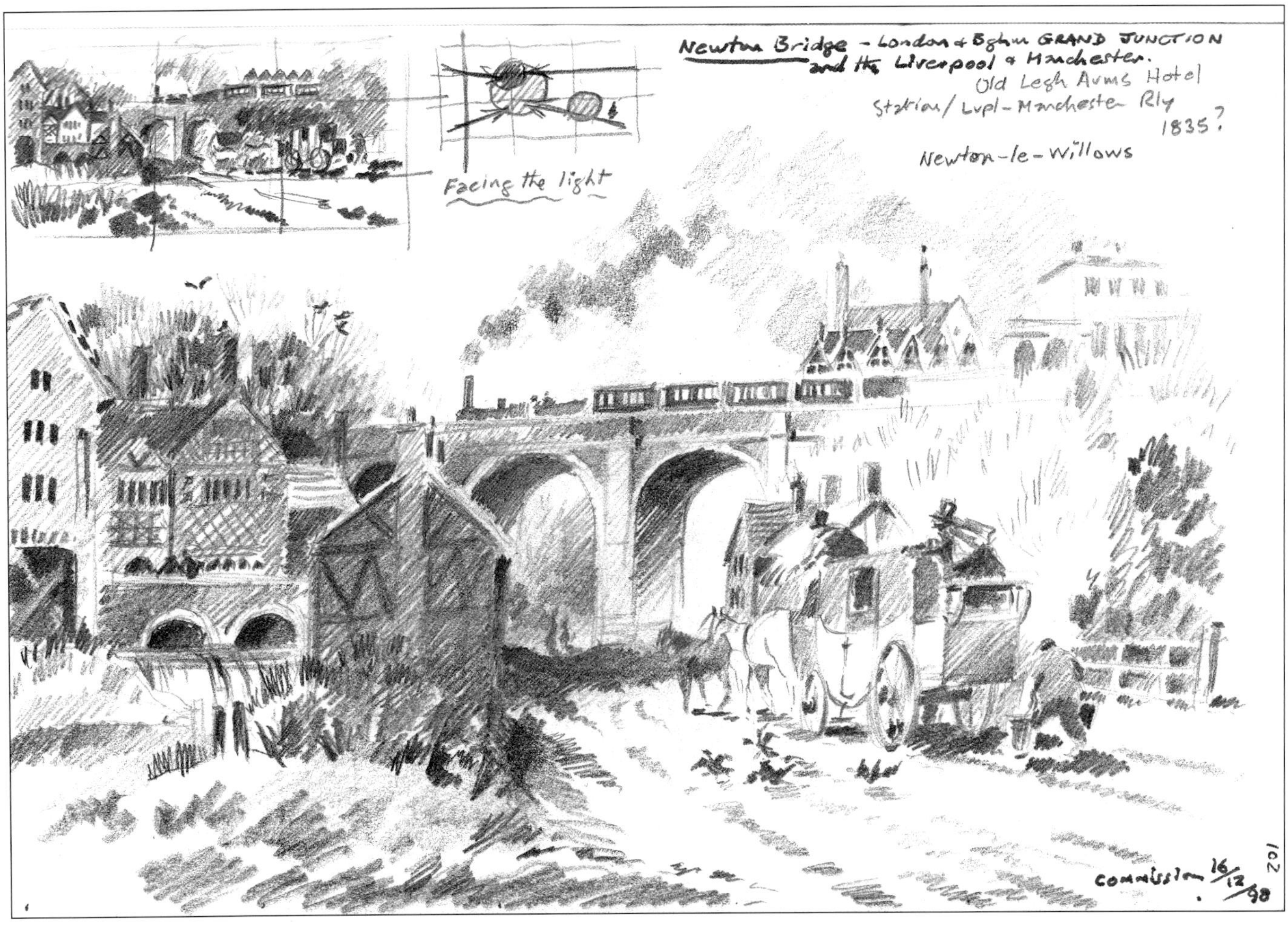
Newton Bridge - London & Bghm GRAND JUNCTION and the Liverpool & Manchester.
Old Legh Arms Hotel
Station/ Lvpl - Manchester Rly
1835?
Newton-le-Willows
Facing the light
commission 16/12/98
102

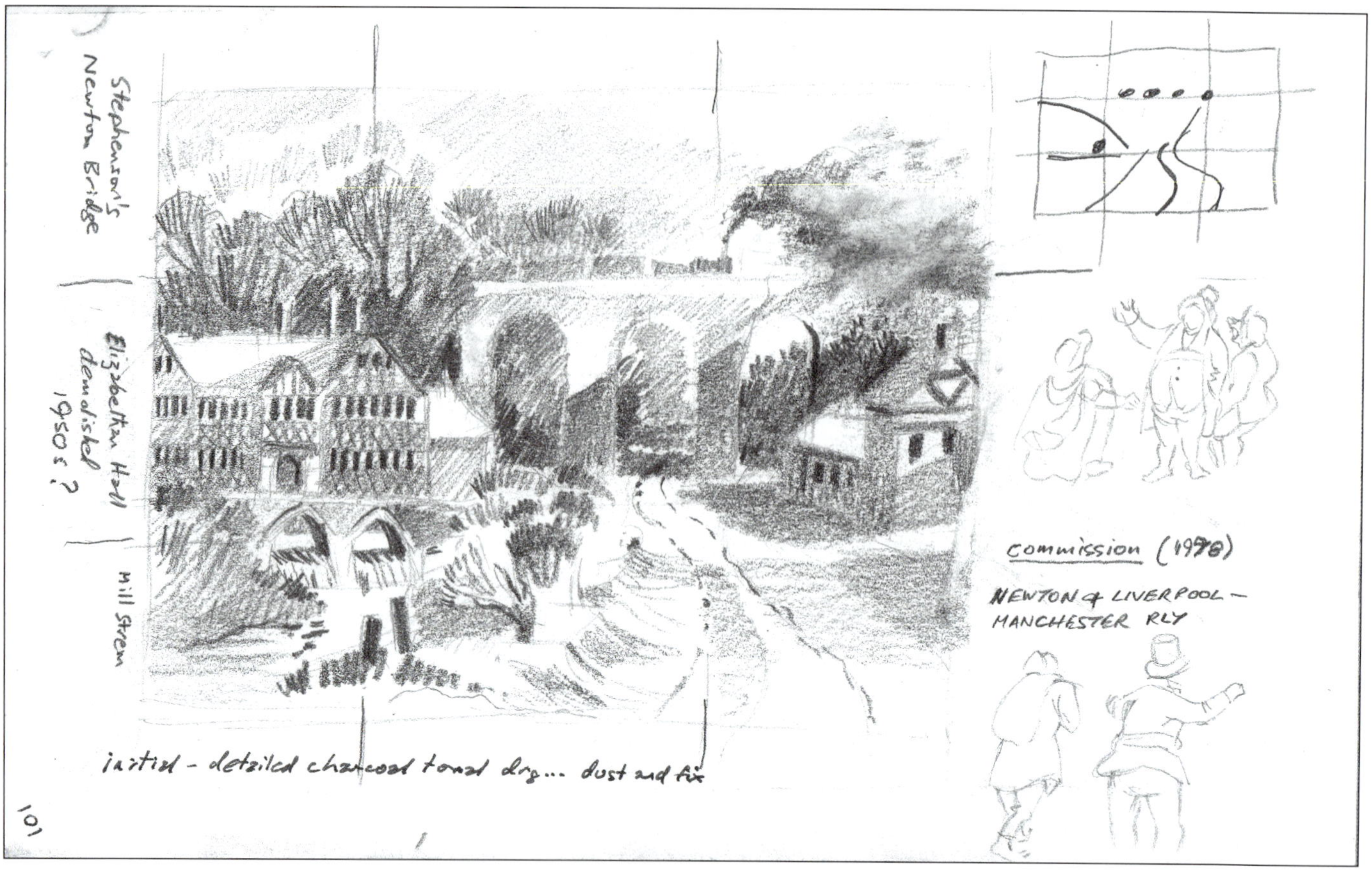
Stephenson's Newton Bridge
Elizabethan Hall demolished 1950s?
Mill Stream
initial - detailed charcoal tonal drg... dust and fix
NEWTON & LIVERPOOL - MANCHESTER RLY

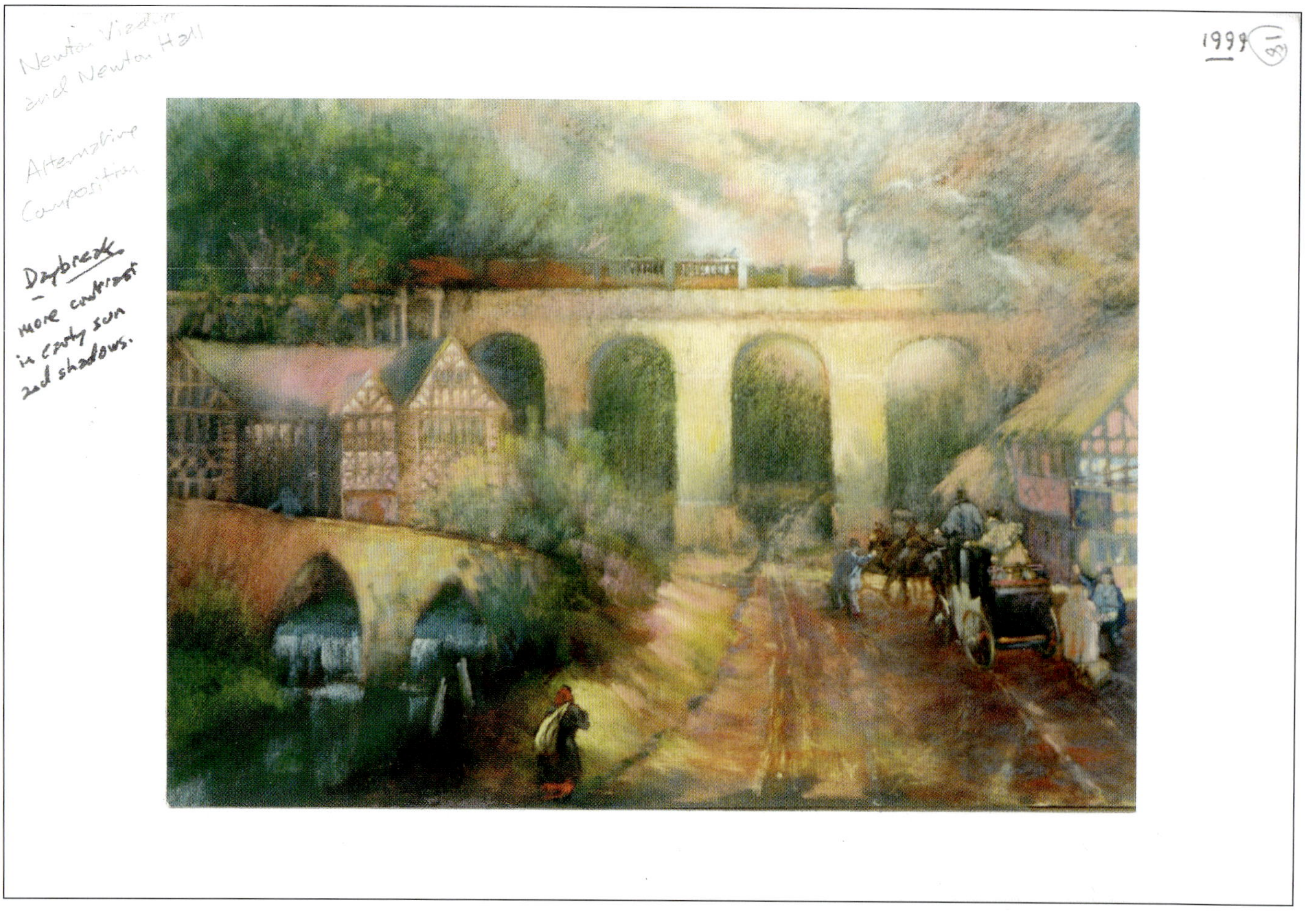
Newton Viaduct and Newton Hall
Alternative Composition
Daybreak
more contrast in early sun and shadows.
1999

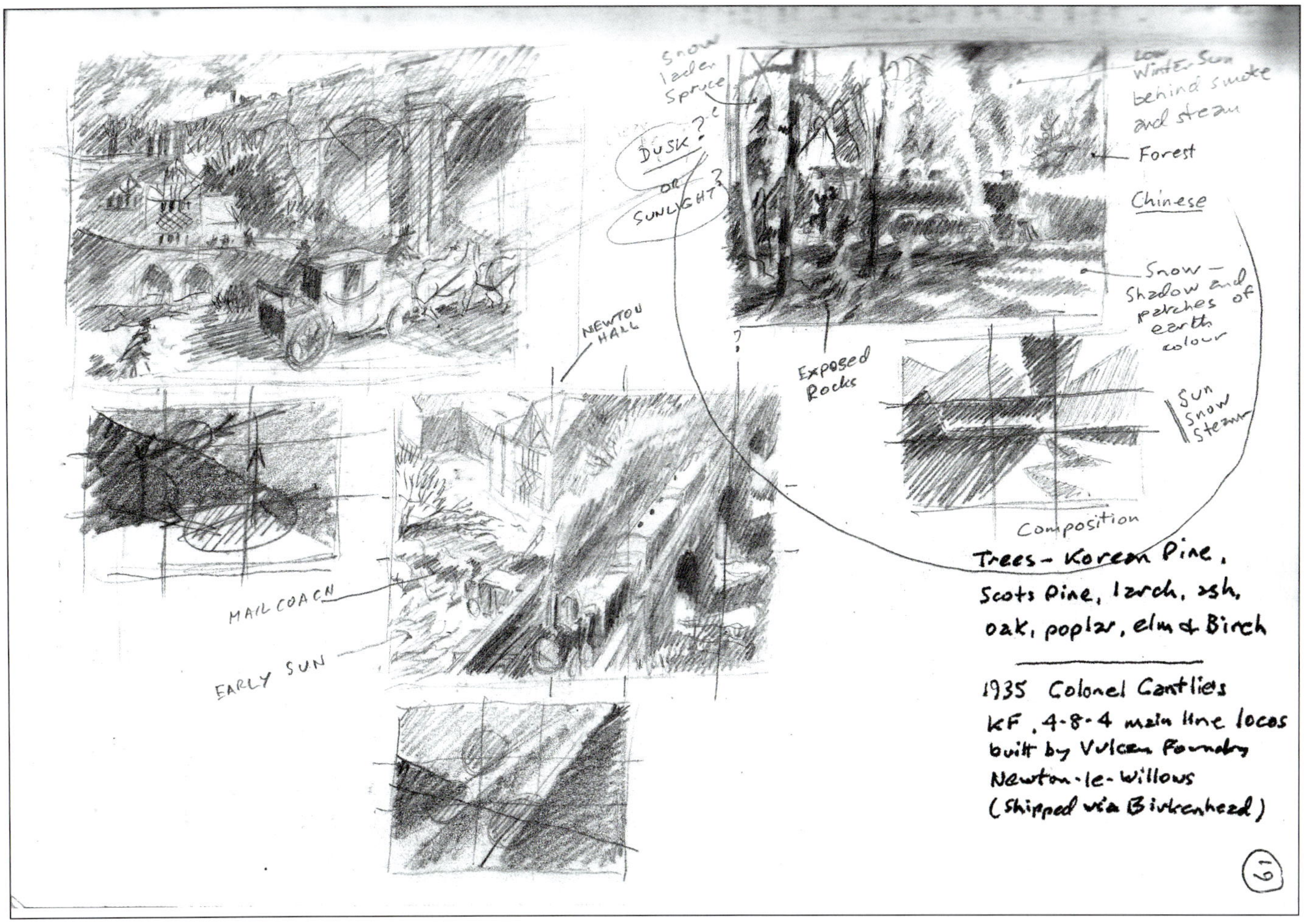
Snow laden Spruce
DUSK?
OR
SUNLIGHT?
Low Winter Sun behind smoke and steam
Forest
Chinese
Snow – Shadow and patches of earth colour
Exposed Rocks
Sun Snow Steam
Composition
NEWTON HALL
MAIL COACH
EARLY SUN
Trees – Korean Pine, Scots Pine, larch, ash, oak, poplar, elm & Birch
1935 Colonel Cantlie's KF, 4-8-4 main line locos built by Vulcan Foundry Newton-le-Willows (Shipped via Birkenhead)
61

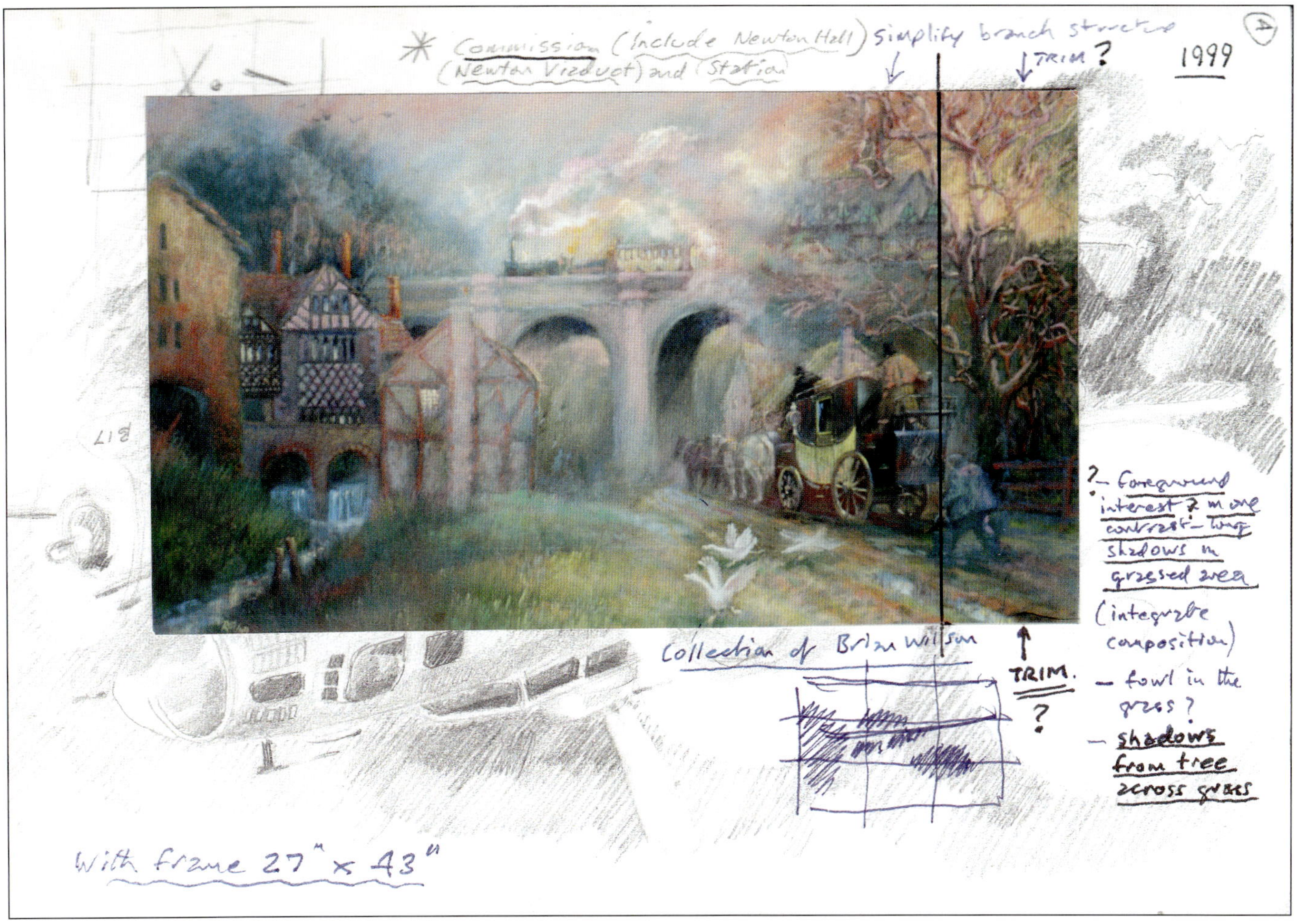
Commission (Include Newton Hall) (Newton Viaduct) and (Station)
simplify branch structure
TRIM?
1999
? – Foreground interest? more contrast – long shadows in grassed area
(integrate composition)
– fowl in the grass?
– shadows from tree across grass
Collection of Brian Wilson
TRIM.
?
With frame 27" x 43"

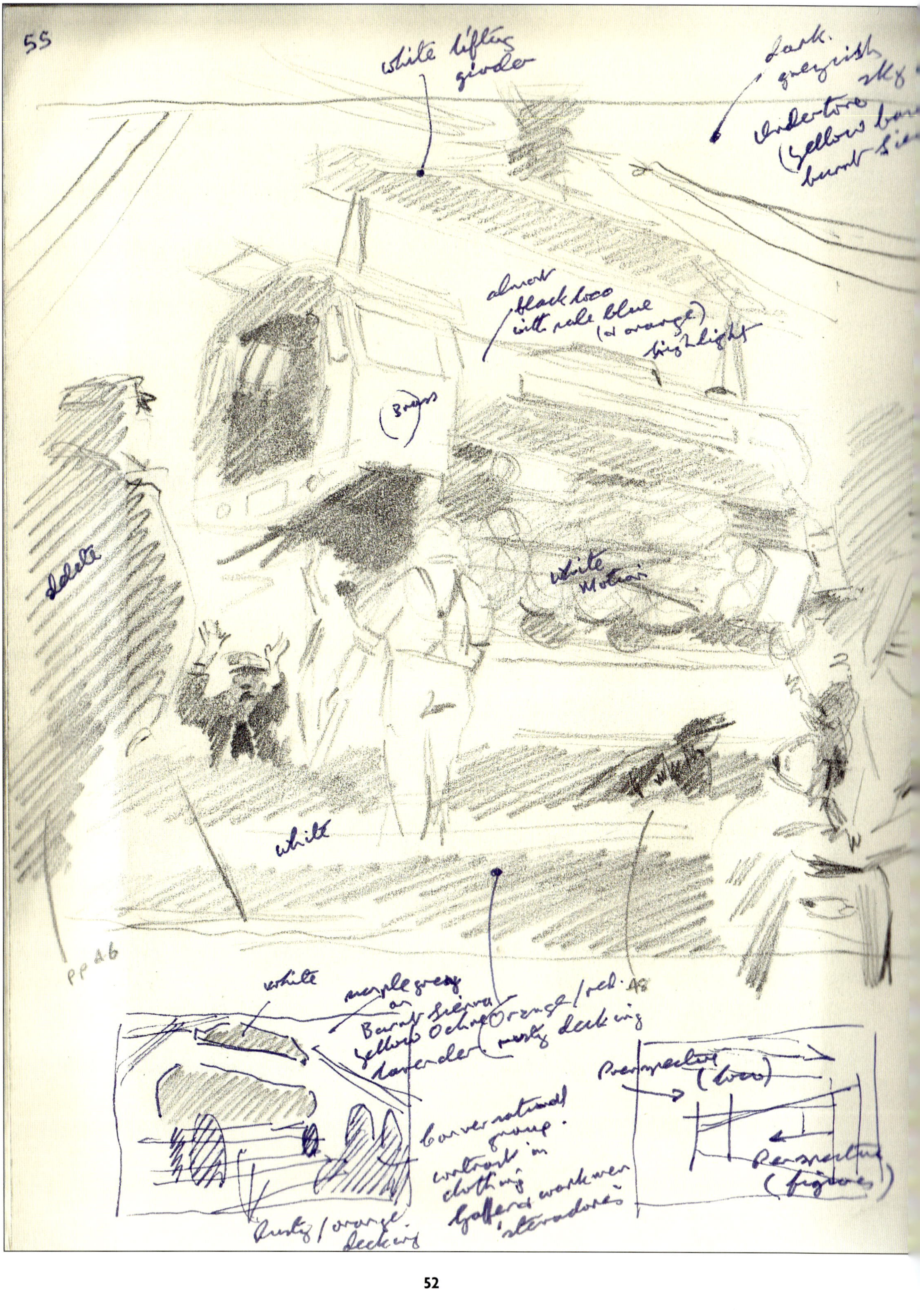
55
white lifting girder
dark greyish
almost black loco with pale blue (or orange) highlight
delete
white motion
white
white
purple grey or
Burnt Sienna
Yellow Ochre
Lavender
Orange/red. rusty decking
Perspective (loco)
Conversational group.
contrast in clothing
Gaffers workwear
Perspective (figures)
Rusty/orange decking

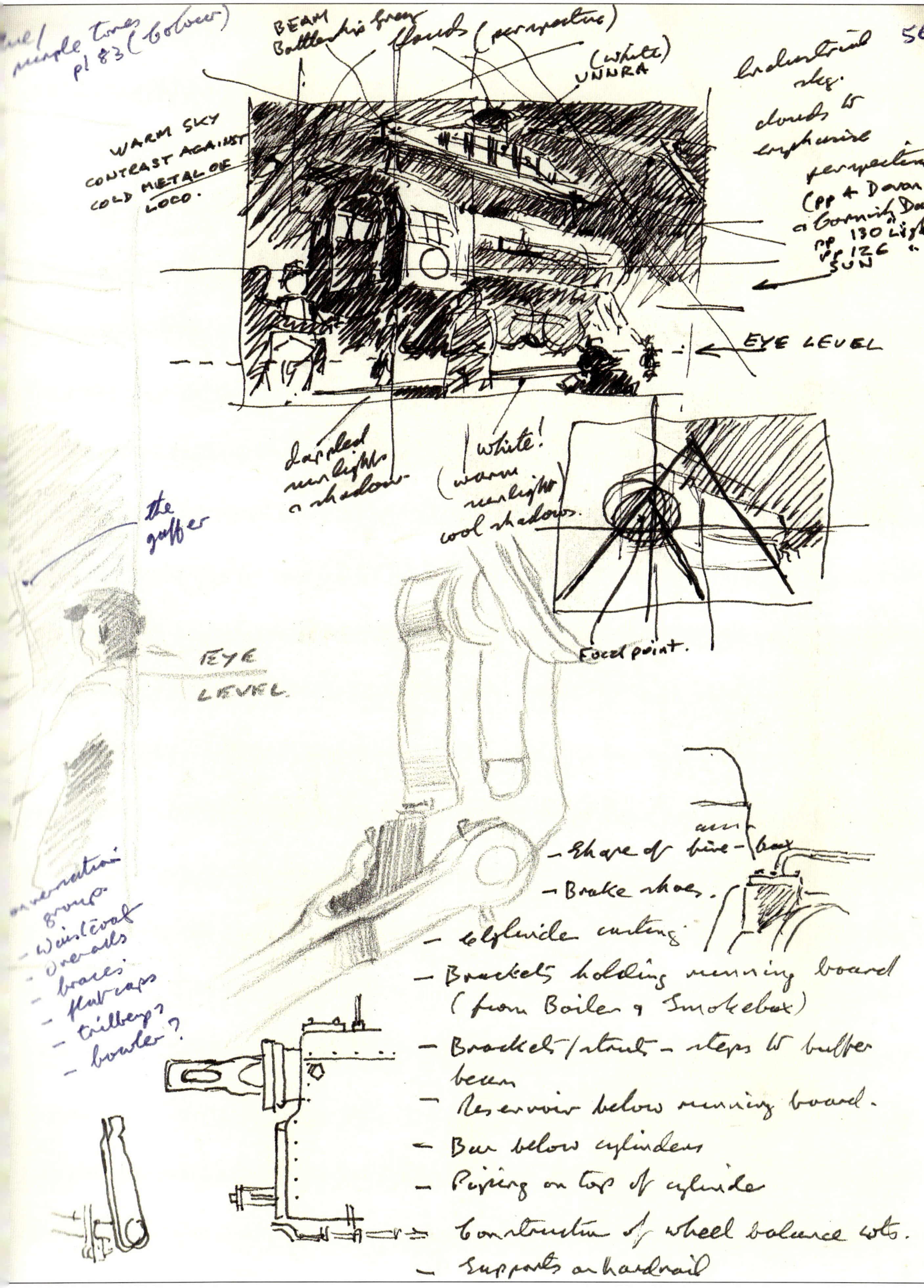
56
BEAM
WARM SKY CONTRAST AGAINST COLD METAL OF LOCO.
(white)
UNNRA
EYE LEVEL
white!
Focal point.
the gaffer
EYE LEVEL
– Brake shoes.
– Brackets holding running board (from Boiler & Smokebox)
– Reservoir below running board.
– Bar below cylinders
– Piping on top of cylinder
– Construction of wheel balance wts.
– Supports on handrail
conversation group.
– Waistcoat
– Overalls
– braces
– flat caps
– trilbeys?
– bowler?

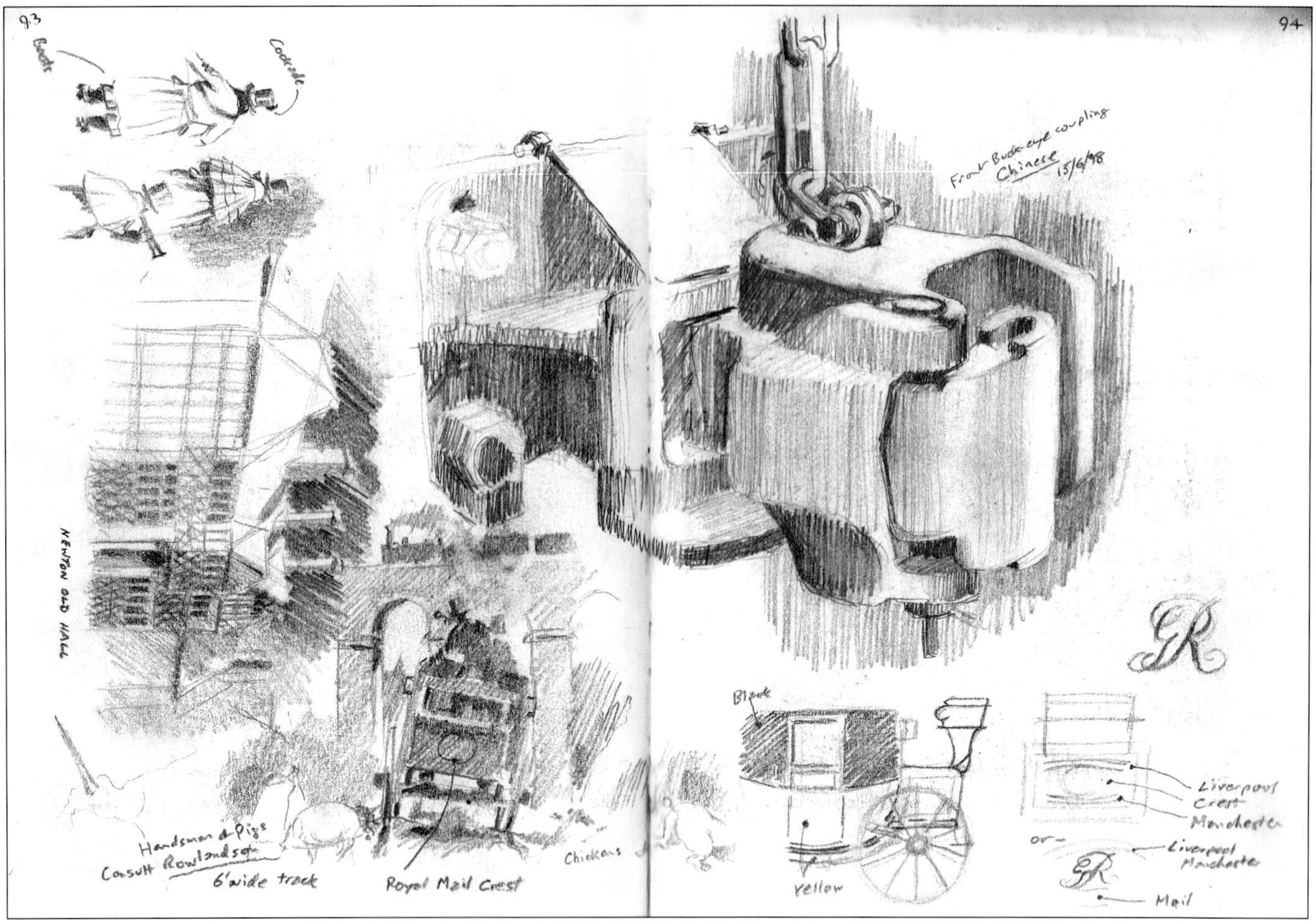
93
94
Boots
Cockade
Front Buck-eye coupling
Chinese 15/6/98
Newton Old Hall
Herdsman & Pigs
Cossutt Rowlandson
6' wide track
Royal Mail Crest
Chickens
Black
Yellow
Liverpool
Crest
Manchester
or
Liverpool
Manchester
Mail

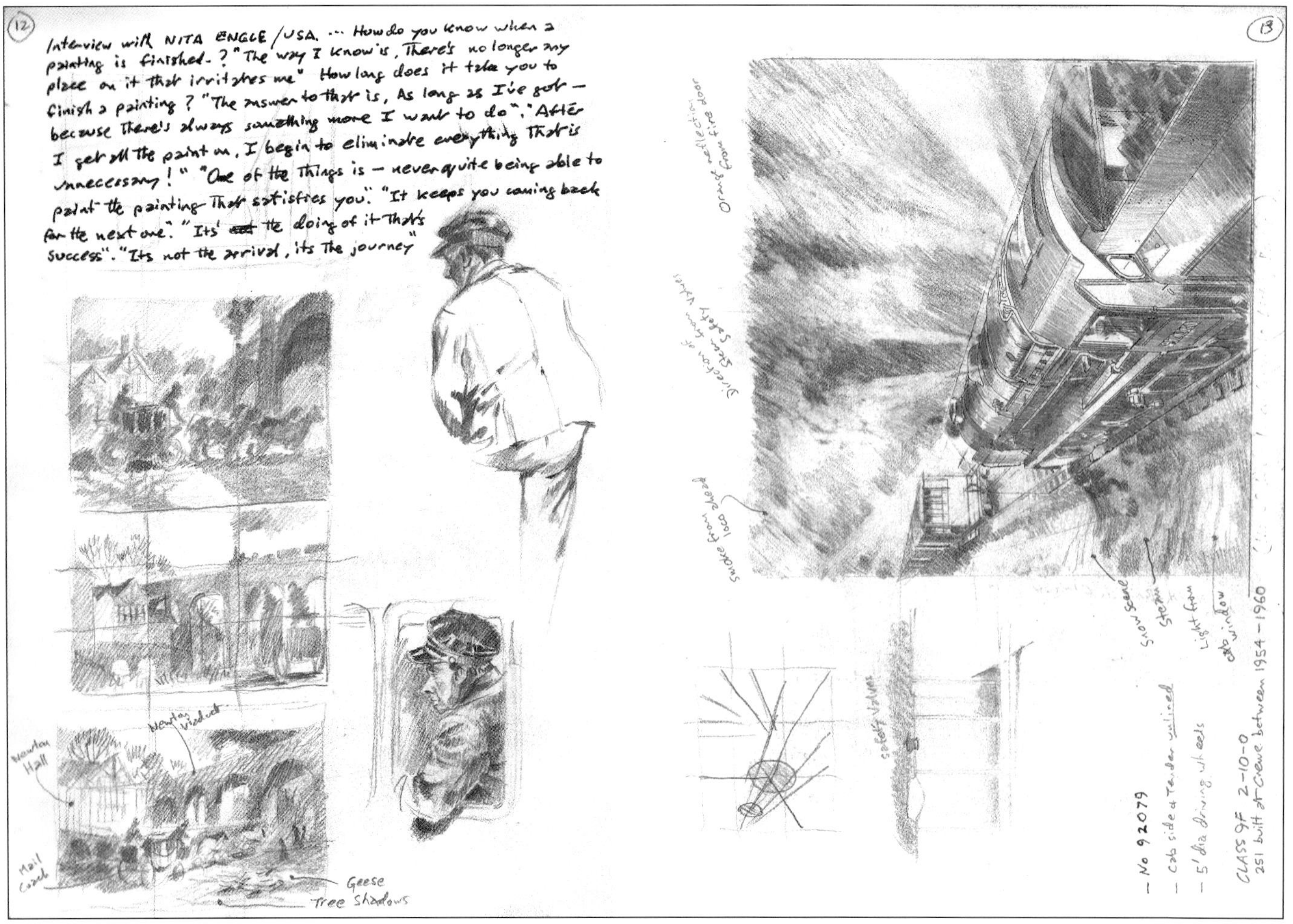
12
13
Interview with NITA ENGLE / USA. ... How do you know when a painting is finished? "The way I know is, There's no longer any place on it that irritates me" How long does it take you to finish a painting? "The answer to that is, As long as I've got — because there's always something more I want to do". "After I get all the paint on, I begin to eliminate everything that is unnecessary!" "One of the things is — never quite being able to paint the painting that satisfies you". "It keeps you coming back for the next one." "Its' the doing of it that's success". "Its not the arrival, its the journey"
Newton Hall
Newton Viaduct
Mail Coach
Geese
Tree Shadows
Orange reflection from fire door
Smoke from ahead loco
Snow scene
Steam
Light from cab window
Safety Valves
— No 92079
— Cab side a Tender unlined
— 5' dia driving wheels
CLASS 9F 2-10-0
251 built at Crewe between 1954–1960

(20)

1999

(SOLD)

Collection of Simon ~~Hossop~~. Moffit

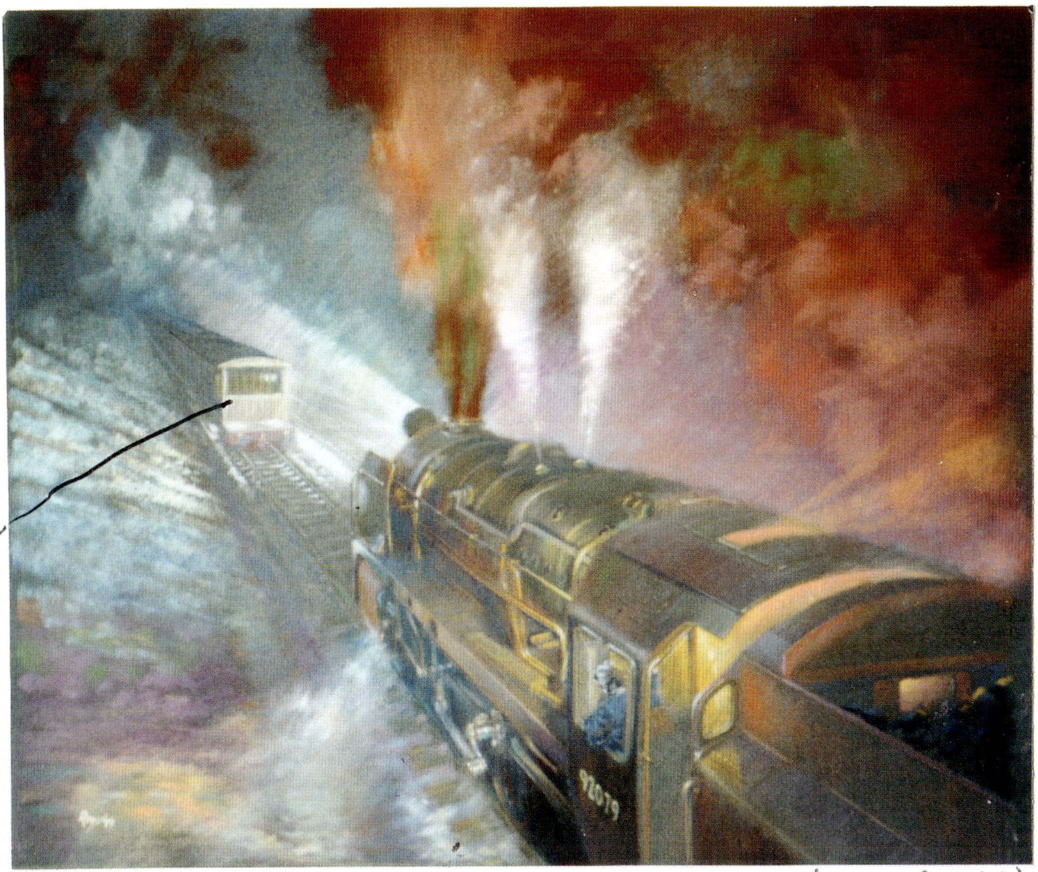

lamp code 2-reds

SOLD – At RAILART '99 (NRM York) to ....

LICKEY BANKER – 9F (with Big Emma's headlight)

(see page 6)

Art is not just a series of techniques on a canvas. Art is an expression of an idea and ~~that~~ technique is nothing more than the vehicle that gets you that expression. Whatever technique you concoct to get to that expression becomes the part of your work that's unique. – Gary Ernest Smith / U.S.A.

My view of Art is that 99% of the people want to be able to understand a work of art, and not have to guess at it. So I try to speak in a language that everybody can understand. In order to speak that language, you have to be able to draw, understand composition and colour, and have all your 'smarts'. Then you can interpret, convey an impression or a feeling – Tom Hill / U.S.A.

Leo Tolstoy said that a work of art has to have emotional content, or it is not a work of art. It is only a craft. This emotional content is very difficult to give to a work. But if you, the artist, are ~~exciting~~ excited about the subject, it transfers to the viewer, and the work becomes lasting – Zoltan Szabo USA

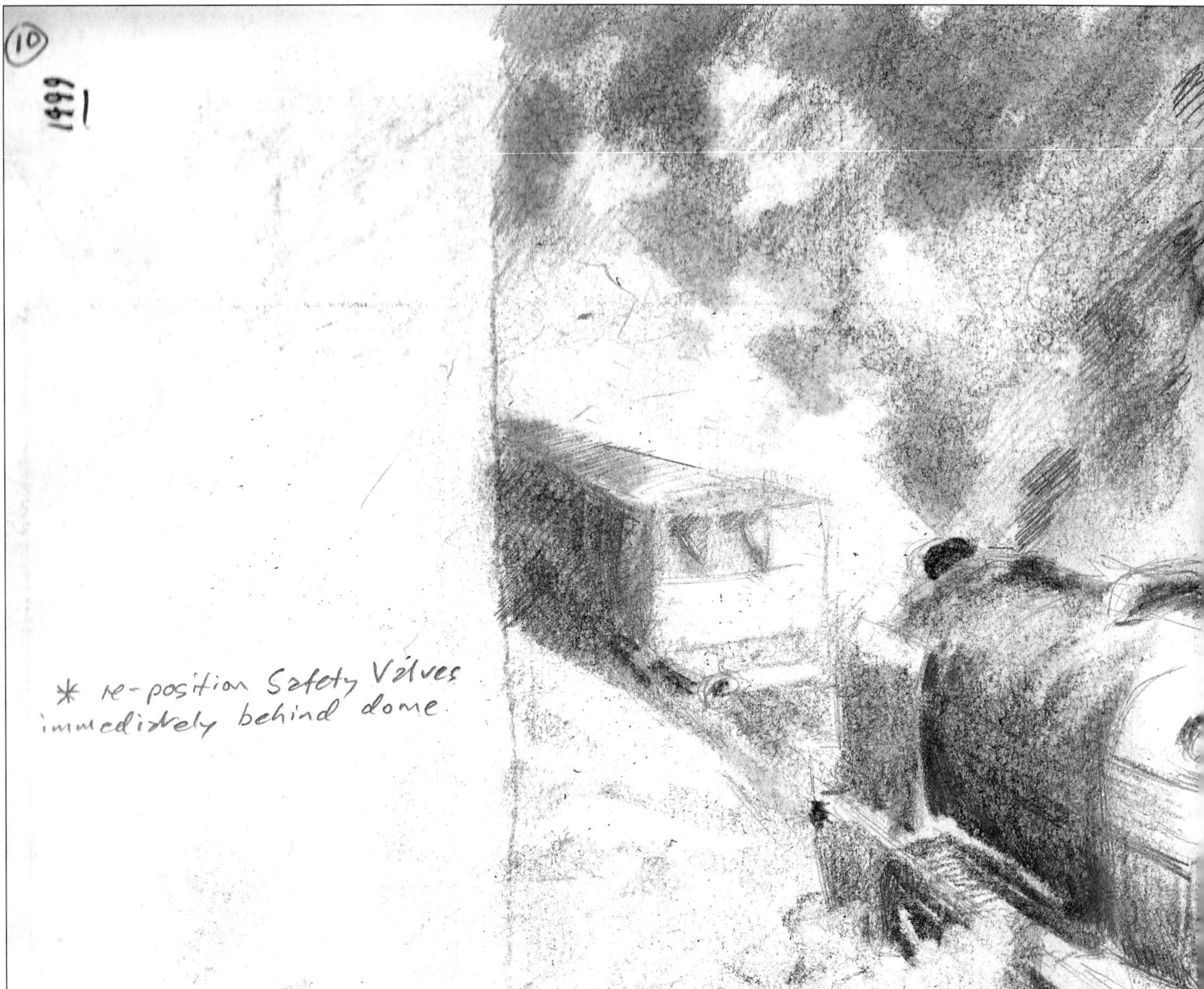
10
1999
* re-position Safety Valves immediately behind dome
"Buffering Up"
9F Replacement for "Big Emma" with 'Big Emma's' headlamp.

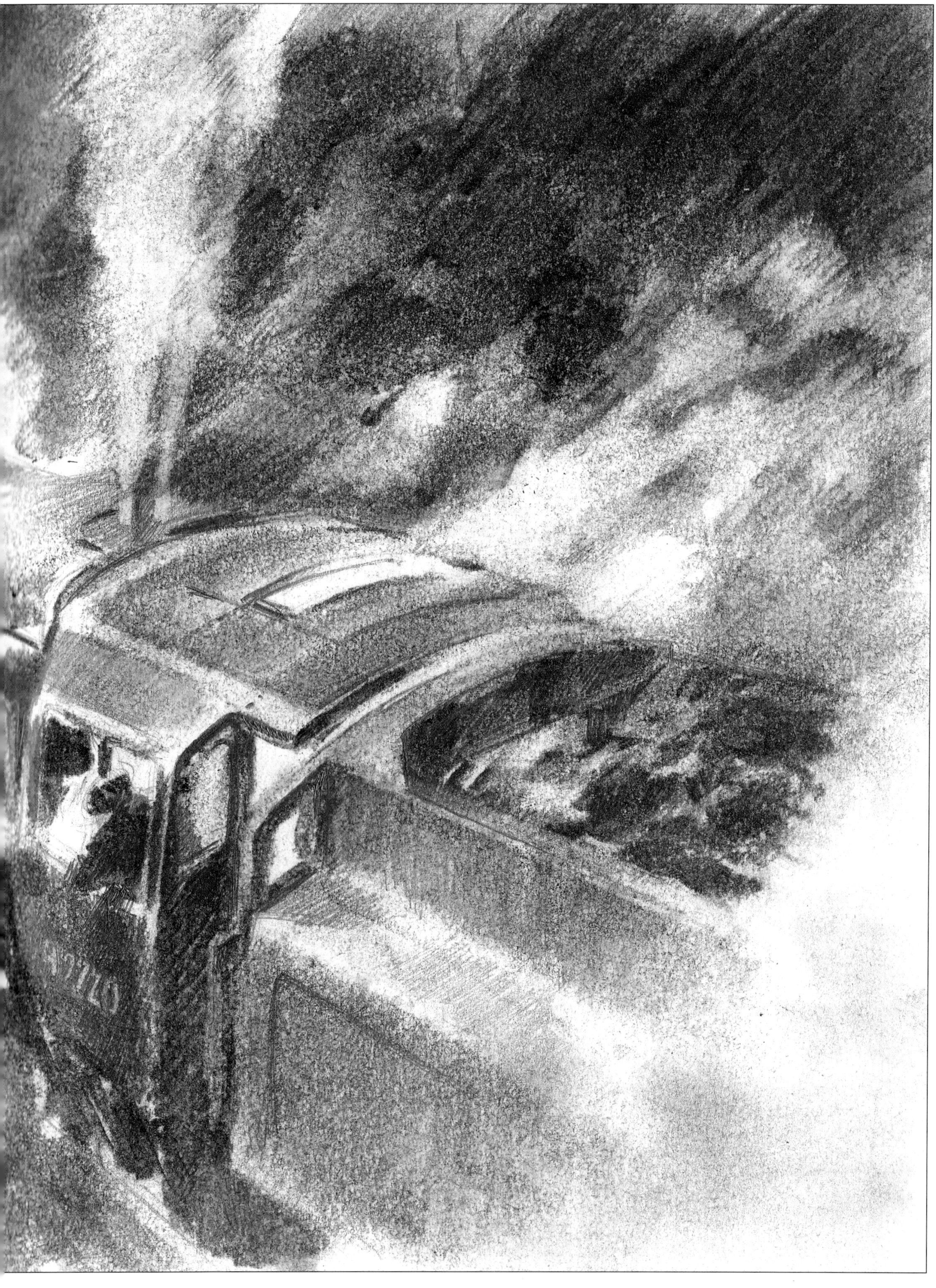

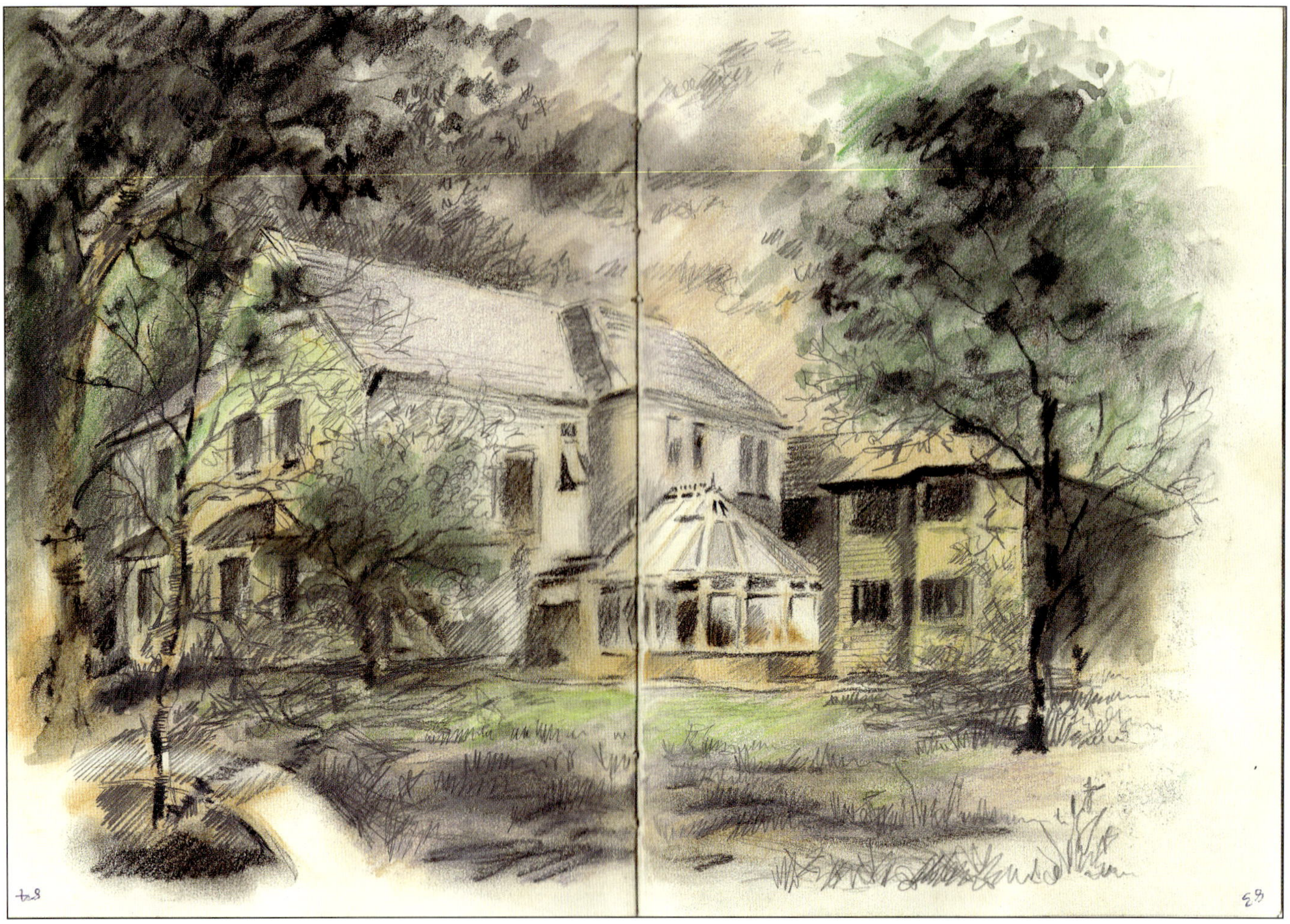

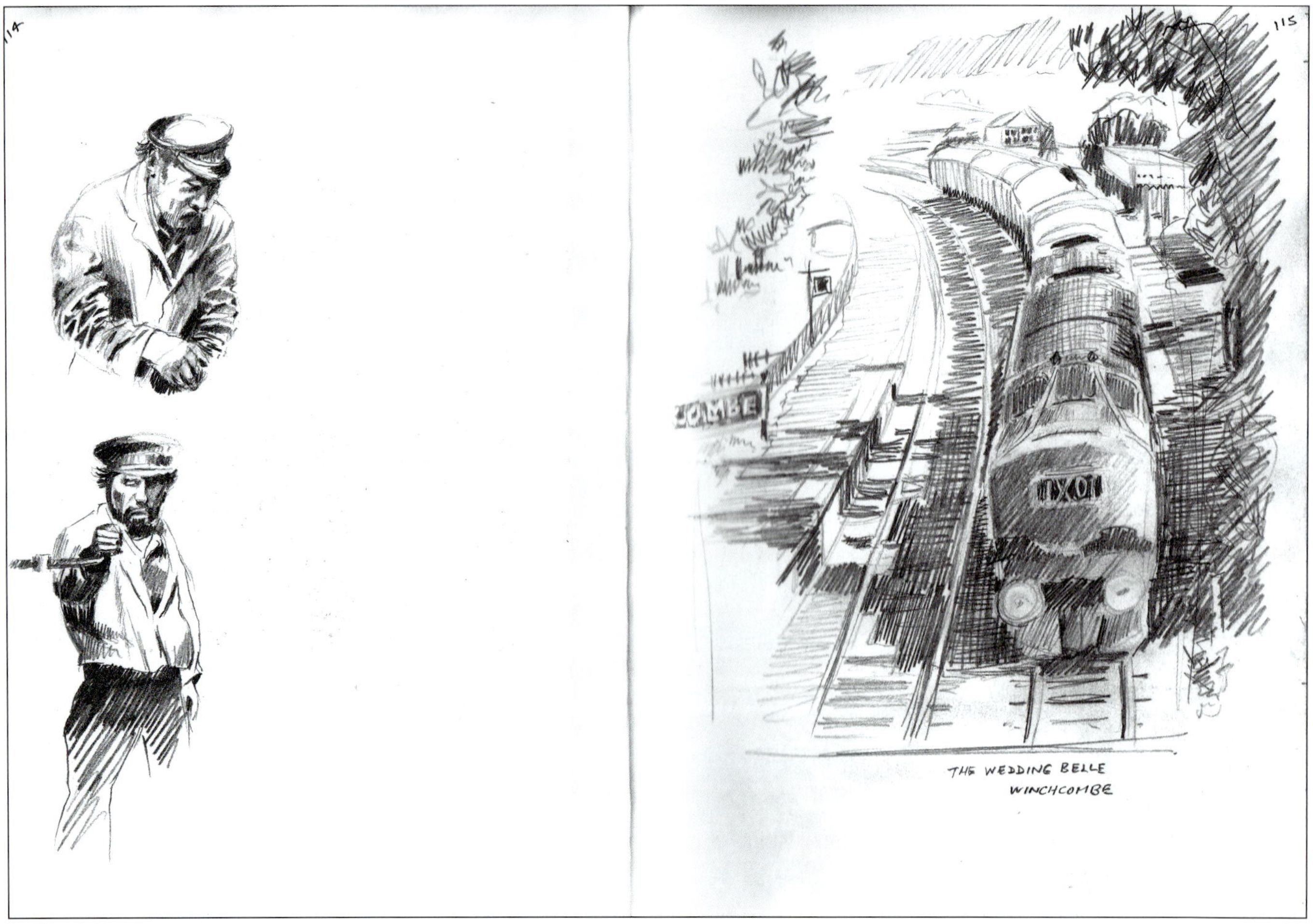
THE WEDDING BELLE
WINCHCOMBE

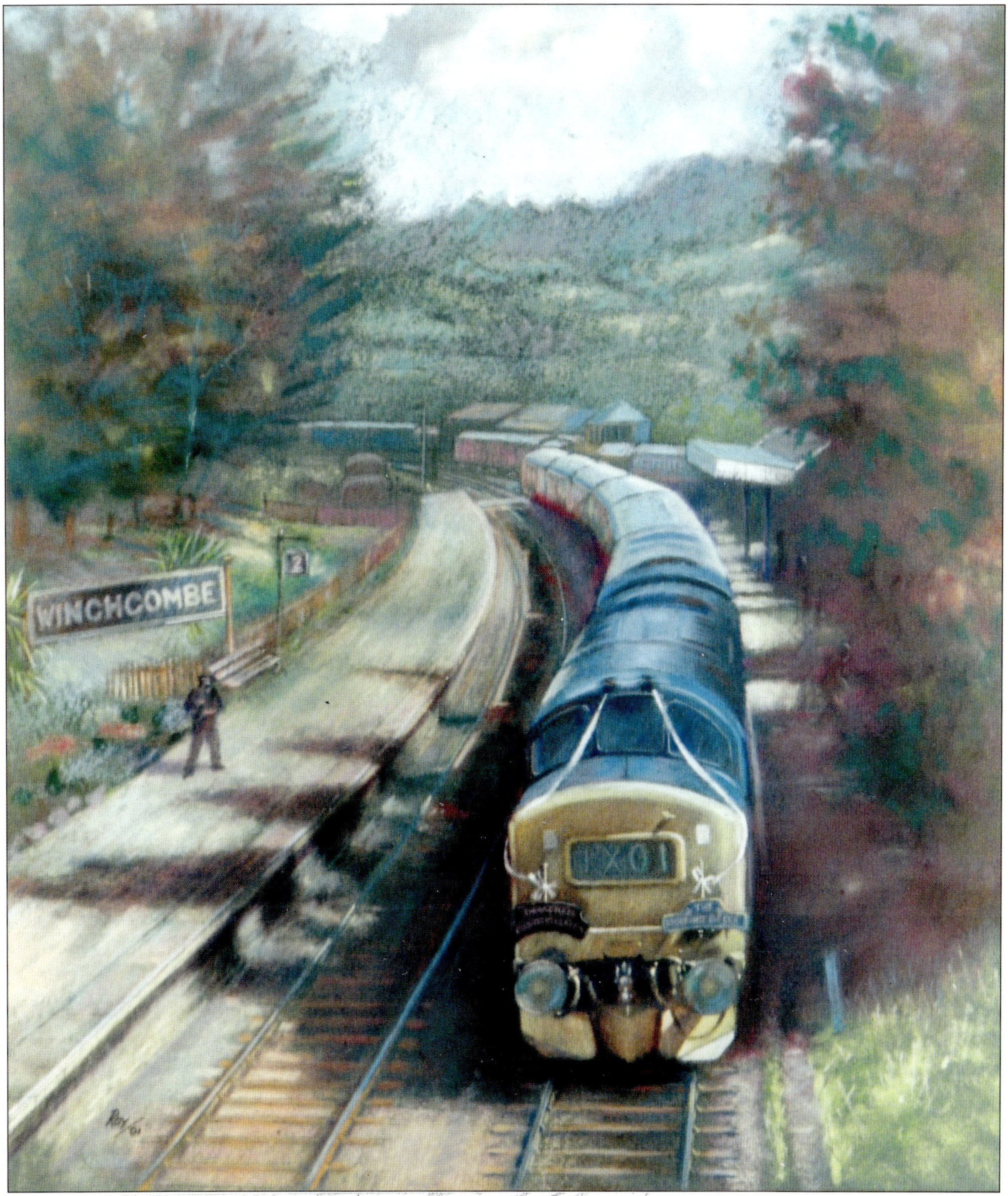

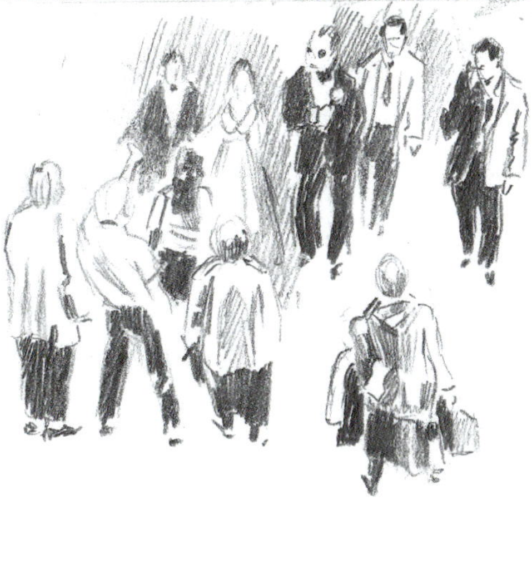

Attention ...
- Purple on platform beneath trees
- Bride - groom and guests
- WINCHCOMBE Station Sign
- Landscape
- Platform edging stones

"THE MAGIC OF STEAM"

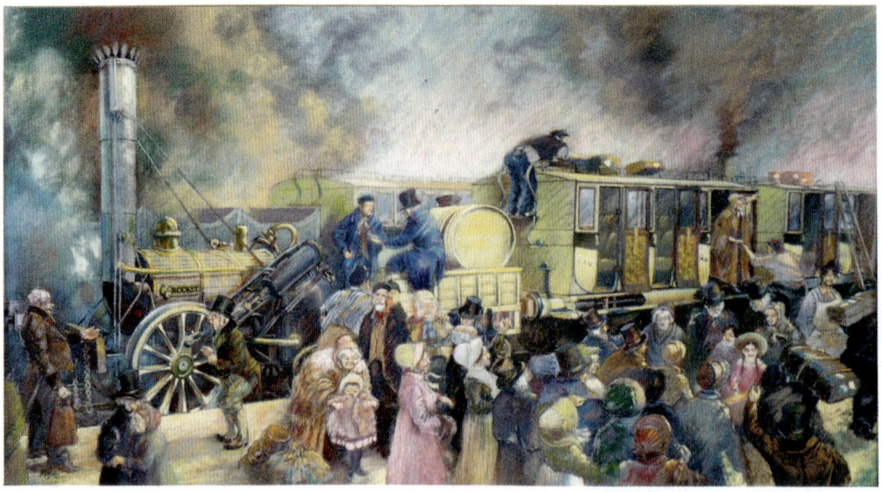

Used in Film production – Los Angeles 1997–98
Film "TRAINS UNLIMITED"

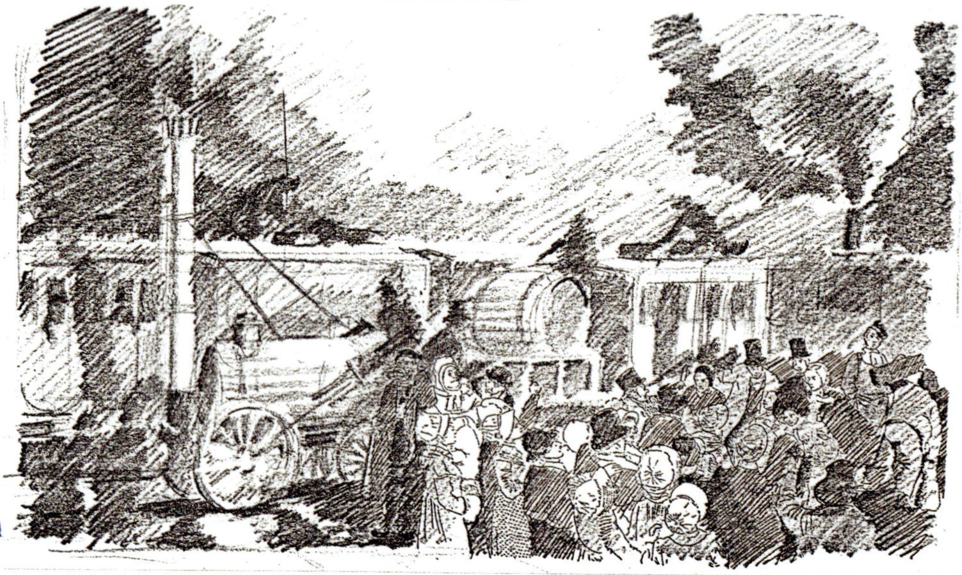

introduce figures to "hold the eye"

introduce figures & luggage ladders

A useful technique is to look through a tinted piece of transparent plastic or glass – red works well. This will minimize the colours and identify the tonal values more easily
– survey with half closed eyes.

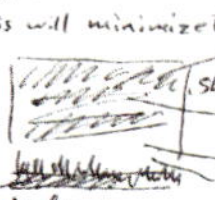

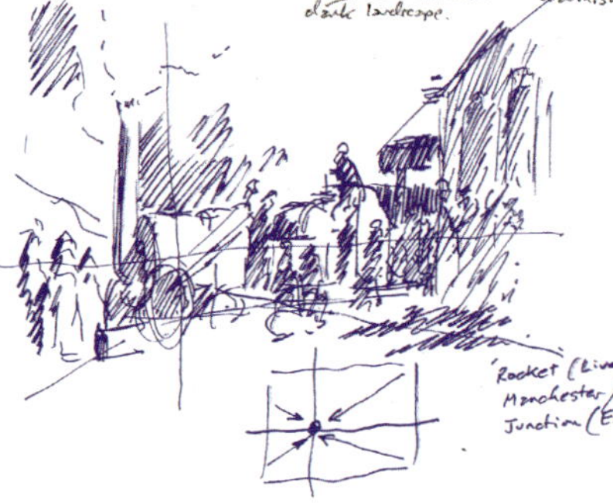

Rocket (Liverpool–Manchester/Newton Junction (Earlestown)

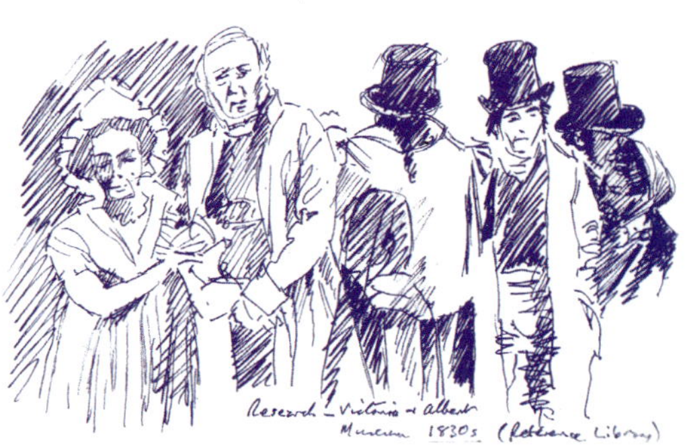

Research – Victoria & Albert Museum 1830s (Reference Library)

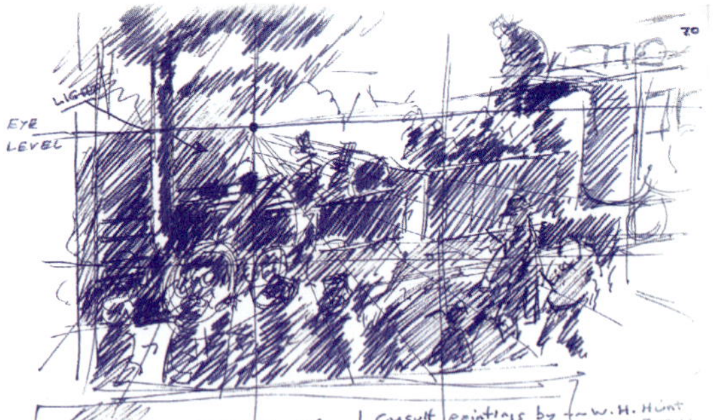

– Luggage – Bags across shoulder
– children

Consult paintings by
W. H. Hunt
F. M. Brown
J. Collinson
W. P. Frith
H. N. O'Neil
J. Tissot
W. Logsdail
W. B. Scott
J. Brett

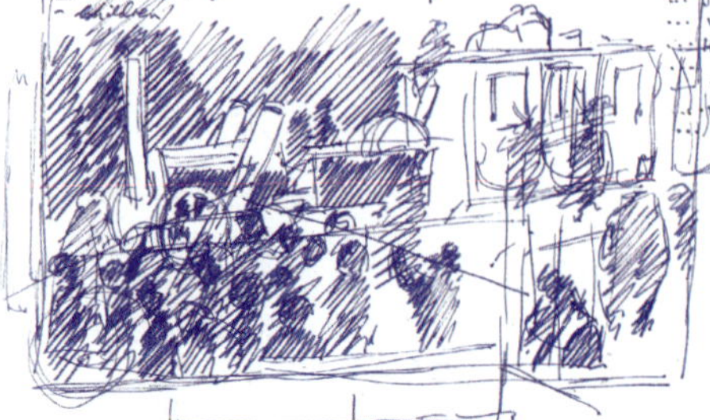

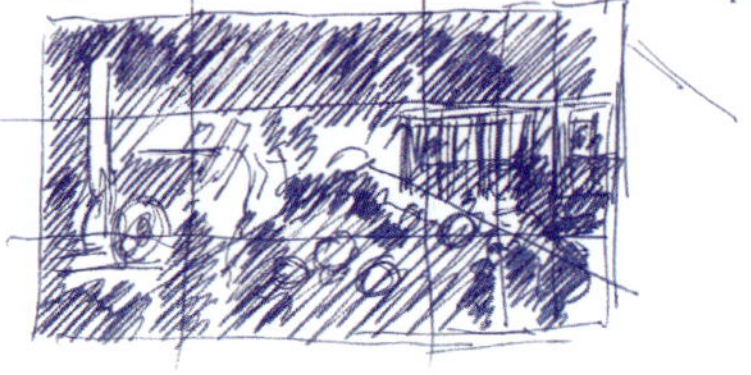

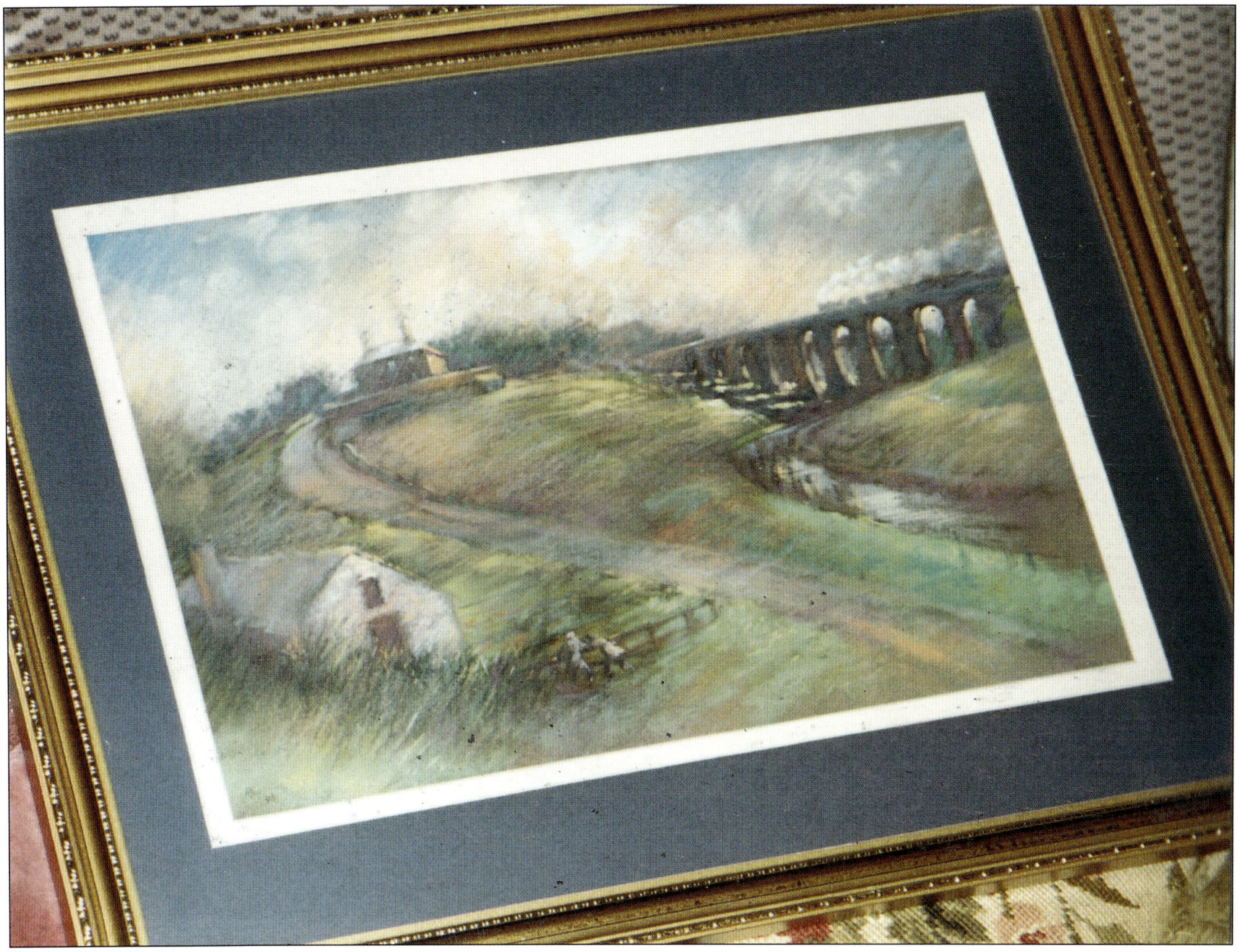

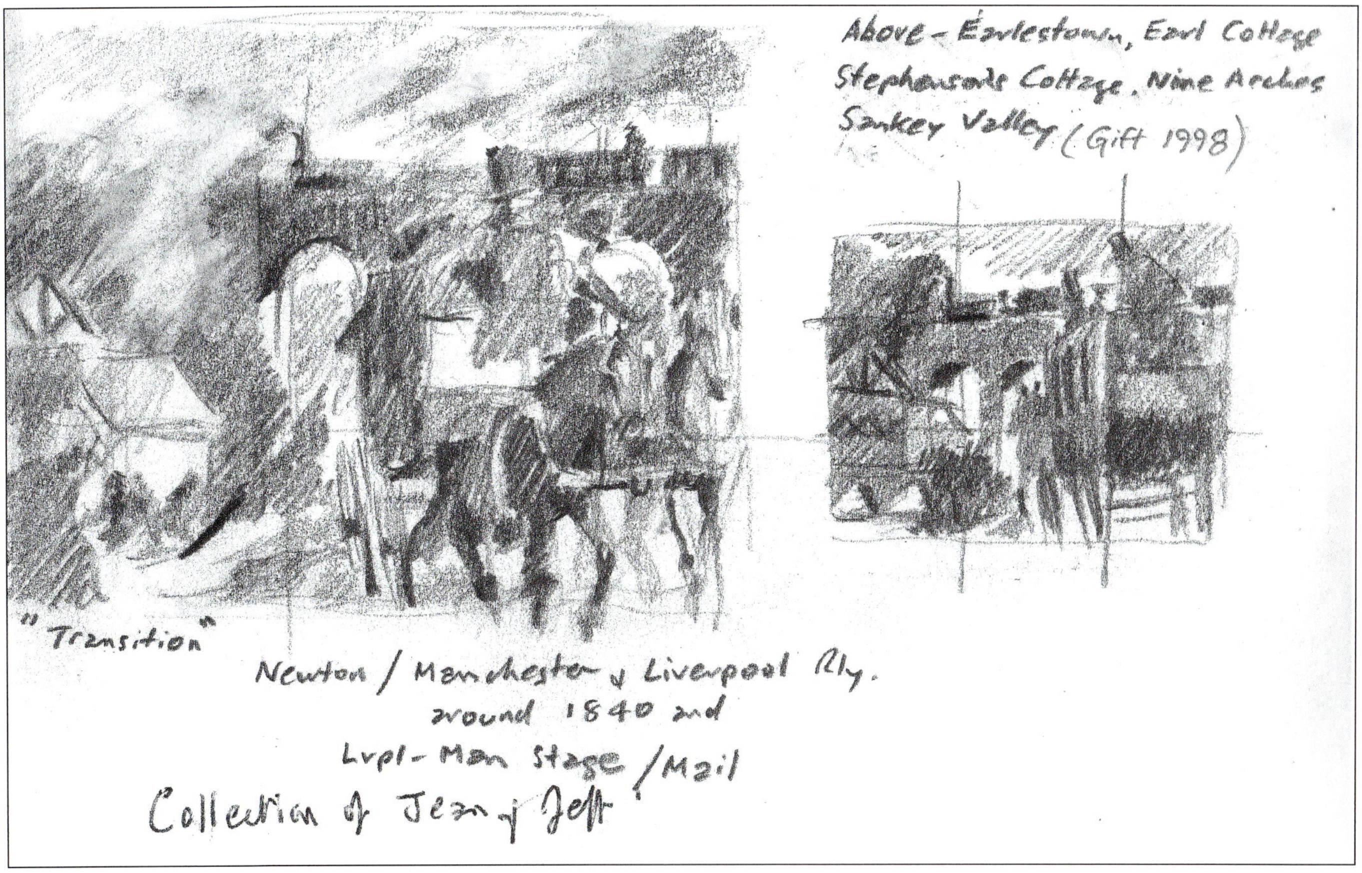
Above – Earlestown, Earl Cottage
Stephenson's Cottage, Nine Arches
Sankey Valley (Gift 1998)
"Transition"
Newton / Manchester & Liverpool Rly.
around 1840 and
Lvpl – Man Stage / Mail
Collection of Jean & Jeff

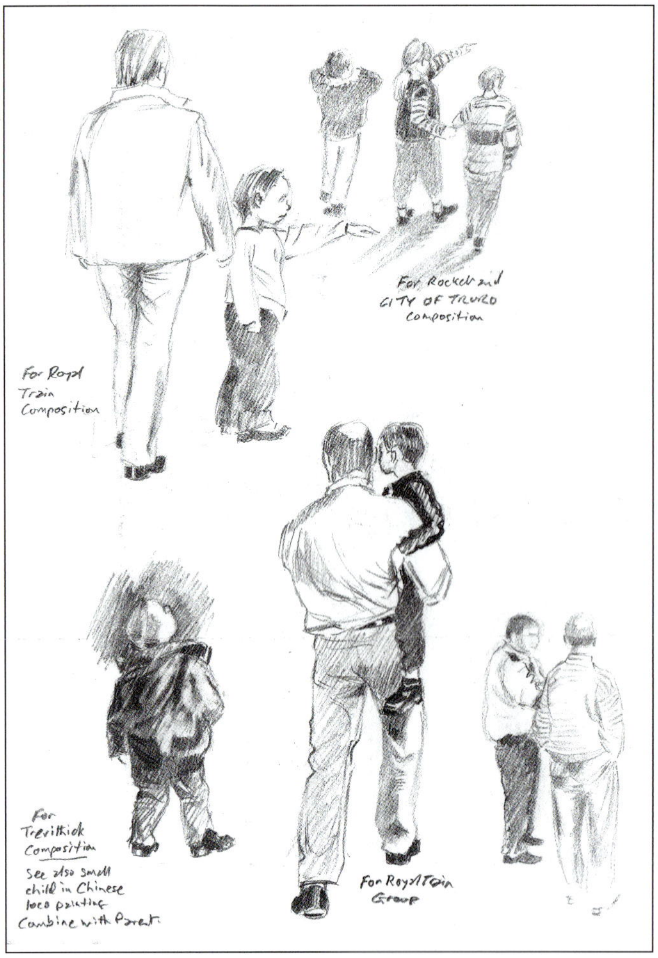

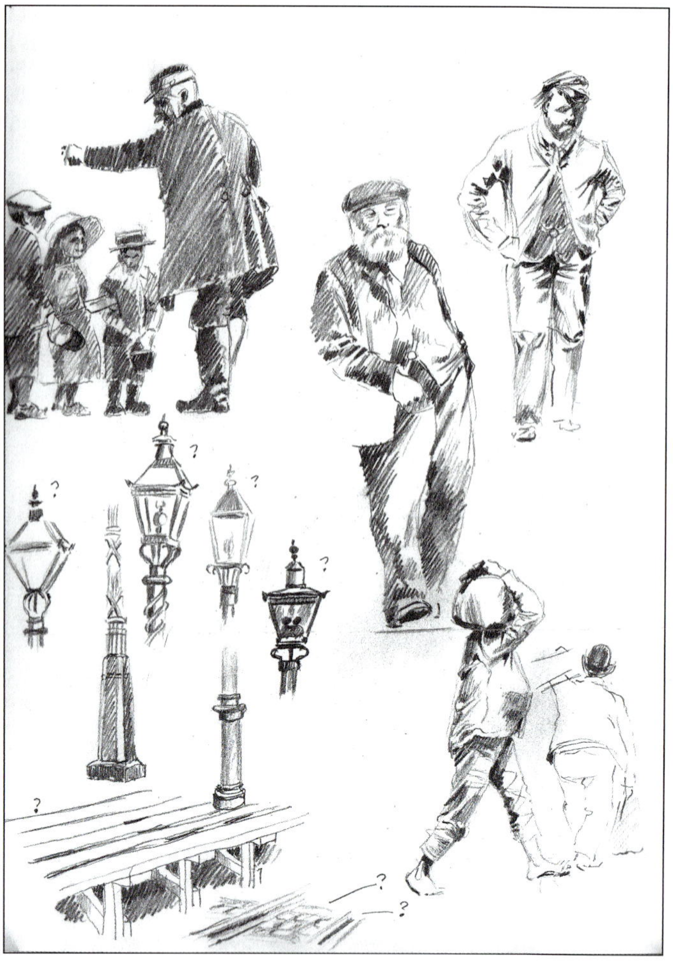

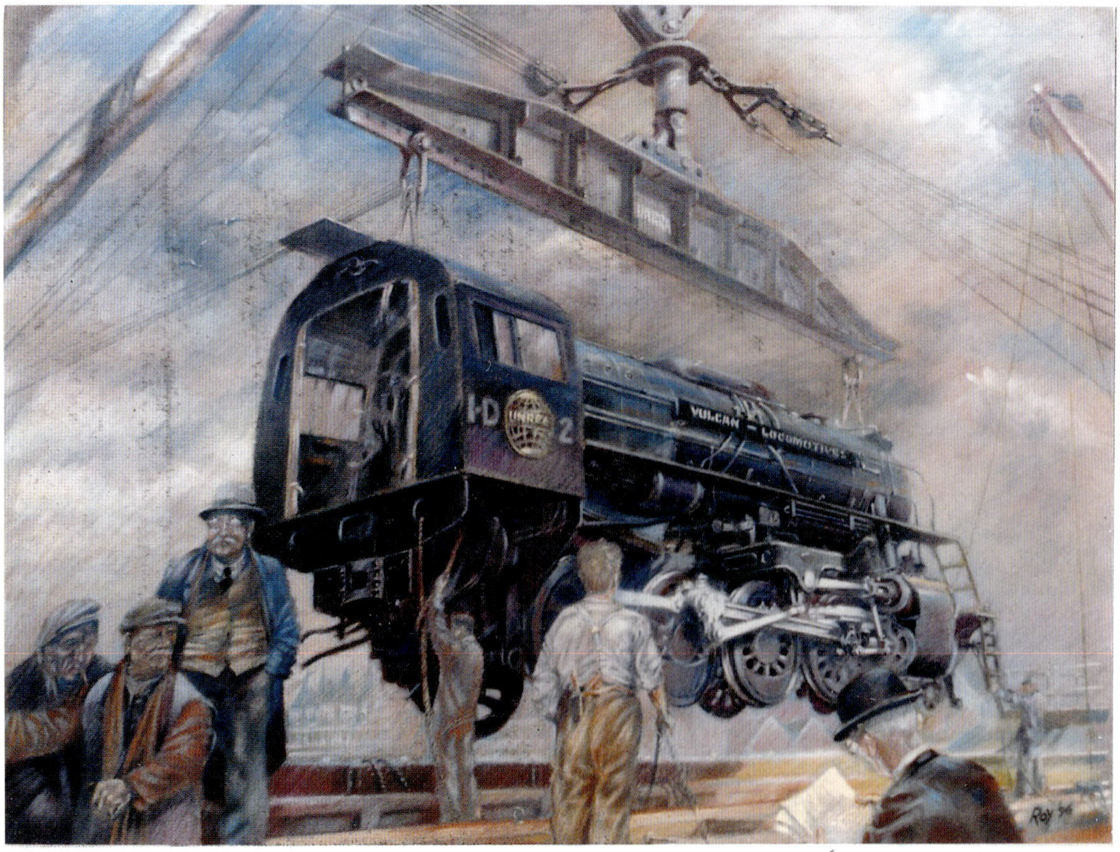

4.25 x 5.75

Liberztion No 2 - (Vulcm Foundry)
One of 30 locos & tenders shipped
zbozd "Empire Wallzce"

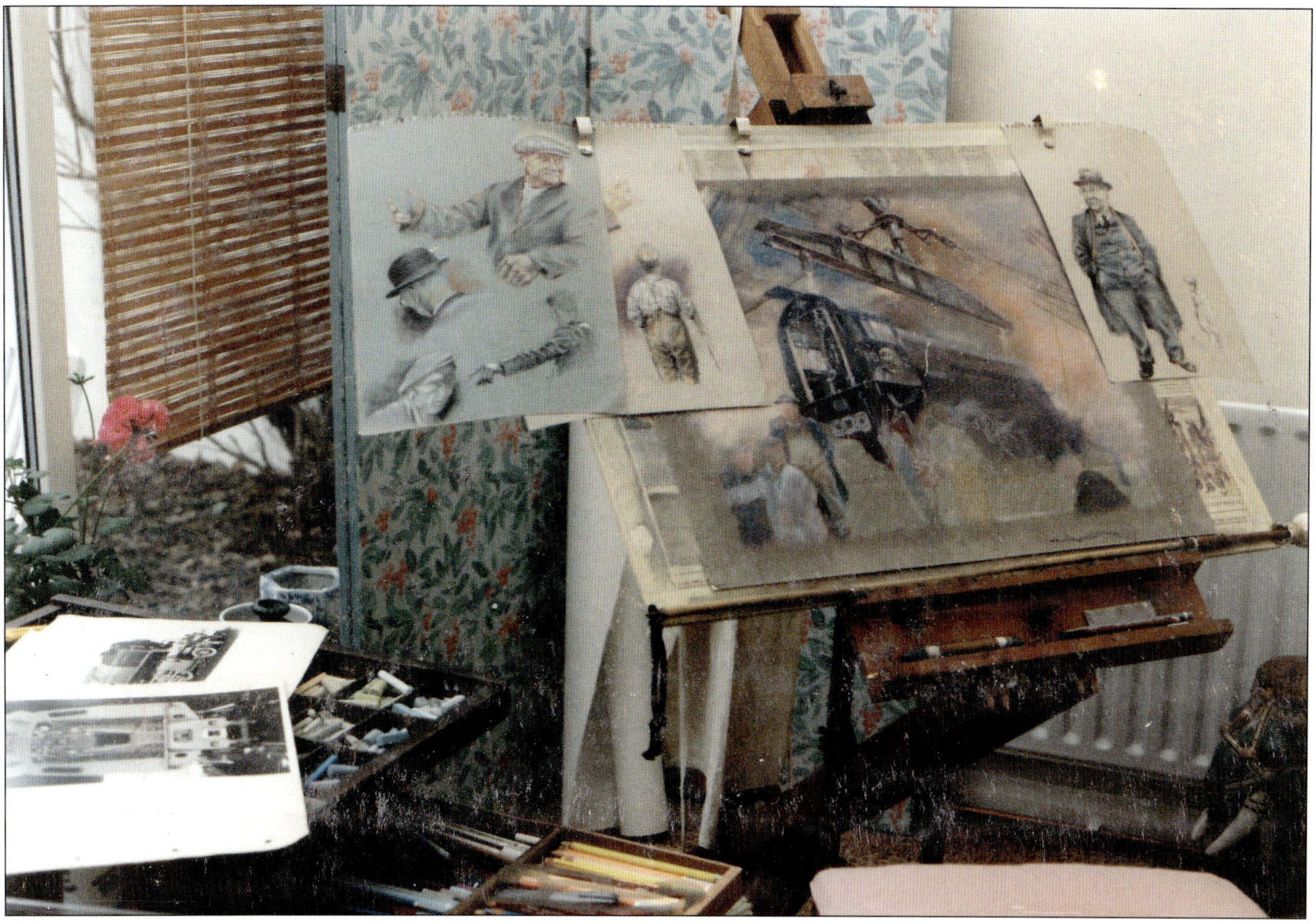

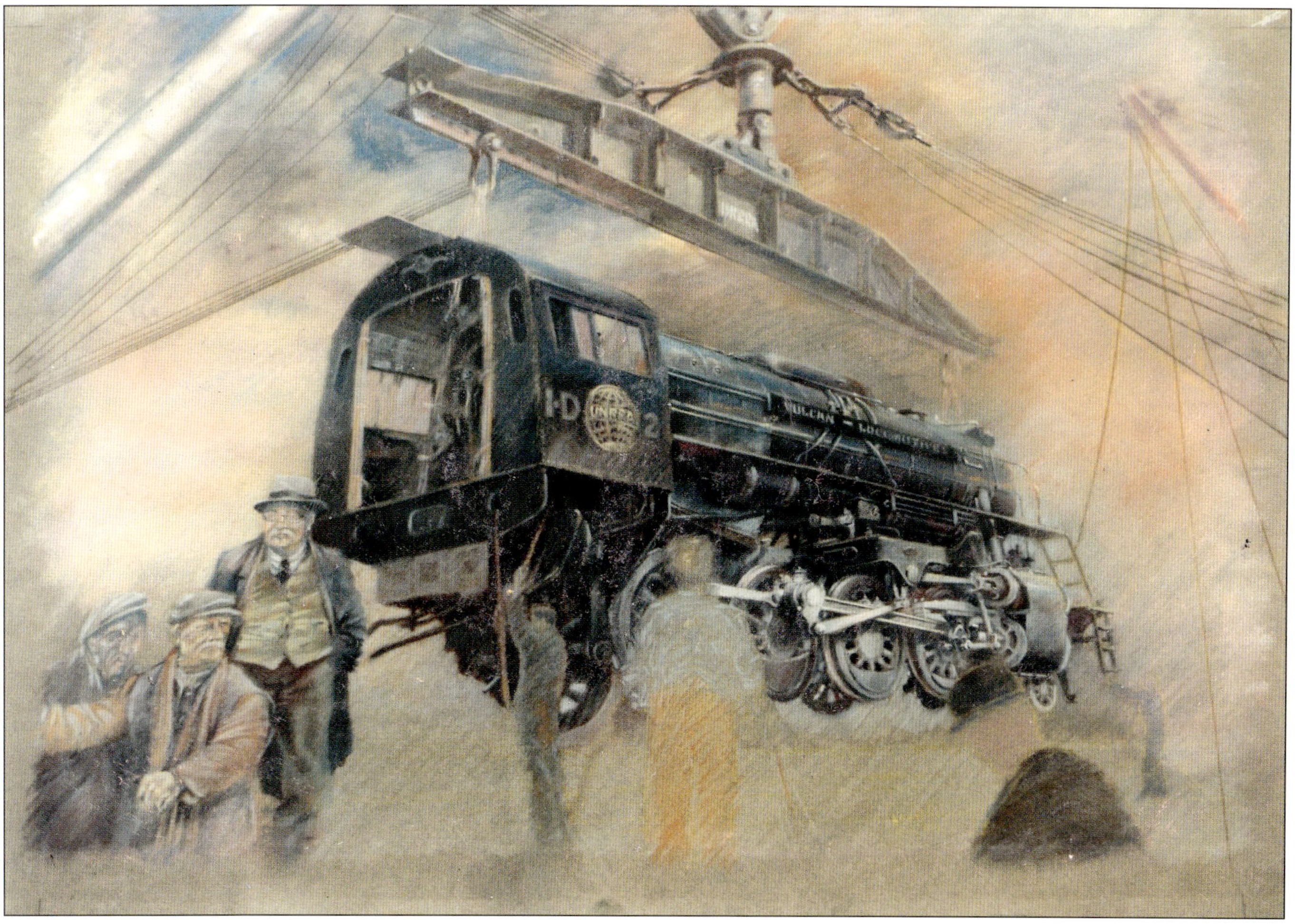

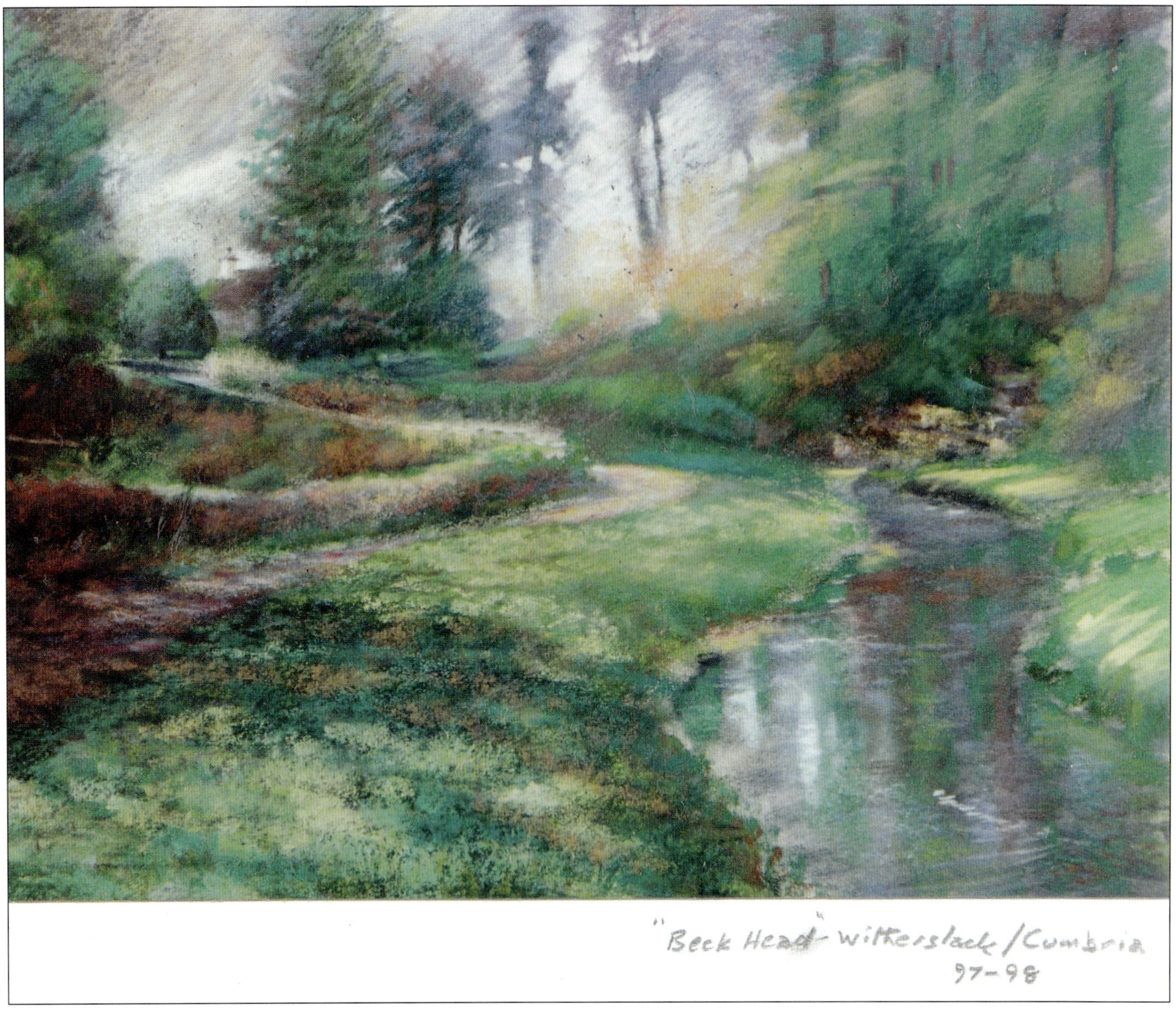
"Beck Head" Witherslack / Cumbria
97–98

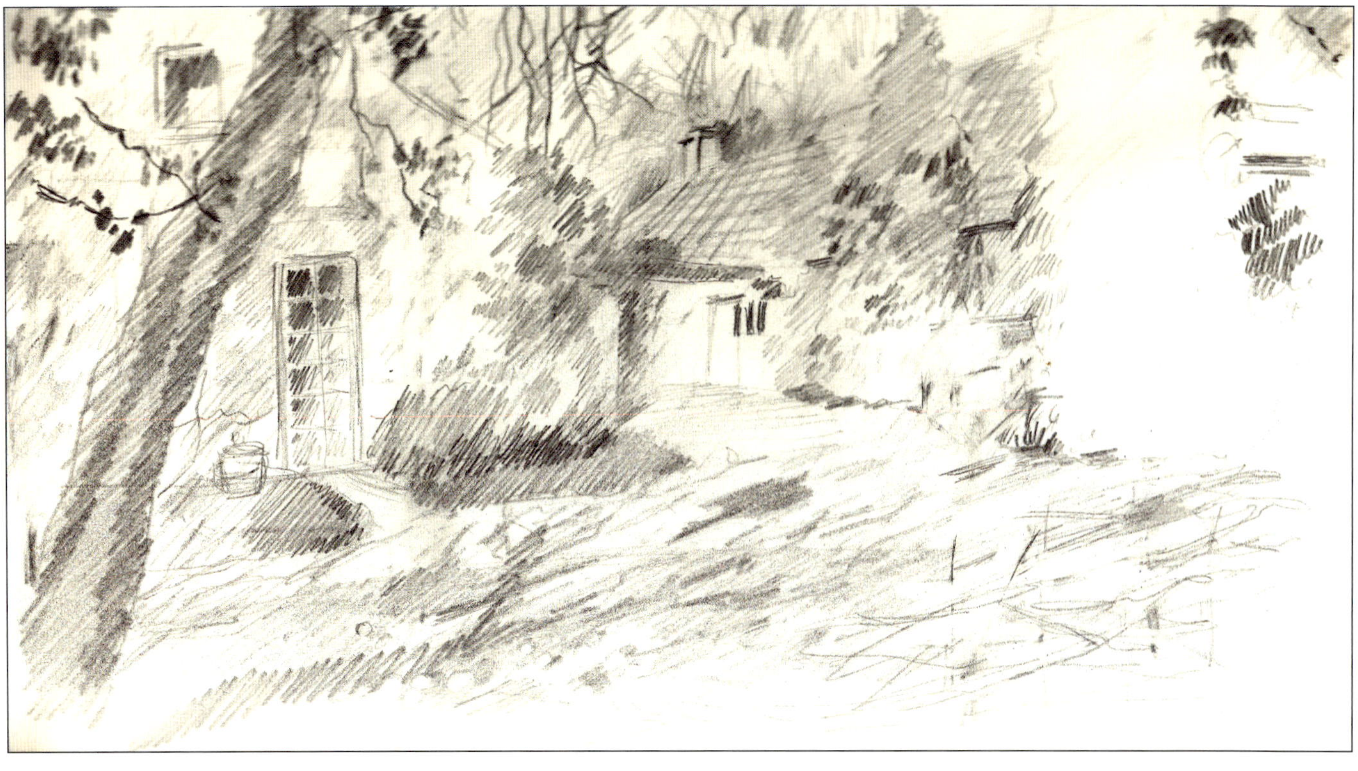

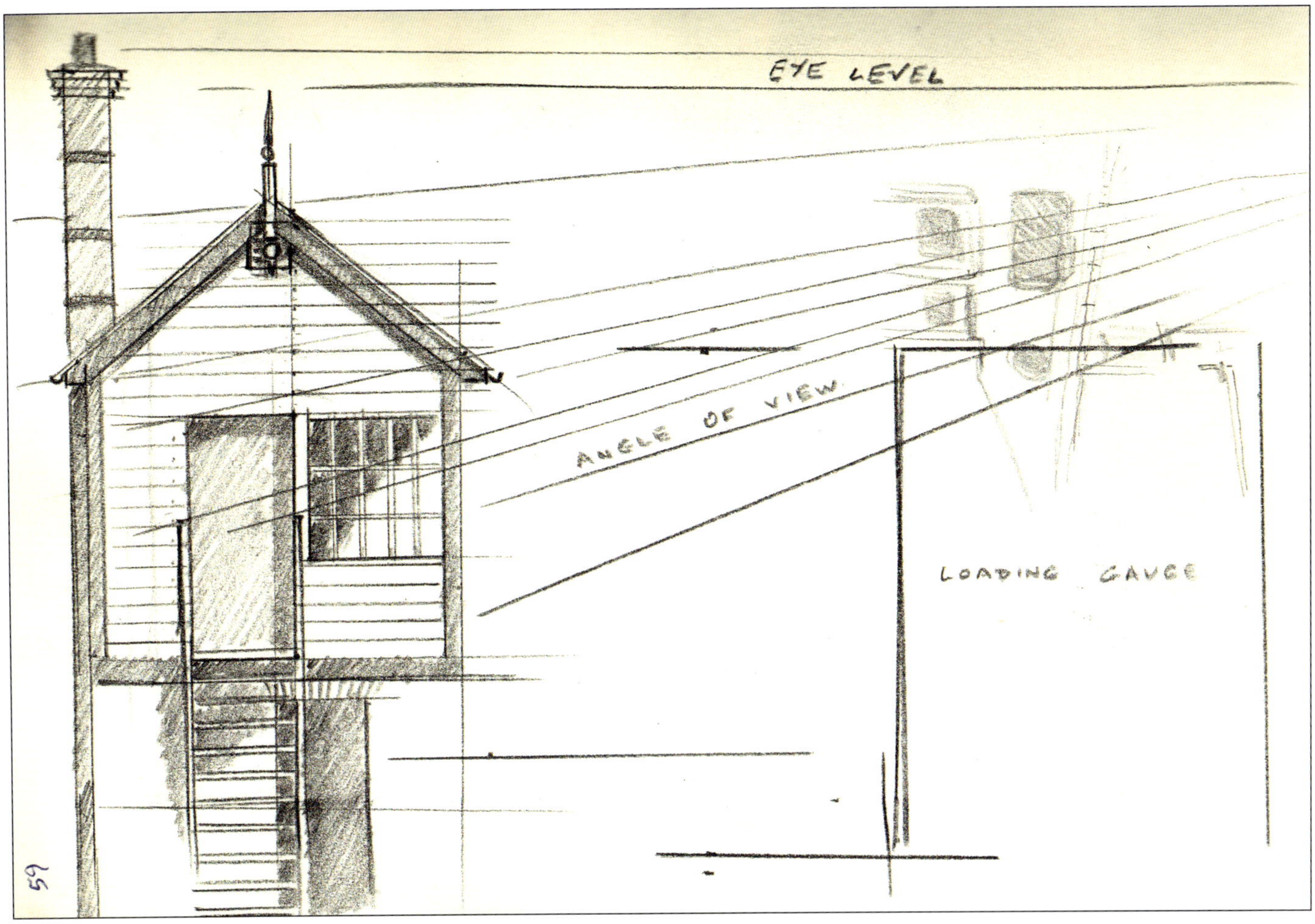
EYE LEVEL
ANGLE OF VIEW
LOADING GAUGE
59

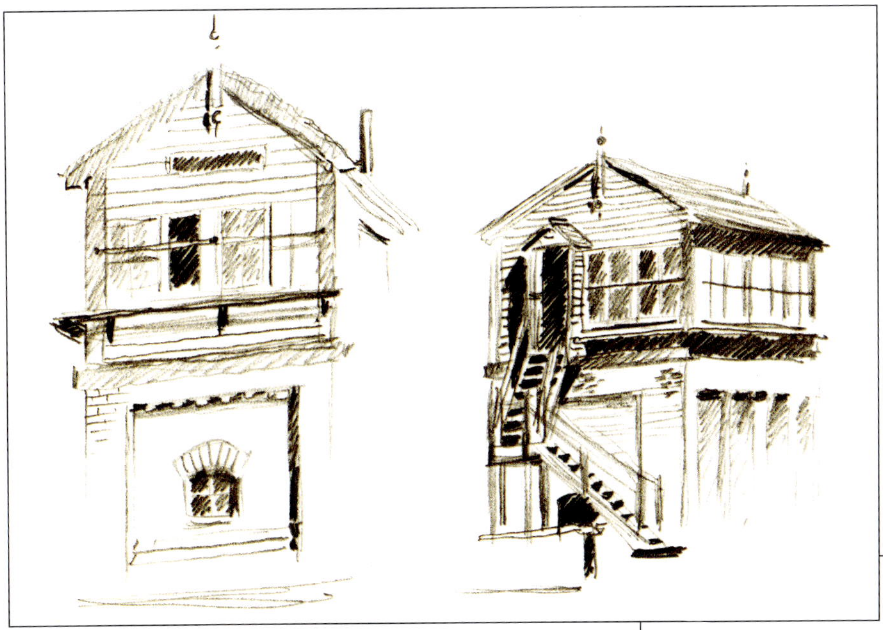

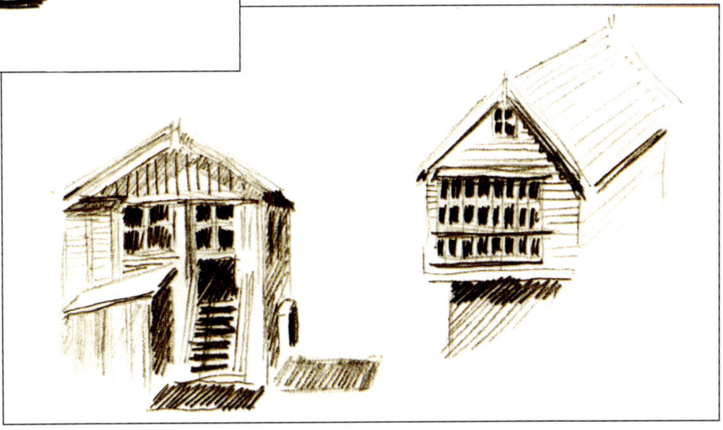

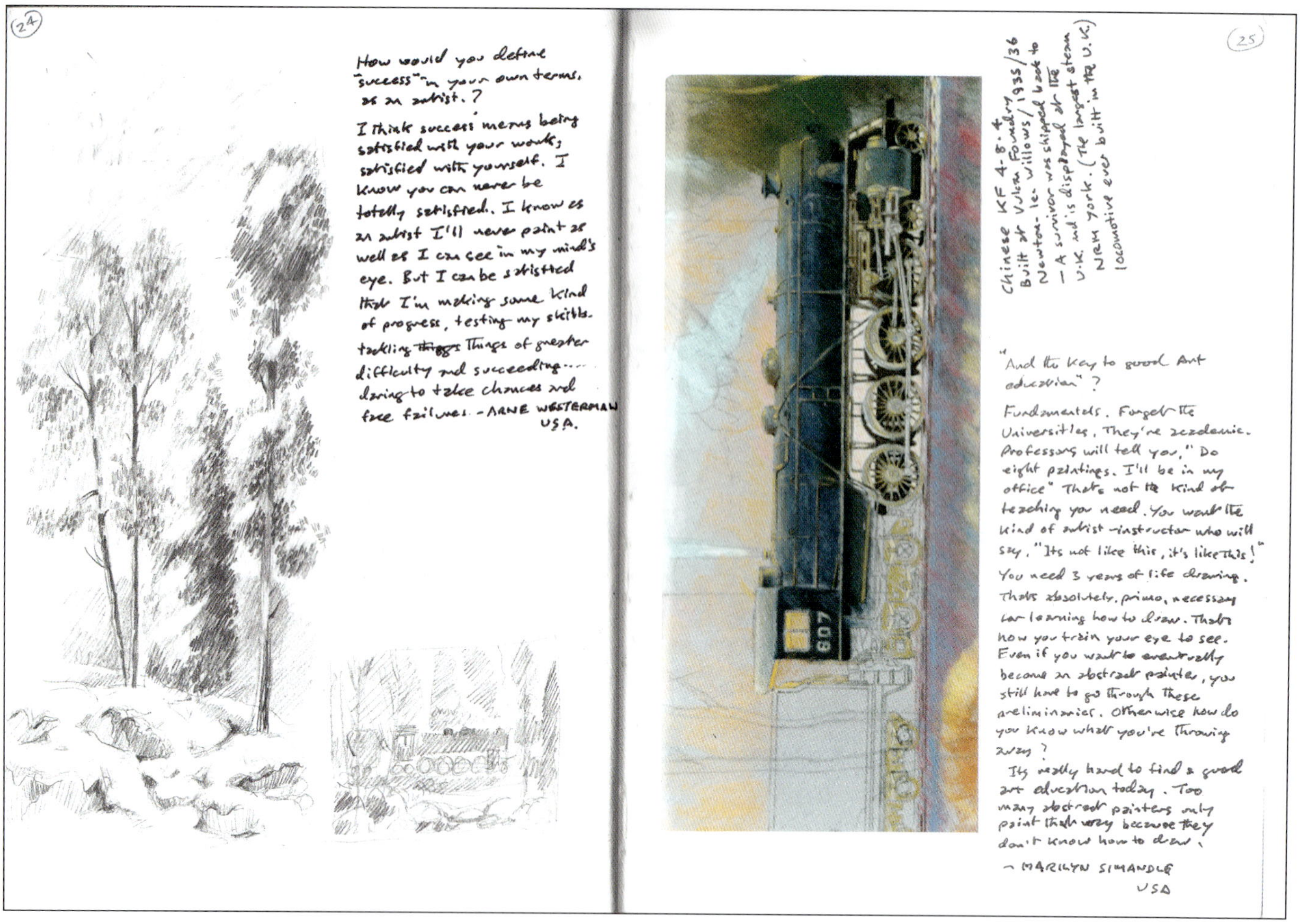
24
How would you define "success" in your own terms, as an artist.?
I think success means being satisfied with your work, satisfied with yourself. I know you can never be totally satisfied. I know as an artist I'll never paint as well as I can see in my mind's eye. But I can be satisfied that I'm making some kind of progress, testing my skills. tackling things of greater difficulty and succeeding.... daring to take chances and face failures. - ARNE WESTERMAN USA.
25
Chinese KF 4-8-4
Built at Vulcan Foundry / 1935/36
Newton-le-Willows / — A survivor was shipped back to U.K. and is displayed at the NRM York. (The largest steam locomotive ever built in the U.K.)
"And the key to good Art education"?
Fundamentals. Forget the Universities, they're academic. Professors will tell you," Do eight paintings. I'll be in my office" That's not the kind of teaching you need. You want the kind of artist-instructor who will say, "It's not like this, it's like this!" You need 3 years of life drawing. That's absolutely, primo, necessary for learning how to draw. That's how you train your eye to see. Even if you want to eventually become an abstract painter, you still have to go through these preliminaries. Otherwise how do you know what you're throwing away?
It's really hard to find a good art education today. Too many abstract painters only paint that way because they don't know how to draw.
— MARILYN SIMANDLE USA

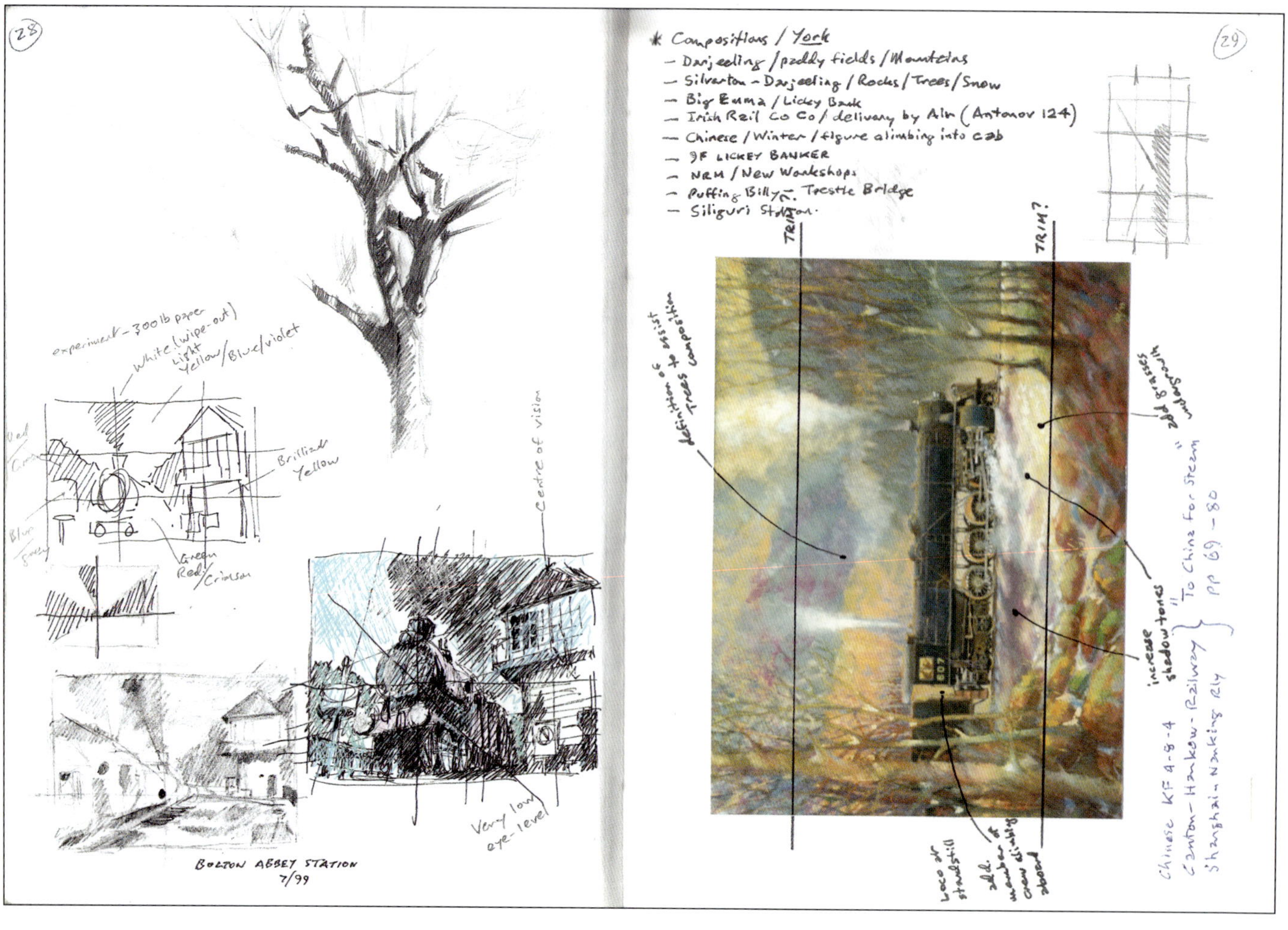
28
experiment - 300lb paper
White (wipe-out)
Light Yellow / Blue/violet
Brilliant Yellow
Green
Red/Crimson
Centre of vision
Very low eye-level
BOLTON ABBEY STATION 7/99
29
* Compositions / York
— Darjeeling / paddy fields / Mountains
— Silverton - Darjeeling / Rocks / Trees / Snow
— Big Emma / Lickey Bank
— Irish Rail Co Co / delivery by Air (Antonov 124)
— Chinese / Winter / figure climbing into cab
— 9F LICKEY BANKER
— NRM / New Workshops
— Puffing Billy / Trestle Bridge
— Siliguri Station.
TRIM?
TRIM?
add grasses undergrowth
increase shadow tones
Loco at standstill
Chinese KF 4-8-4
Canton-Hankow-Railway
Shanghai-Nanking Rly
"To China for Steam" pp 69-80

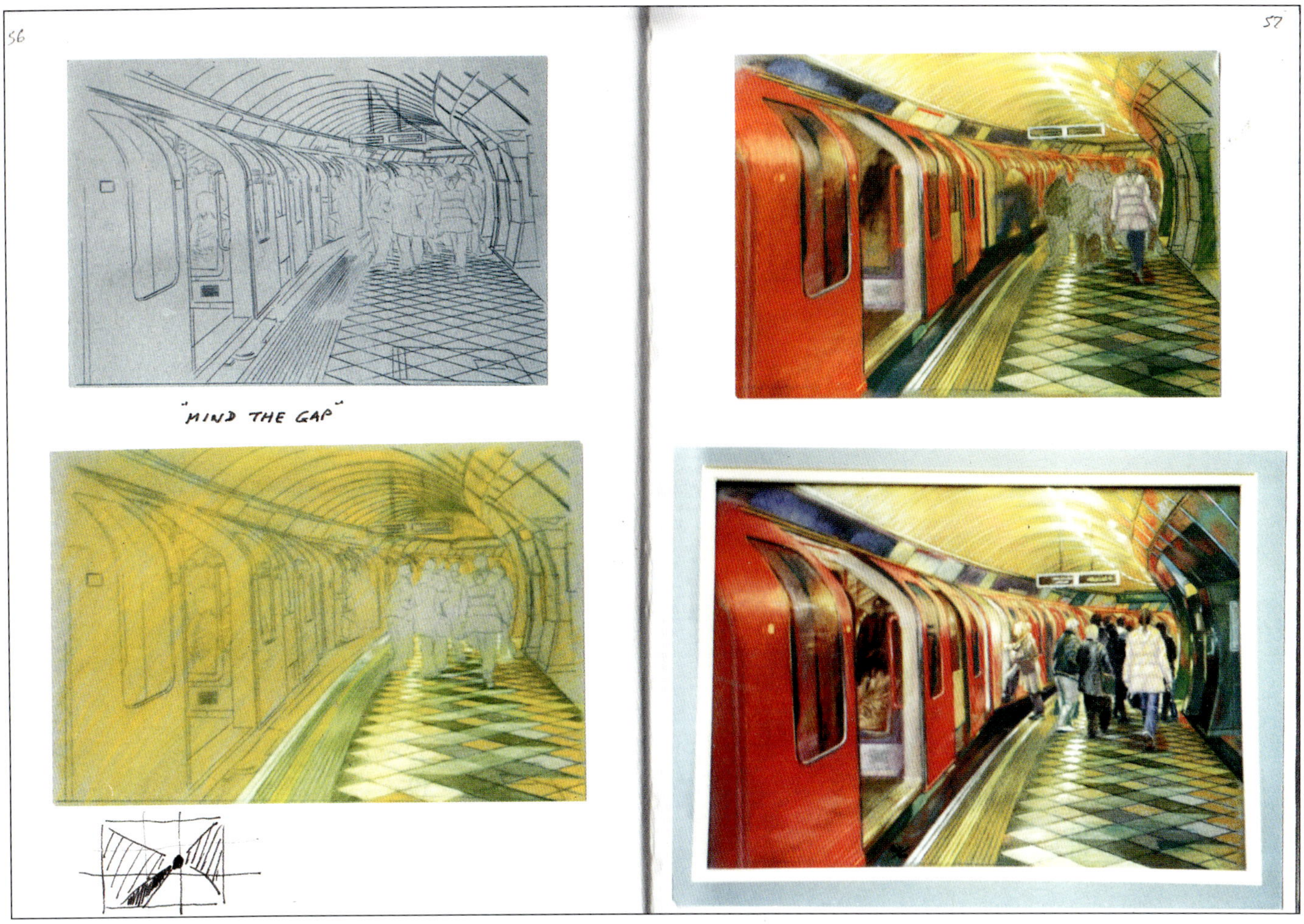
56
57
"MIND THE GAP"

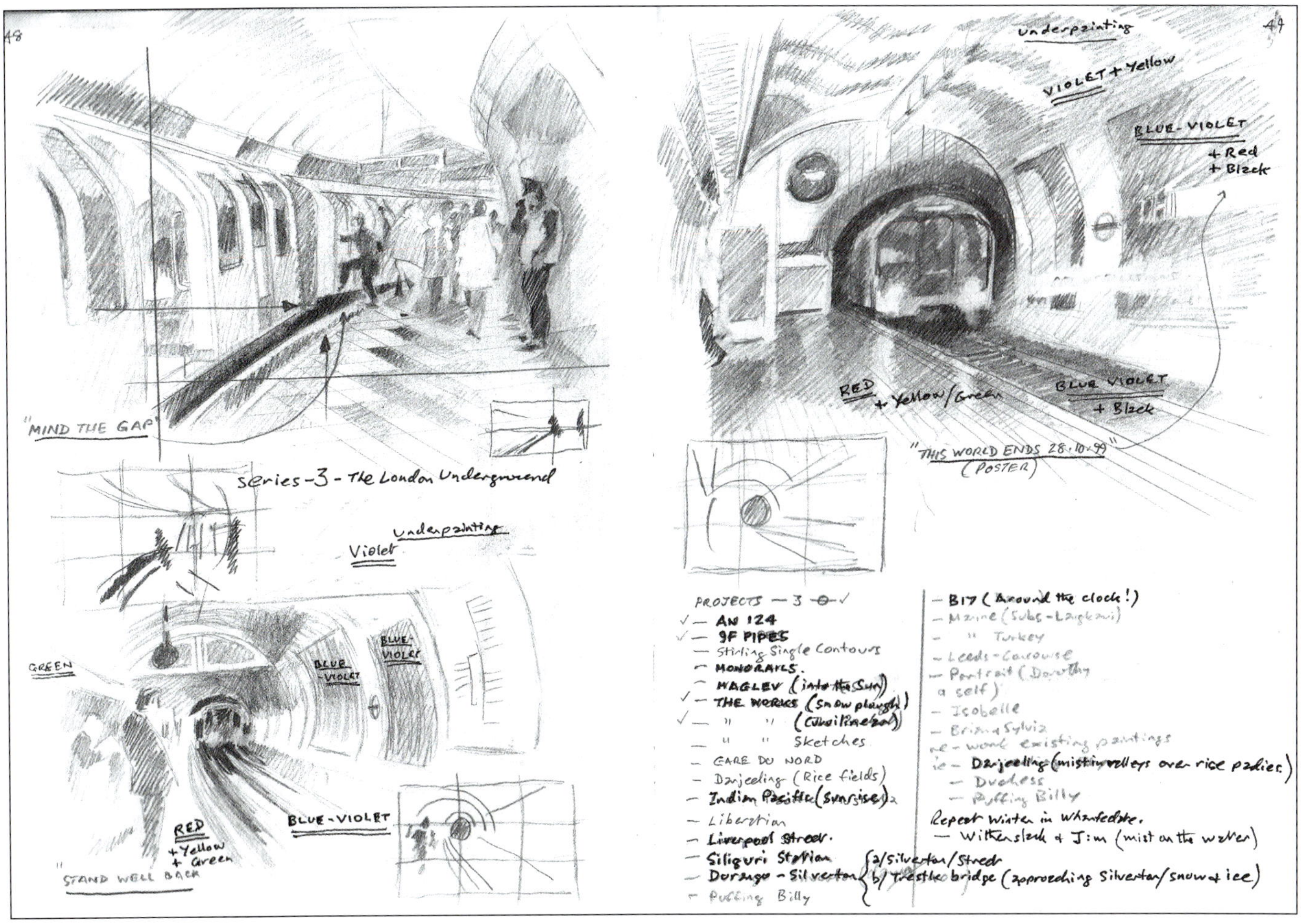
48
49
"MIND THE GAP"
Series-3 - The London Underground
Underpainting
Violet
GREEN
BLUE-VIOLET
BLUE-VIOLET
RED
+Yellow
+ Green
BLUE-VIOLET
"STAND WELL BACK"
Underpainting
VIOLET + Yellow
BLUE-VIOLET
+ Red
+ Black
RED
+ Yellow/Green
BLUE VIOLET
+ Black
"THIS WORLD ENDS 28.10.99"
(POSTER)
PROJECTS — 3
— AN 124
— 9F PIPES
— Stirling Single Contours
— MONORAILS.
— MAGLEV (into the Sun)
— THE WORKS (Snow plough)
— " " Sketches
— GARE DU NORD
— Darjeeling (Rice fields)
— Indian Pacific (Sunrise)
— Liberation
— Liverpool Street.
— Siliguri Station
— Durango - Silverton
a/Silverton/Street
b/ Trestle bridge (approaching Silverton/snow + ice)
— Puffing Billy
— B17 (Around the clock!)
— Marine (Subs - Langkawi)
— " Turkey
— Leeds - Carousel
— Portrait (Dorothy a self)
— Isobelle
— Brian + Sylvia
re-work existing paintings
— Darjeeling (misty valleys over rice padies.)
— Duchess
— Puffing Billy
Repeat Winter in Wharfedale.
— Wittenslack + Jim (mist on the water)

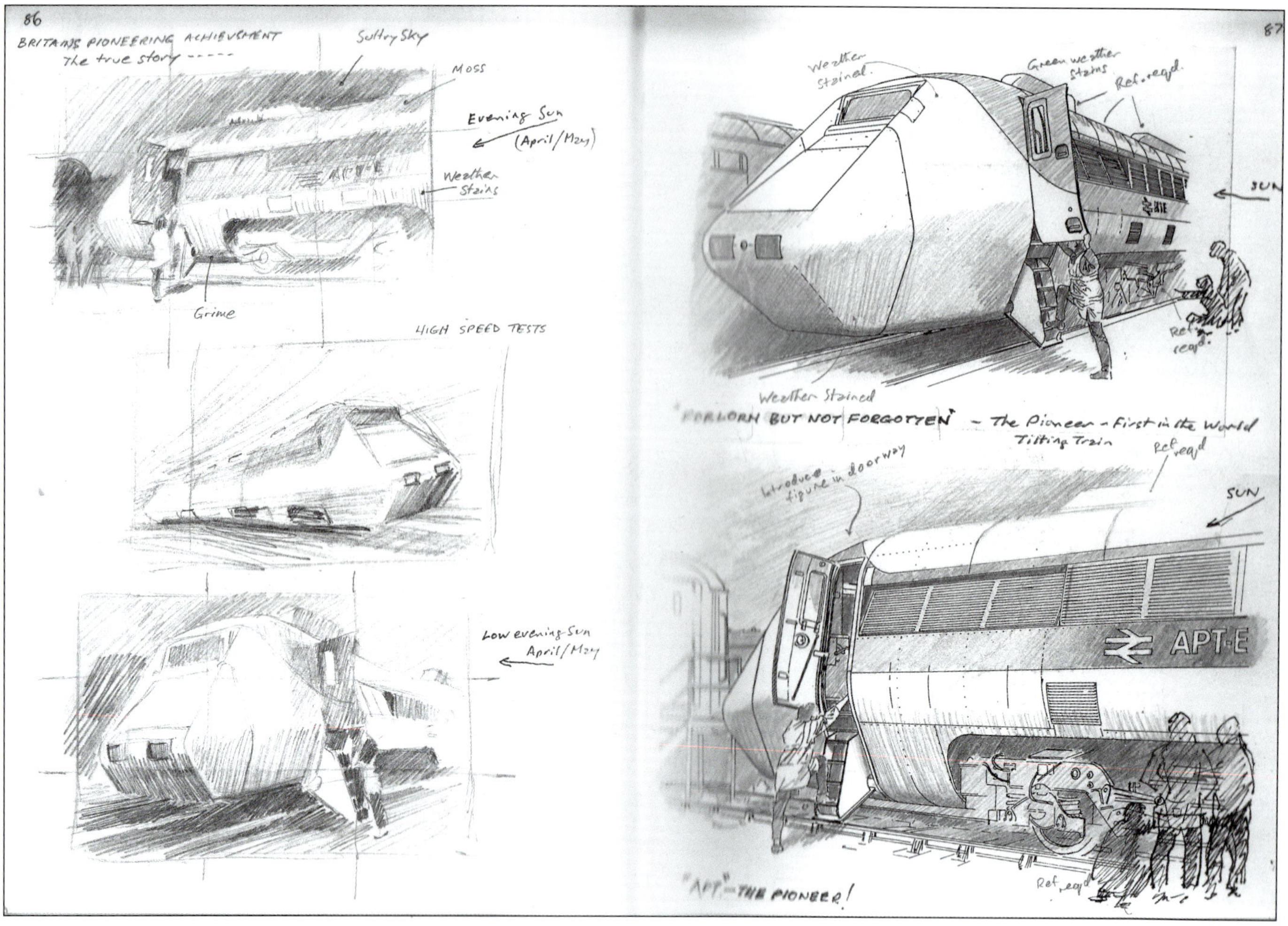
86
BRITAINS PIONEERING ACHIEVEMENT
The true story -----
Sultry Sky
Moss
Evening Sun
(April/May)
Weather Stains
Grime
HIGH SPEED TESTS
Low evening Sun
April/May
87
Weather Stained.
Green weather Stains
Ref. reqd.
SUN
Weather Stained
"FORLORN BUT NOT FORGOTTEN" – The Pioneer – First in the World
Tilting Train
Ref reqd
Introduce figure in doorway
SUN
APT-E
"APT"—THE PIONEER!
Ref. reqd.

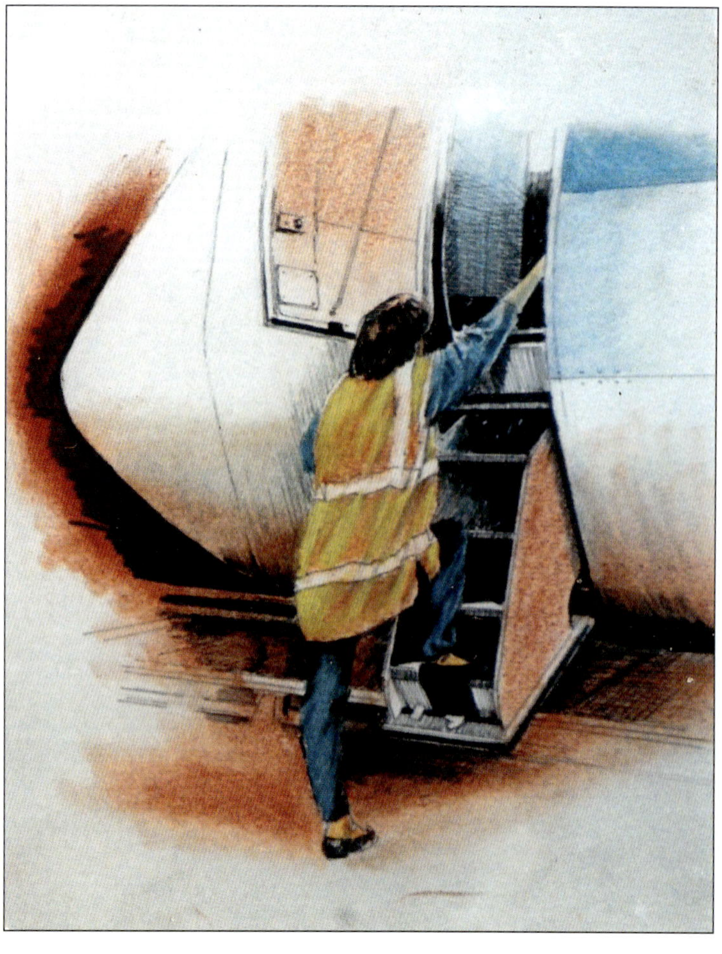

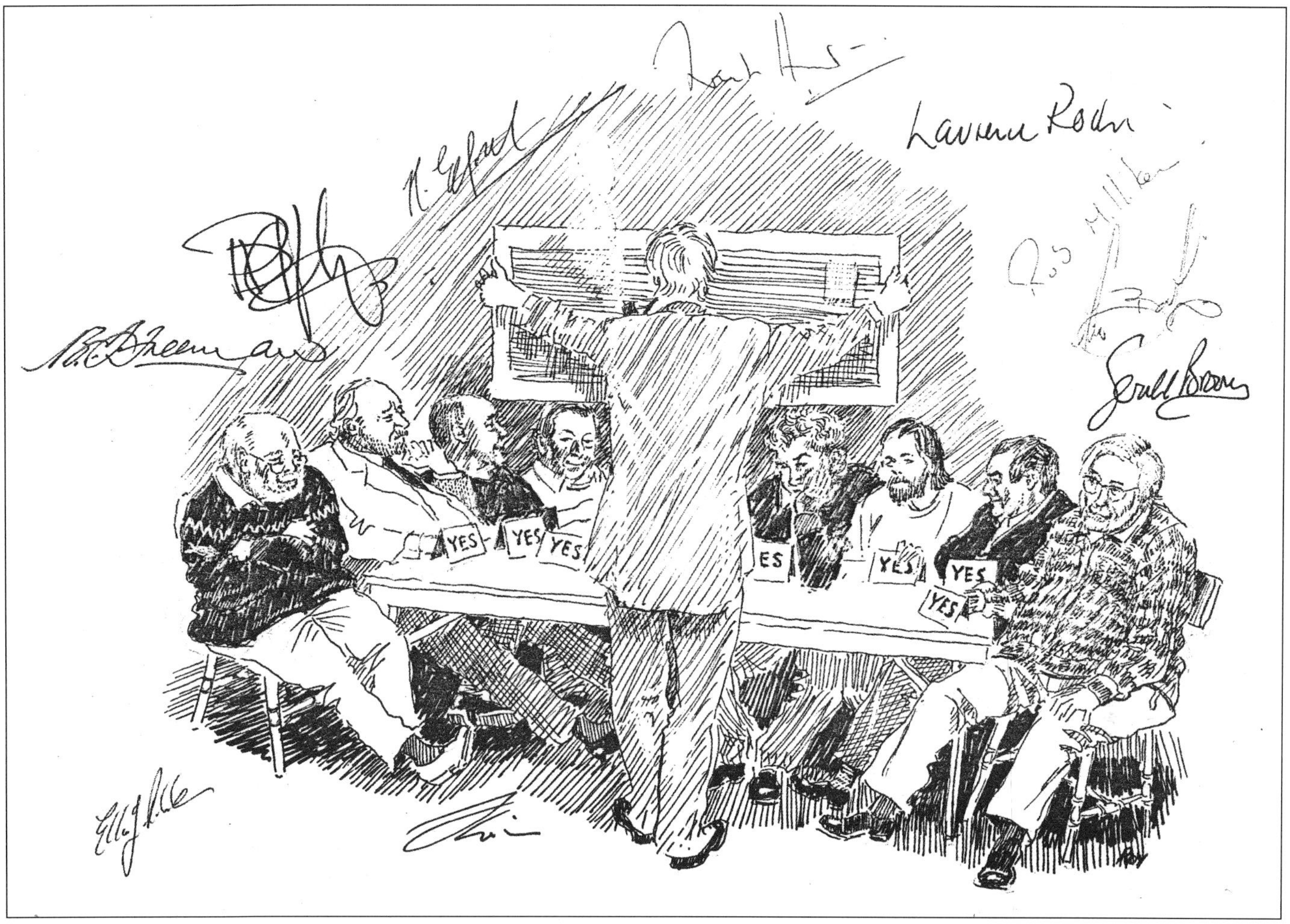
YES
YES
YES
ES
YES
YES
YES

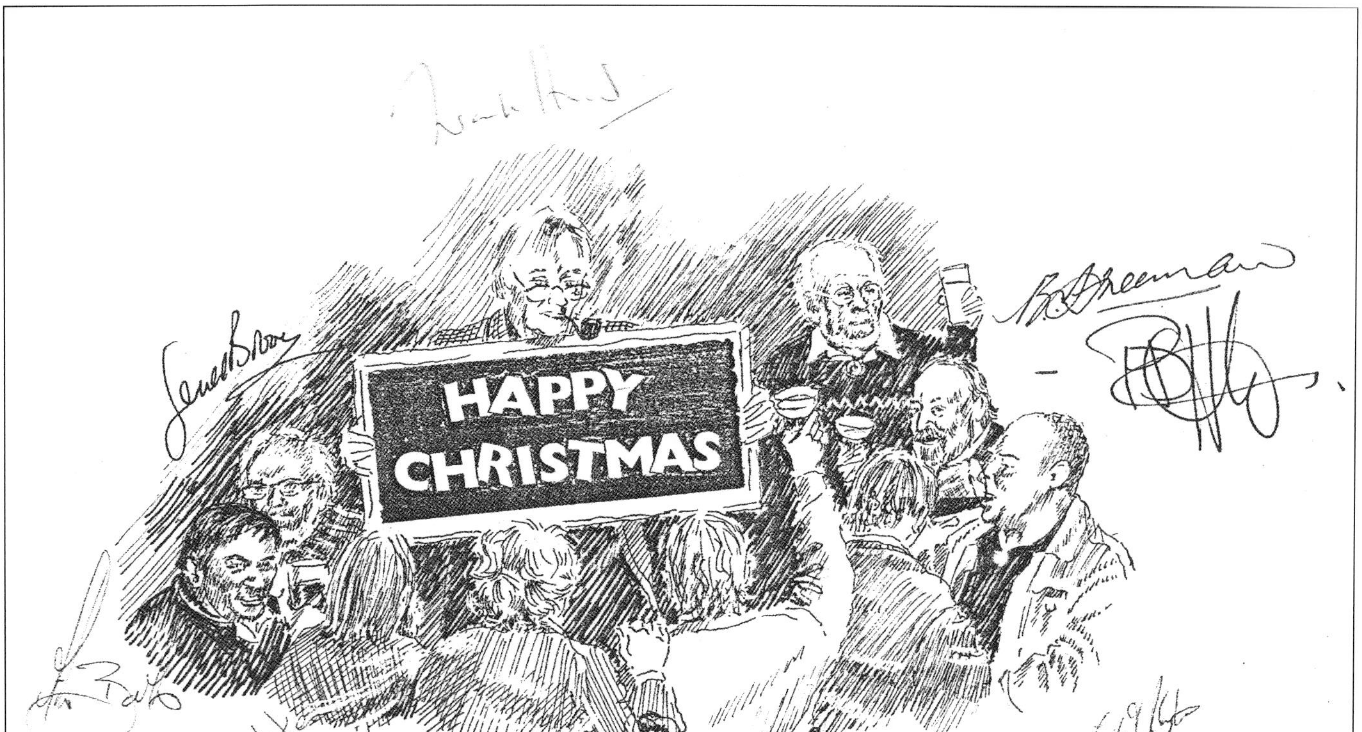
HAPPY
CHRISTMAS

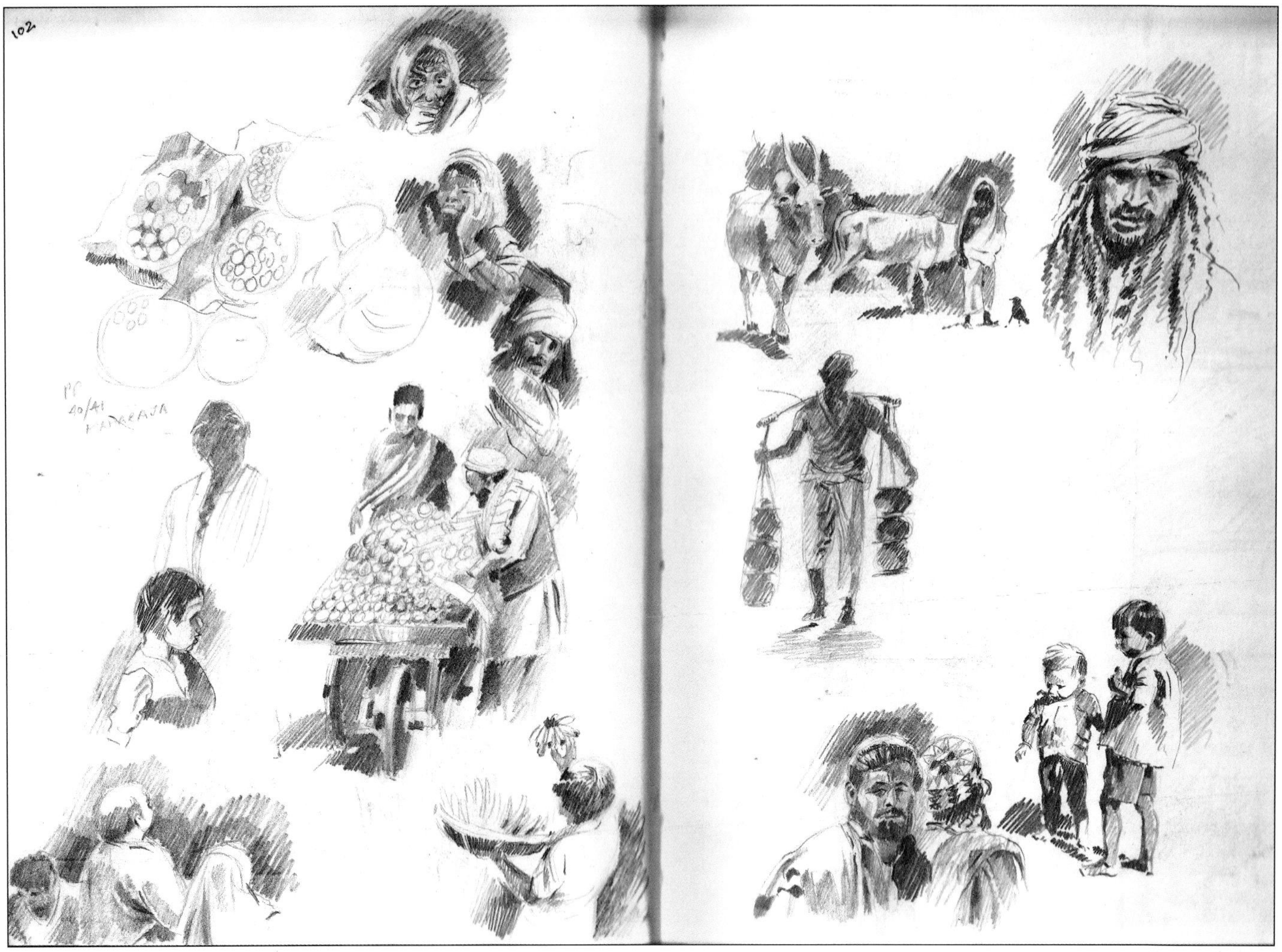
102

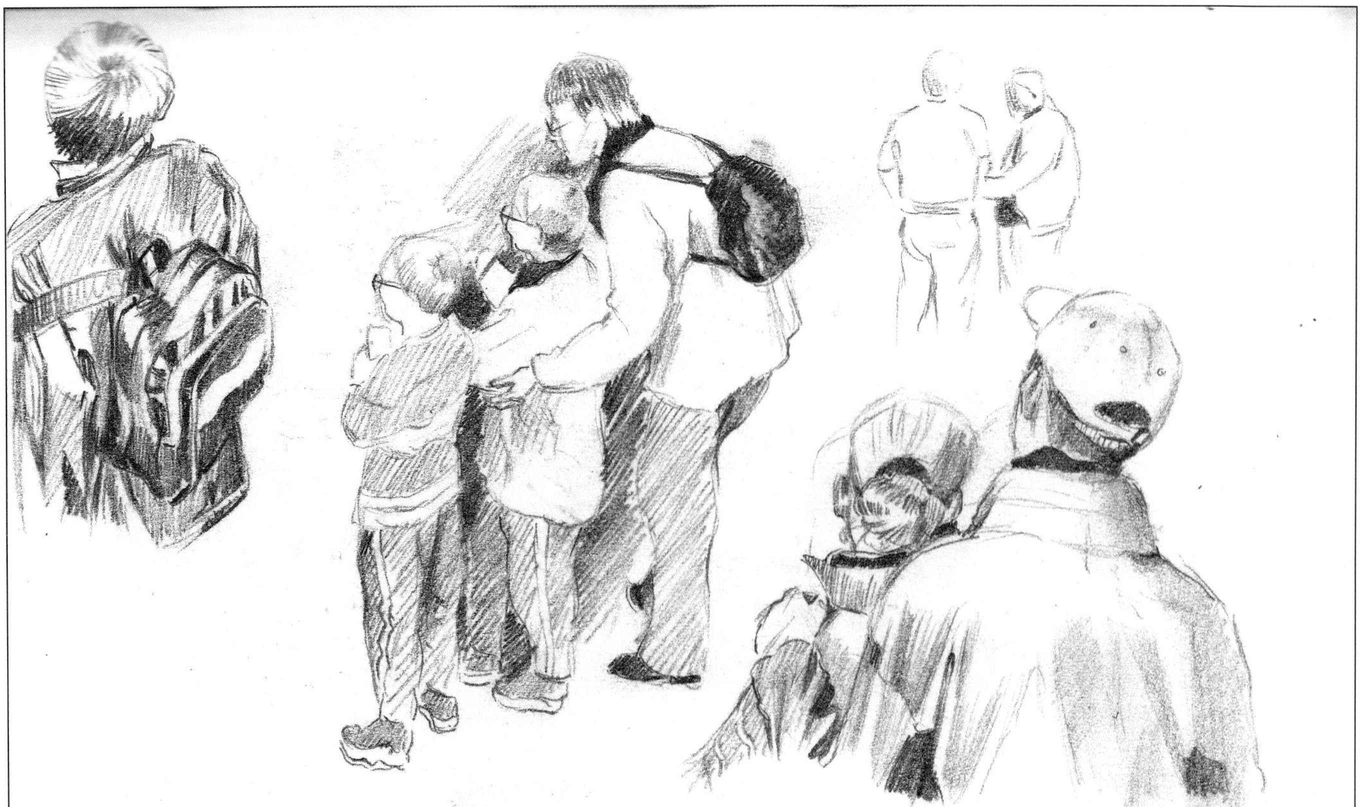
Jack – Sam – Ruth

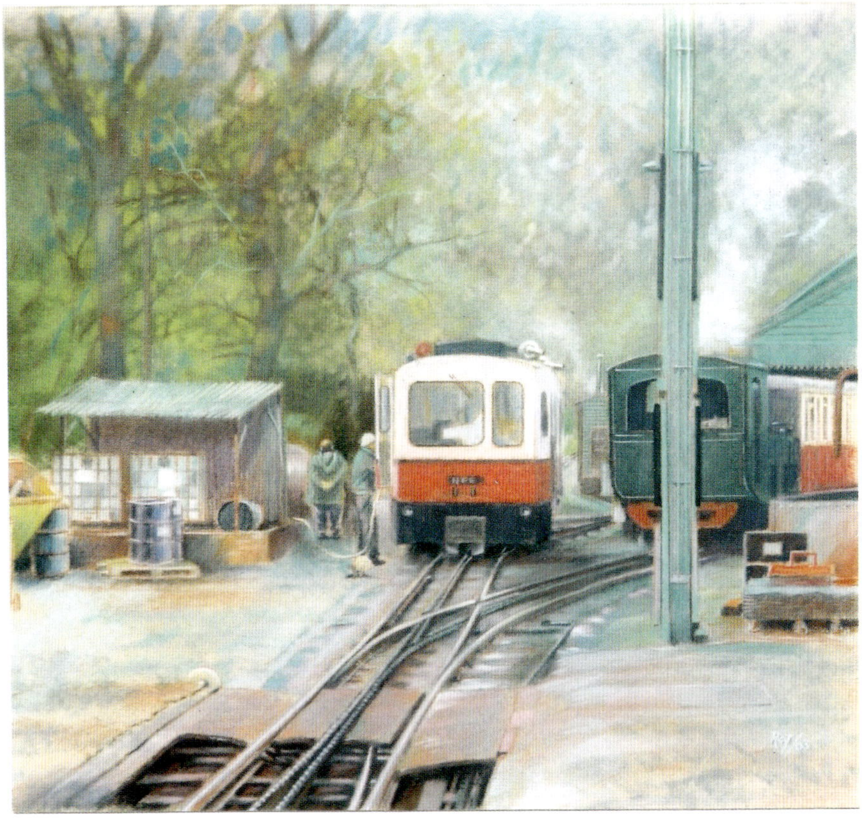

Llanberis .... Snowdon Mountain Railway / 2003

SNOWDON MOUNTAIN RLY

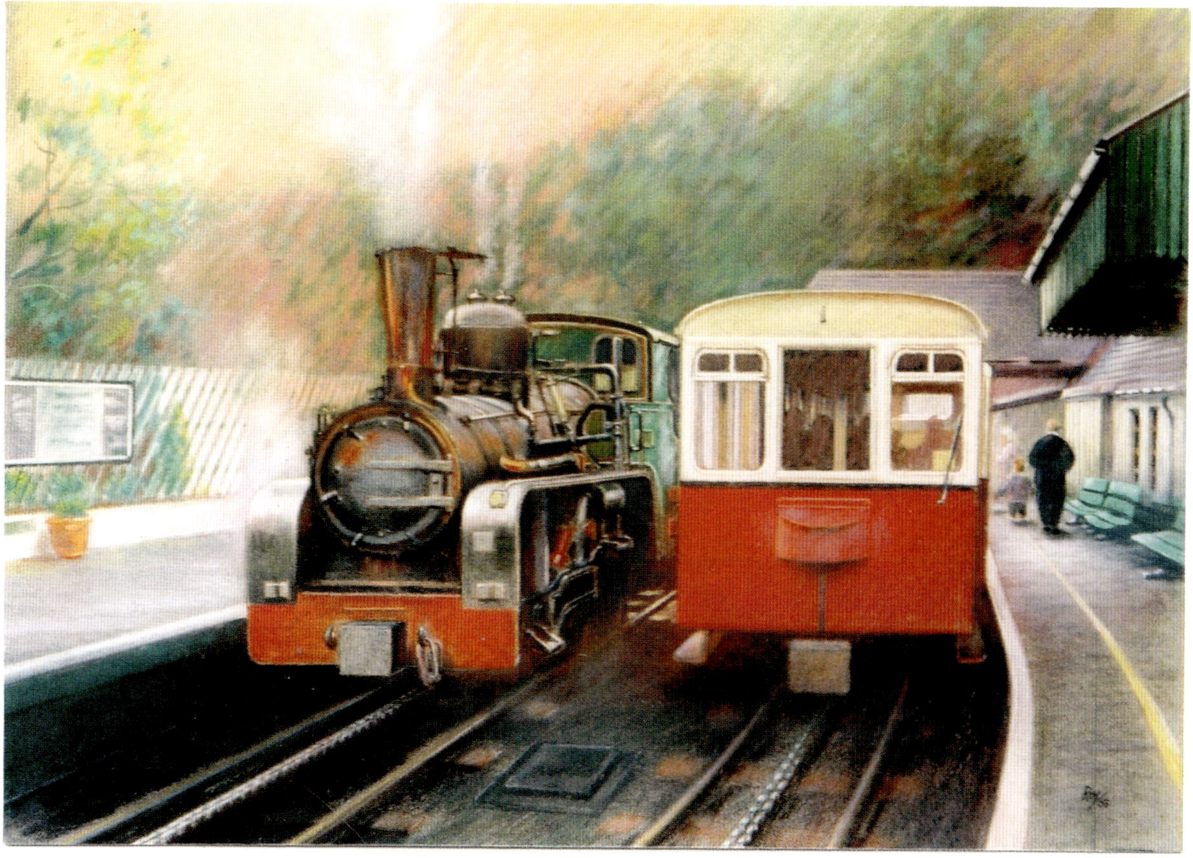

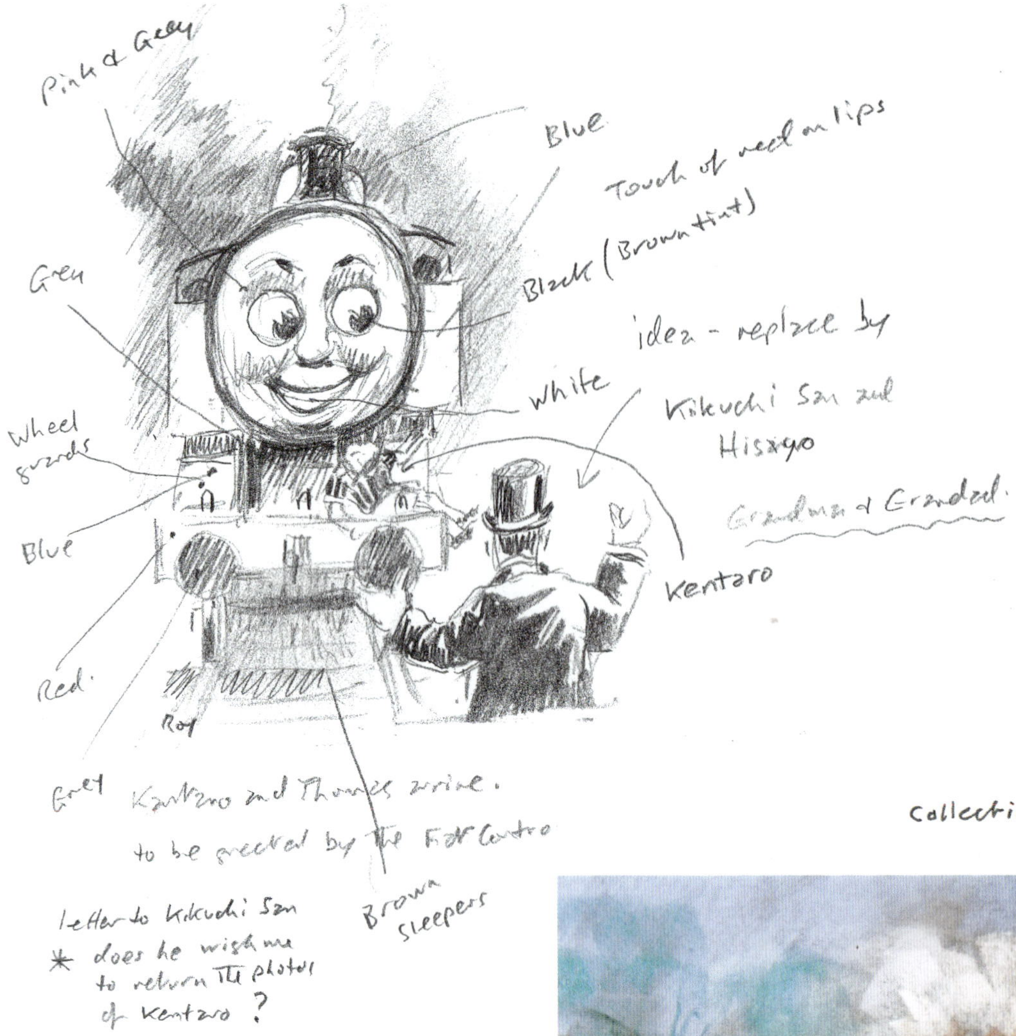
Pink & Grey
Blue
Touch of red on lips
Black (Brown tint)
Green
White
idea - replace by
Kikuchi San and
Hisayo
Grandma & Grandad.
Wheel guards
Blue
Kentaro
Red.
Roy
Grey
Kentaro and Thomas arrive.
to be greeted by the Fat Controller
Brown sleepers
letter to Kikuchi San
* does he wish me
to return the photos
of Kentaro ?

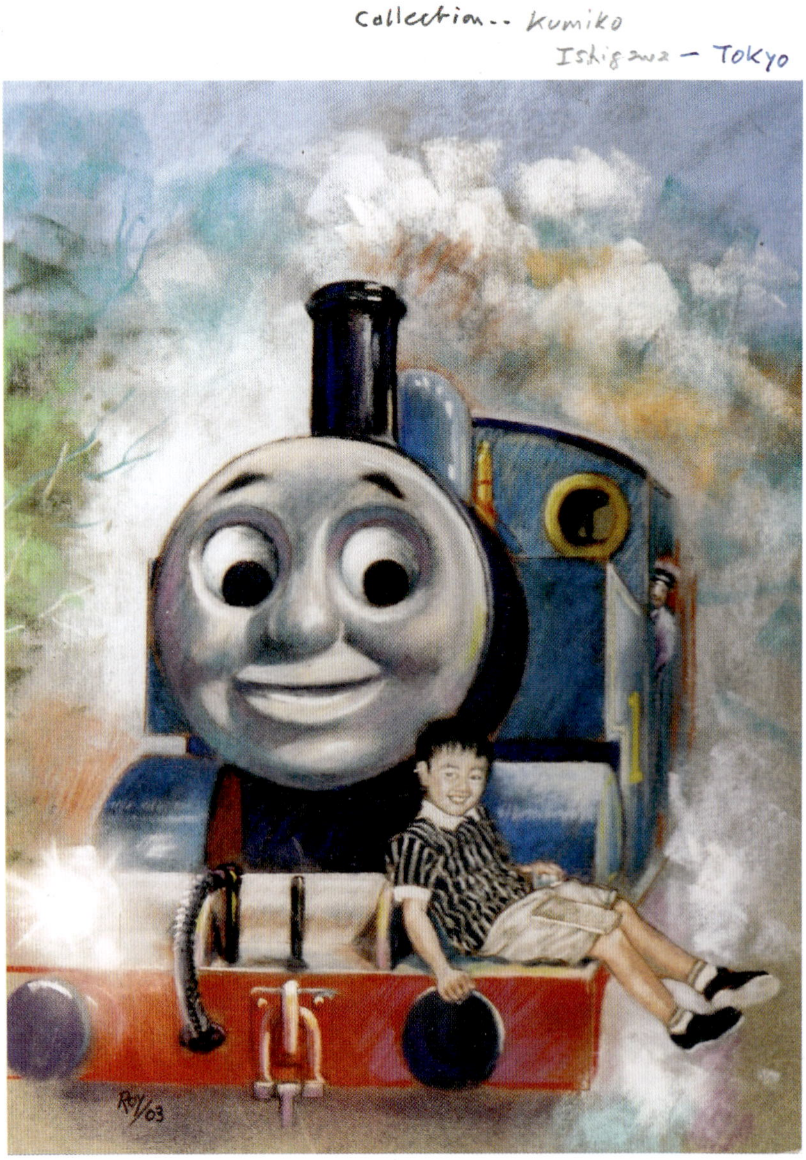
Collection.. Kumiko
Ishigawa - Tokyo
Roy/03

(34)

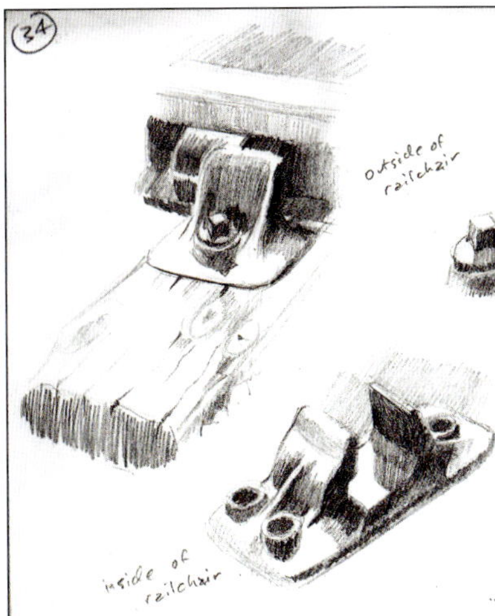

Sally Strand. ("American Artist / Aug '99)
Basic drg drafted on 140-lb cold-pressed Arches watercolour paper which she scrubs with water and stretches on a board with padding underneath – she then sprays the drg. to fix and does an underpainting in acrylic, watercolour or gouache. This serves a number of purposes: laying down a tone to eliminate the white of the paper, setting up the values, and creating a foundation for painting in complementary colours (so that the viewer sees the vibrancy of the colour coming through. Sometimes she leaves areas of the underpainting untouched by pastel, so they remain exposed in the final painting .... Working up from the dark tones and leaving the lights untouched until the final end of the process

(35)

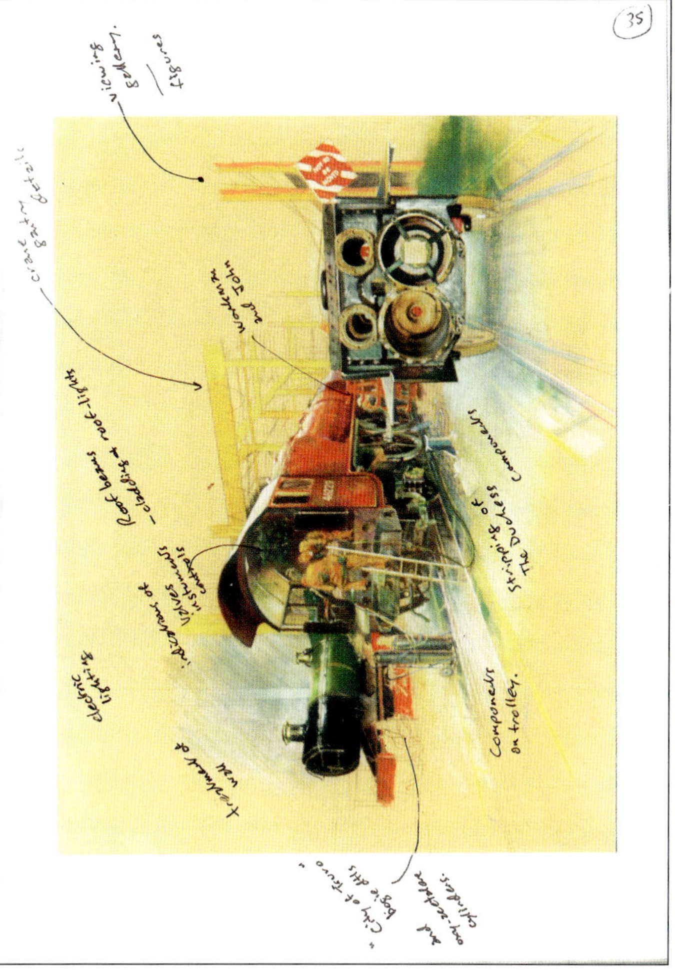

(36)

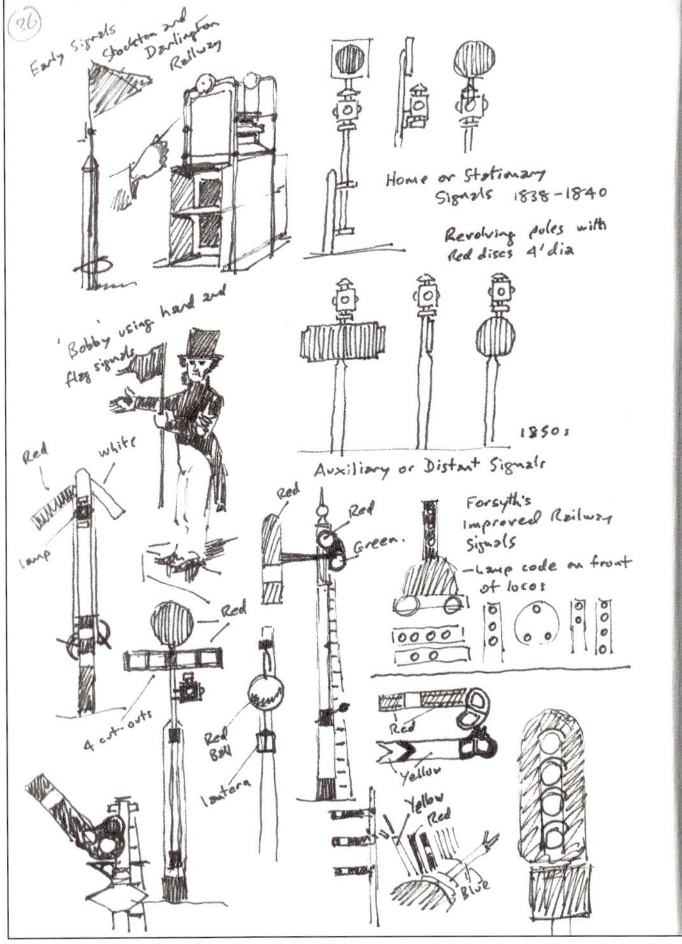

(37)

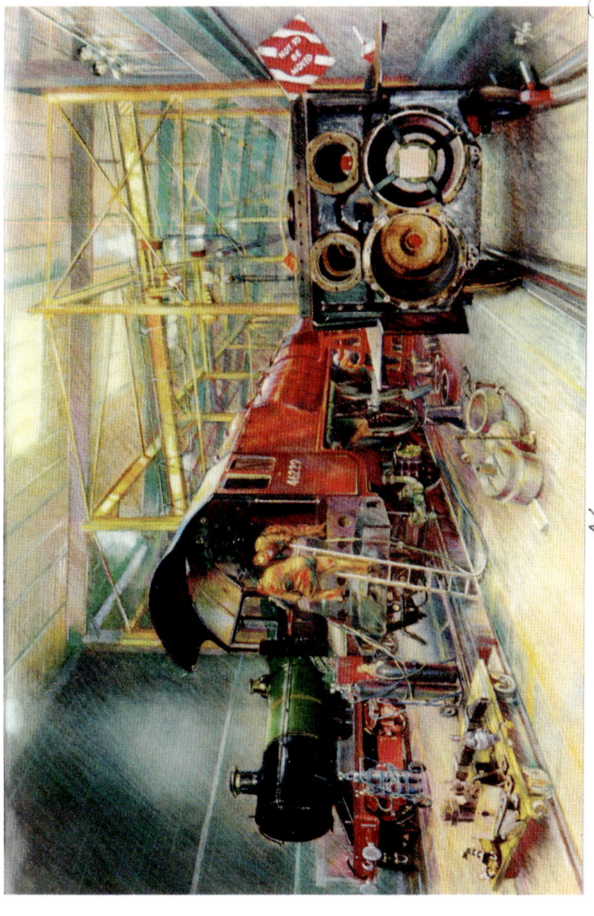

40 cm x 62 cm The Stripping of 46229 Pastel/Pastel Pencil

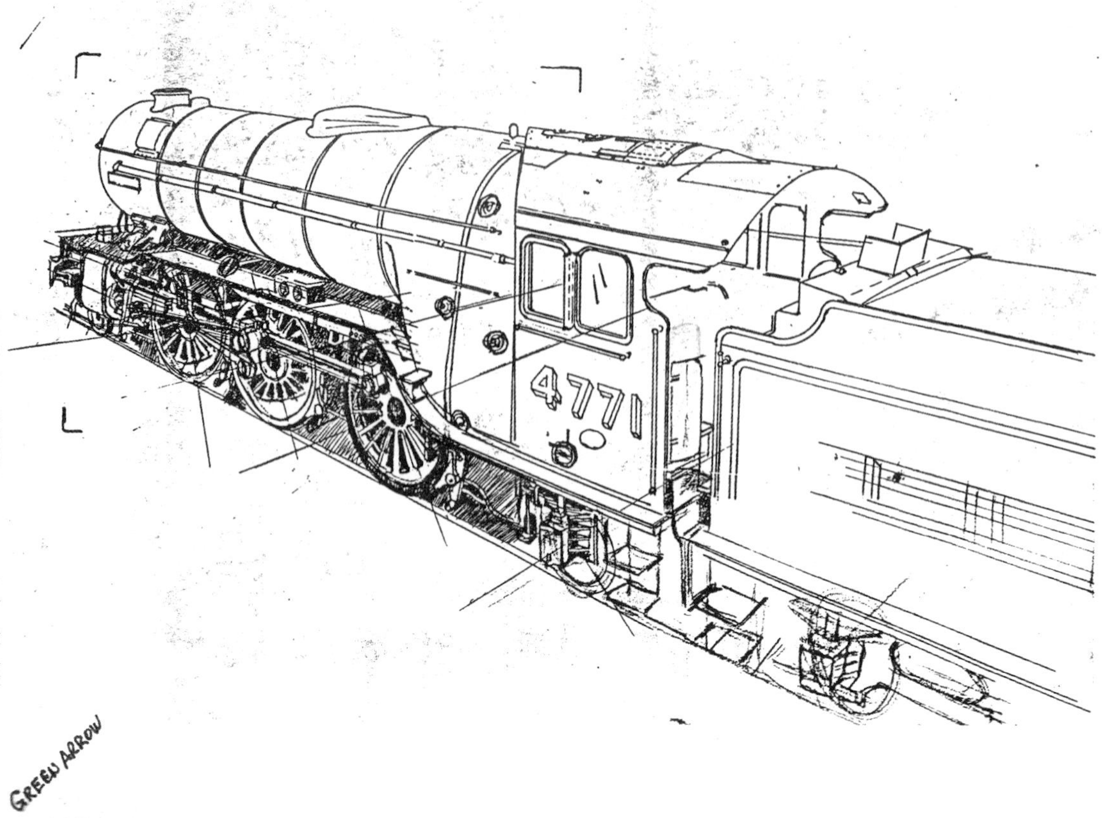
4771
GREEN ARROW

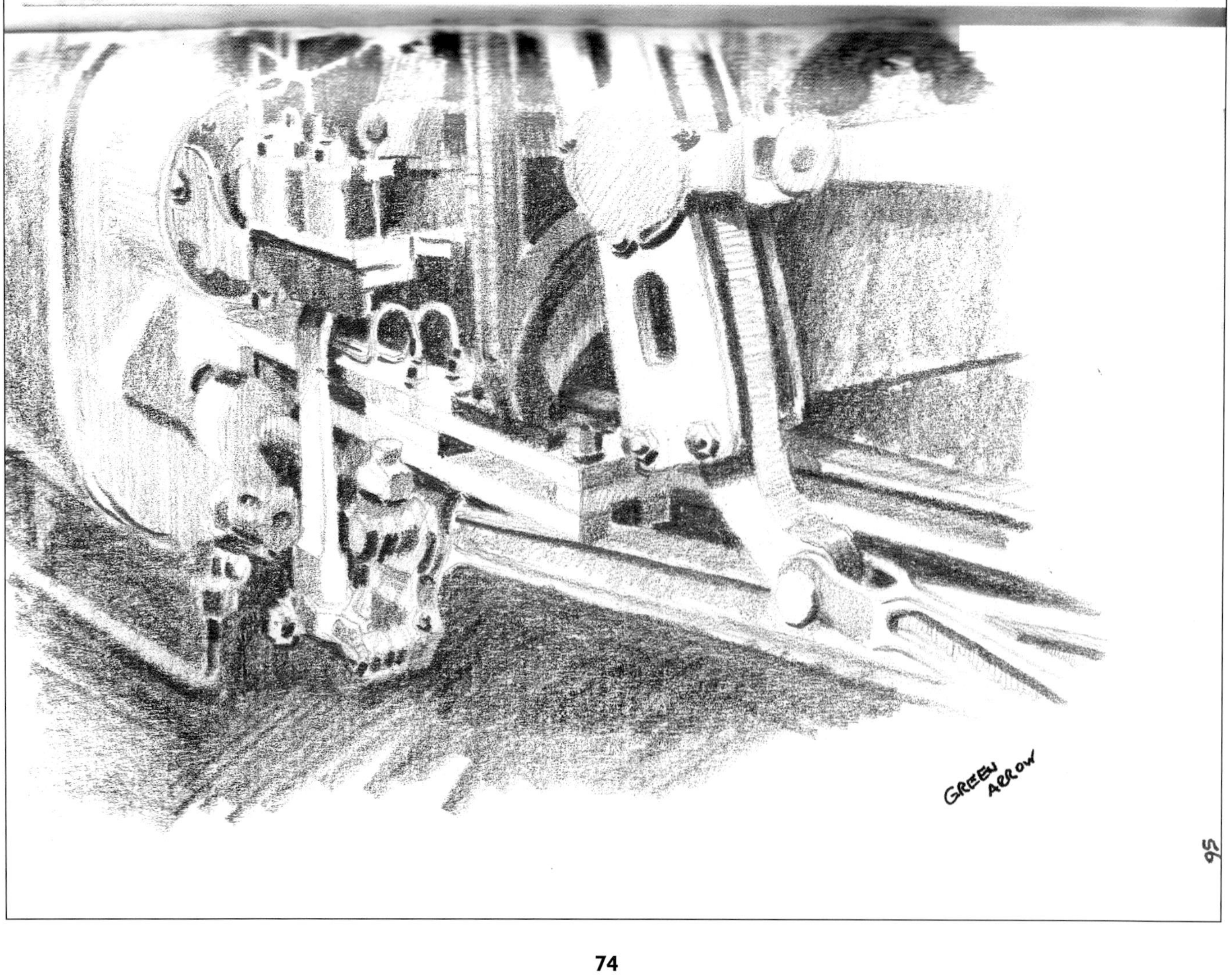
GREEN ARROW

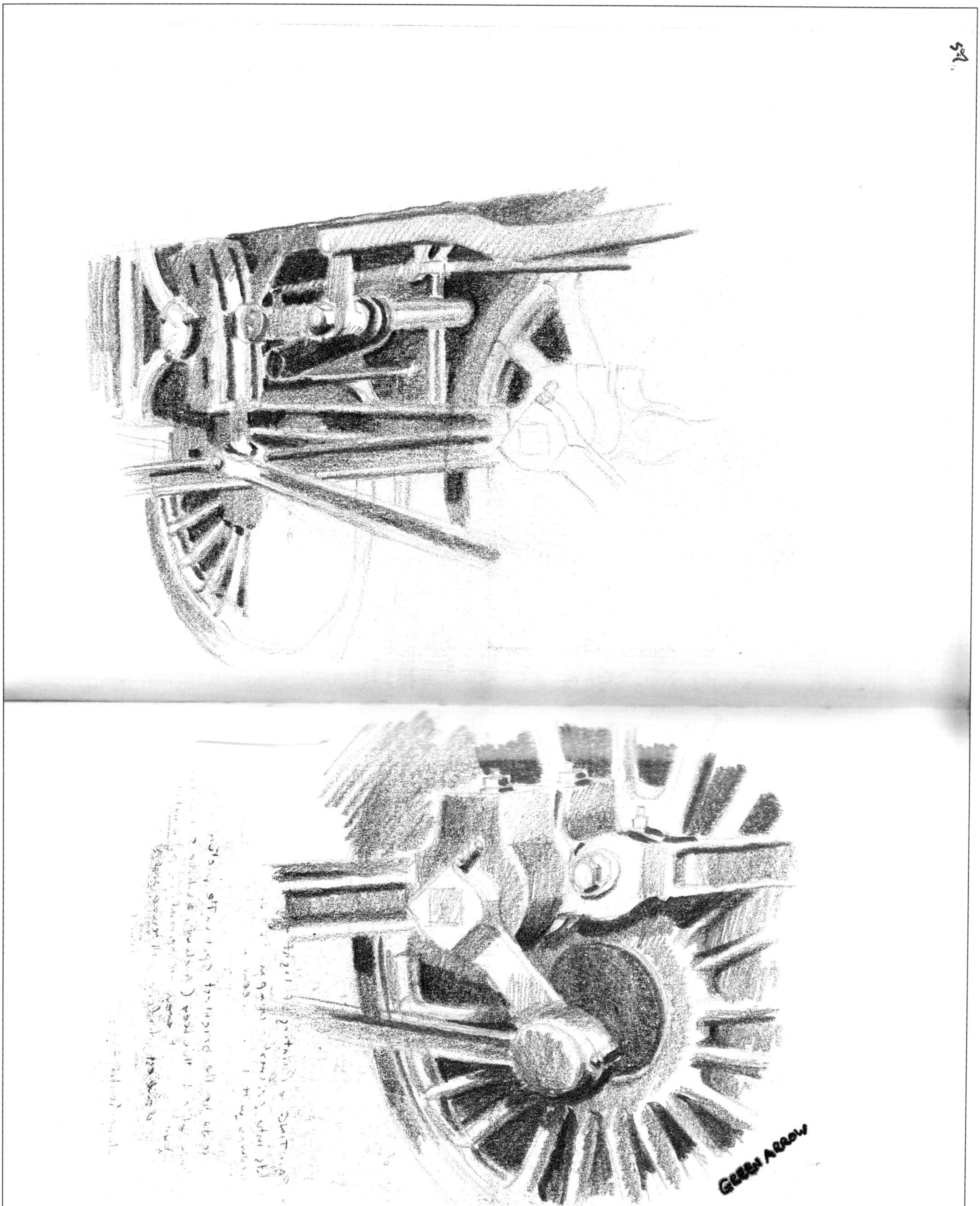
GREEN ARROW

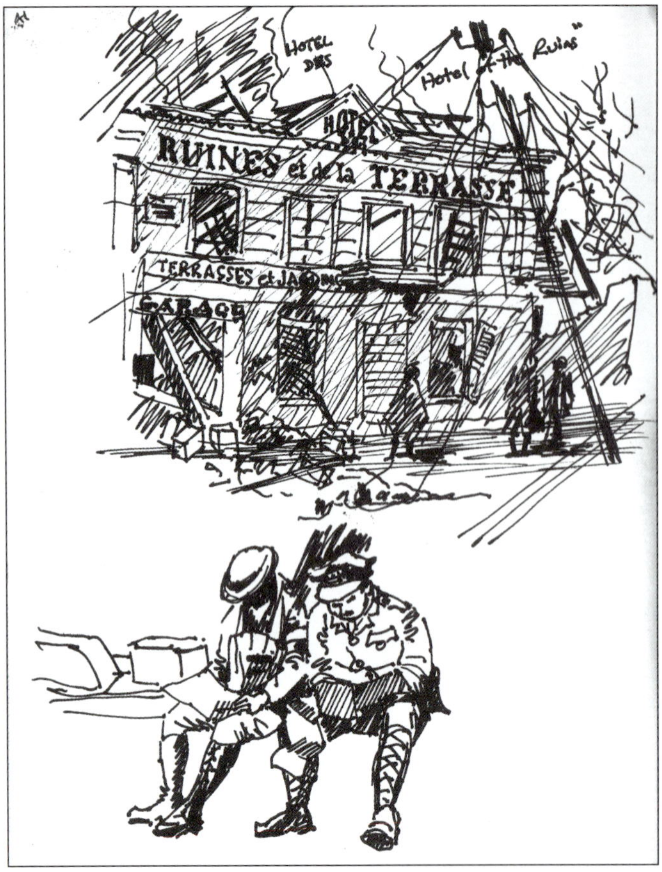
Hotel des
Hotel of the Ruins
HOTEL
RUINES et de la TERRASSE
TERRASSES et JARDINS
GARAGE

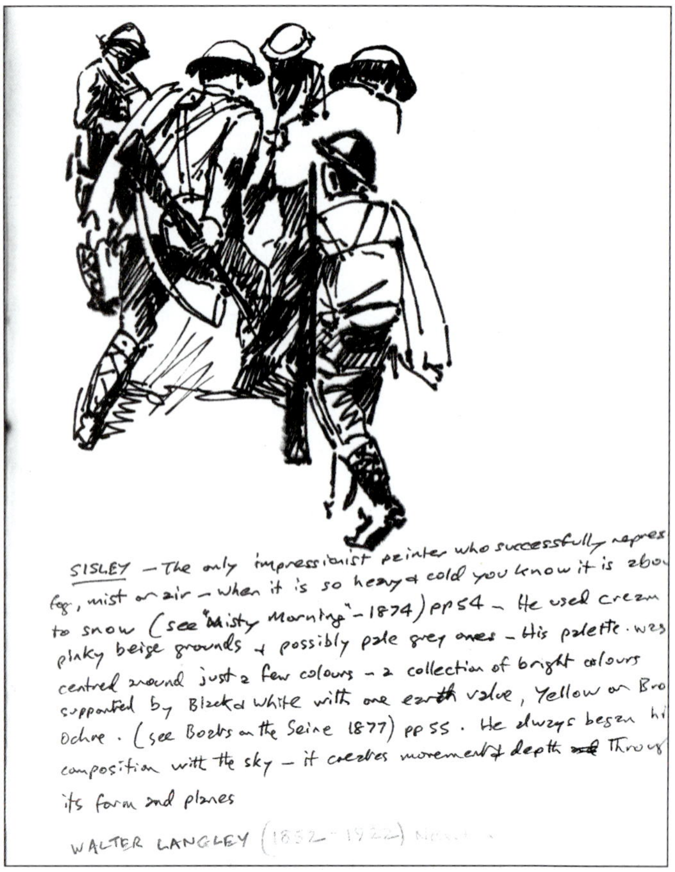
SISLEY – The only impressionist painter who successfully repres
fog, mist or air – when it is so heavy & cold you know it is abou
to snow (see "Misty Morning" – 1874) pp54 – He used cream
pinky beige grounds + possibly pale grey ones – His palette was
centred around just a few colours – a collection of bright colours
supported by Black & White with one earth value, Yellow or Bro
Ochre. (see Boats on the Seine 1877) pp55. He always began hi
composition with the sky – it creates movement & depth Throug
its form and planes
WALTER LANGLEY (1852 – 1922)

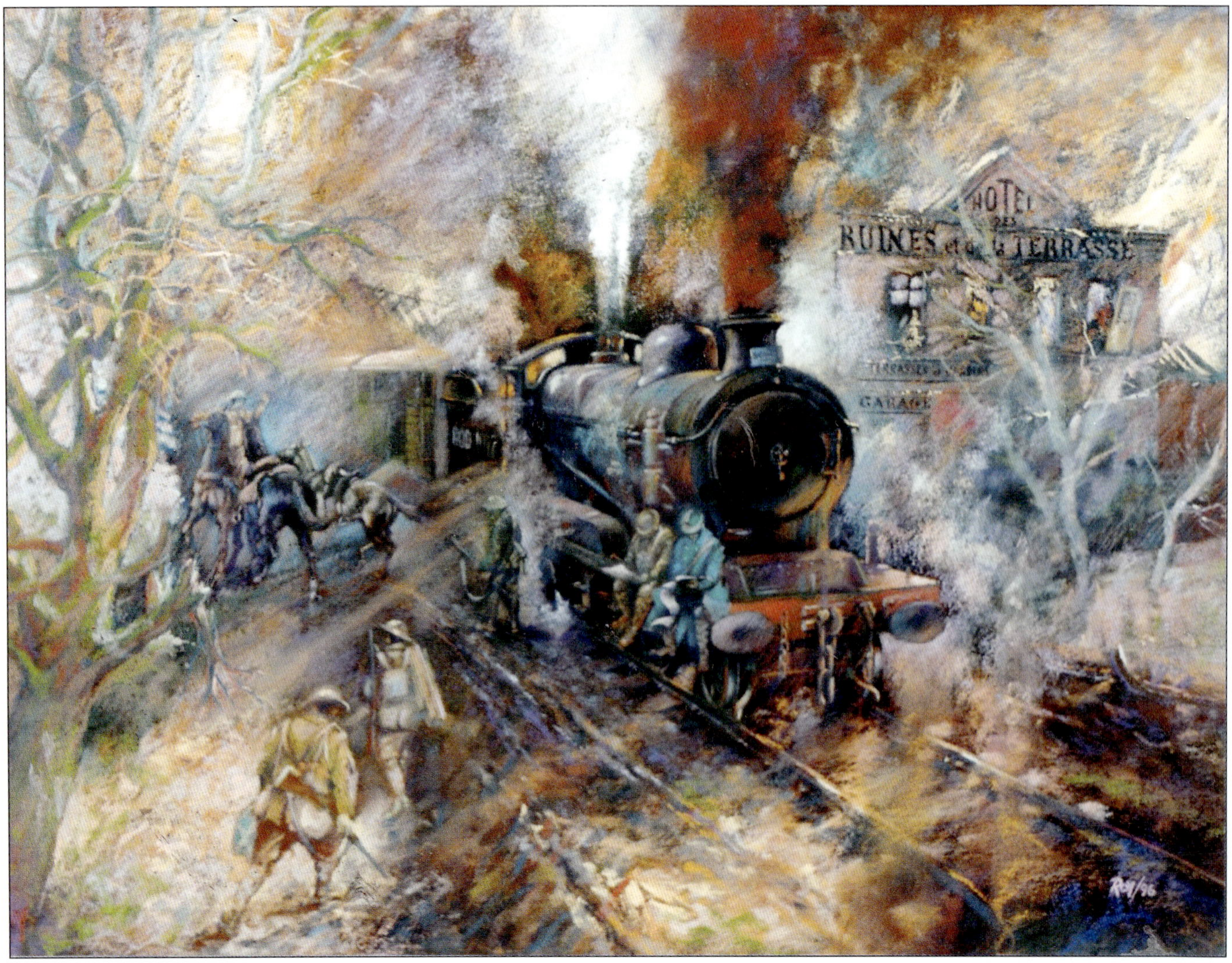
HOTEL
RUINES et de la TERRASSE
GARAGE

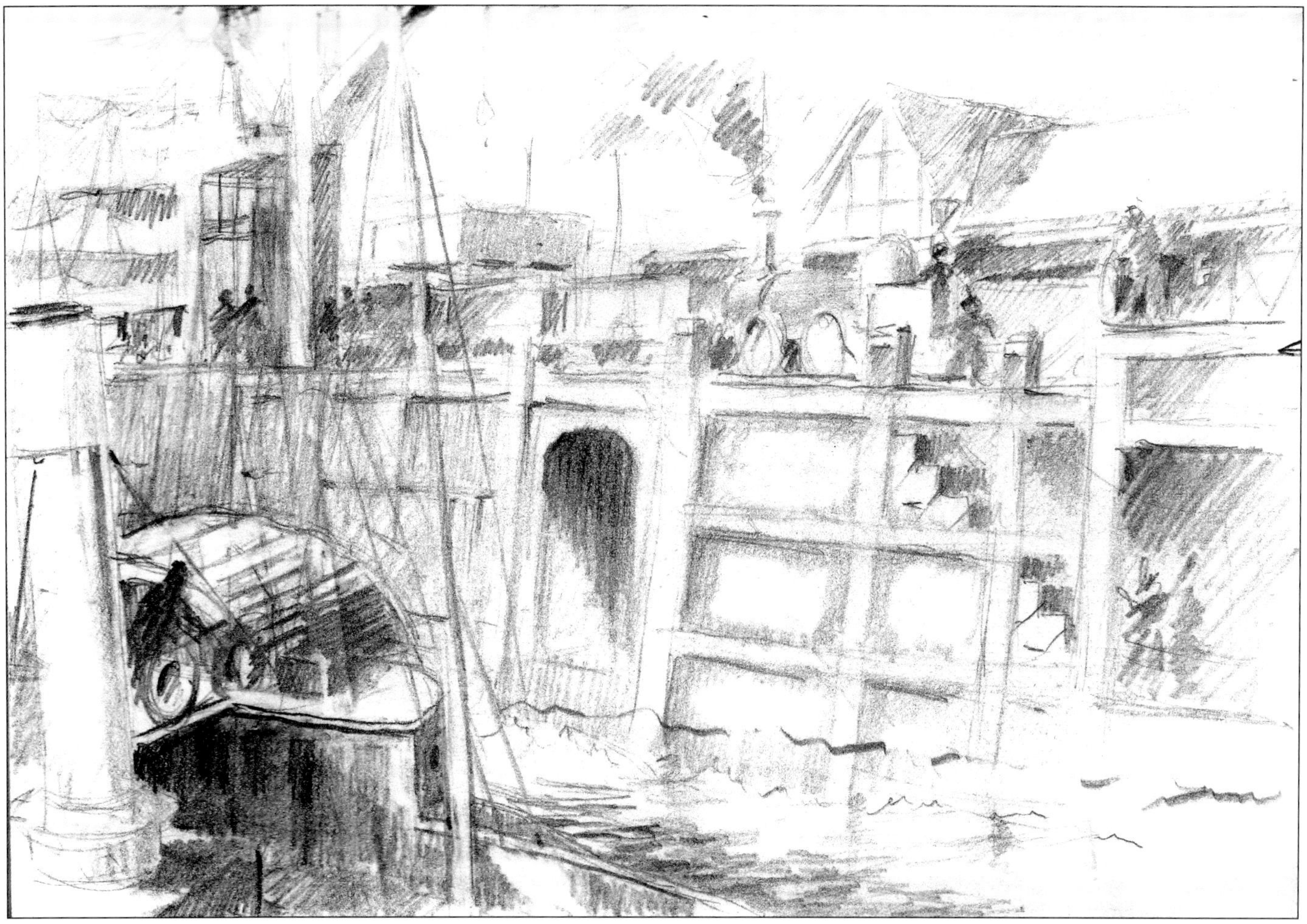

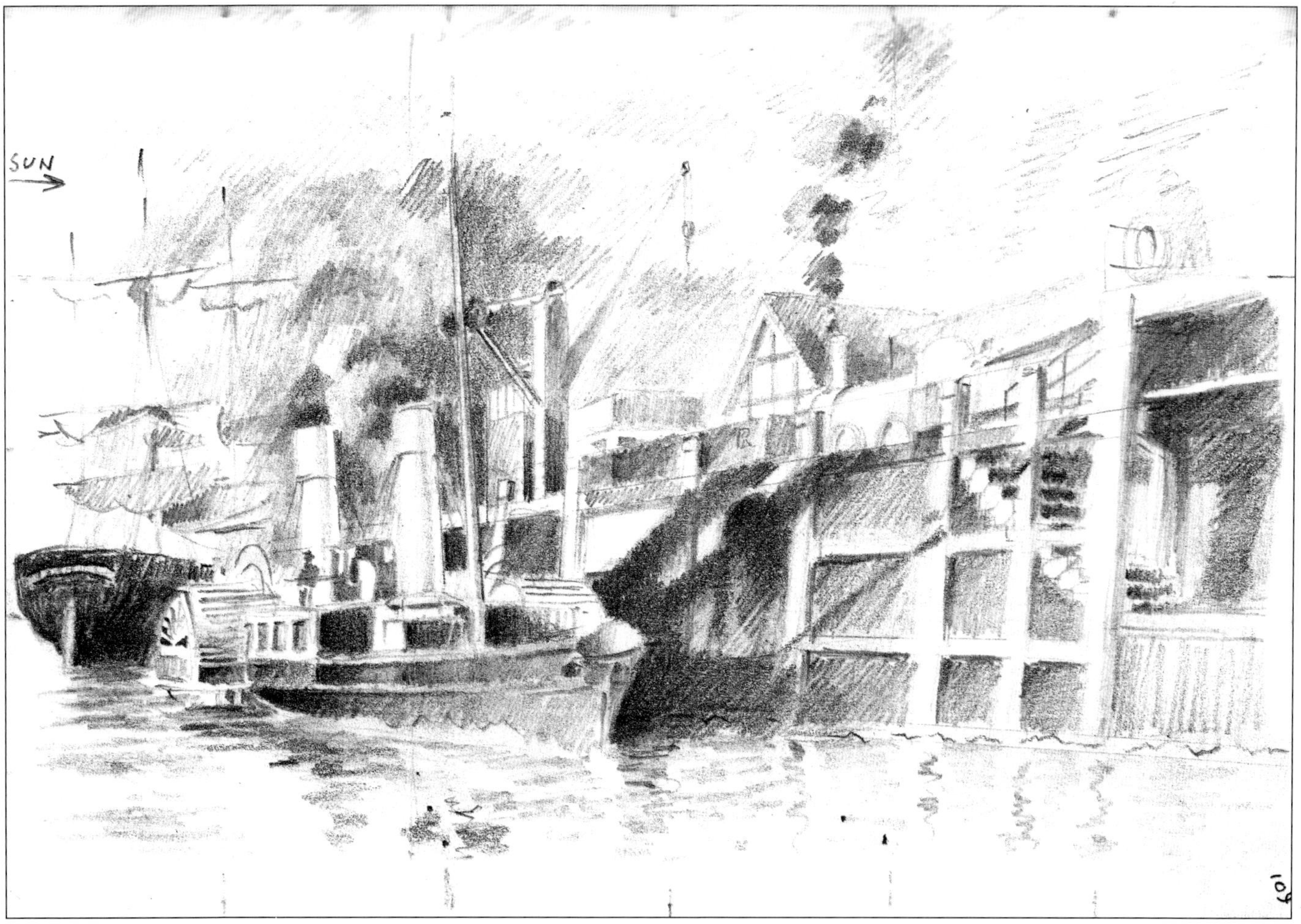
SUN
109

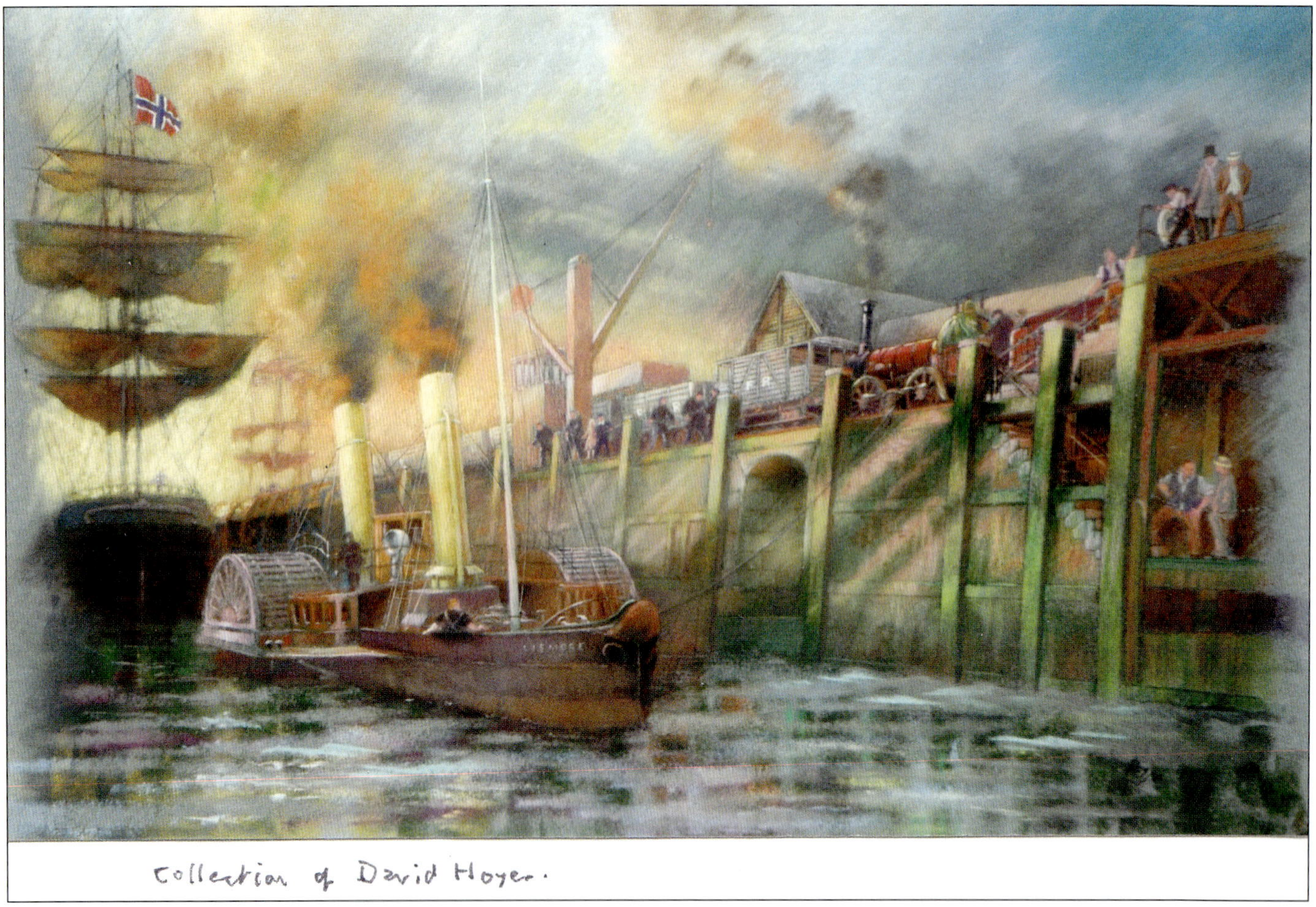
Collection of David Hoyer.

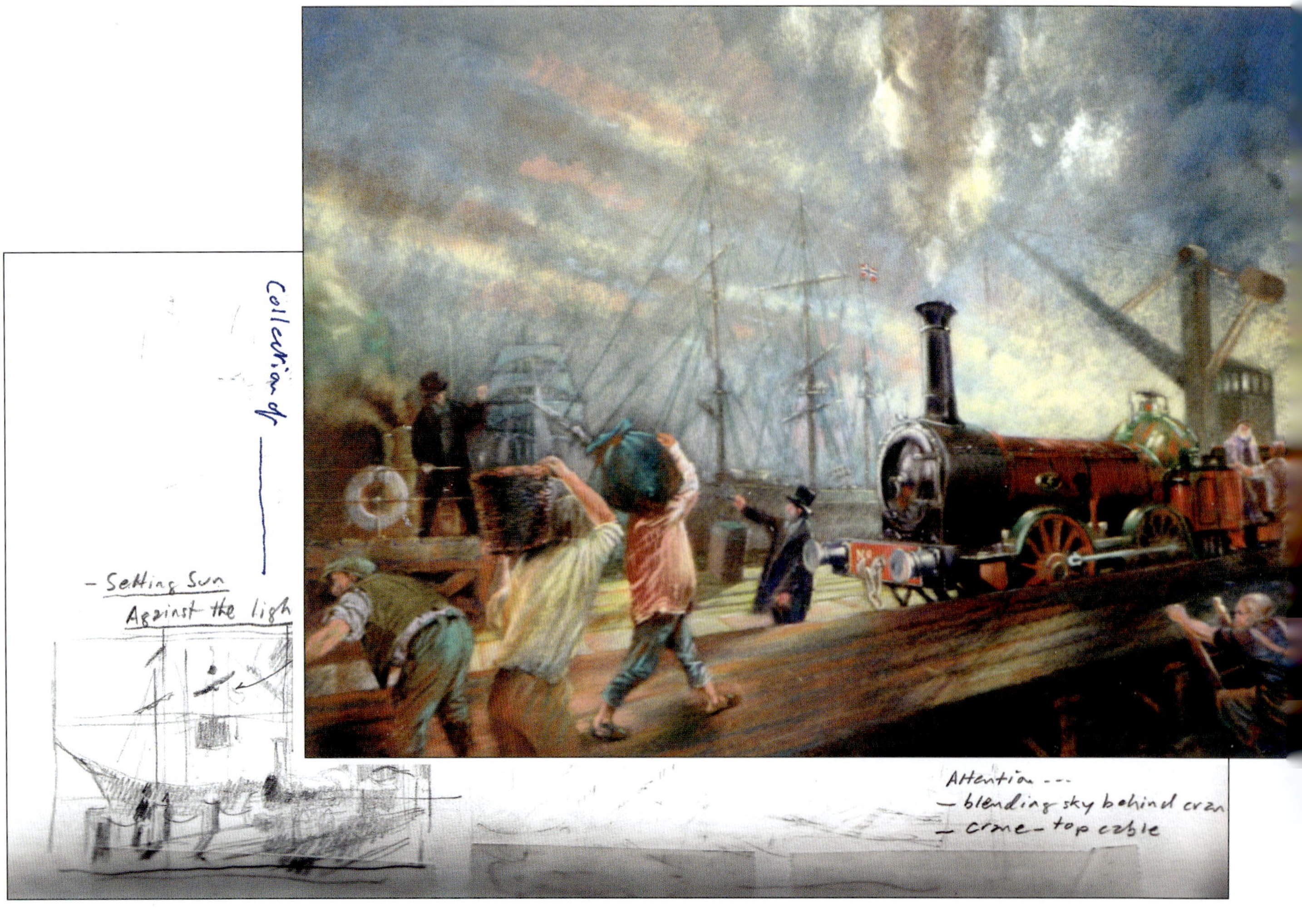
Collection of
– Setting Sun
Against the ligh
Attention ---
– blending sky behind cran
– crane – top cable

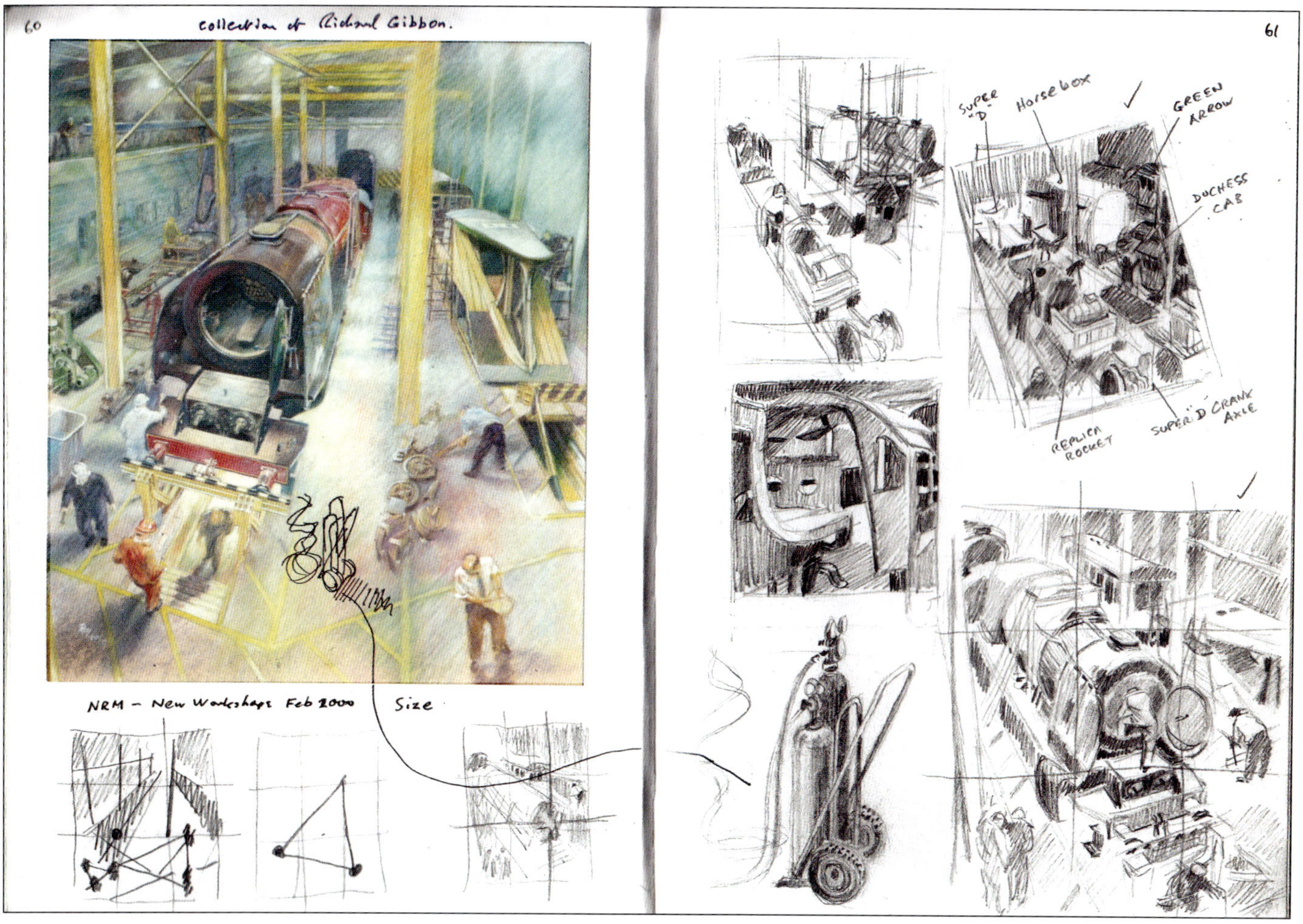
60
Collection of Richard Gibbon.
61
Super "D"
Horse box
GREEN ARROW
DUCHESS CAB
REPLICA ROCKET
SUPER 'D' CRANK AXLE
NRM – New Workshops Feb 2000
Size

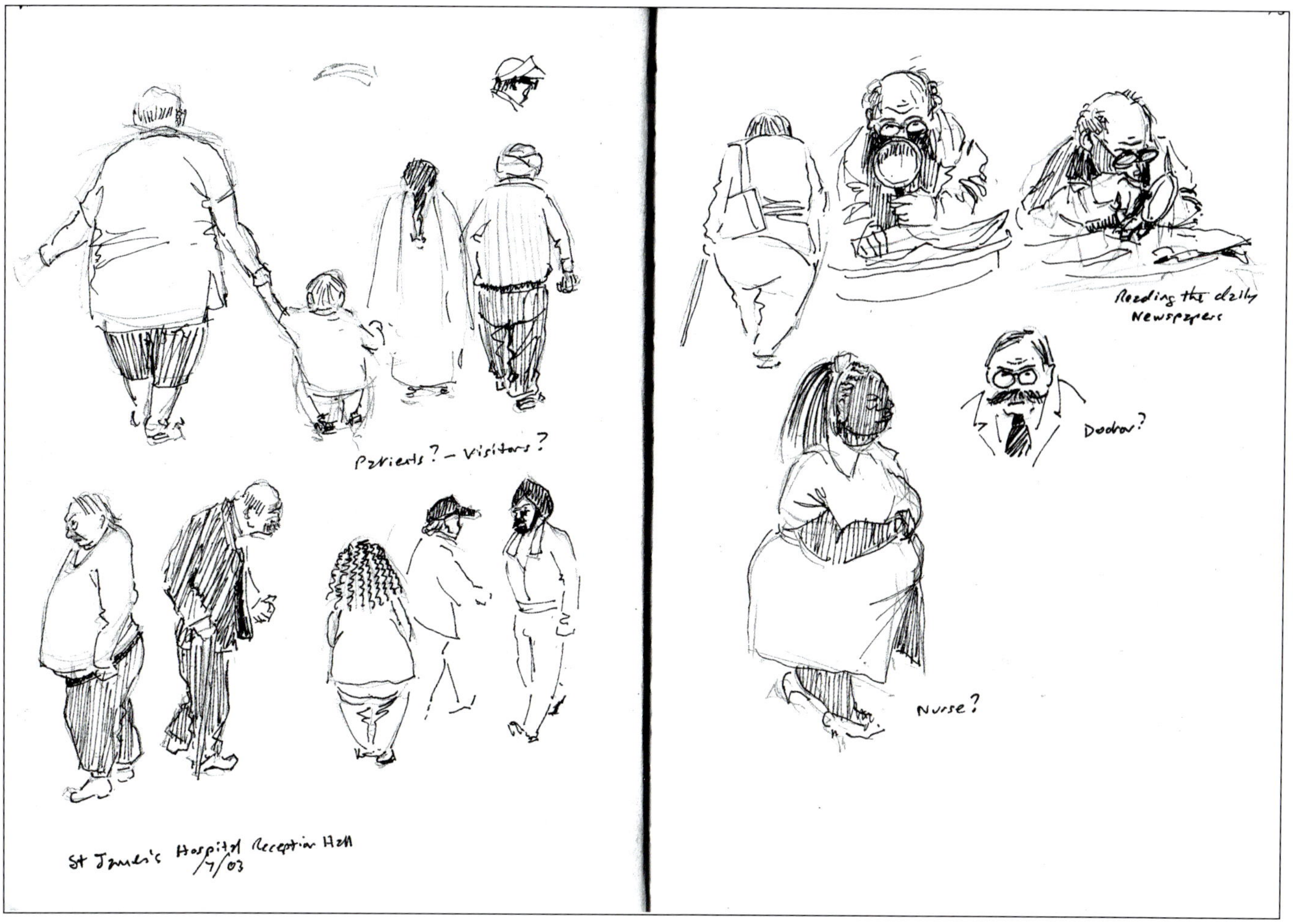
Patients? – Visitors?
St James's Hospital Reception Hall 7/03
Reading the daily Newspapers
Doctor?
Nurse?

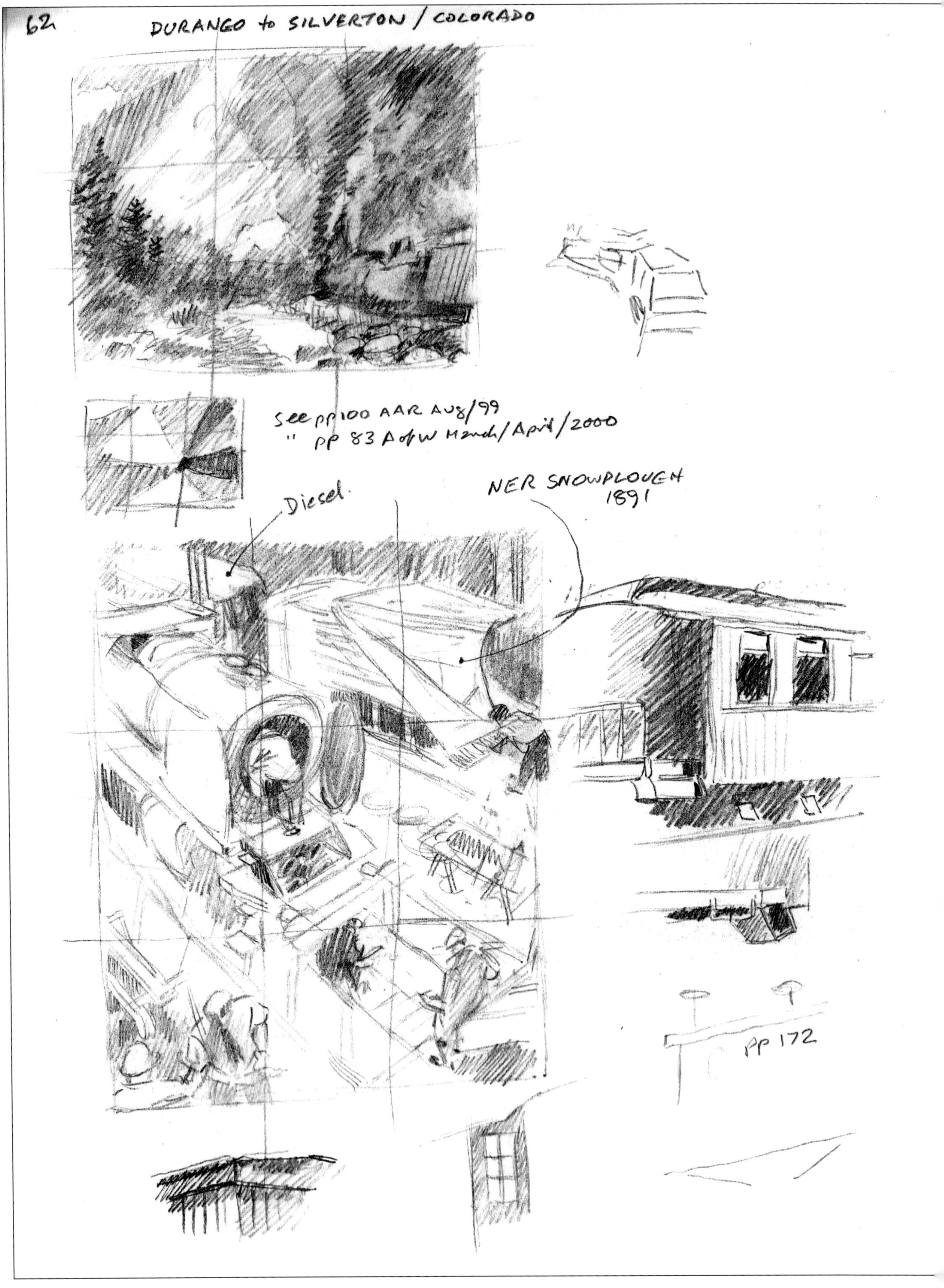
62
DURANGO to SILVERTON / COLORADO
see pp 100 AAR Aug/99
" pp 83 A of W March/April/2000
Diesel
NER SNOWPLOUGH
1891
pp 172

63

- service pits open
- Flow lighter
- Welding gear x indicated

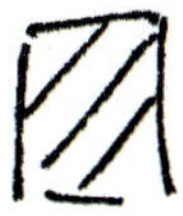

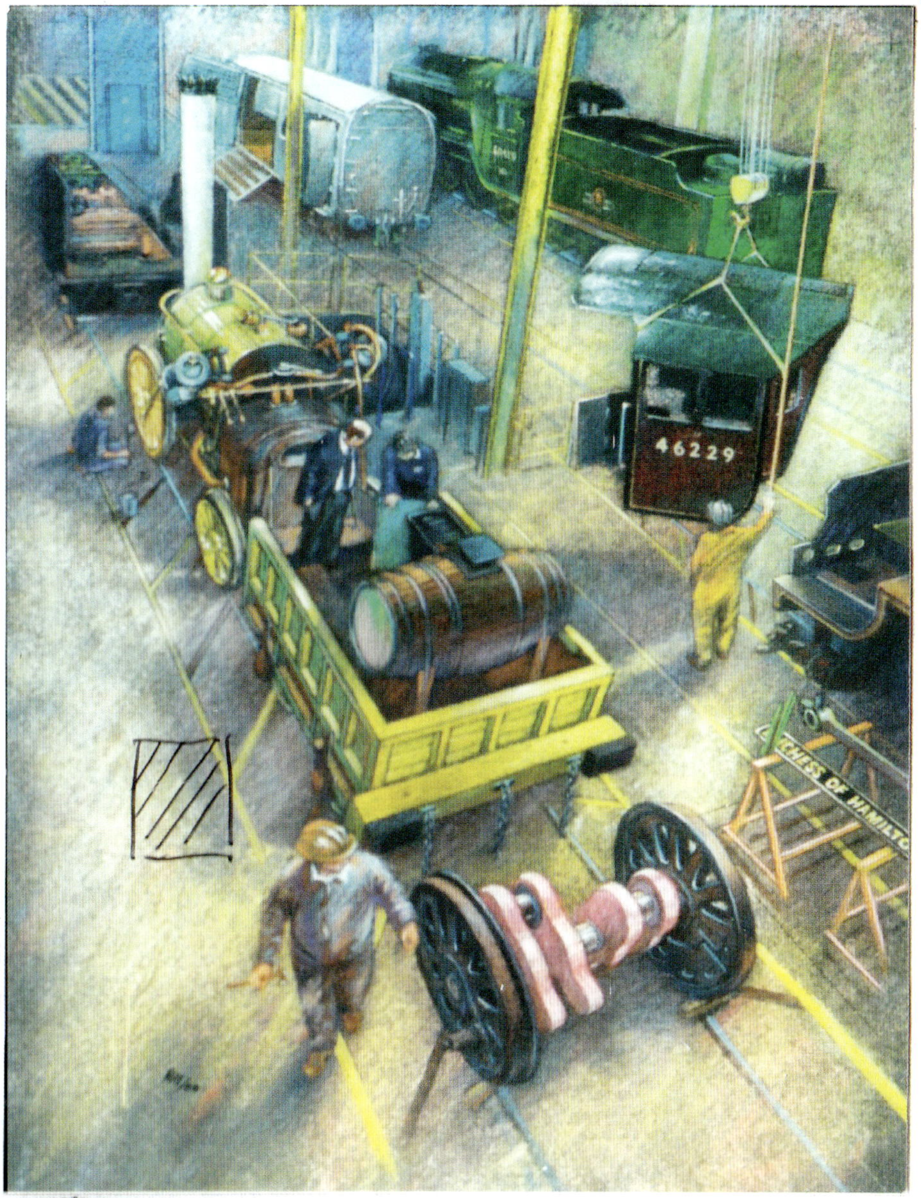

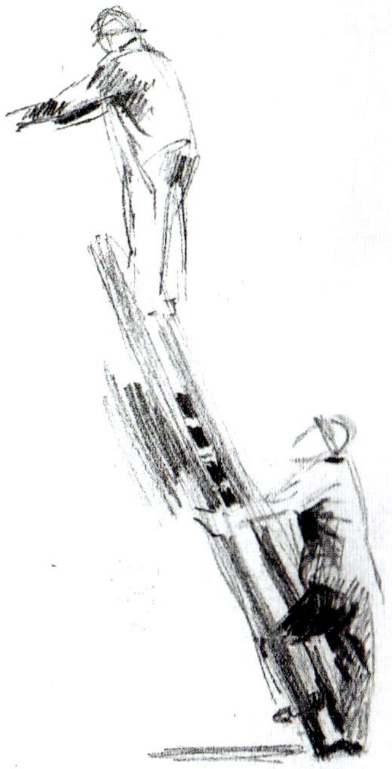

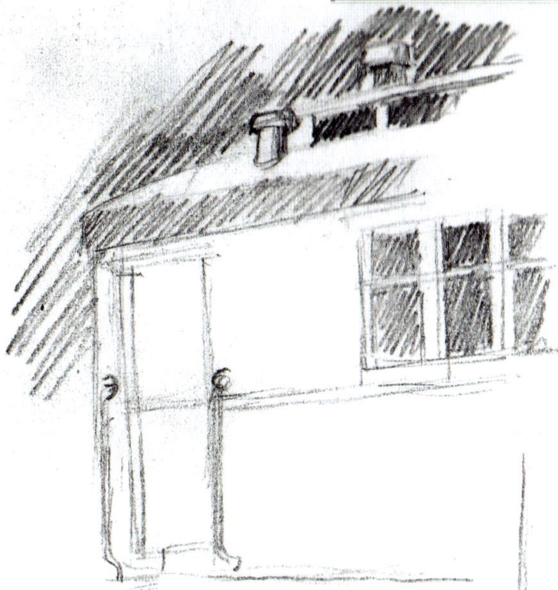

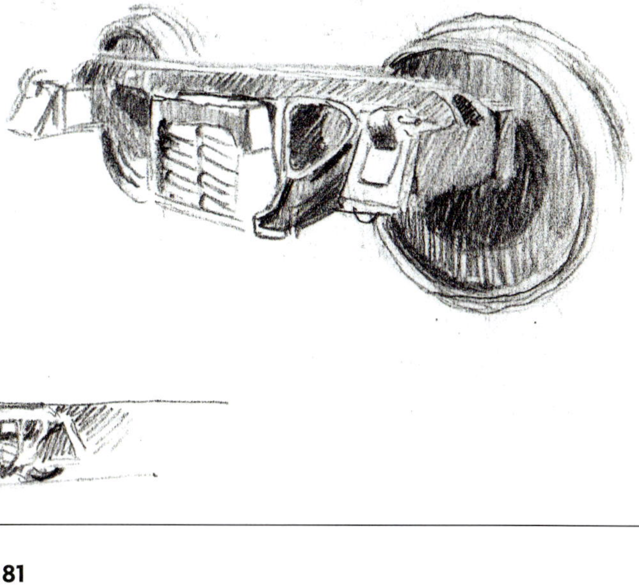

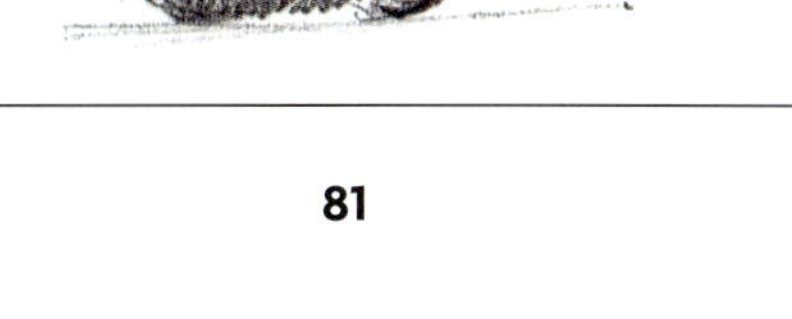

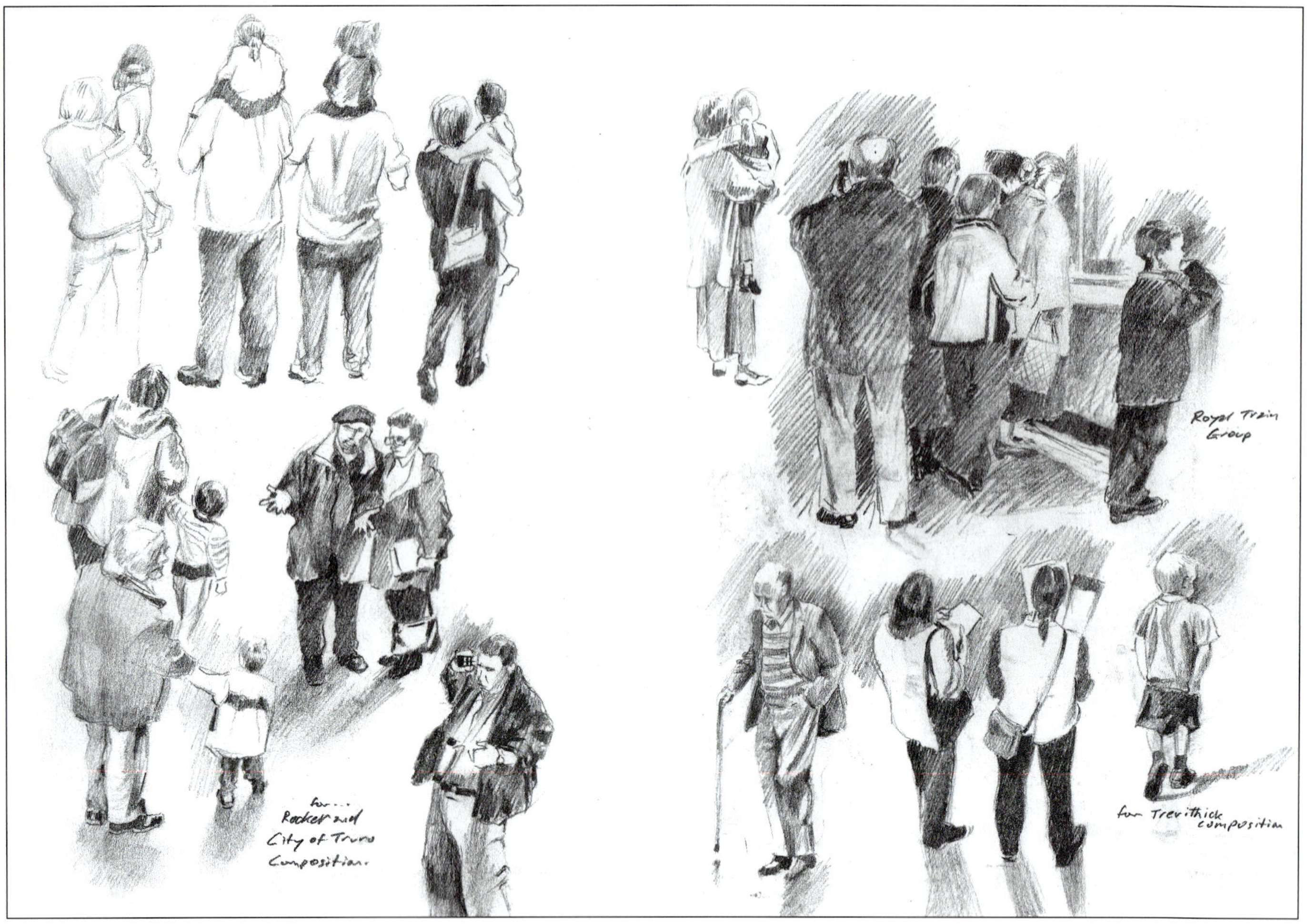
for...
Rocket and
City of Truro
Composition.
Royal Train
Group
for Trevithick
composition

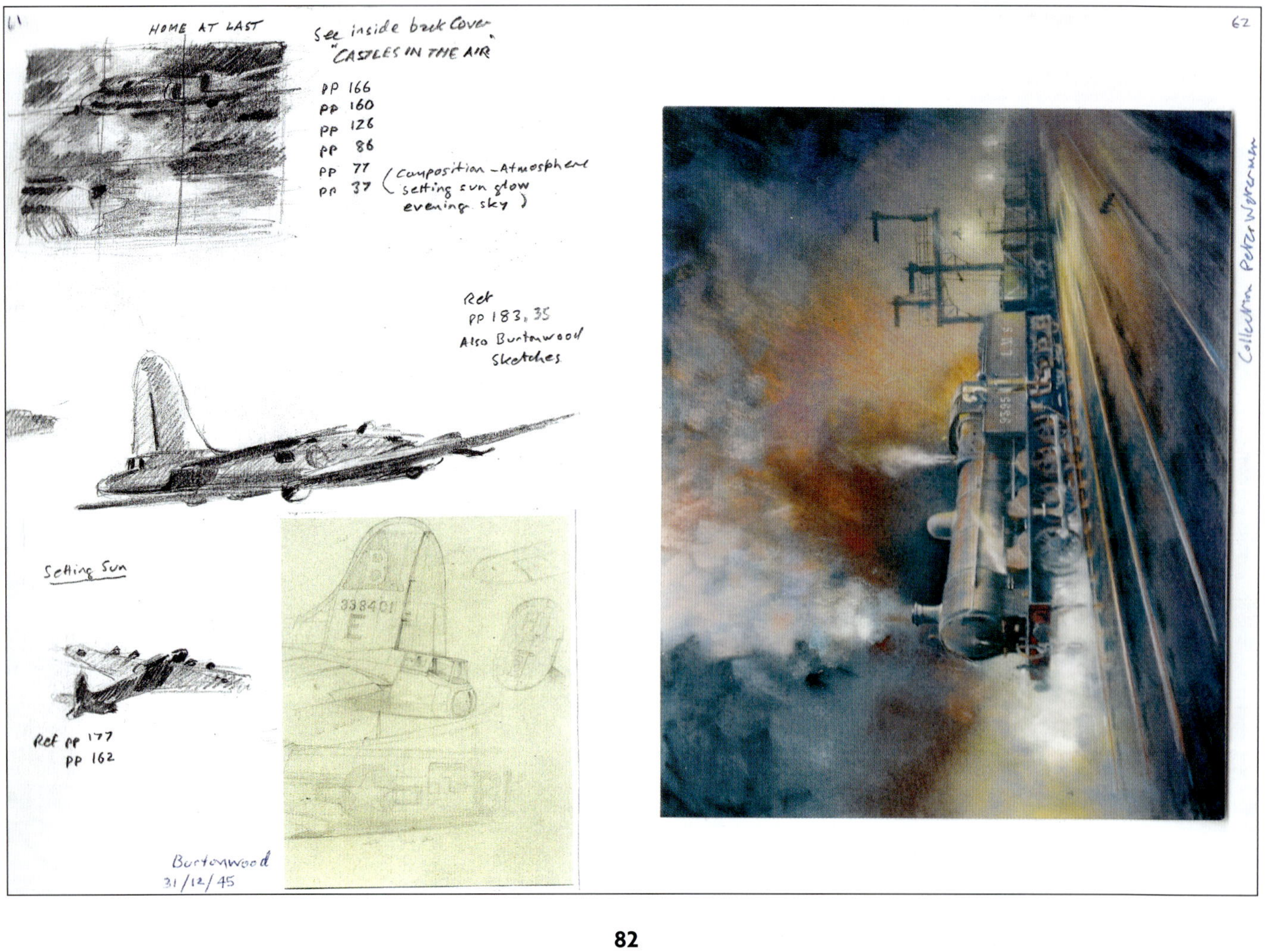
61
HOME AT LAST
See inside back Cover.
"CASTLES IN THE AIR"
PP 166
PP 160
PP 126
PP 86
PP 77
PP 37
(Composition - Atmosphere
setting sun glow
evening sky)
62
Ref
PP 183, 35
Also Burtonwood
Sketches
Setting Sun
338401
E
Ref PP 177
PP 162
Burtonwood
31/12/45
Collection Peter Waterman

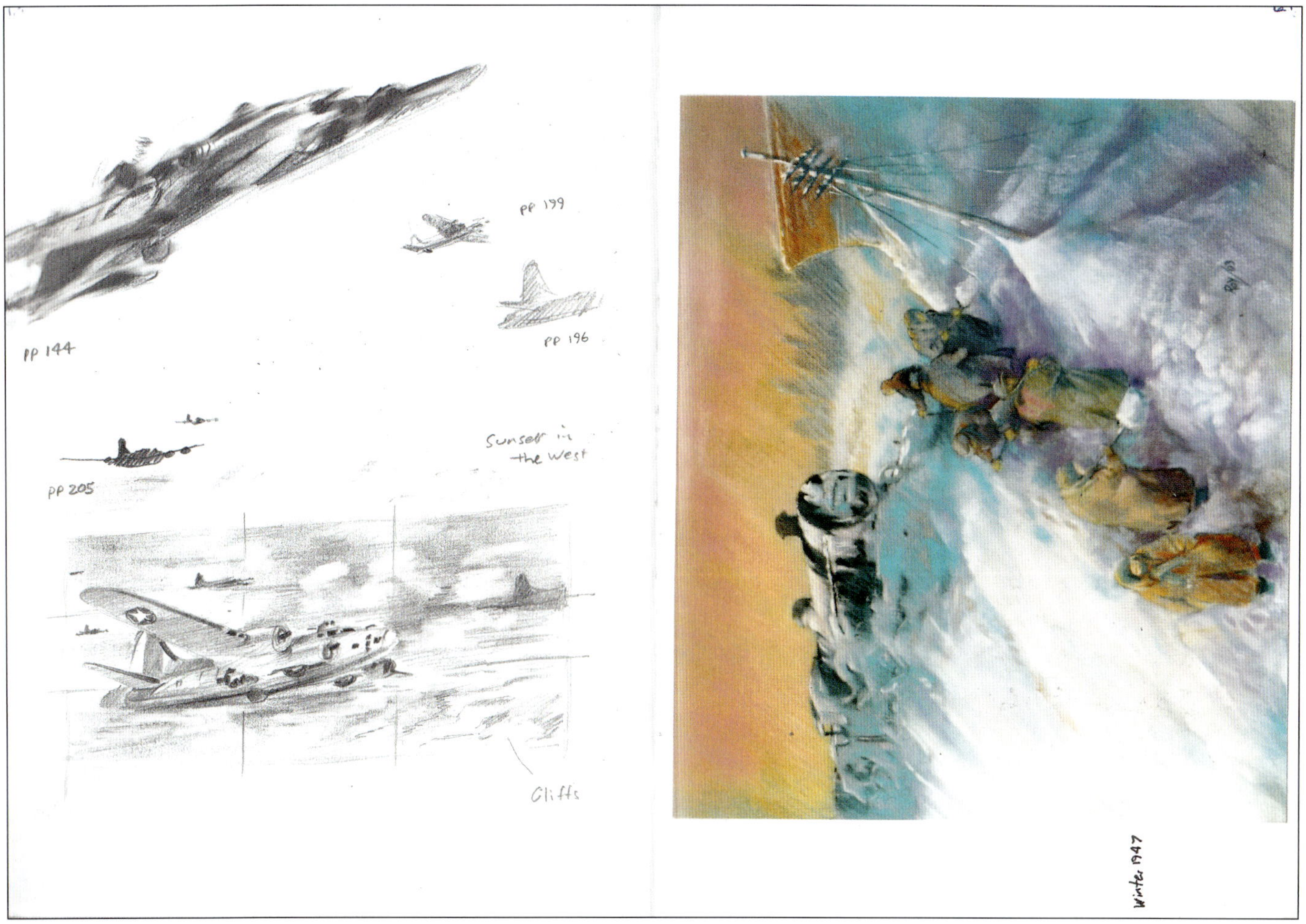
PP 199
PP 144
PP 196
Sunset in the West
PP 205
Cliffs
Winter 1947

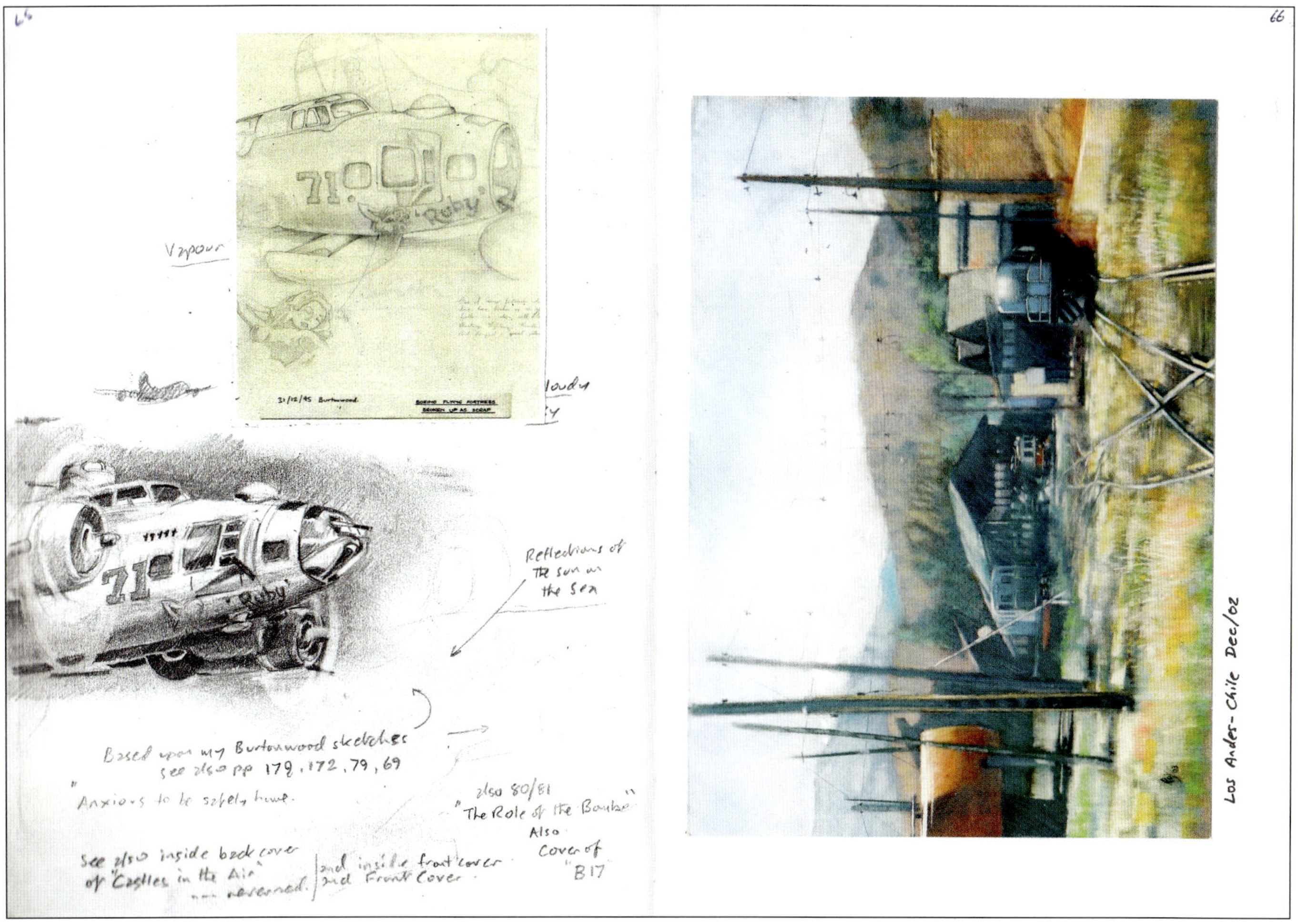
66
Vapour
71
Ruby
31/12/45 Burtonwood
Reflections of the sun on the sea
Based upon my Burtonwood sketches
see also pp 179, 172, 79, 69
"Anxious to be safely home.
also 80/81
"The Role of the Bomber"
Also
Cover of
"B17"
See also inside back cover
of "Castles in the Air"
... reversed.
and inside front cover
and Front Cover
Los Andes-Chile Dec/02

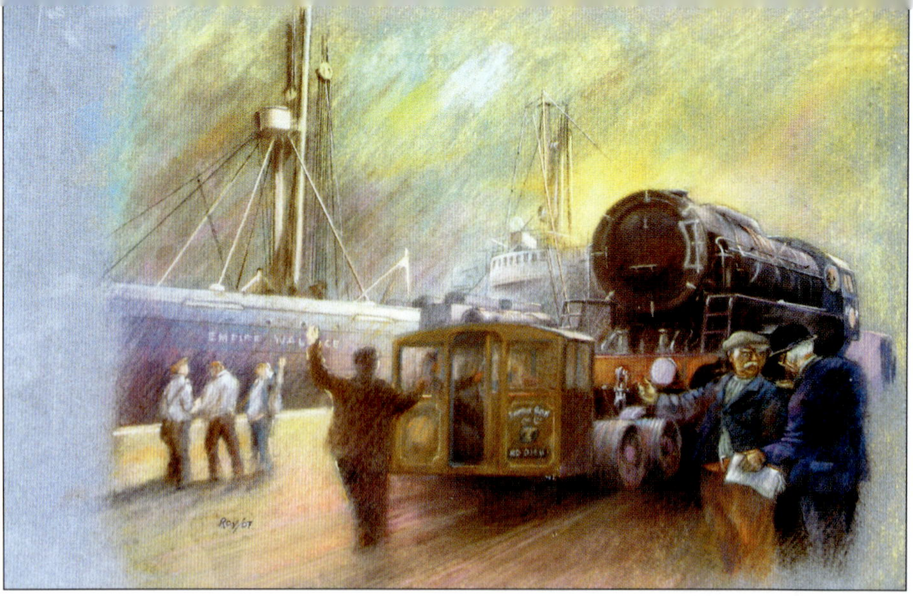

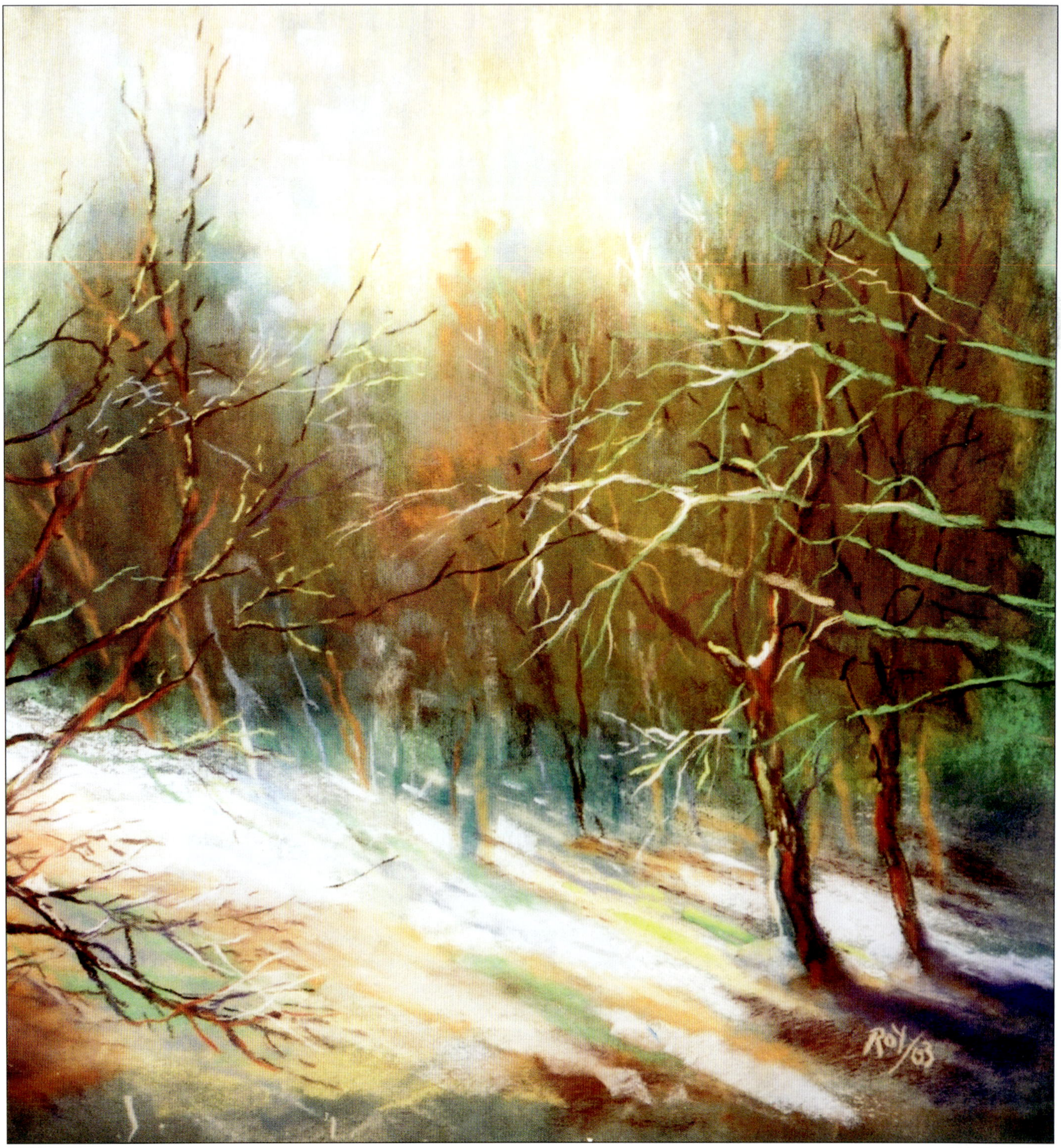

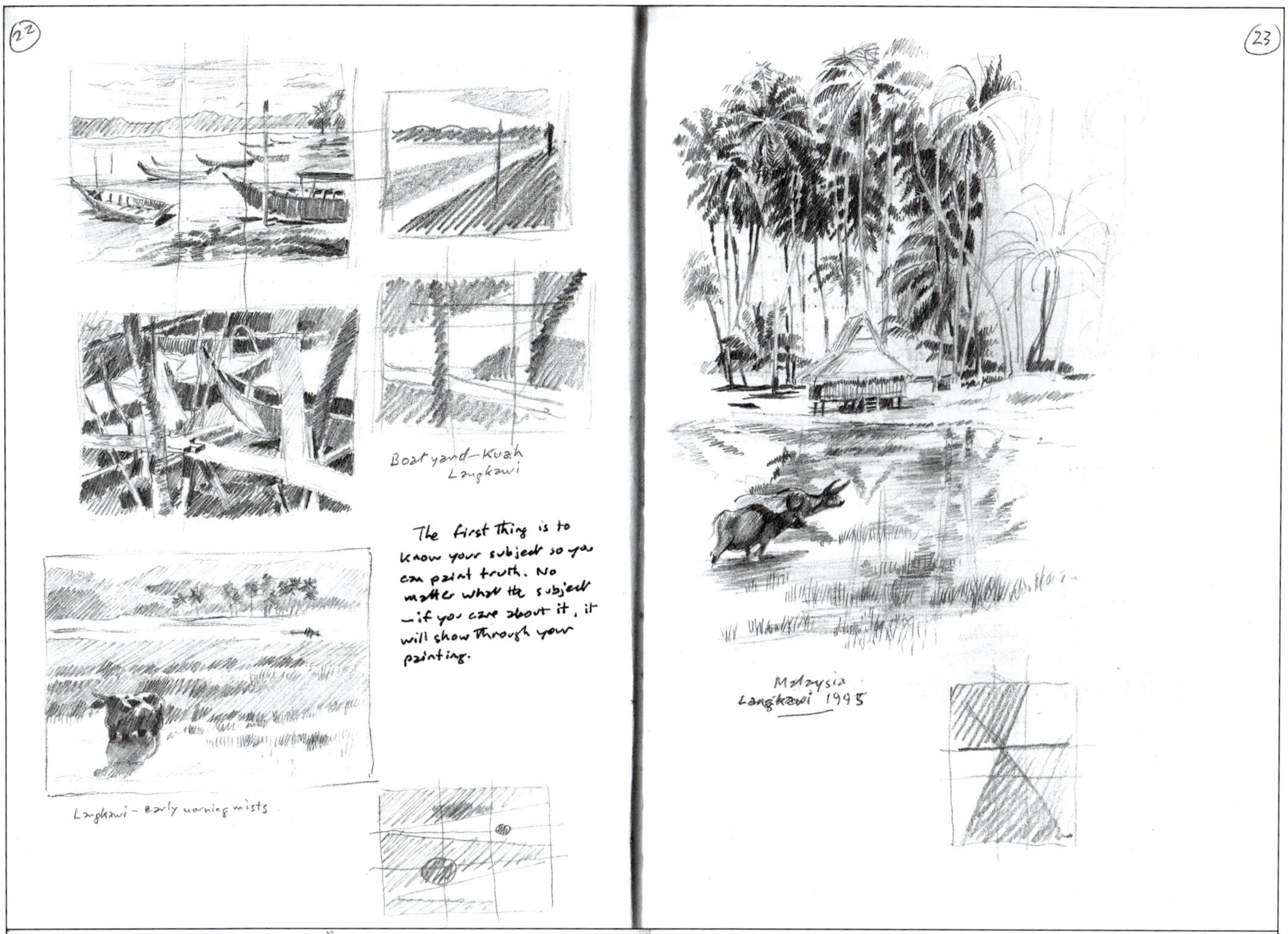
22
Boat yard—Kuah Langkawi
The first thing is to know your subject so you can paint truth. No matter what the subject — if you care about it, it will show through your painting.
Langkawi – early morning mists
23
Malaysia Langkawi 1995

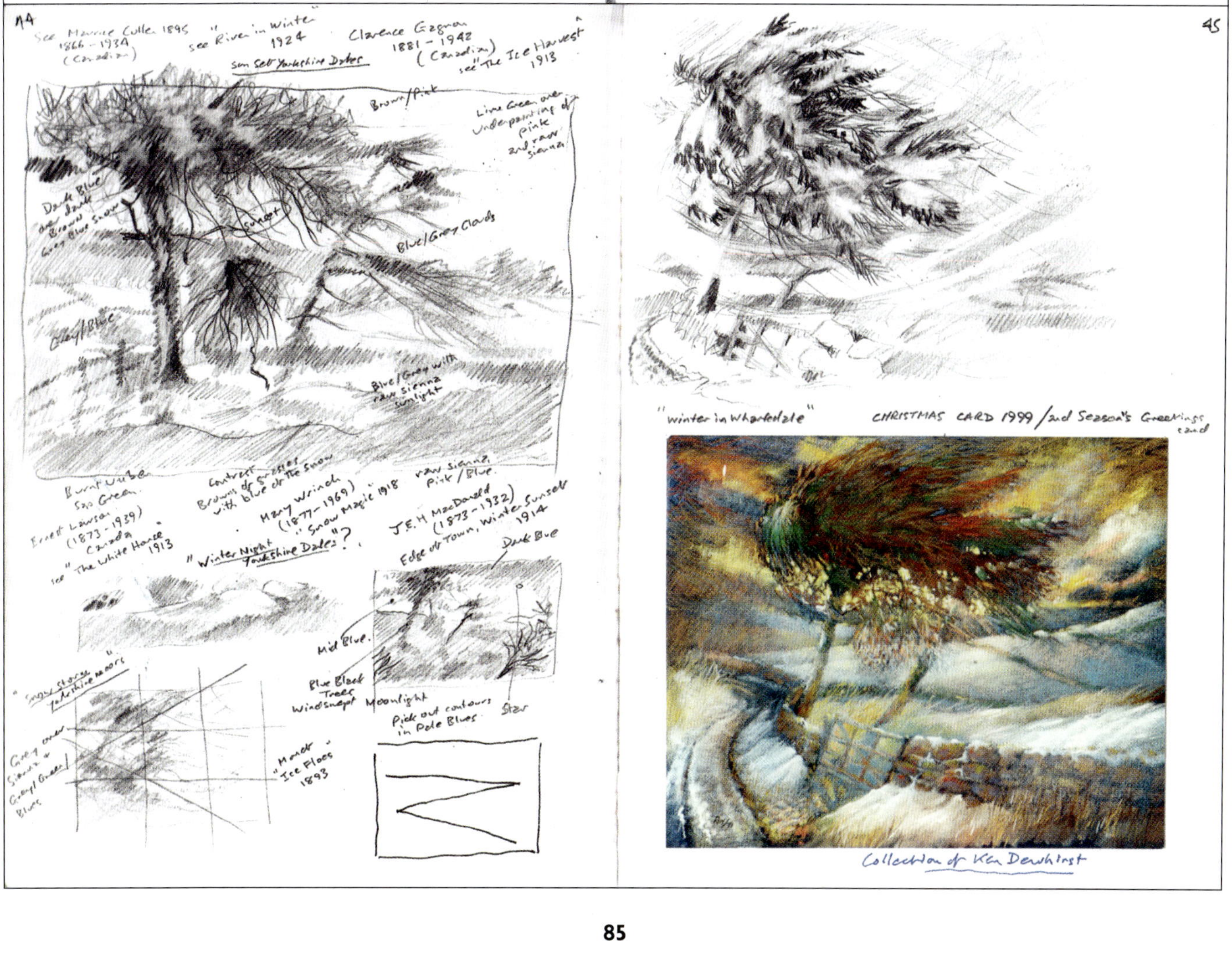
44
See Maurice Cullen 1895 1866 – 1934 (Canadian)
see "River in Winter" 1924
Clarence Gagnon 1881 – 1942 (Canadian)
see "The Ice Harvest" 1913
Sun Set Yorkshire Dales
Brown/Pink
Lime Green over under-painting of pink and raw sienna
Sunset
Blue/Grey Clouds
Grey/Blue
Blue/Grey with raw sienna sunlight
Burnt Umber Sap Green
Contrast Browns of grasses with blue of the snow
Mary Wrinch (1877 – 1969) "Snow Magic" 1918
raw sienna Pink / Blue
Ernest Lawson (1873 – 1939) Canada see "The White Horse" 1913
J.E.H. MacDonald (1873 – 1932) Edge of Town, Winter Sunset 1914
"Winter Night Yorkshire Dales"?
Dark Blue
Mid Blue
Blue Black Trees Windswept
Moonlight
Pick out contours in Pale Blues
Star
"Monet Ice Floes 1893"
45
"Winter in Wharfedale"
CHRISTMAS CARD 1999 / and Season's Greetings card
Collection of Ken Dewhirst

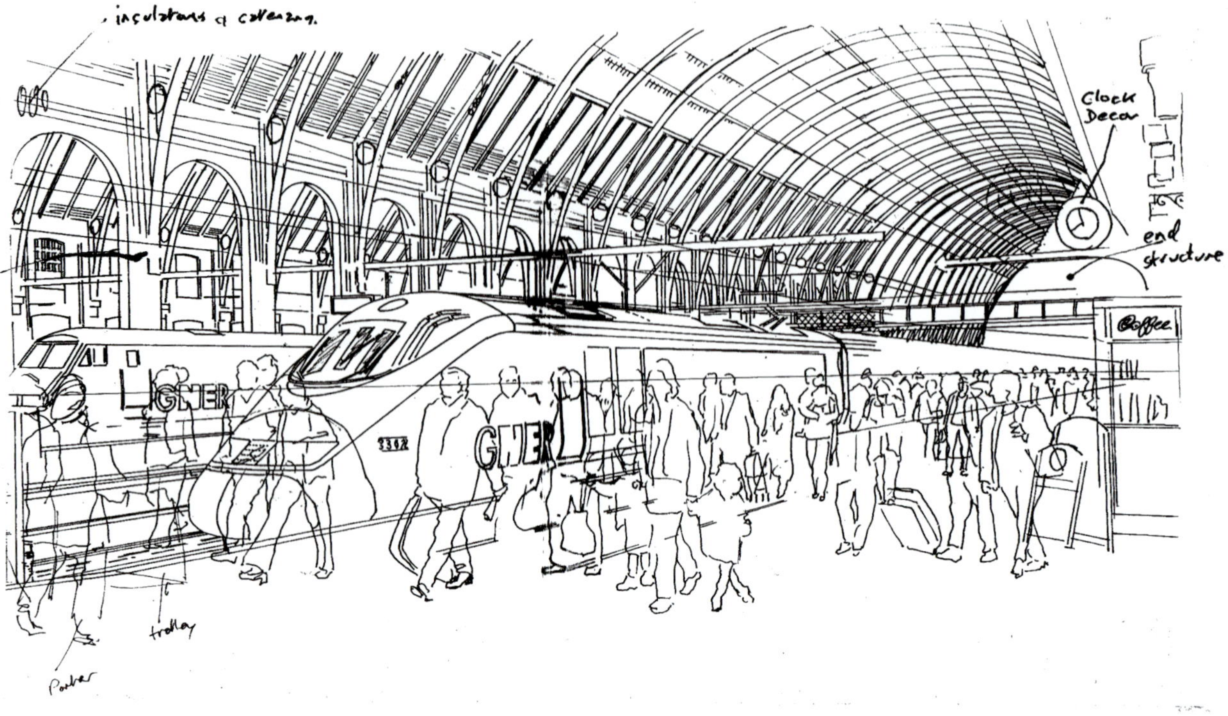
Clock
Decor
end
structure
Base?
Coffee
GNER
3302
trolley
Porter

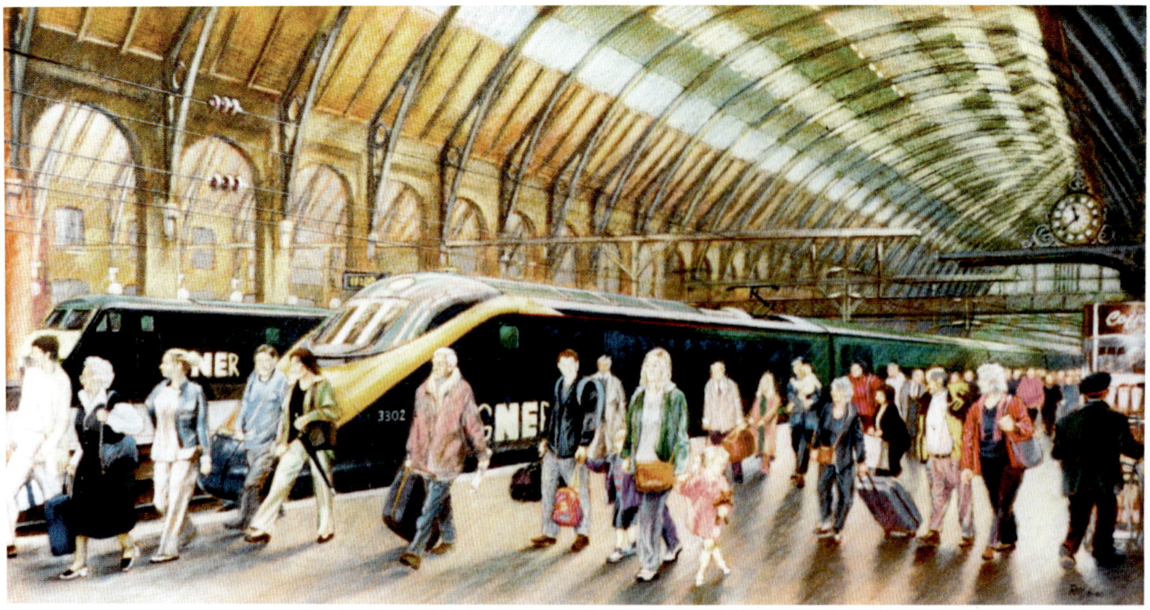
GNER
3302

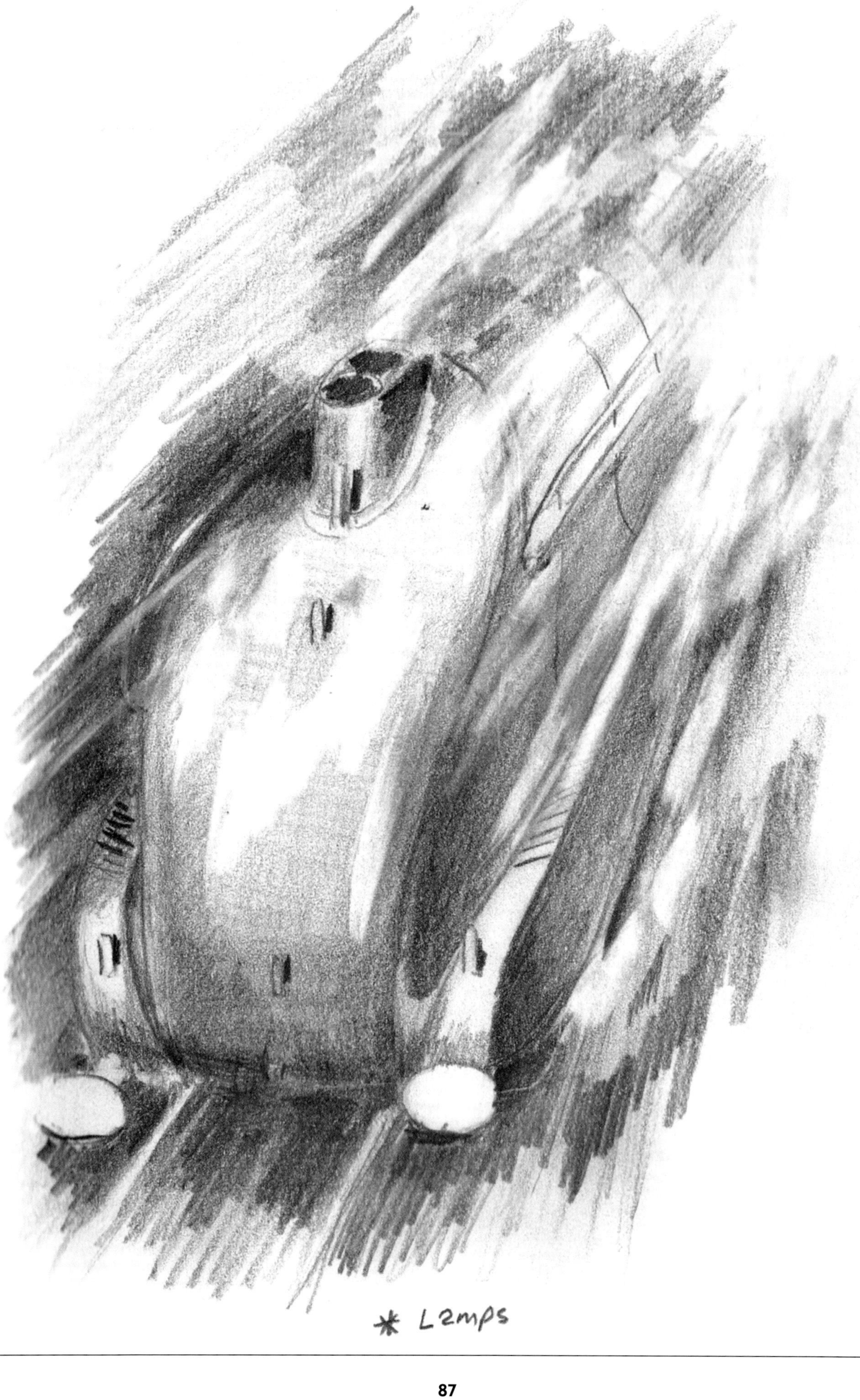

* Lamps

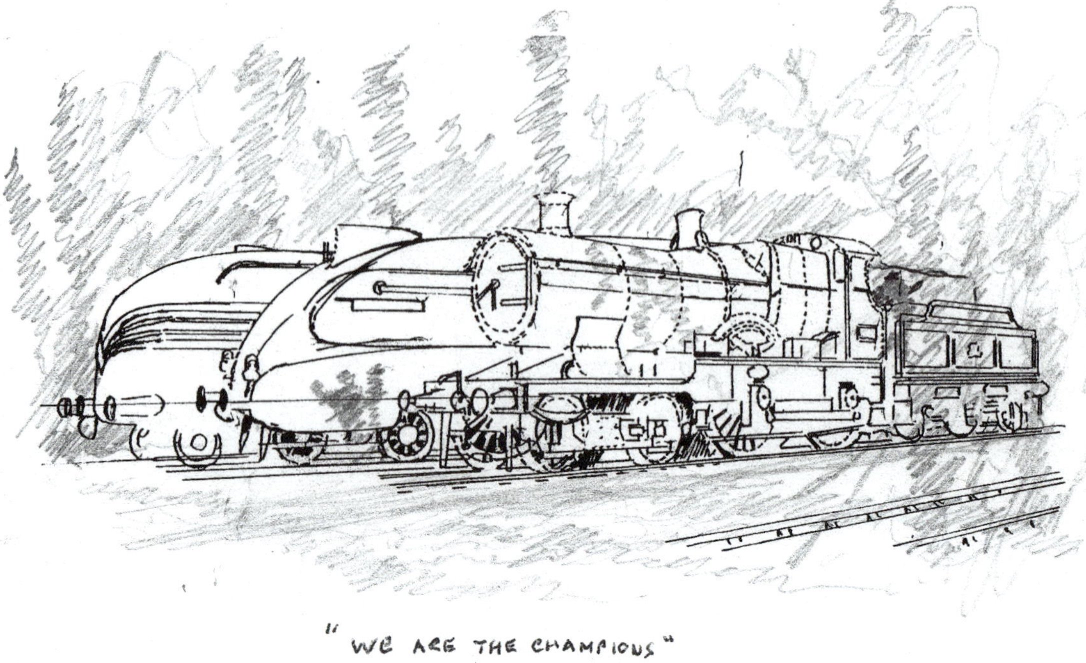
"WE ARE THE CHAMPIONS"

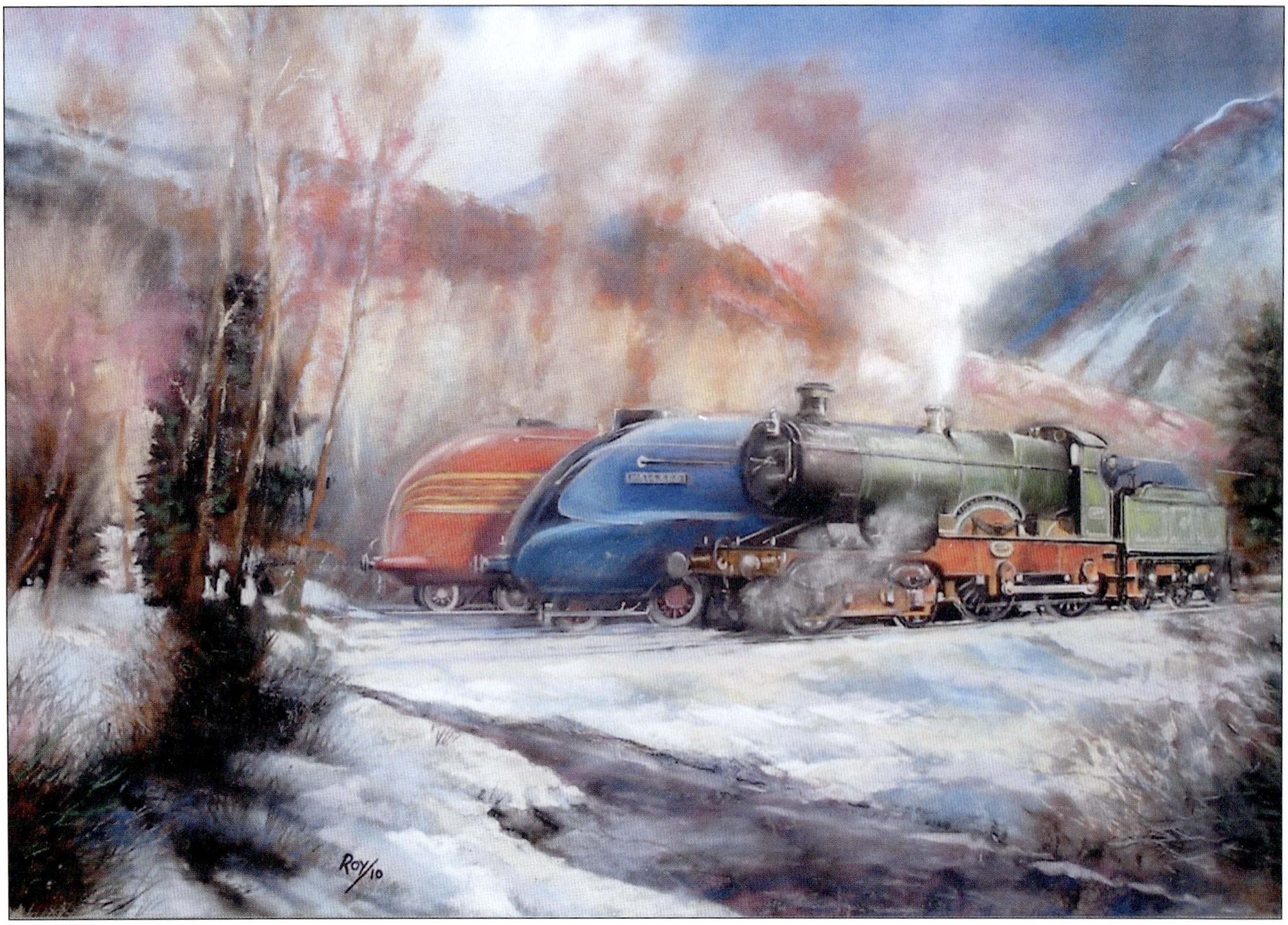
ROY/10

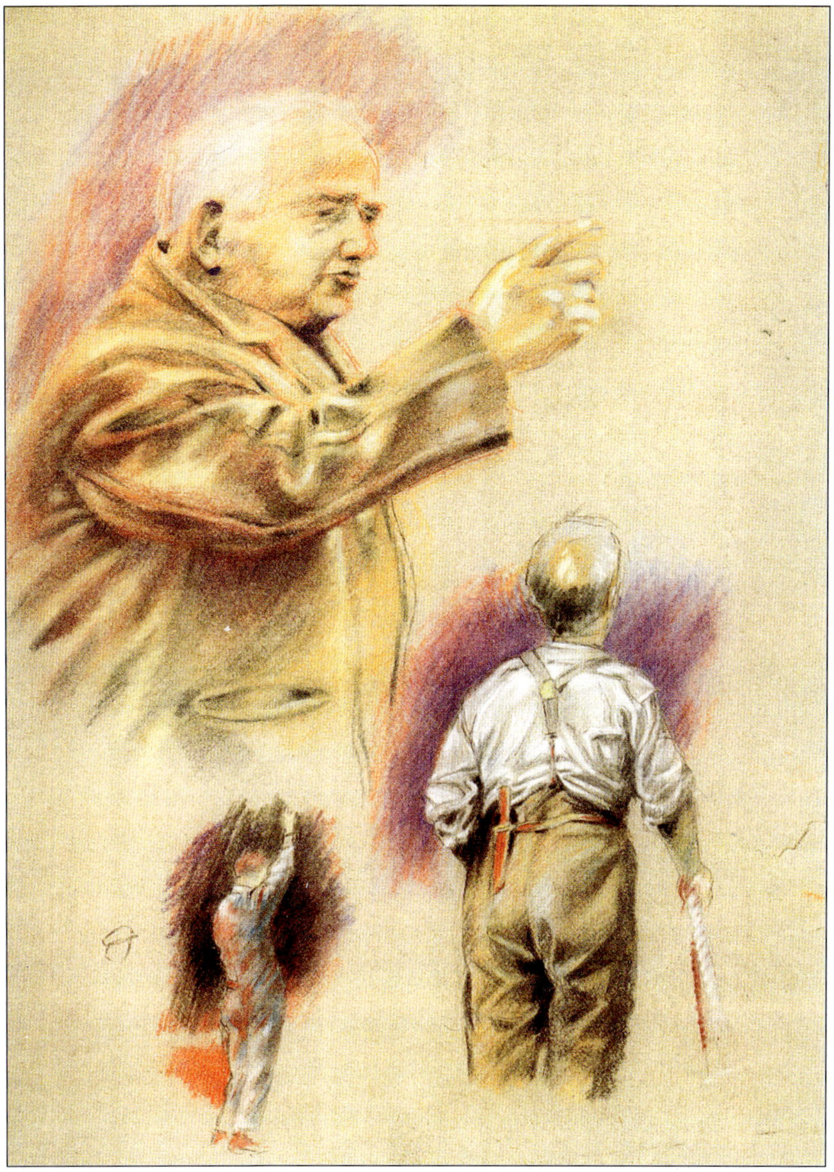

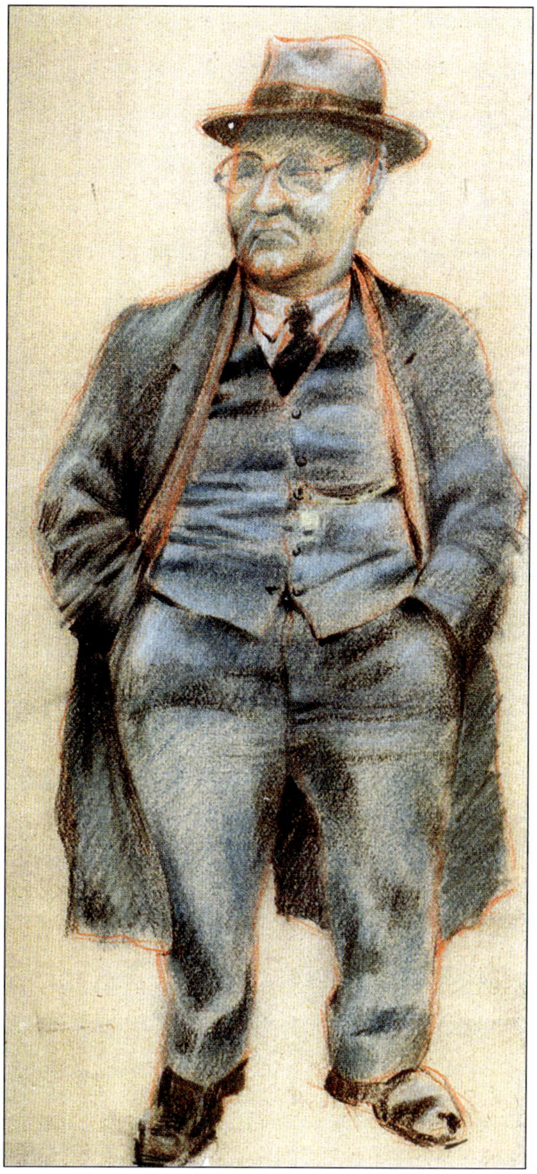

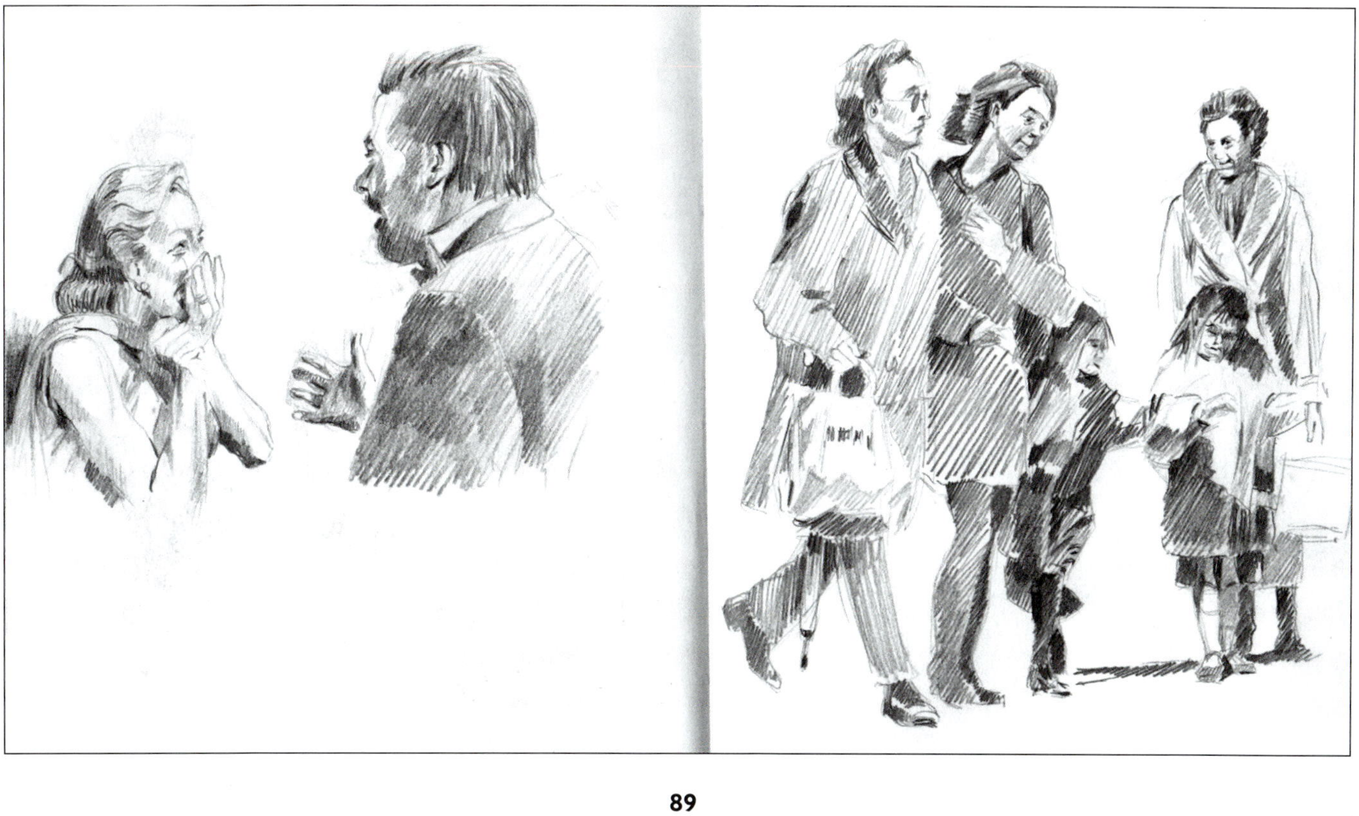

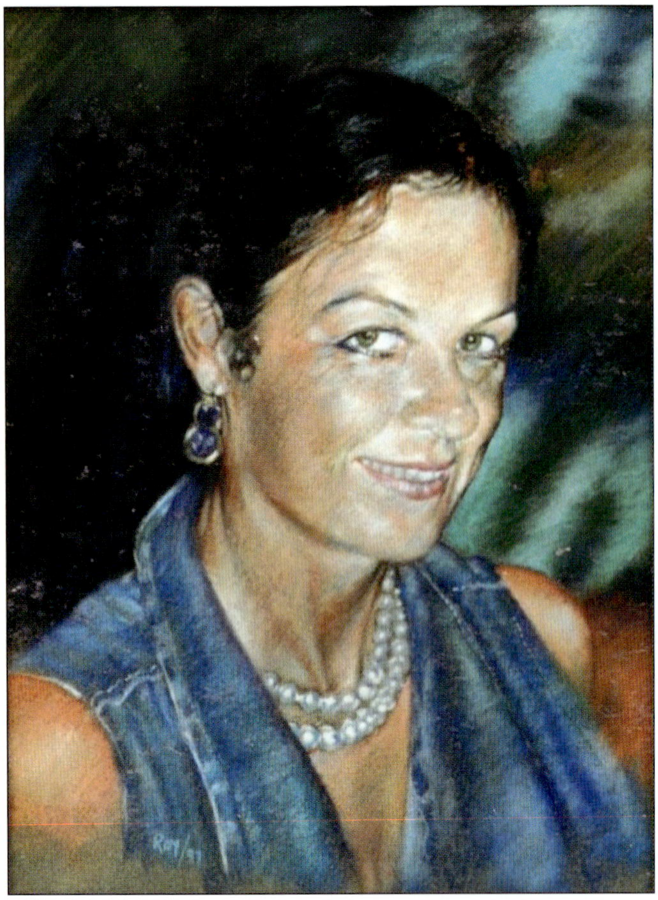

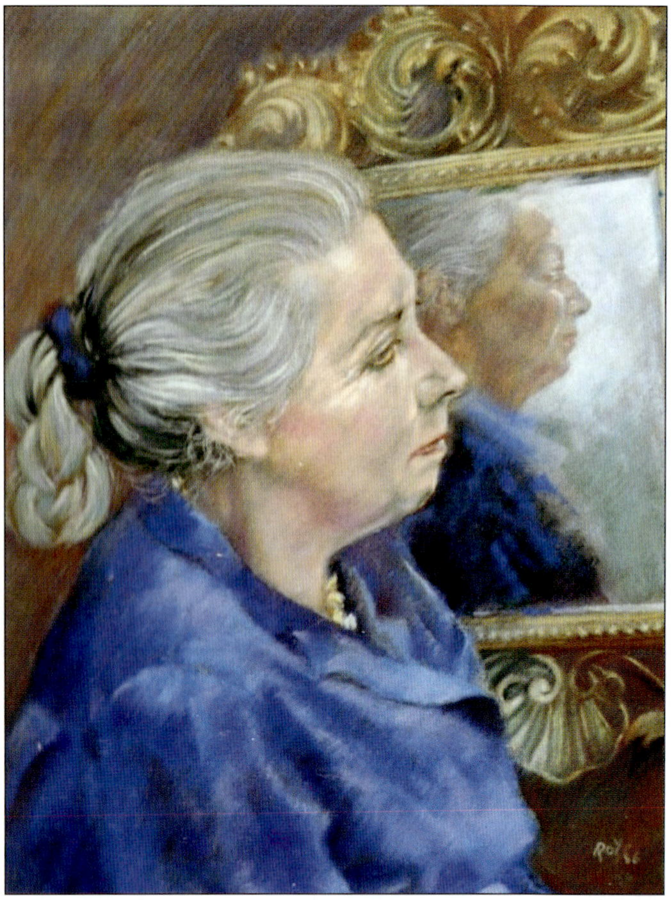

Roy also painted a few portraits beyond the self-portraits he produced when at art school.

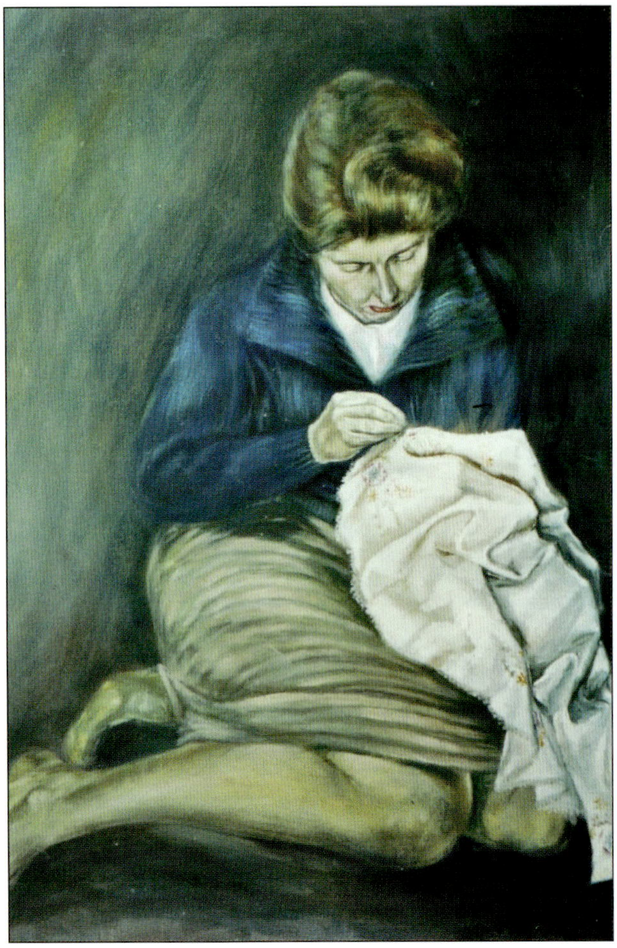

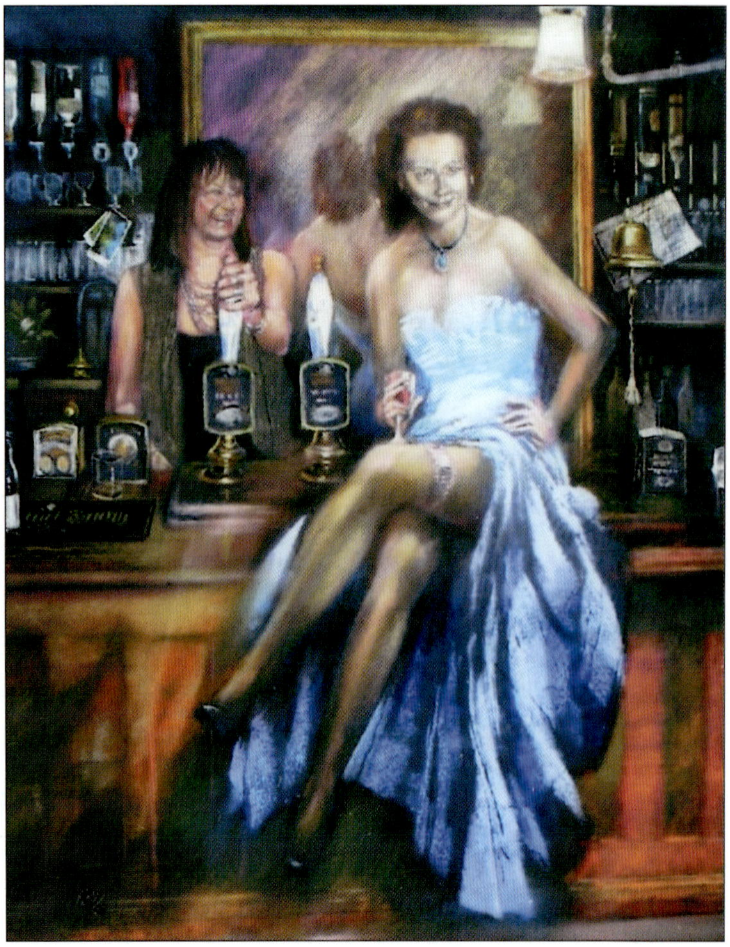

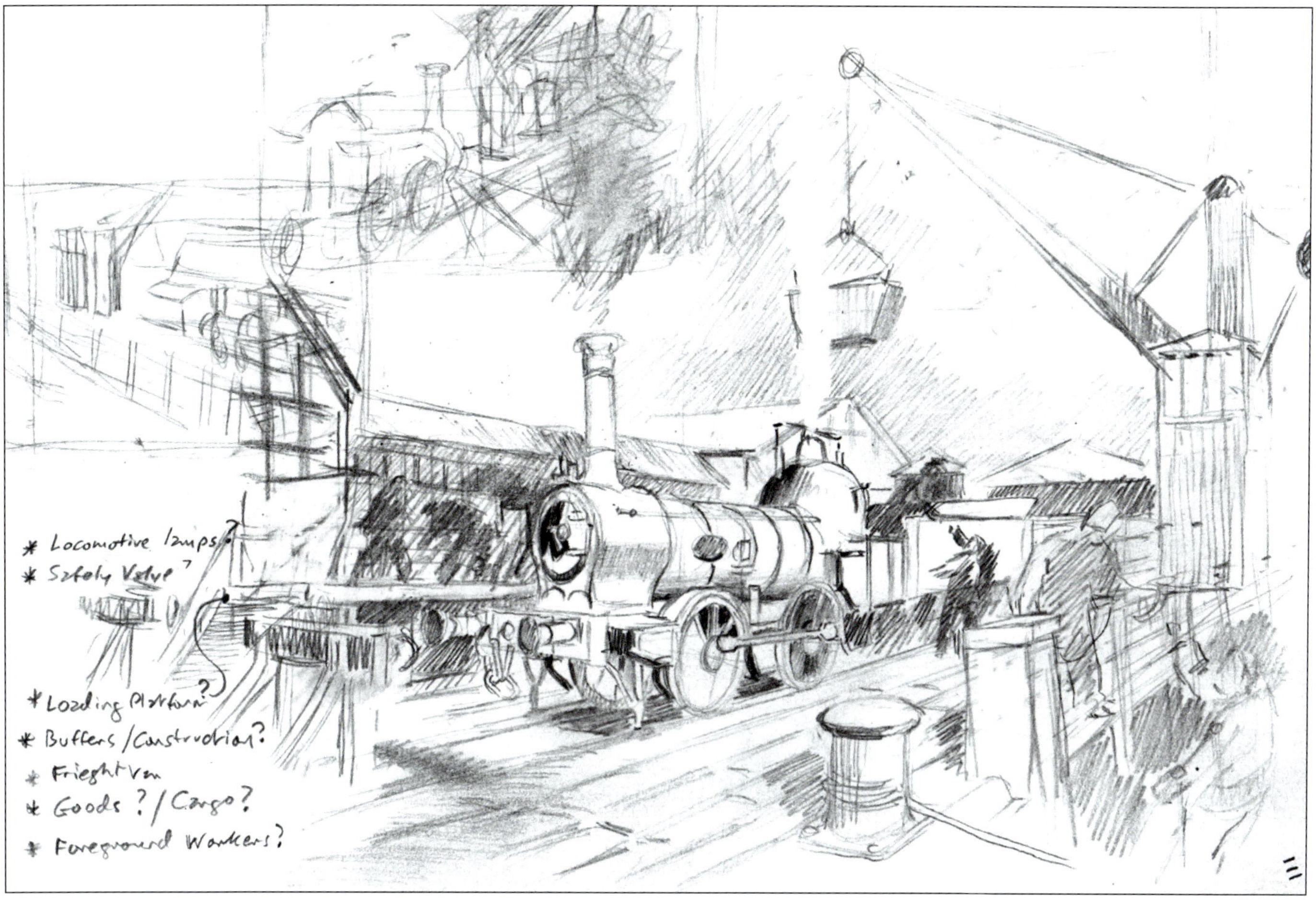

There are also some examples of initial railway studies that never made it to finished paintings.

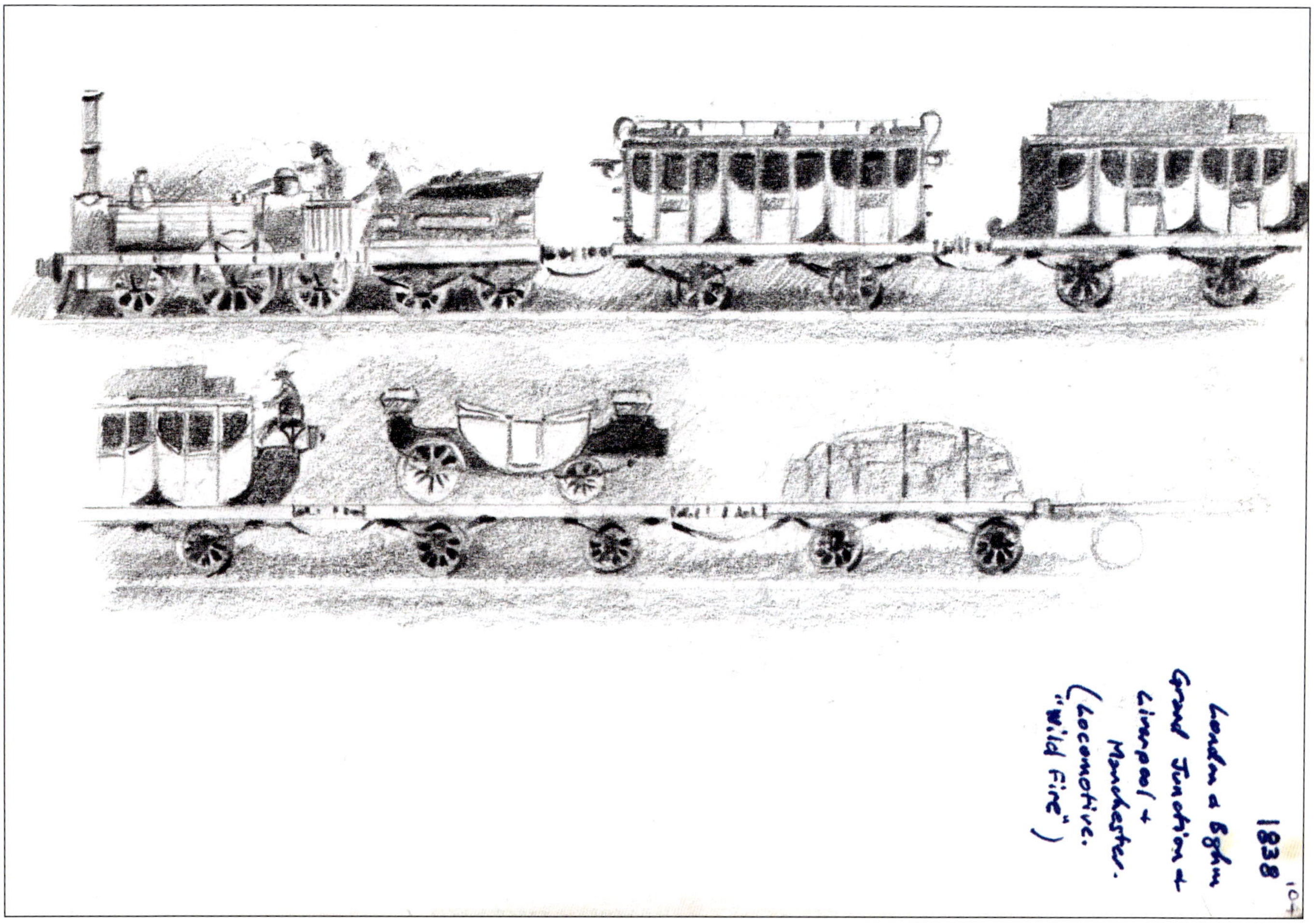

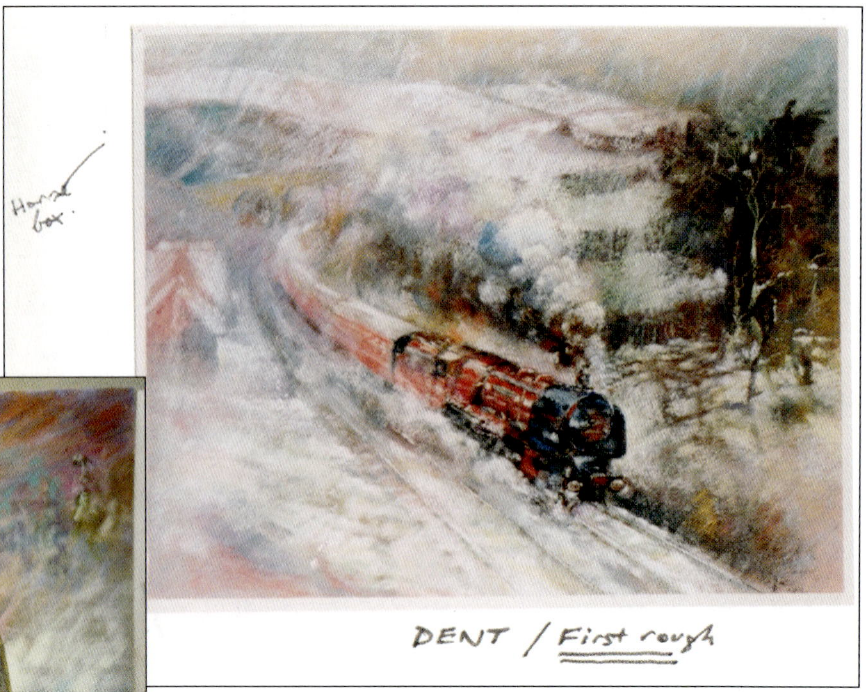

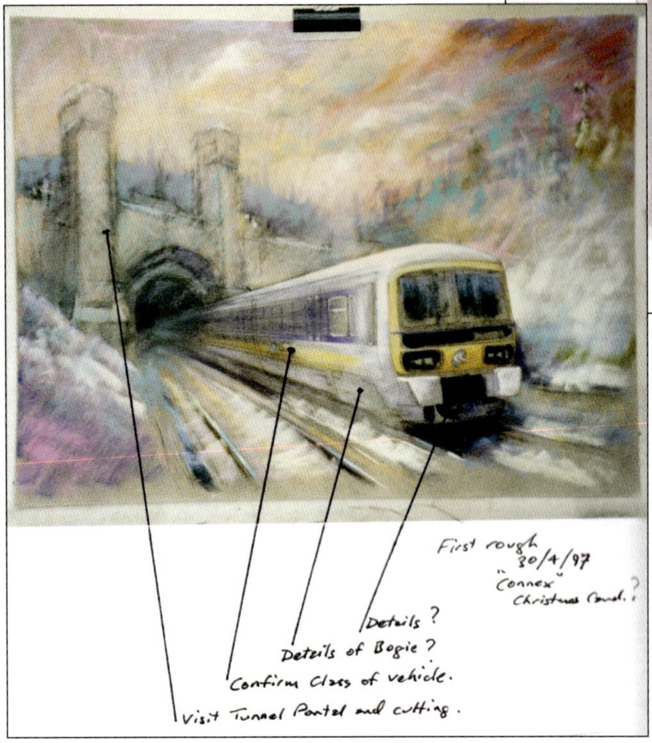

Rocket at Lime Street.

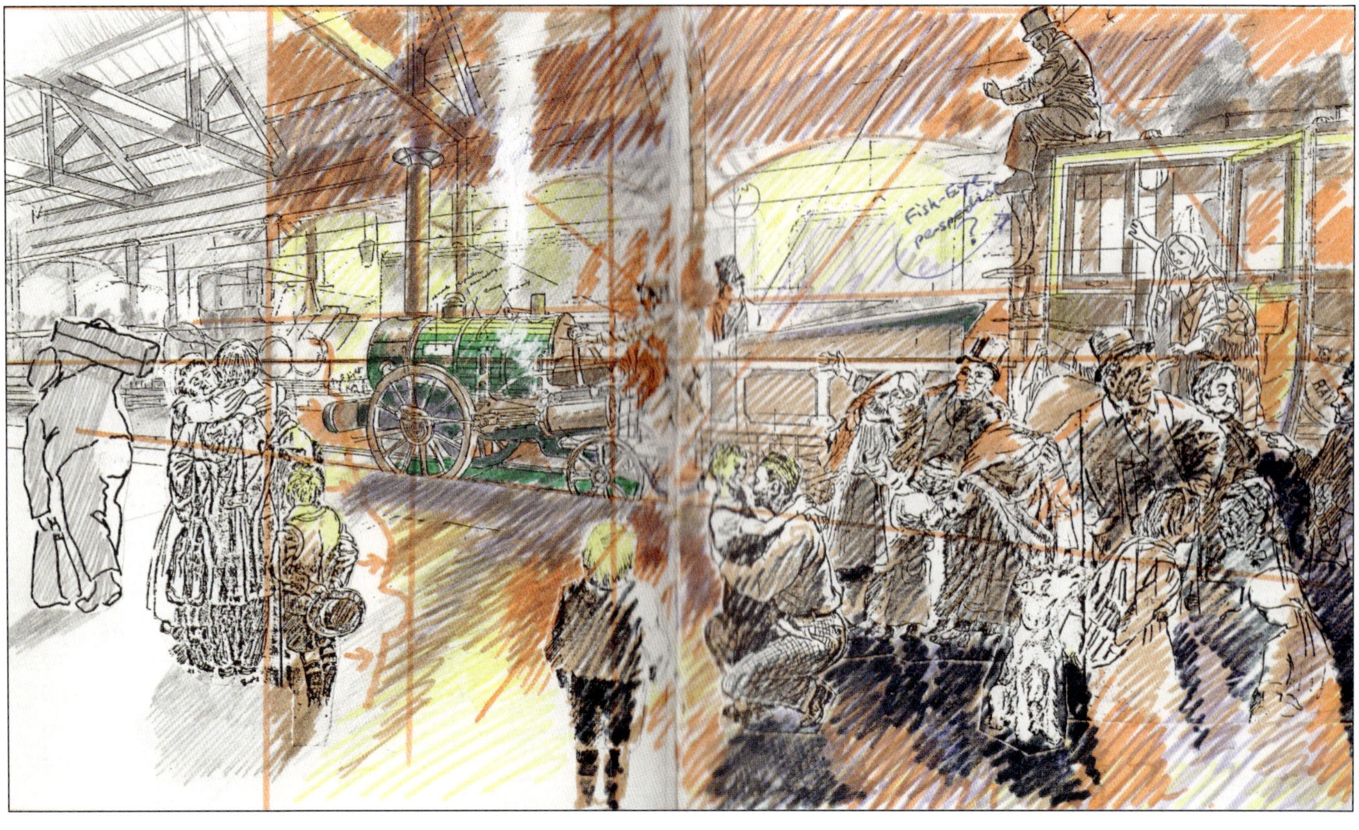

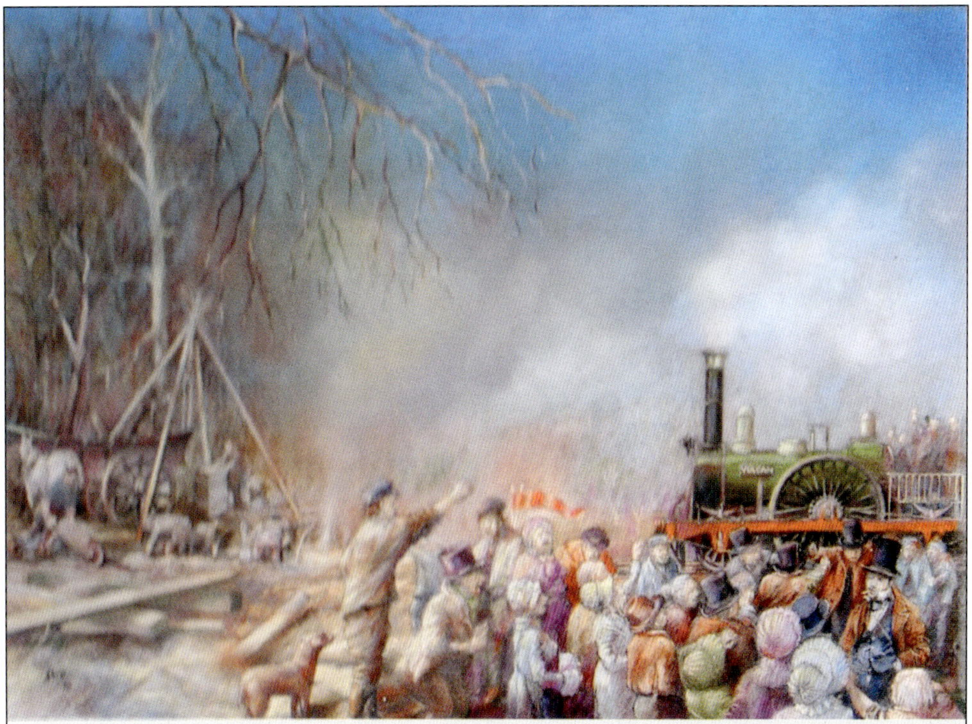

"VULCAN" Broad Gauge loco – First on-test run from St Pancras

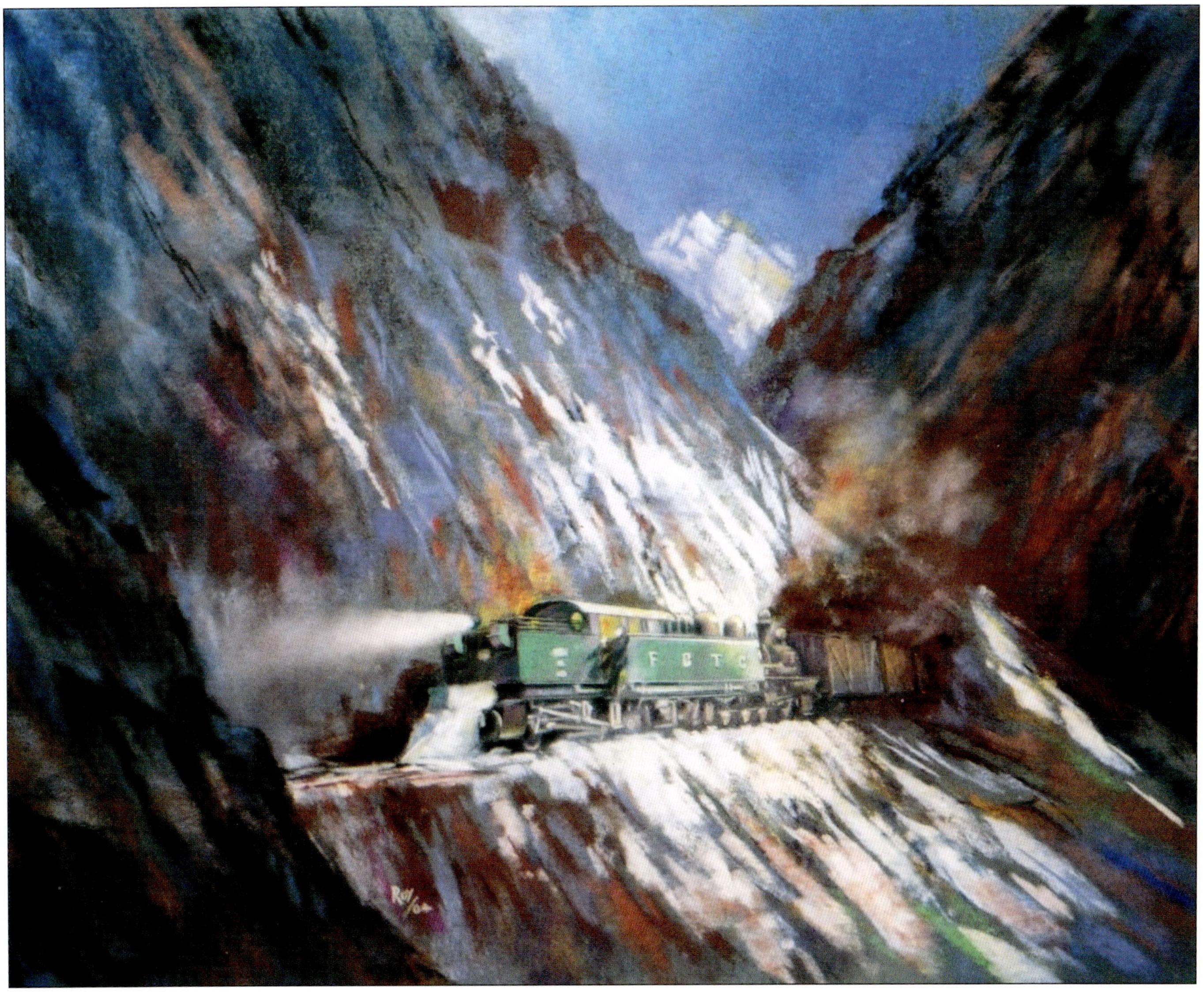

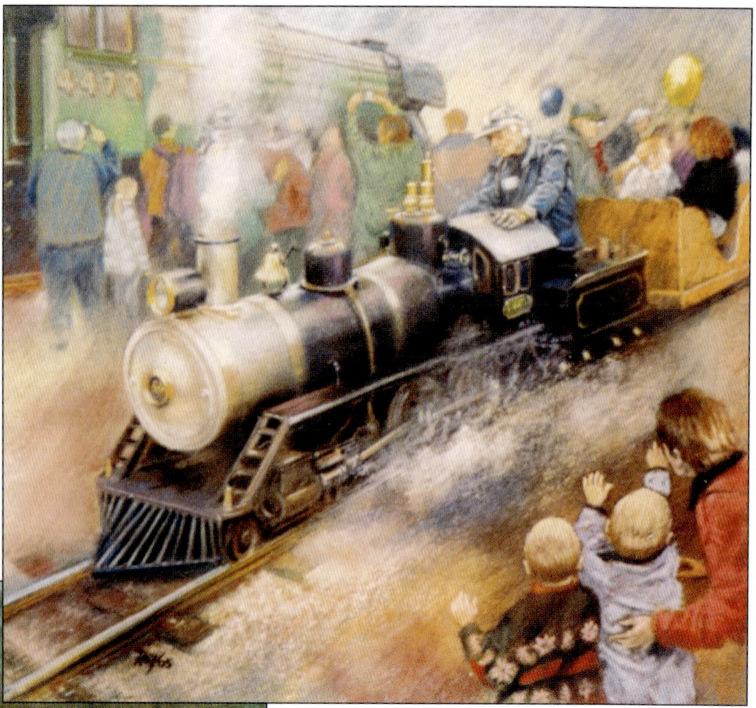

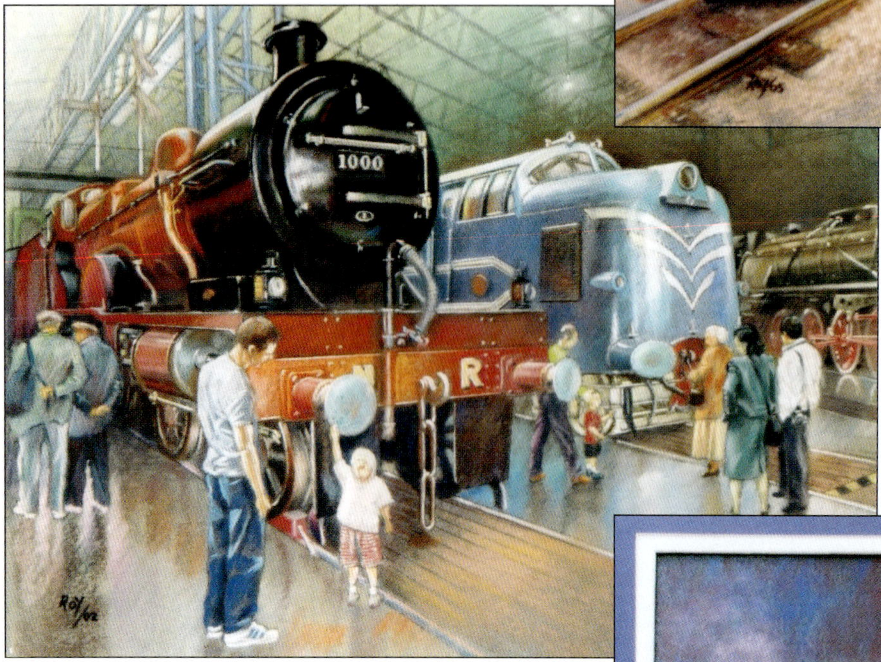
1000

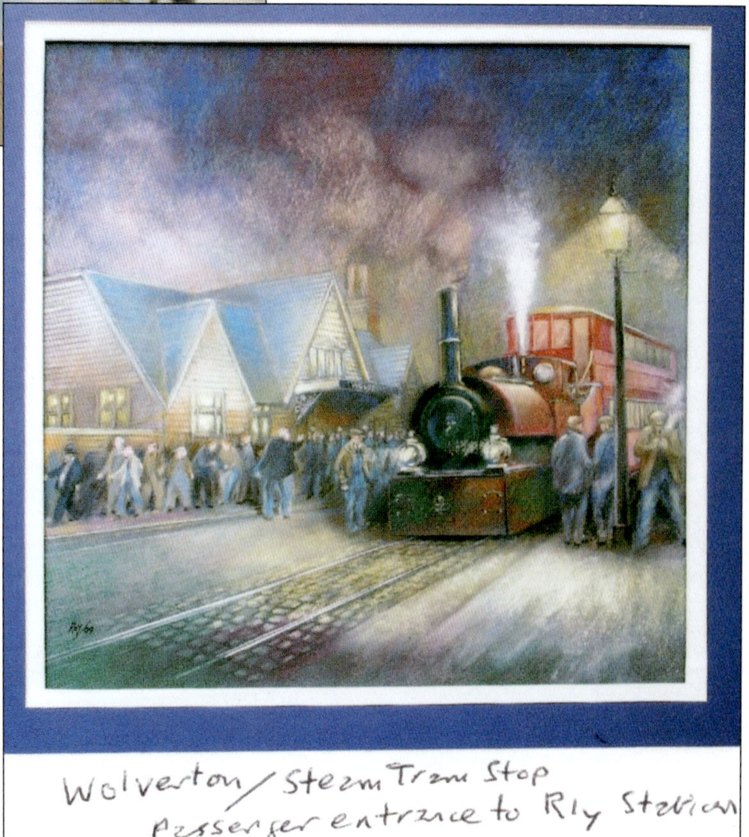
Wolverton / Steam Tram Stop
passenger entrance to Rly Station

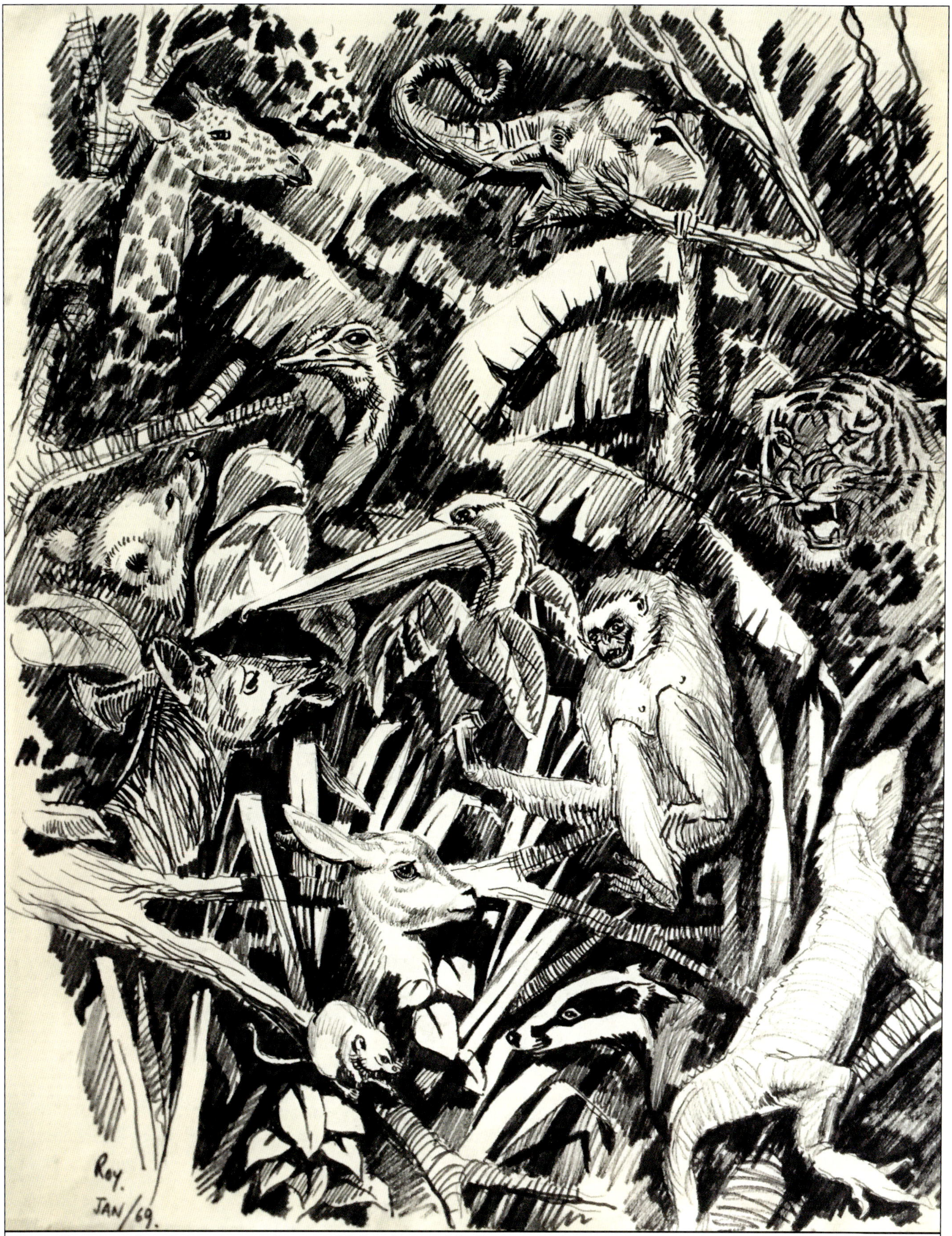

This collage was in a letter to my 6 year-old daughter with the instruction:

Now I have done a little sketch for you – you have to find 12 animals. – not nearly so clever as yours but I hope you will like it

The trawl through Roy's log books illustrates the range and variety of subjects and scenes that define the vast representational capability that he had developed over his artistic lifetime. Be it an individual, a tree, a hand or even a building he manages to bring a purpose, or a character, to its inclusion within a painting; adding to the overall concept and expression of the scene.

His representation of people is, I believe one of his greatest skills and this combined with his previous engineering experience enables him to create a life and an overall character within each of his railway-oriented paintings.

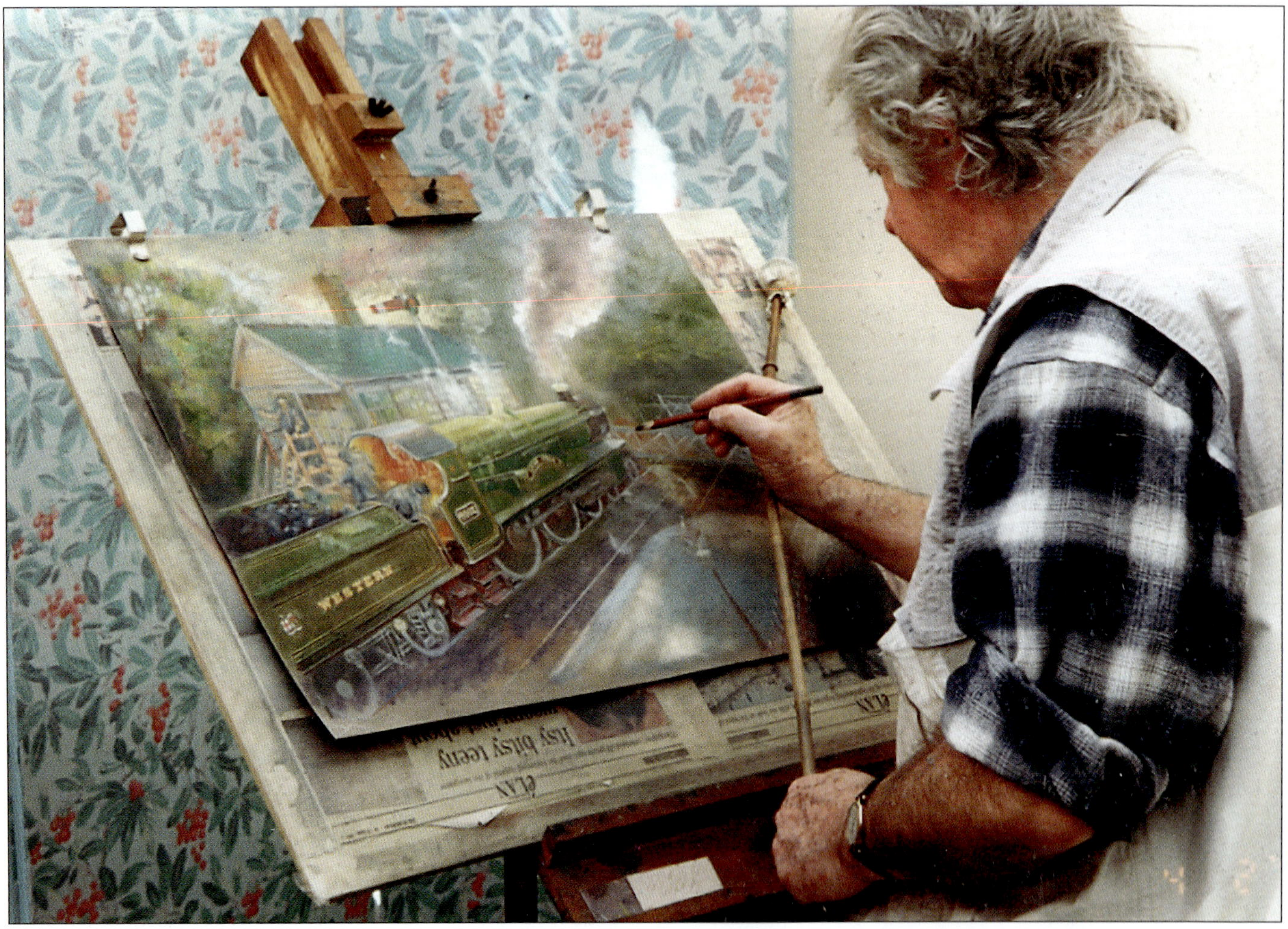

CHAPTER FIVE represents a selection of the paintings produced within the span of his retirement. They are chosen to show his ability to represent:

(a) a locomotive at speed,
(b) the variety of occasions which bring together people and the railways and
(c) the various times of day, which requires the integration of mechanical, light and other environmental features needed for the desired atmosphere

Here he is shown at work in his attic. The painting shows the G.W.R. "Lode Star" at a level crossing.

CHAPTER FIVE

SELECTION OF RAILWAY PAINTINGS

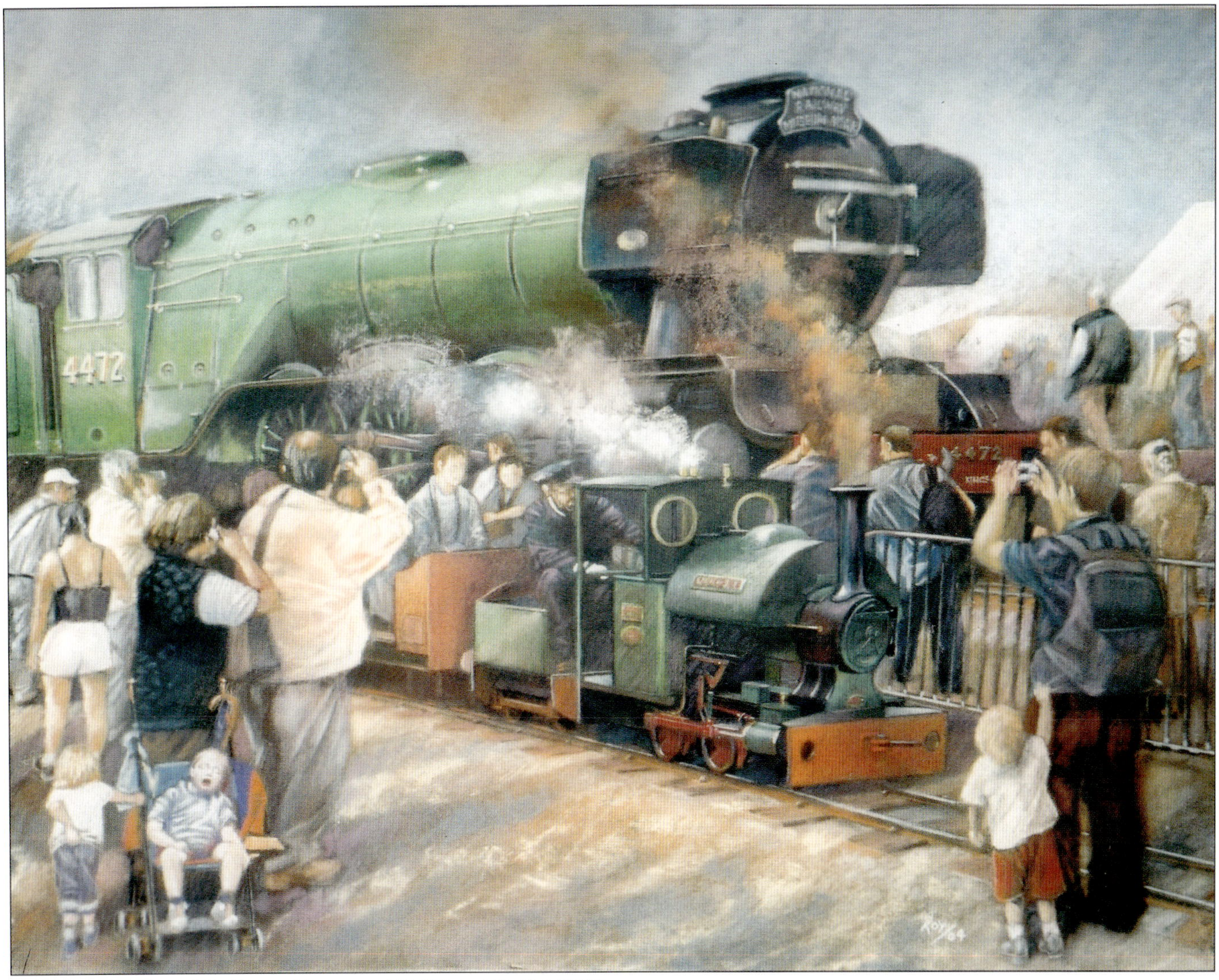

Railart at National Railway Museum, 20/03 to 30/06 2002.

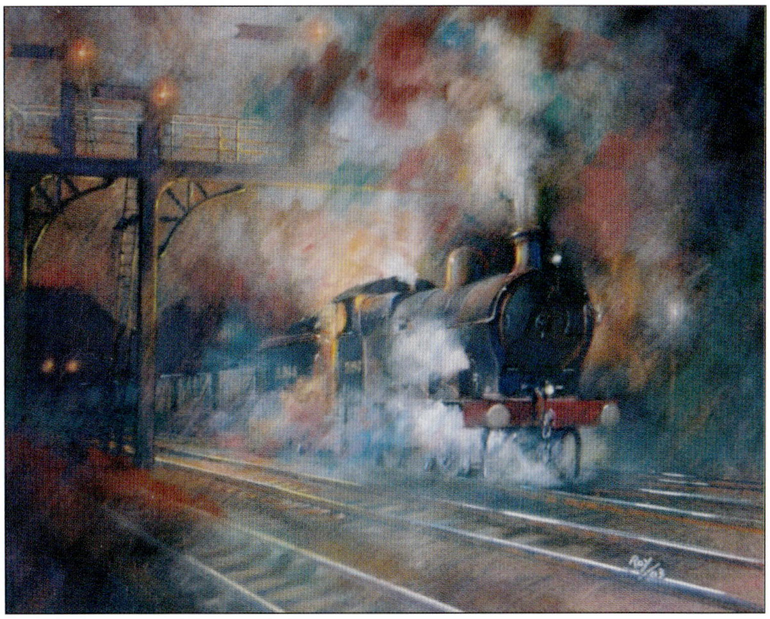

The Nightly Wigan Alps Colliery Triangle – 1940s.

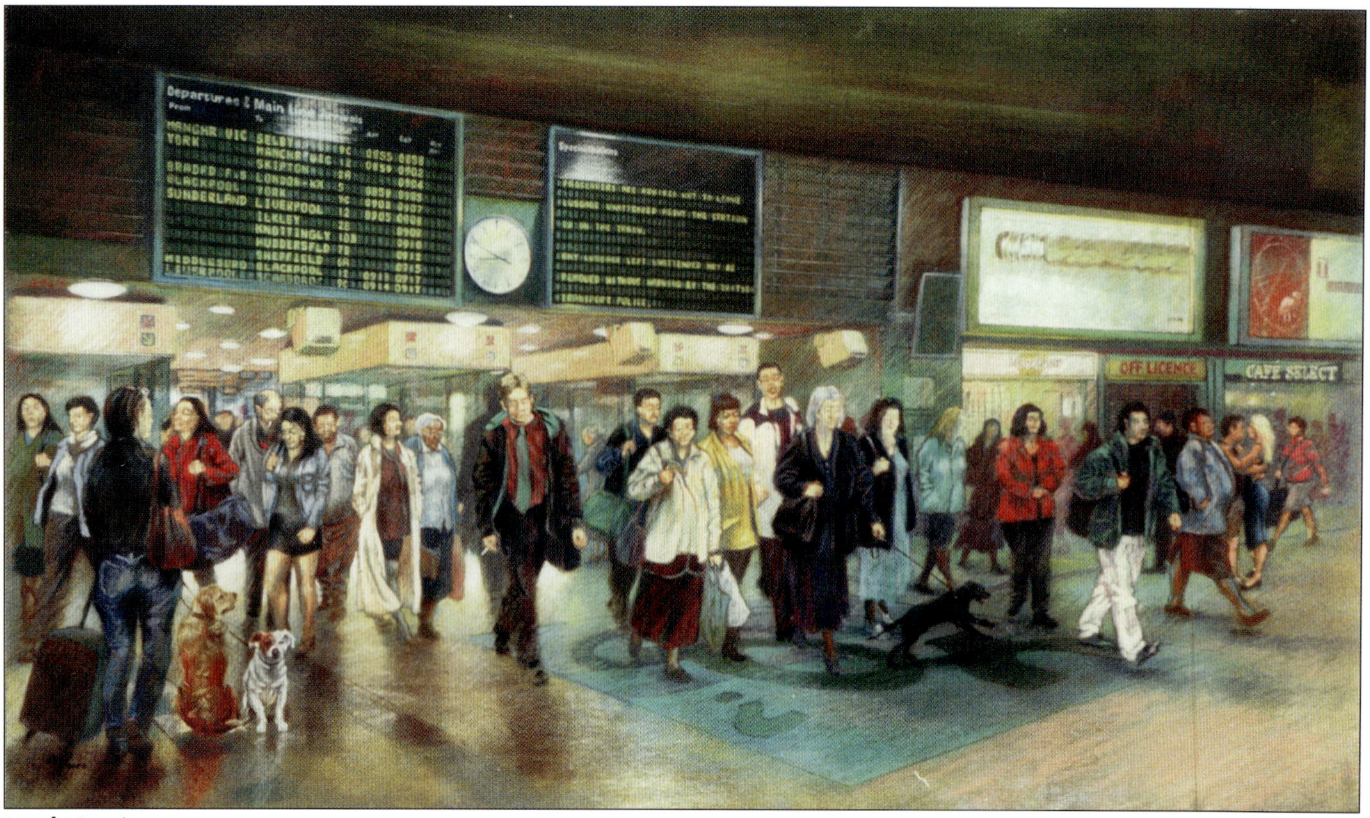

Leeds Station concourse.

Black Five.

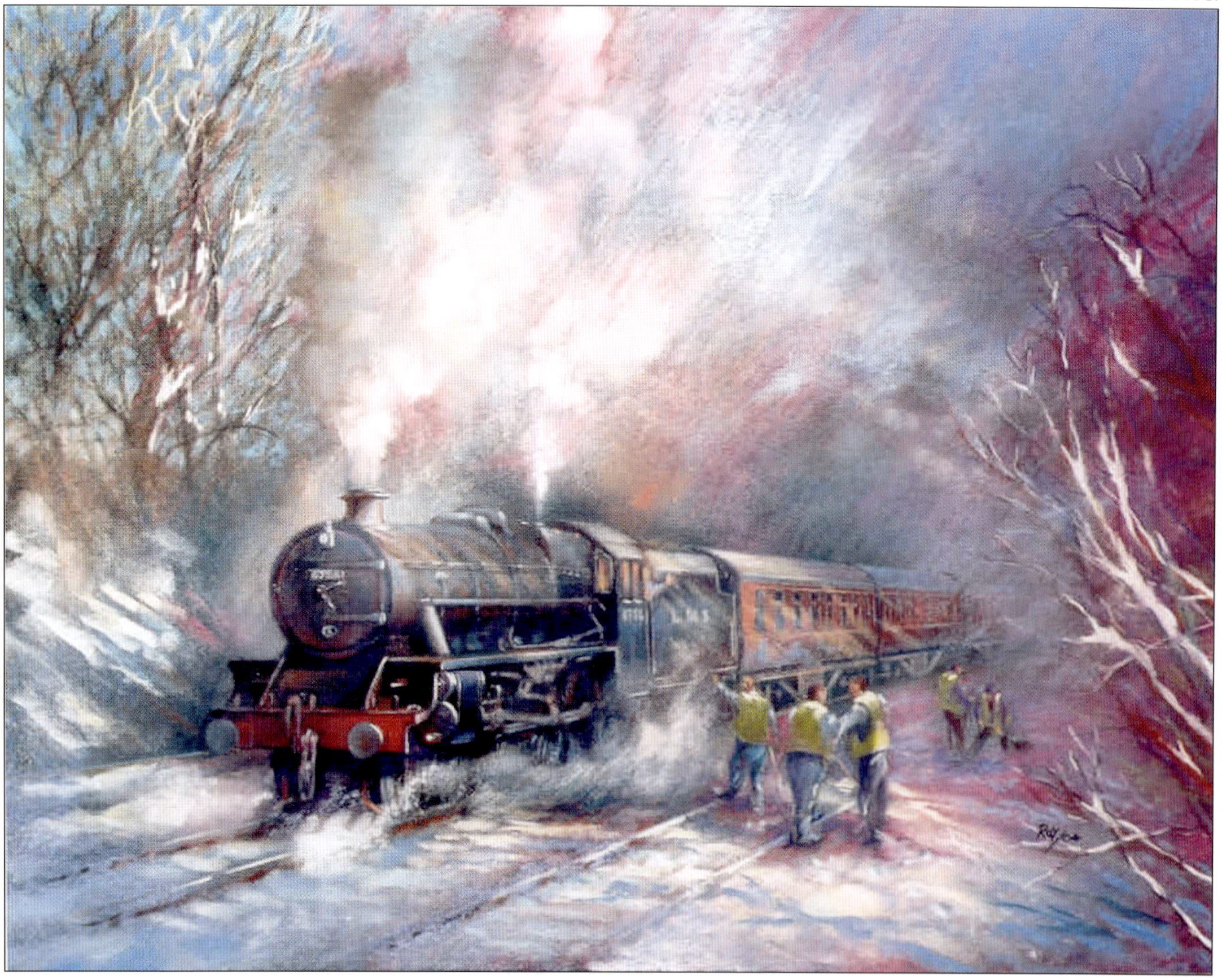

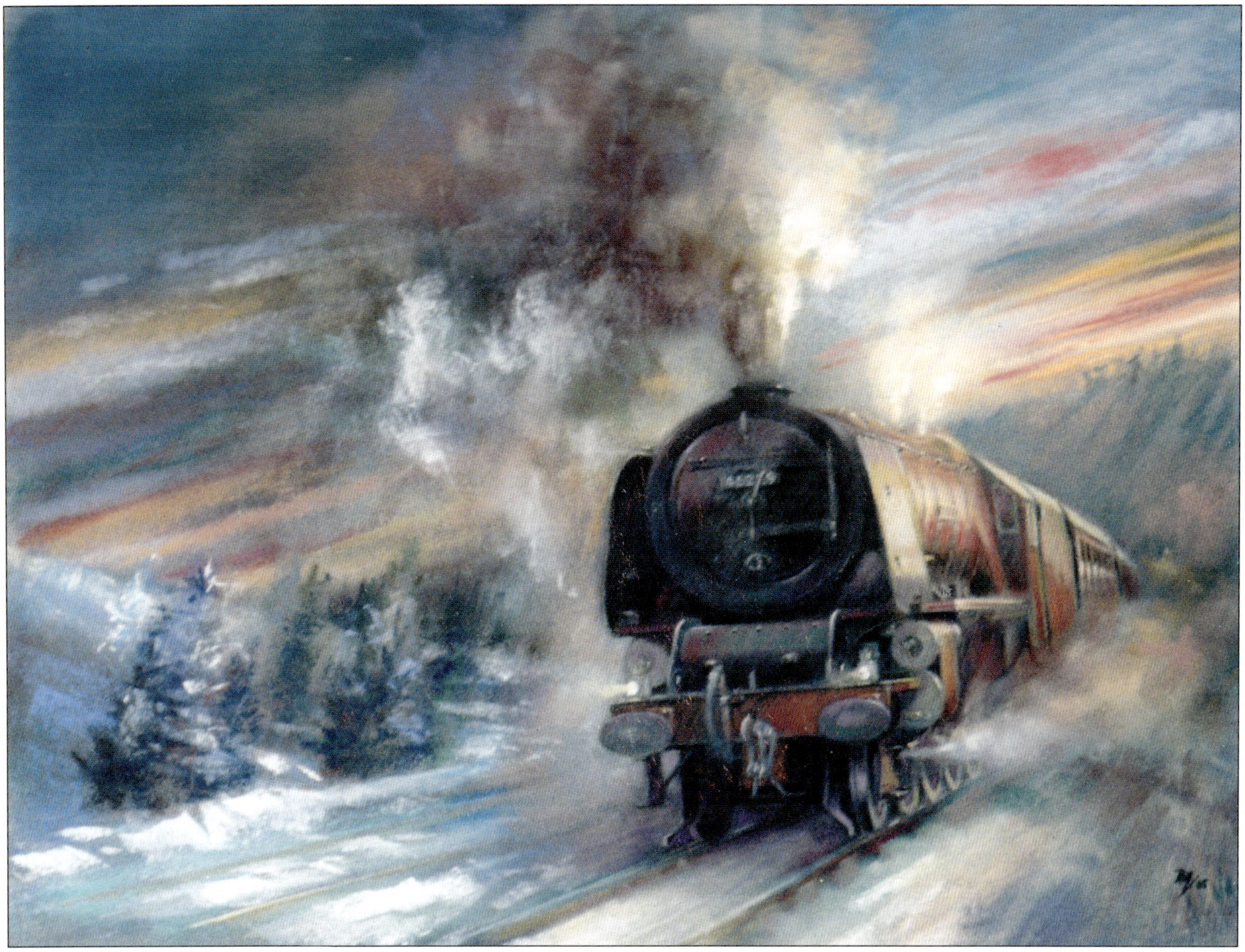

Duchess at Shap.

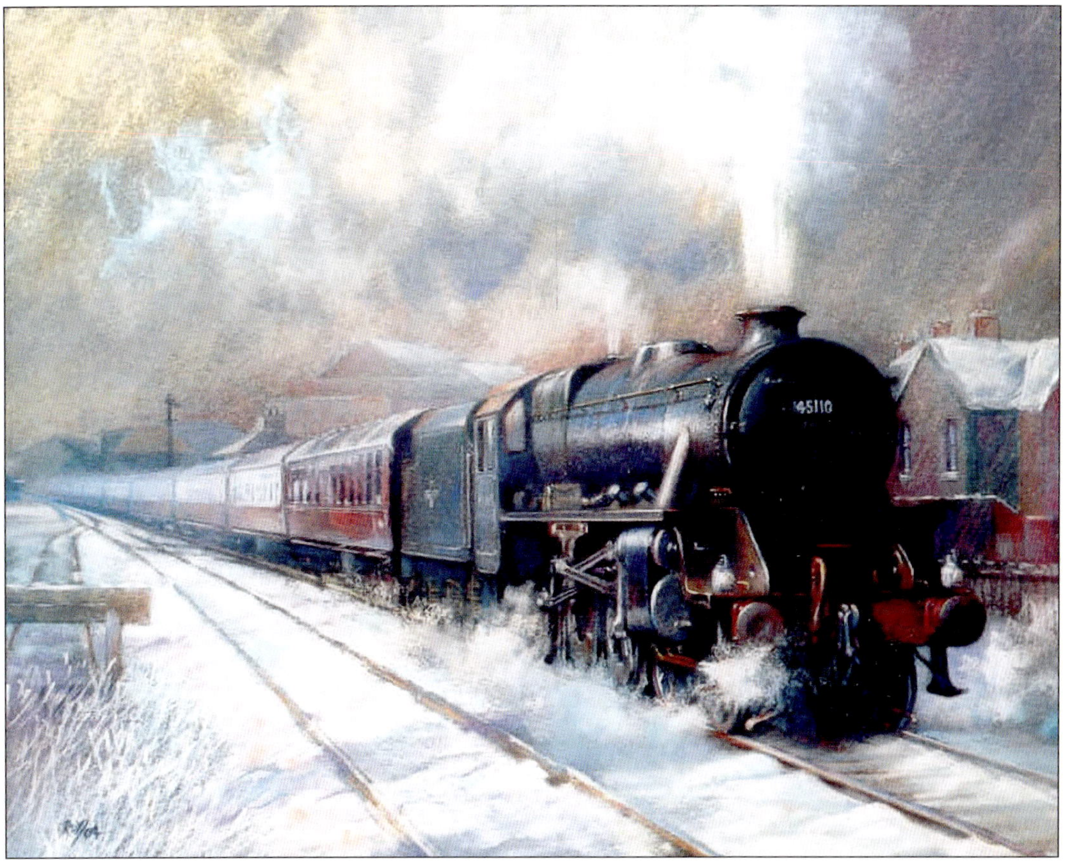

Earlestown Black Five.

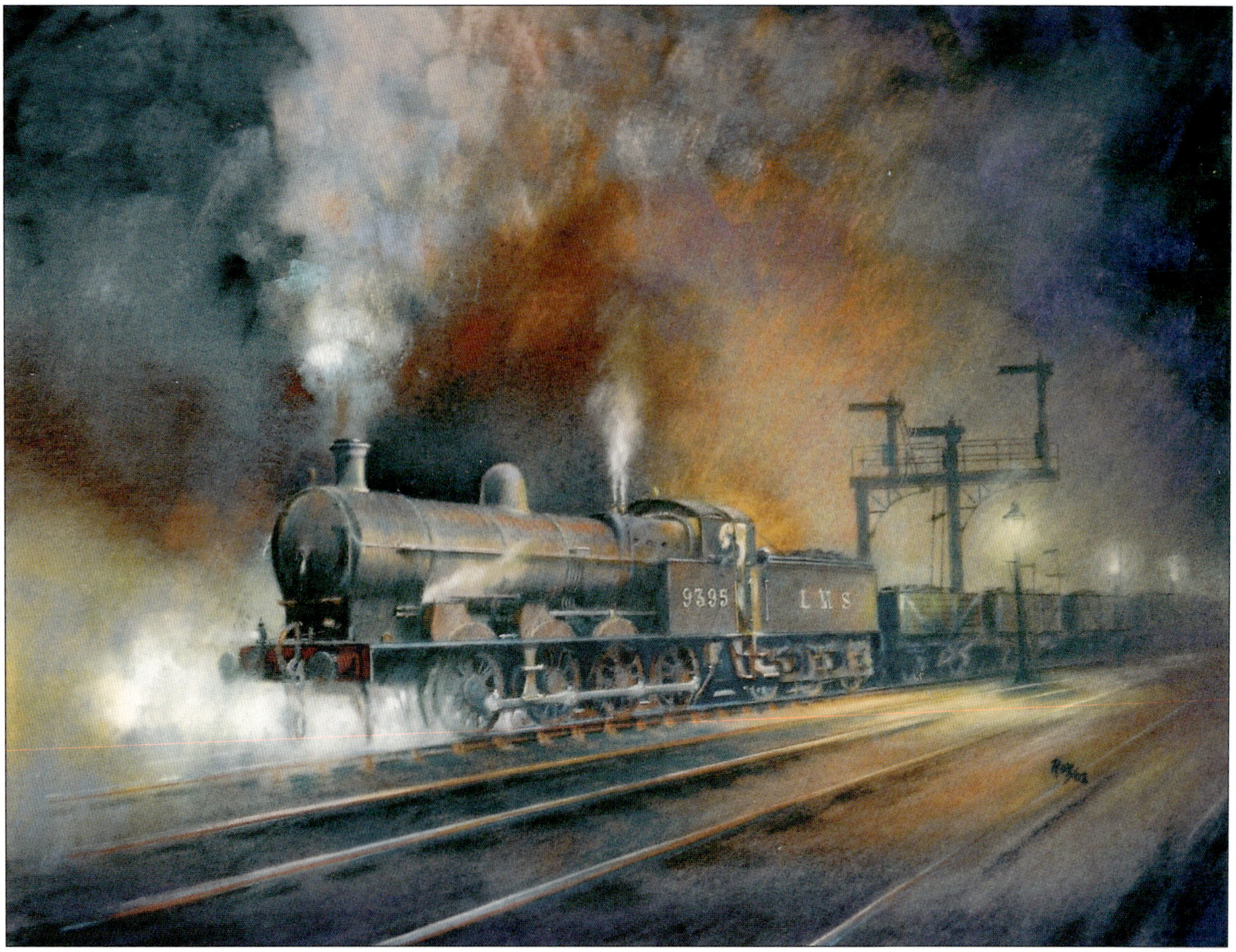

Night goods.

Workshop.

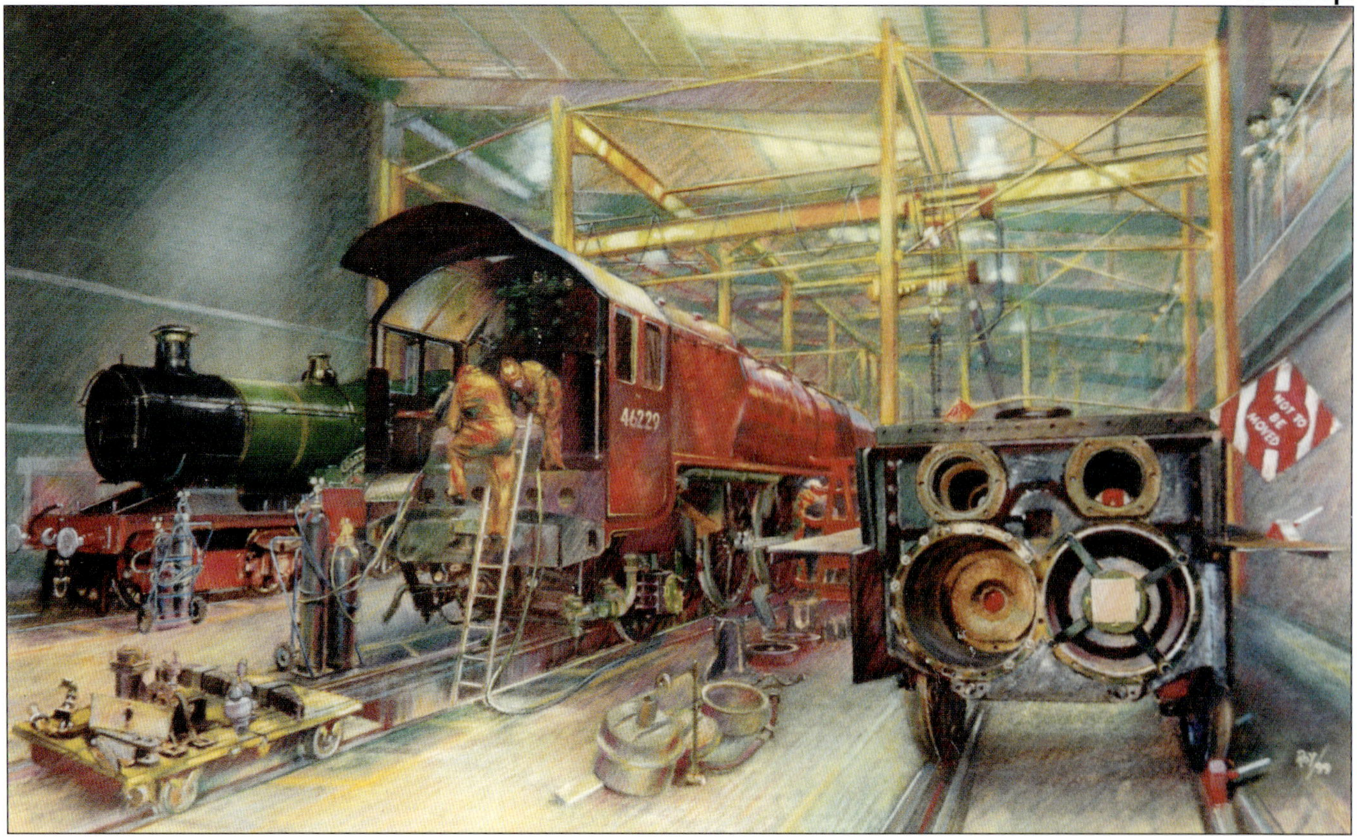

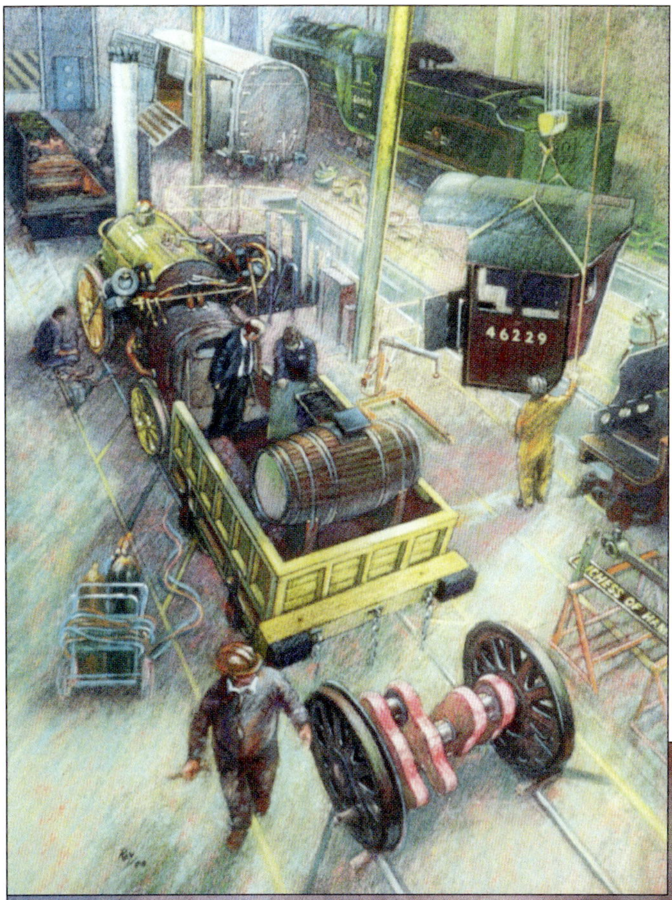

Workshop (Rocket).

Big Bertha – Banking Engine.

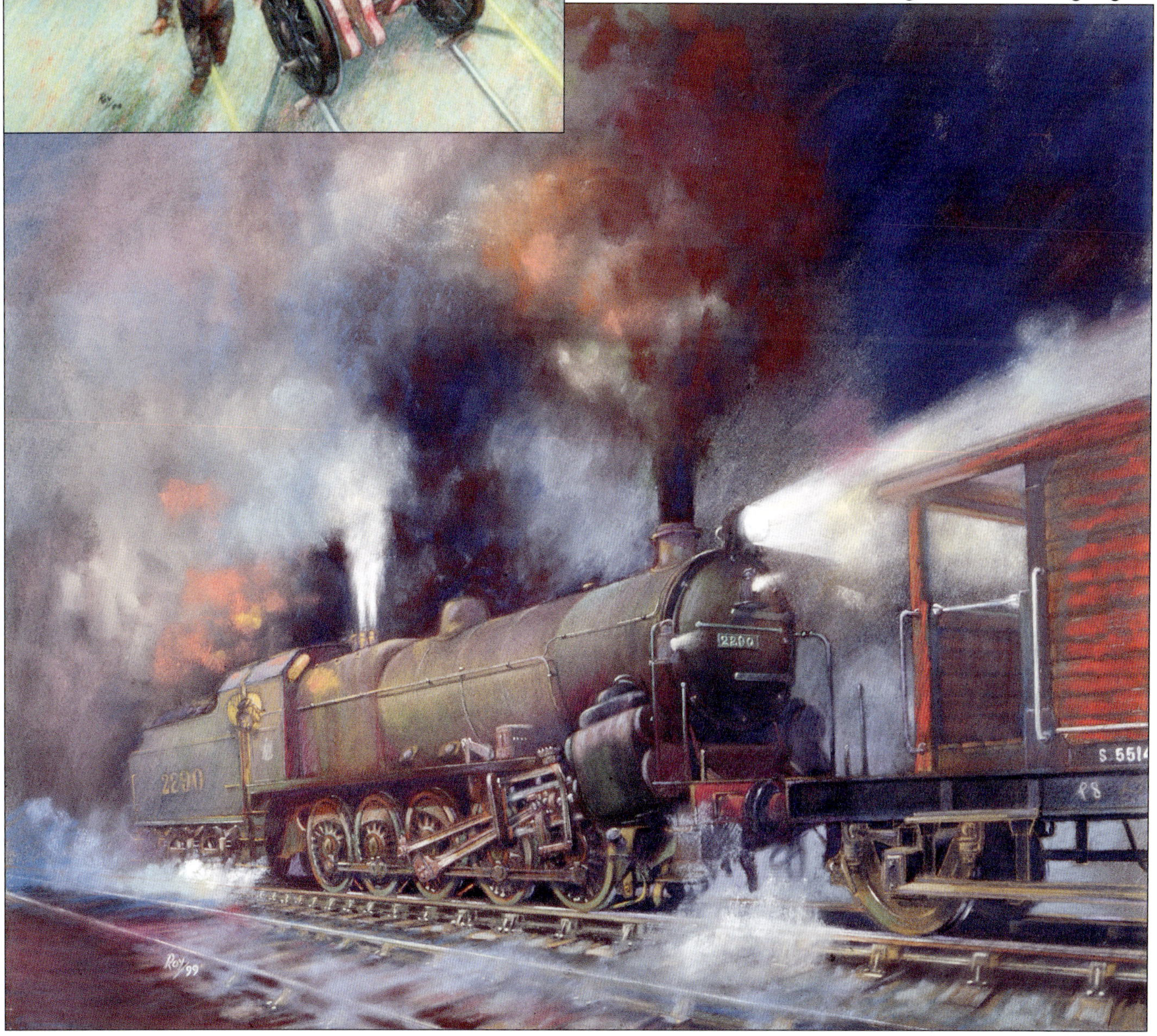

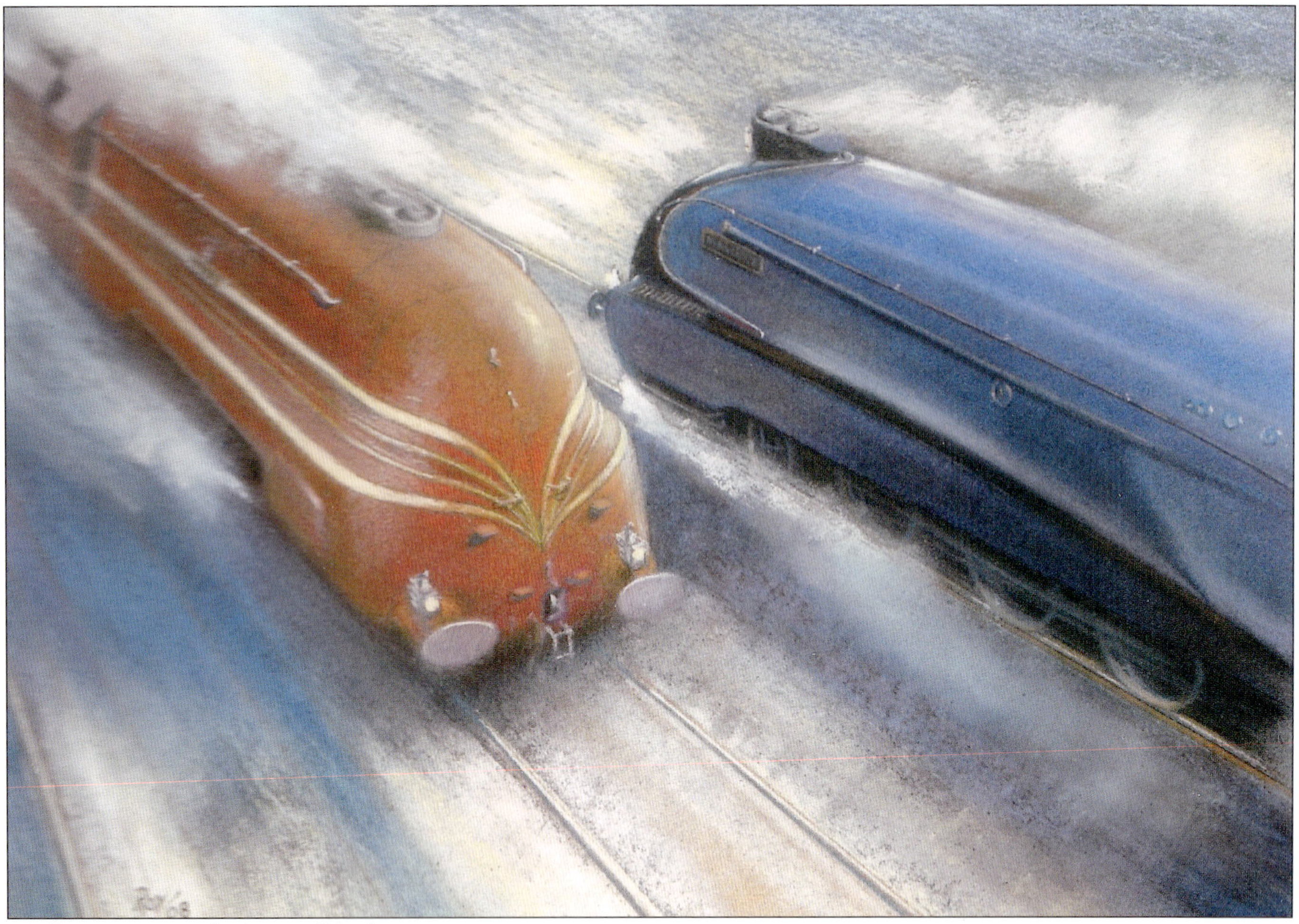

Brief Encounter – the impossible dream.

Still Dreaming.

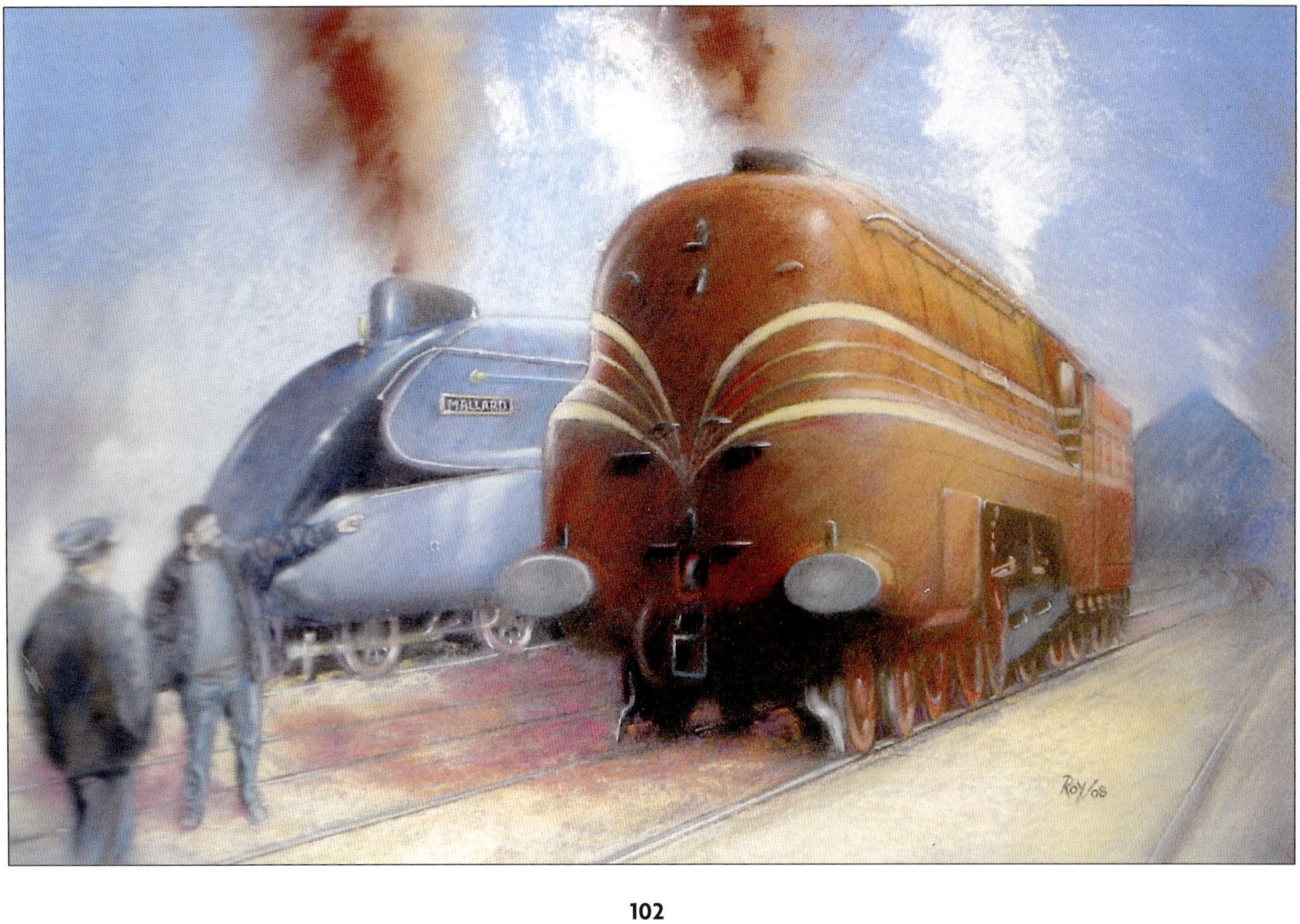

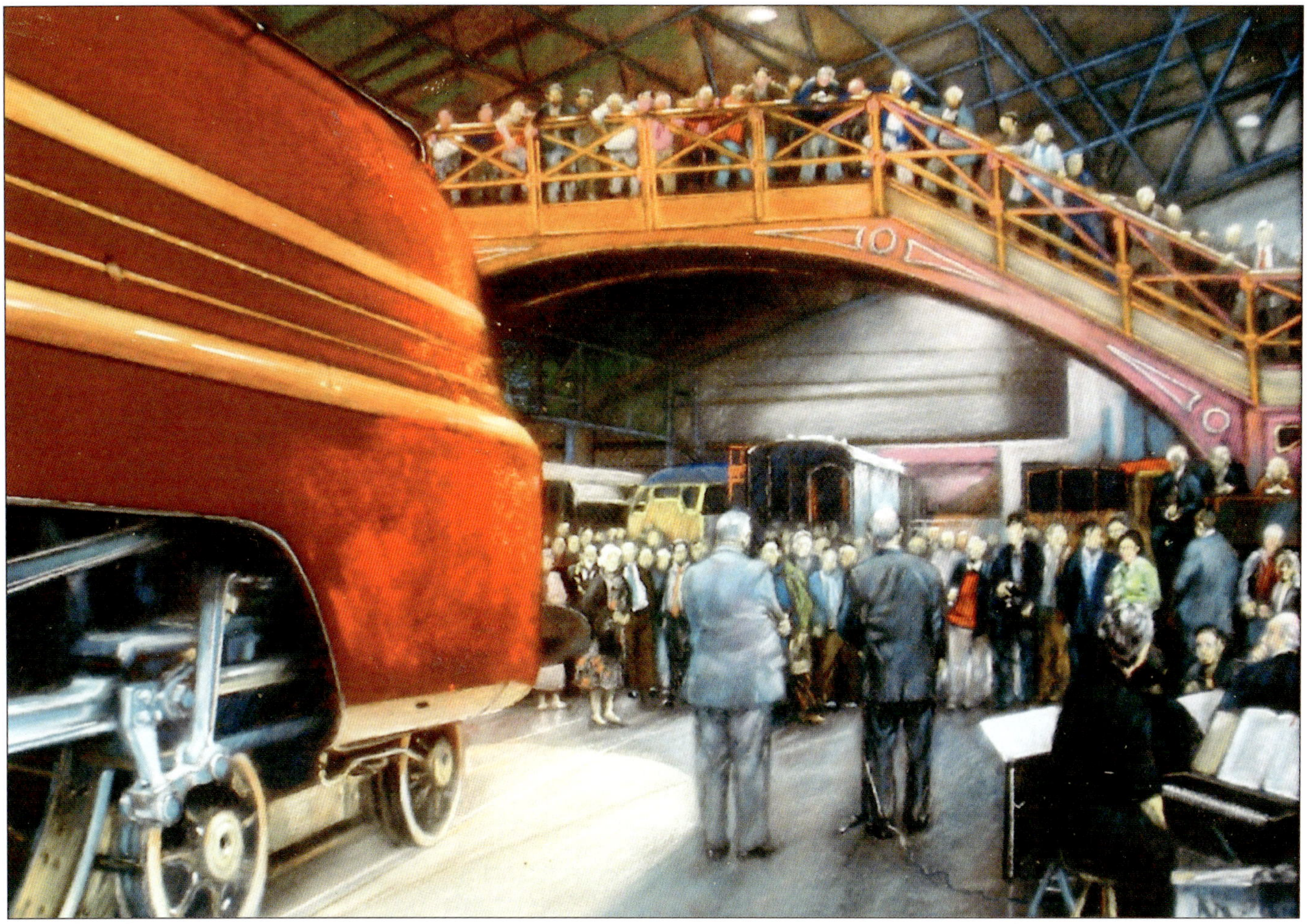

Arrival at the NRM.

Flying Scotsman at NRM.

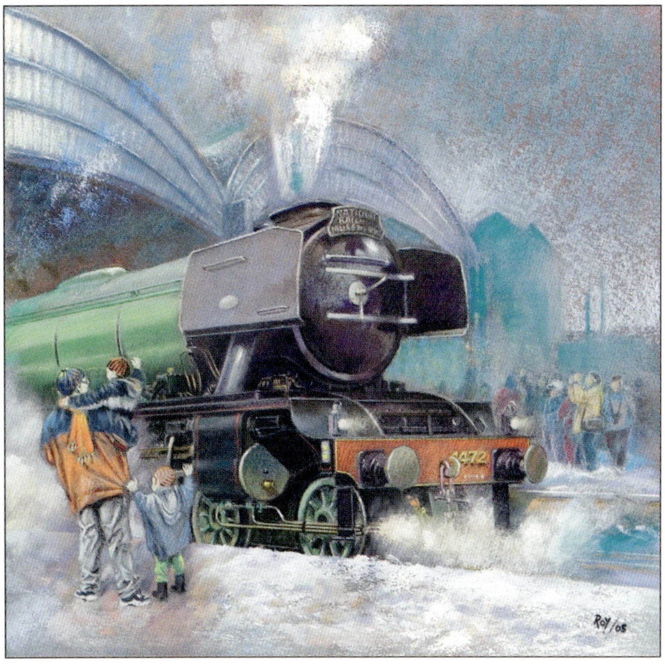

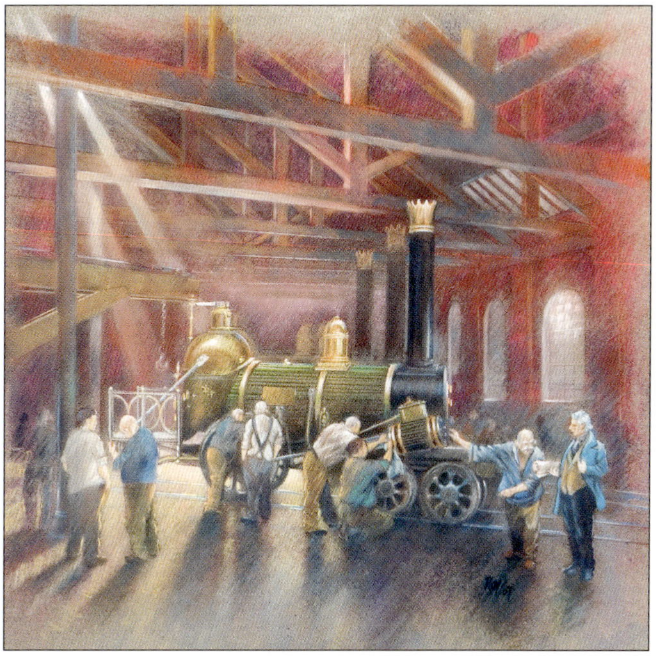

"Austria" – inspection.

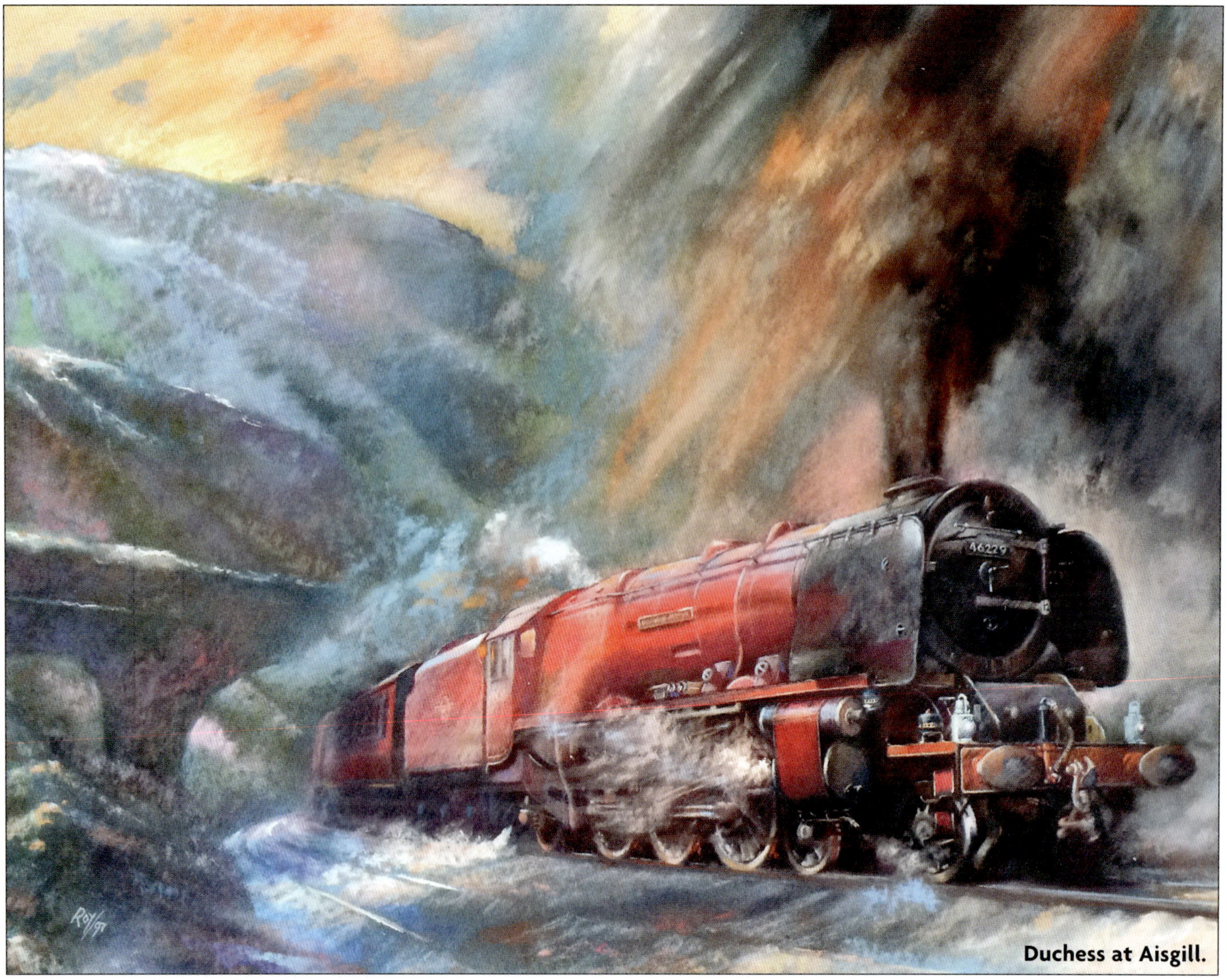
Duchess at Aisgill.

Banker approaching Lickey.

An afternoon outing by the railway.

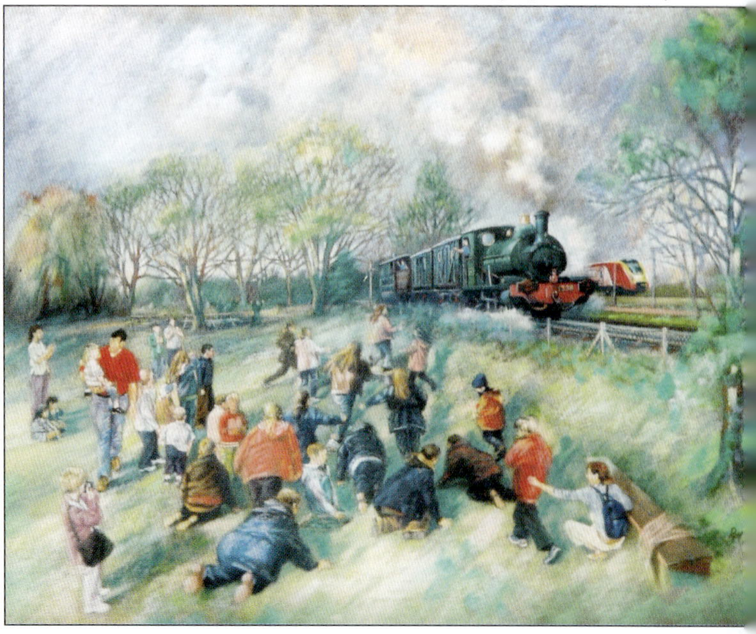

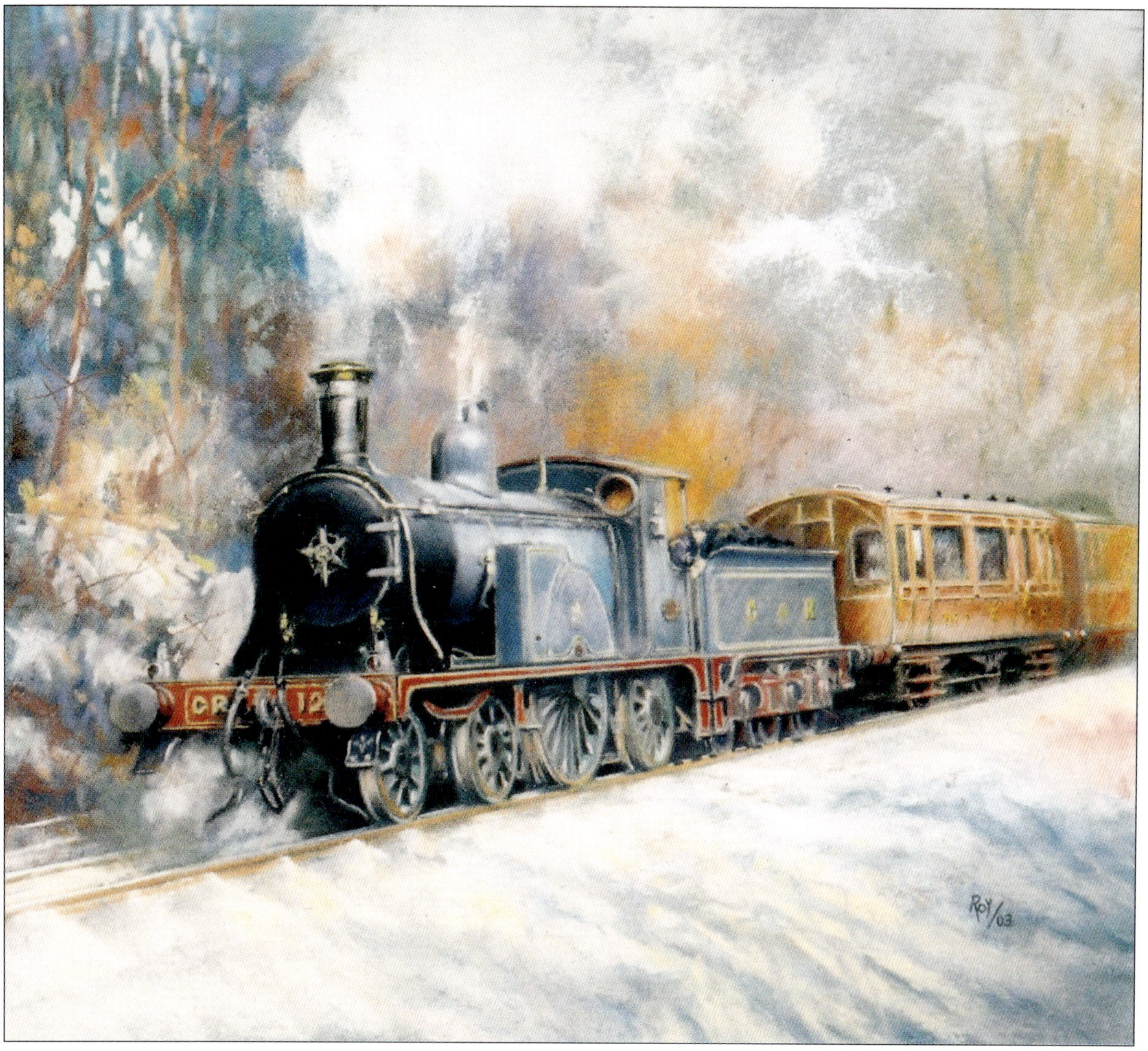

Caledonian Railways 4-4-2.

Driver Arthur.

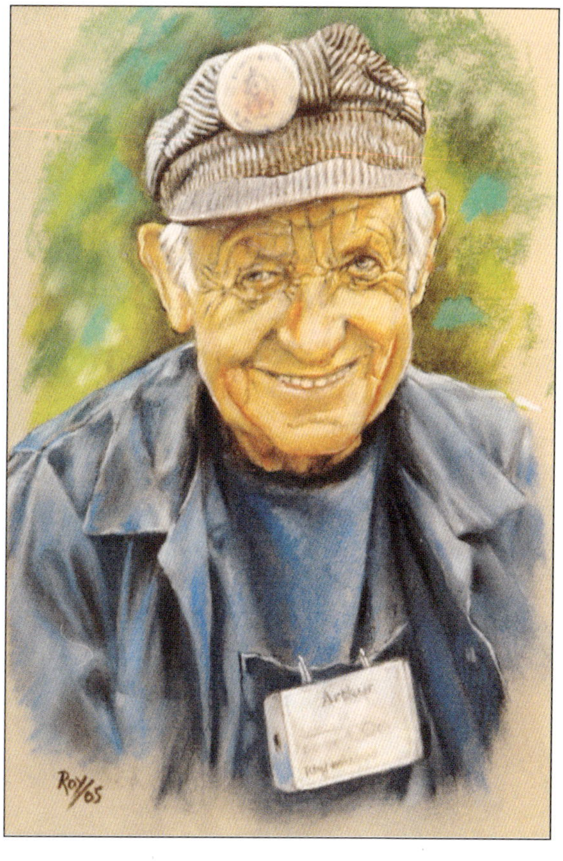

Driver Frank.

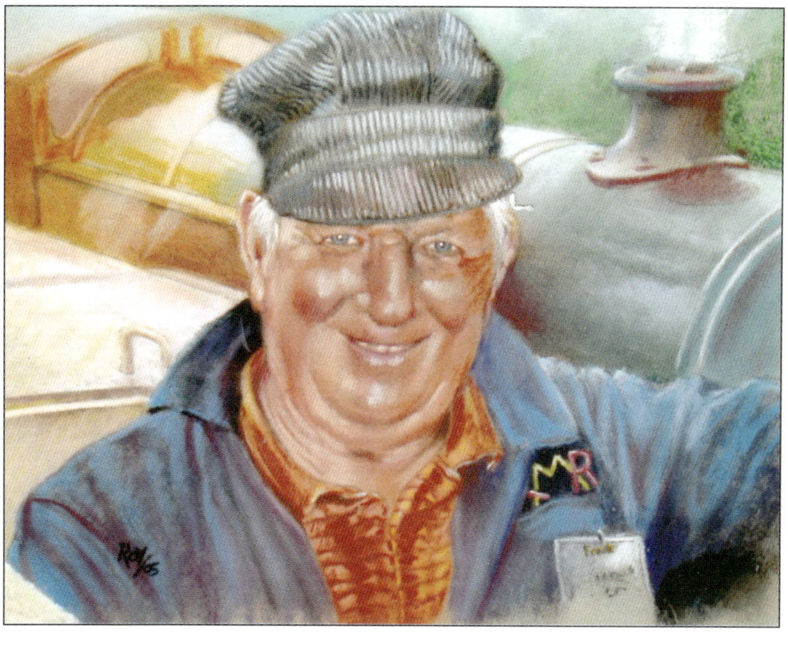

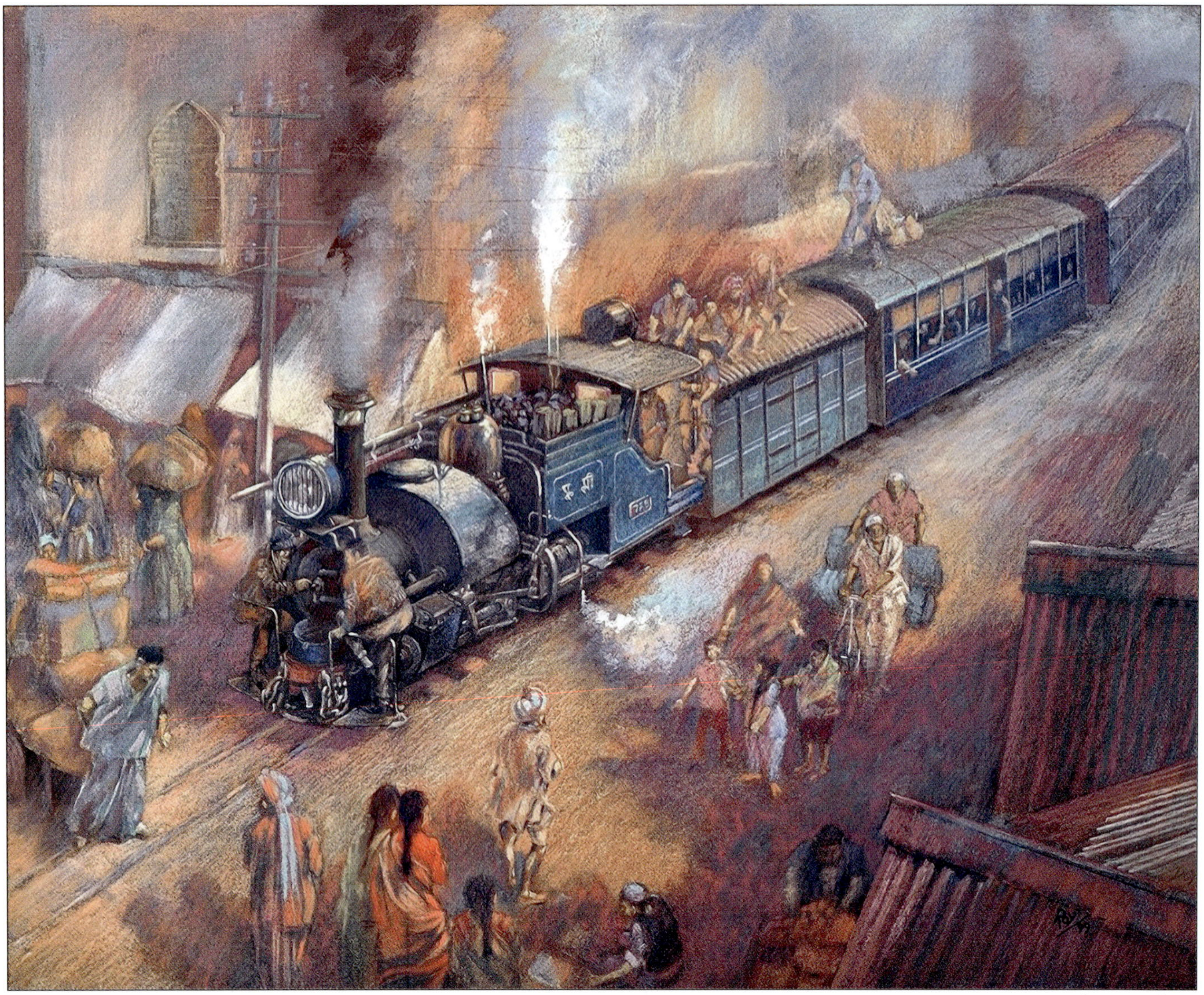

Darjeeling tanker.

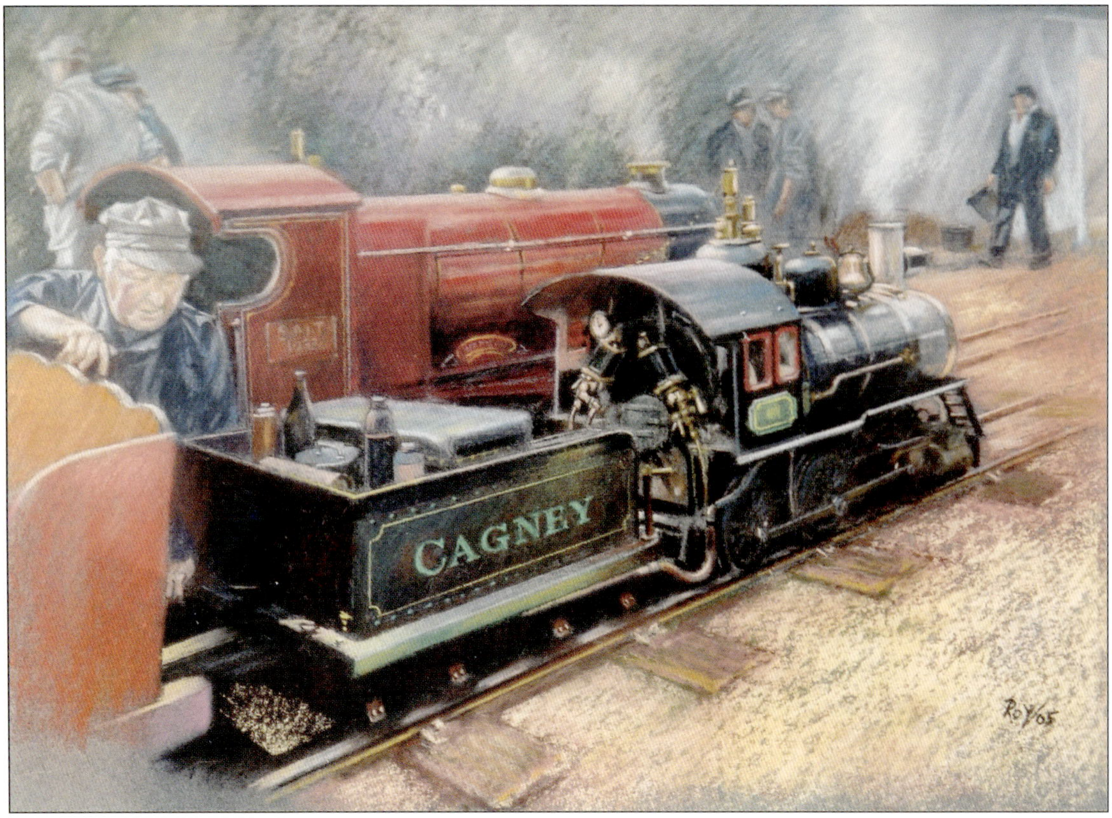

Small scale at NRM.

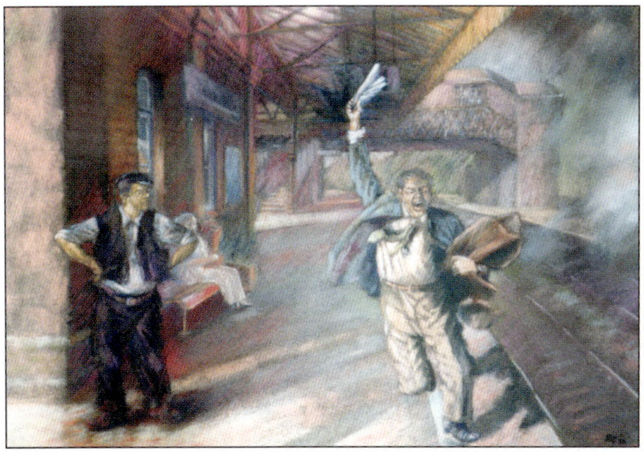

Missed the train!

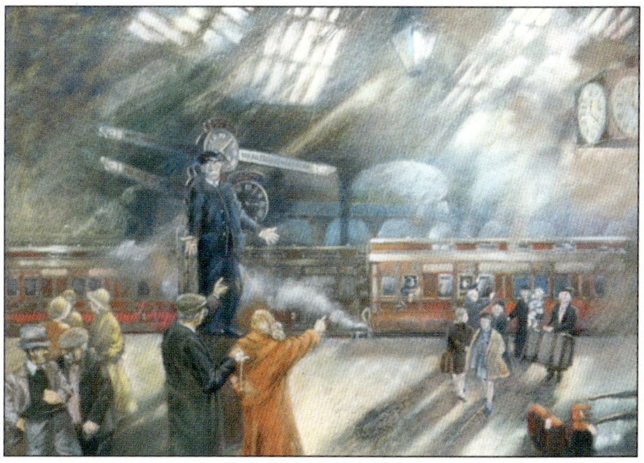

The controls.

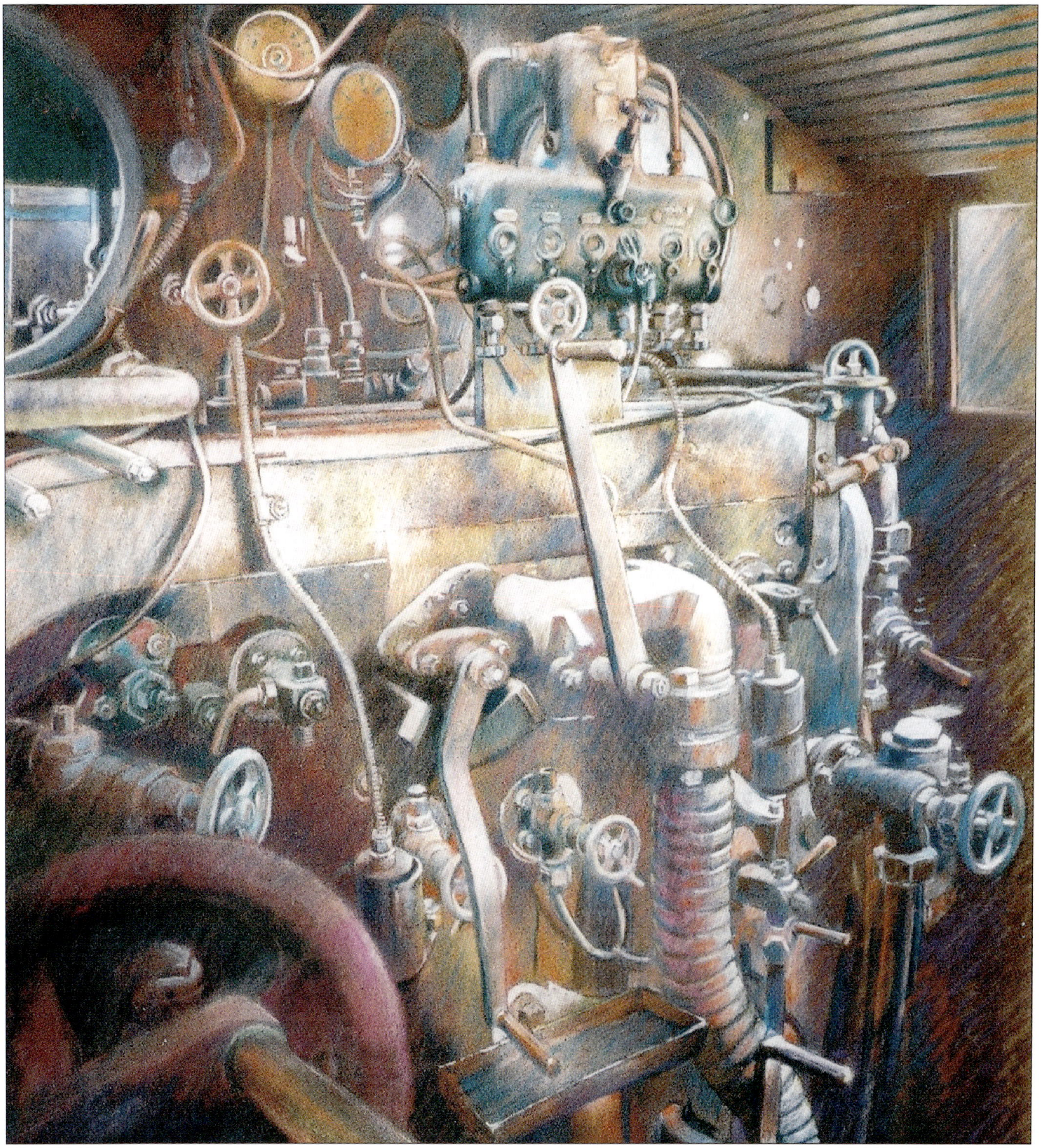

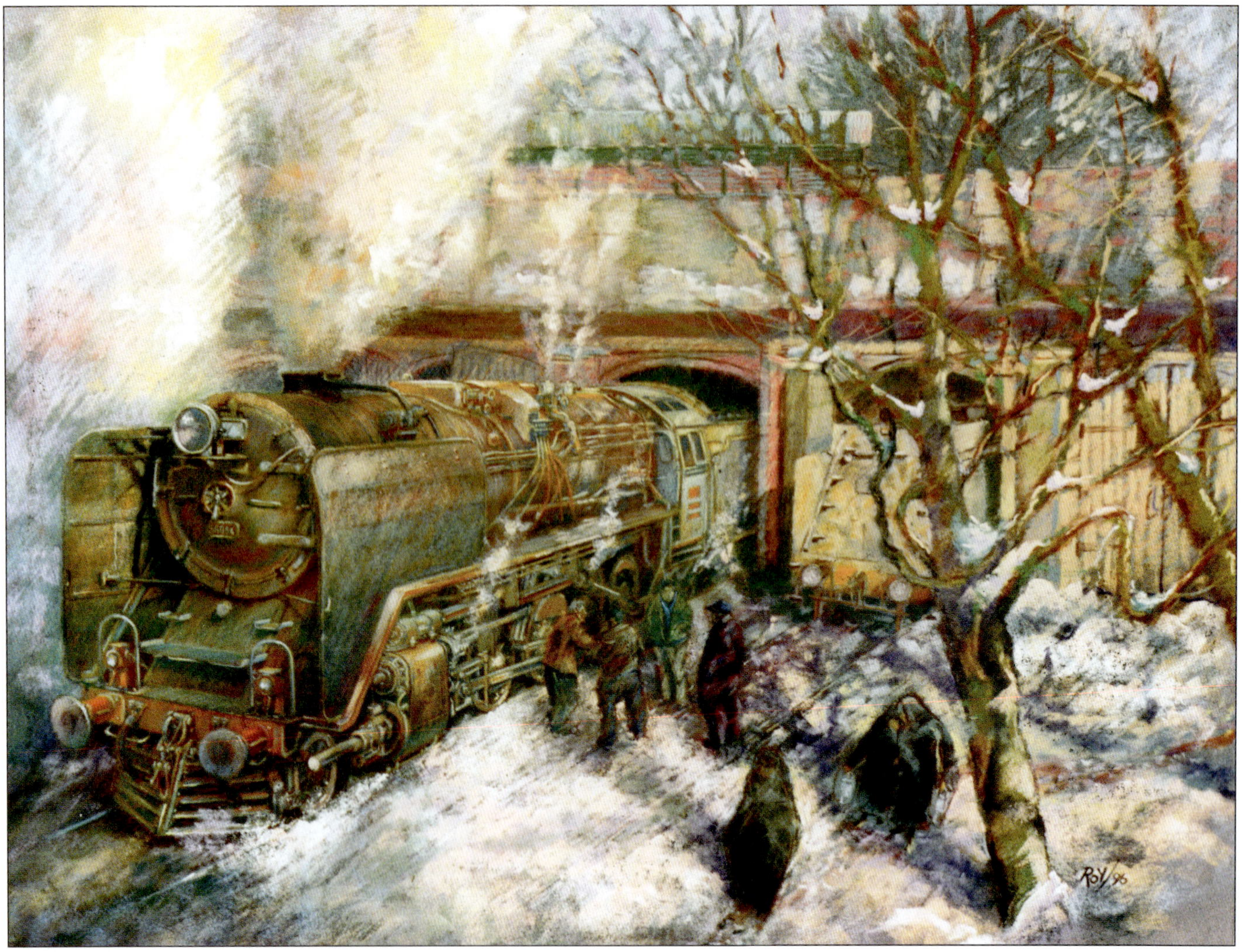

Konya sheds, Turkey 1980s.

"Coppernob" Ramsden Dock, Barrow-in-Furness. Historical reconstruction.

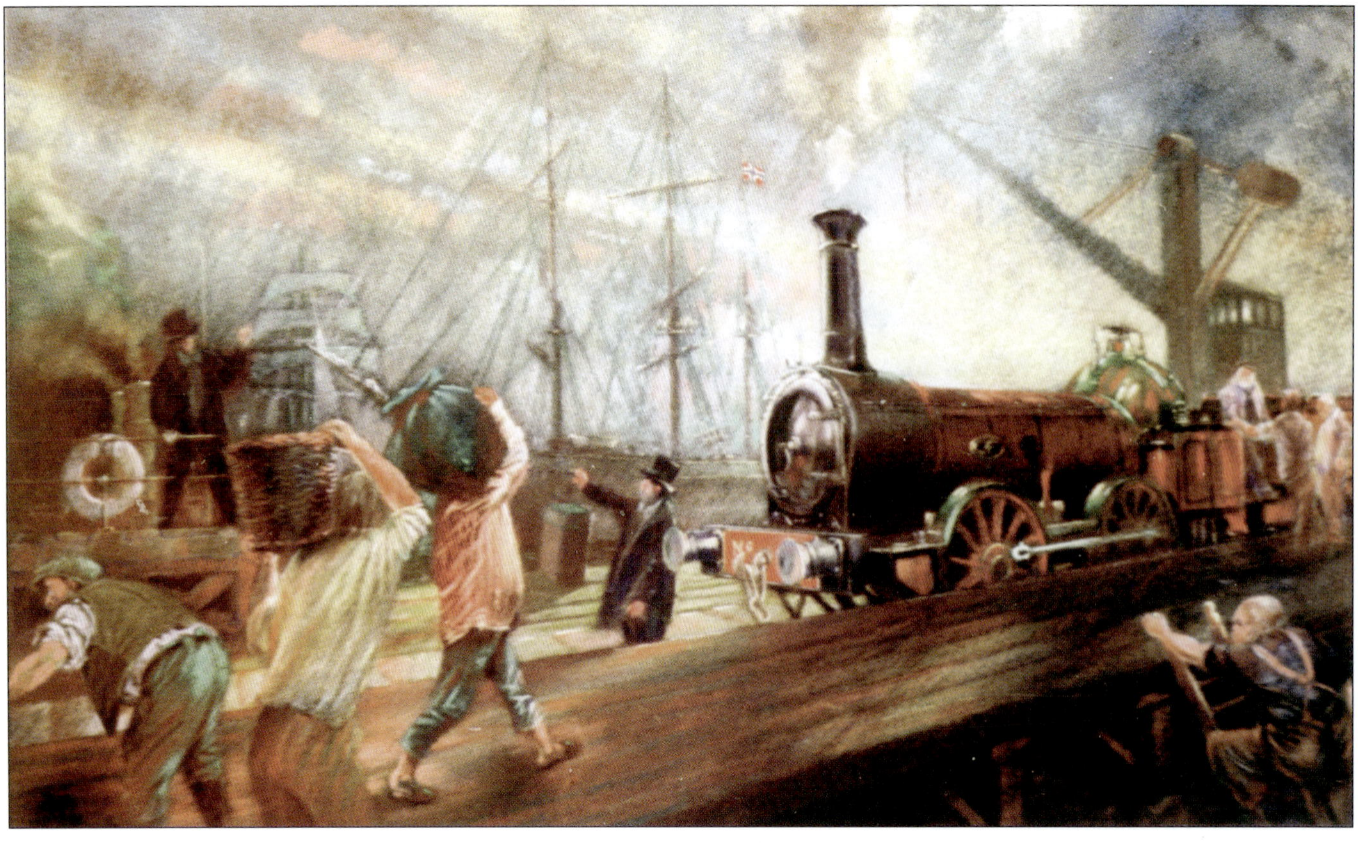

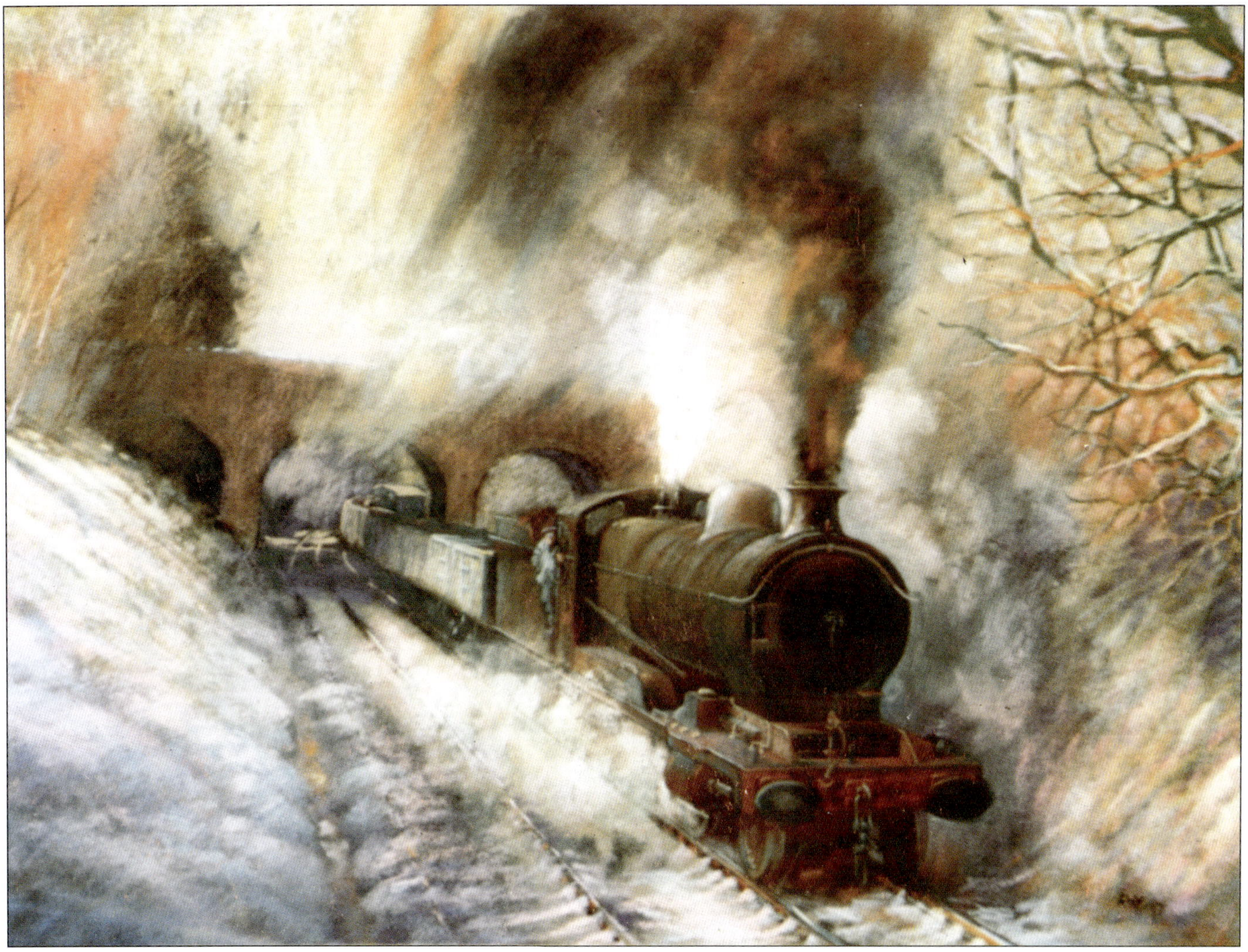

Robinson freight.

Chinese 4-8-4 class in operation.

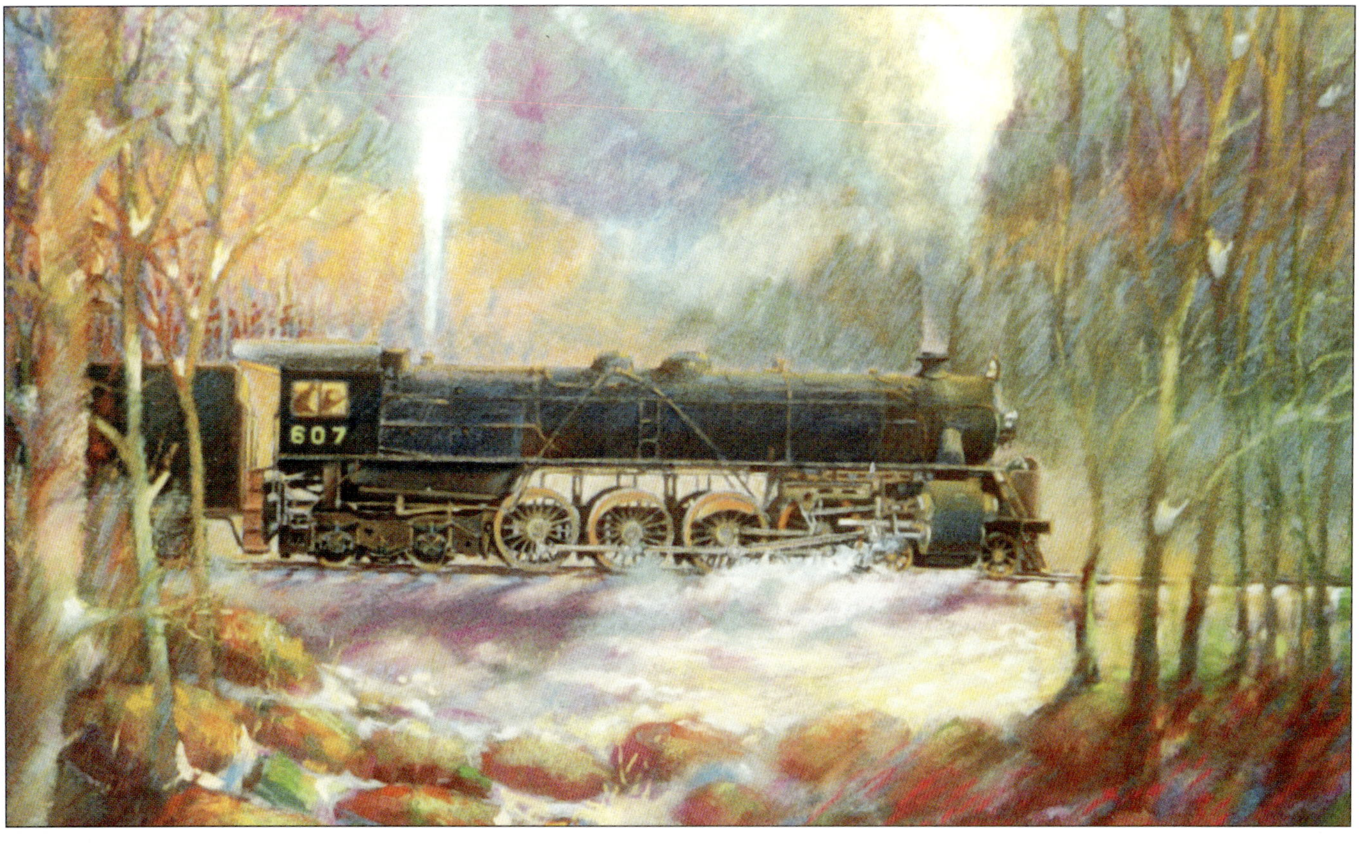

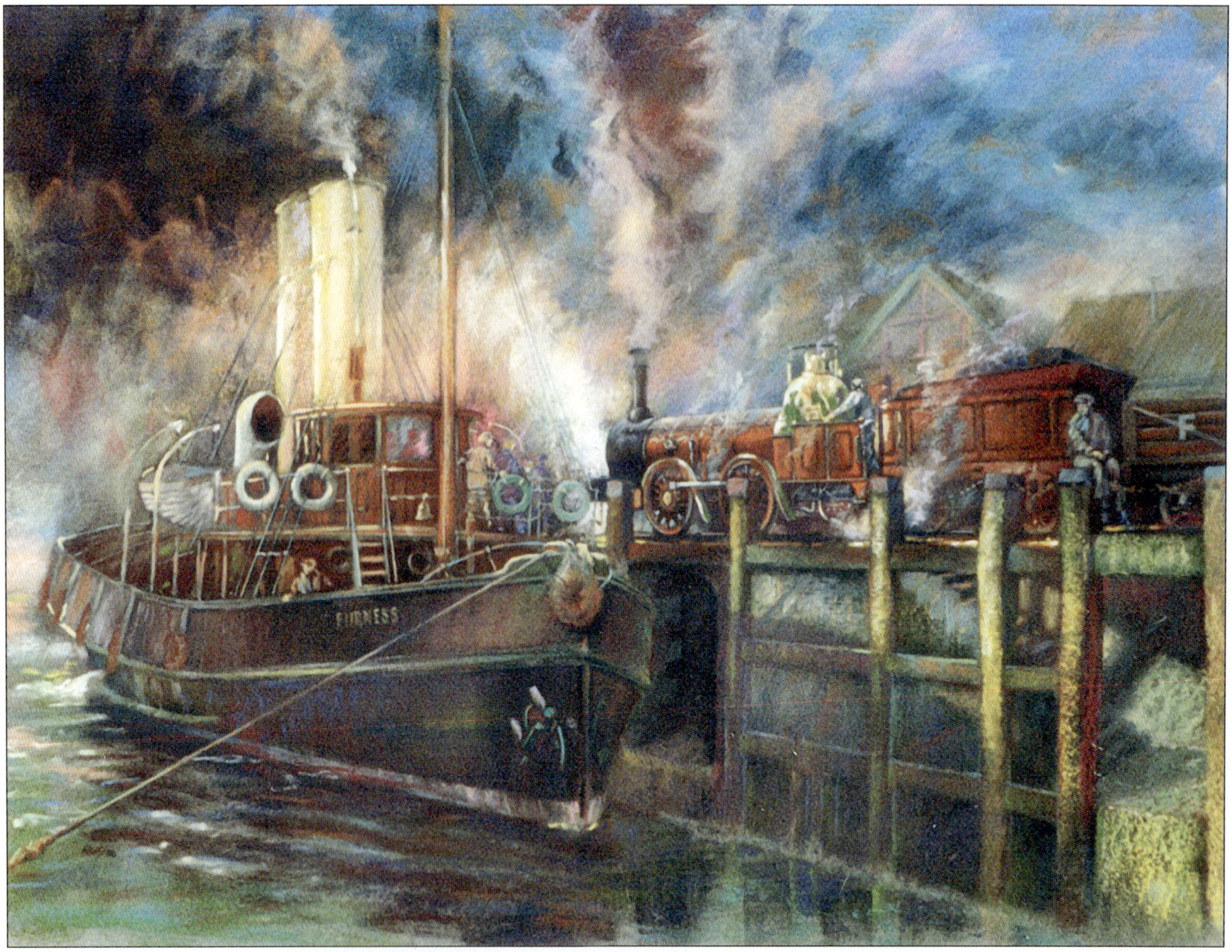

"Coppernob"
Ramsden Dock,
Barrow, 1896.

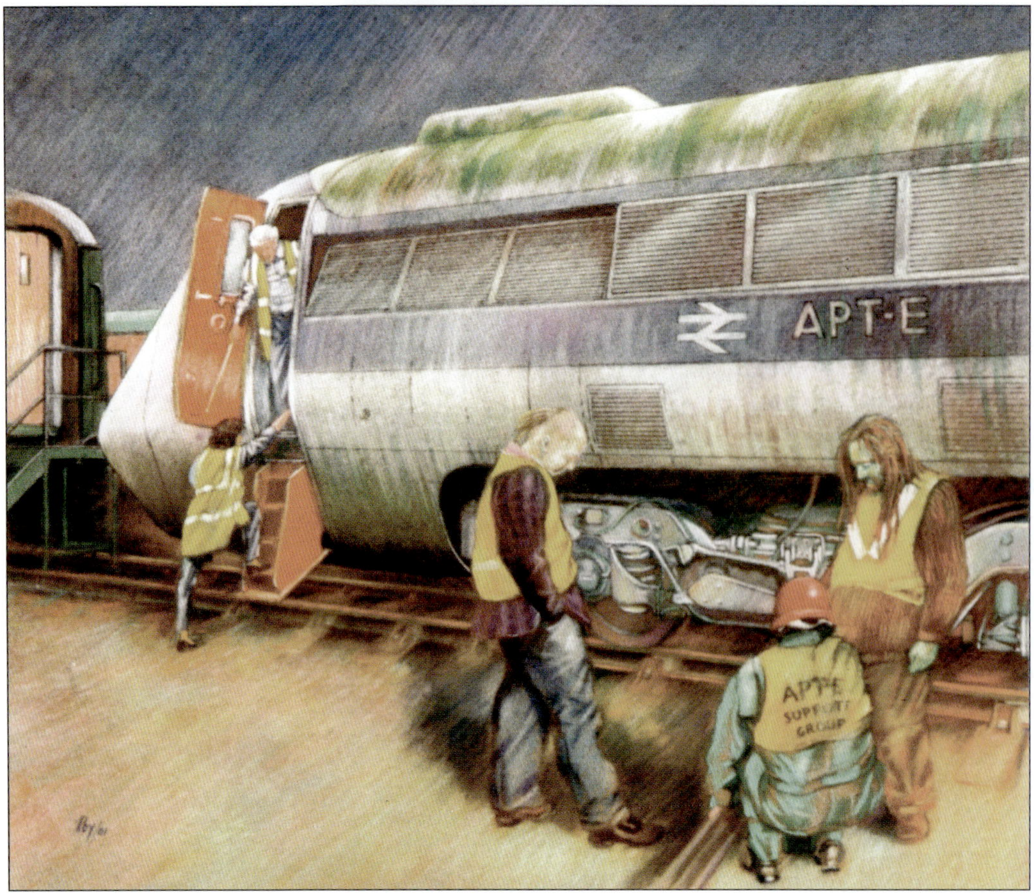

APT and workers.

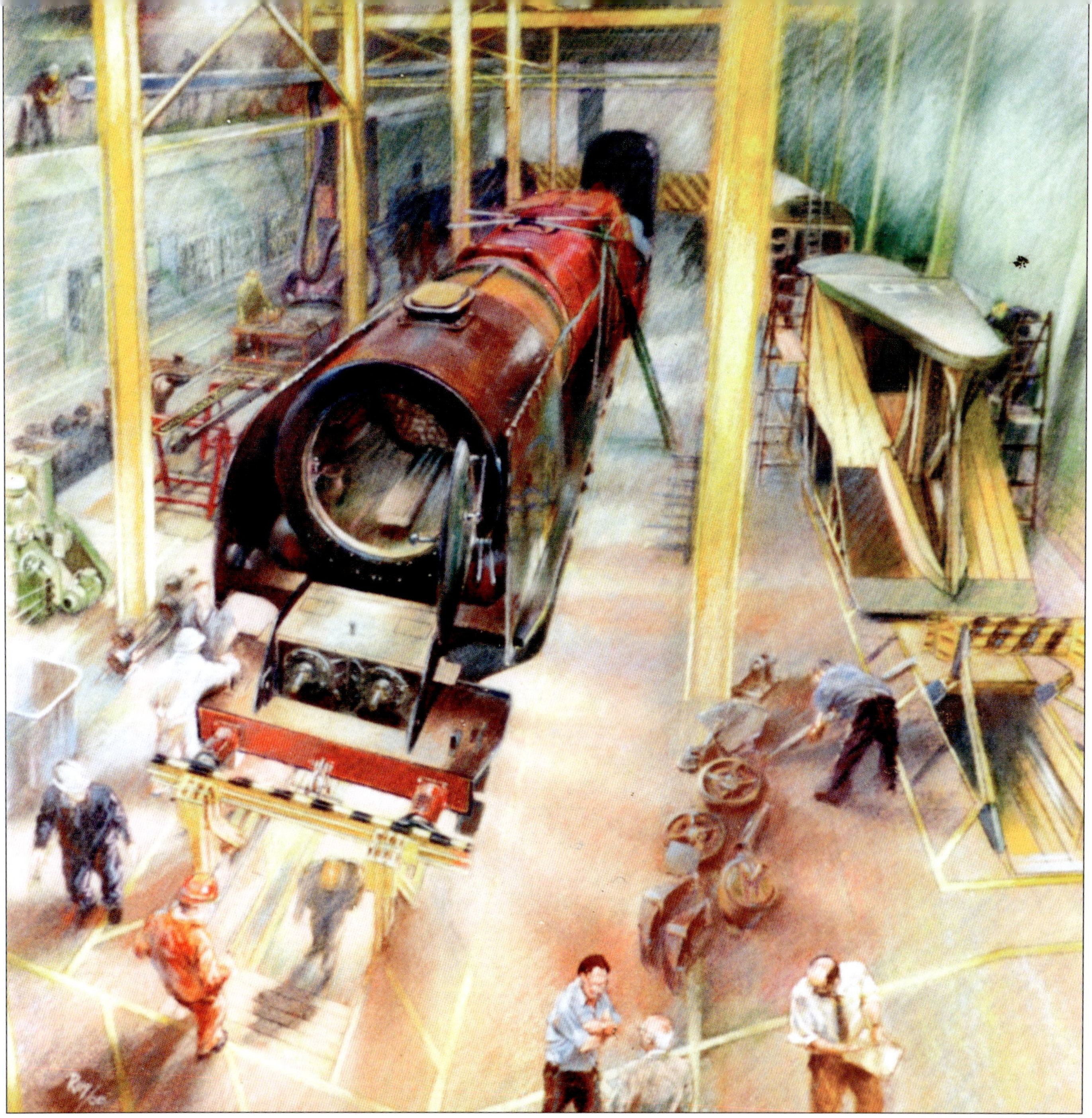

National Railway Museum, York. The new workshop restoration of "Duchess of Hamilton" and rebuilding the NER 1891 Snowplough No. 12.

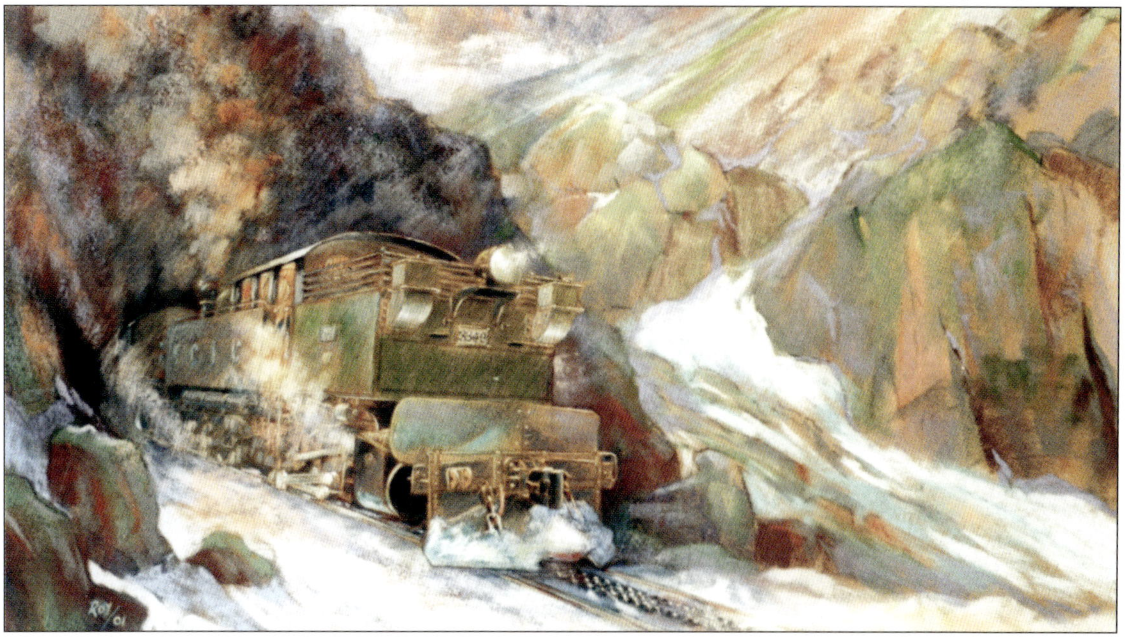

Chilean Transandine Railroad, Kitson-Meyer adhesion rack locomotive, built Leeds 1909.

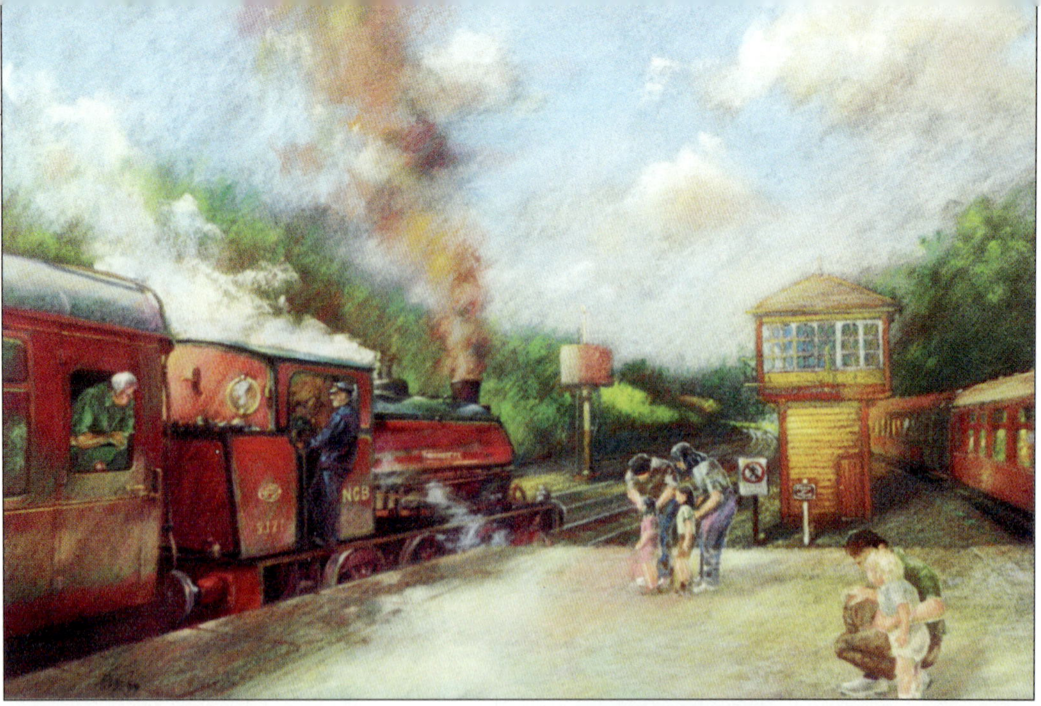

Embsay Railway, Skipton.

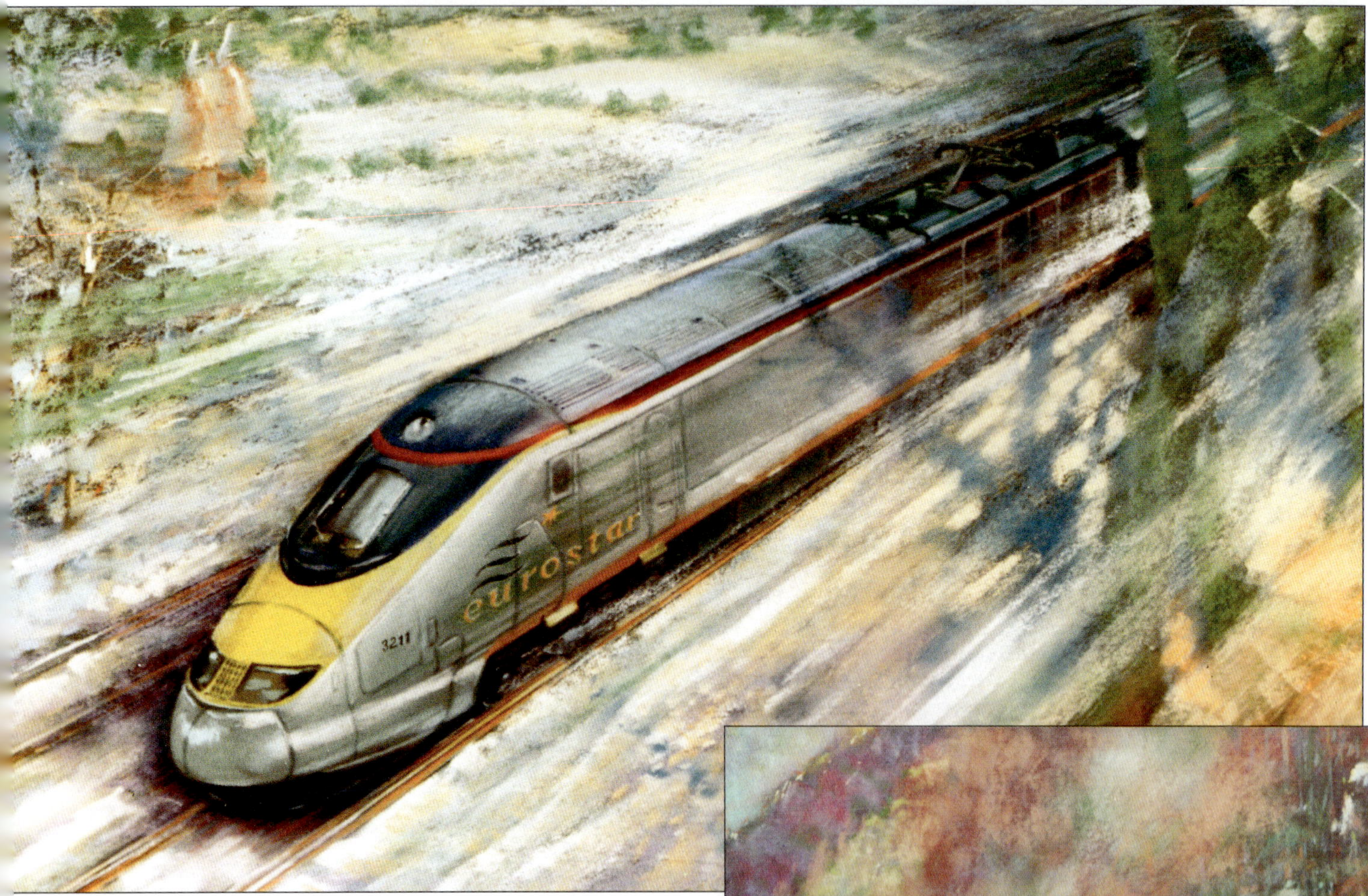

Eurostar.

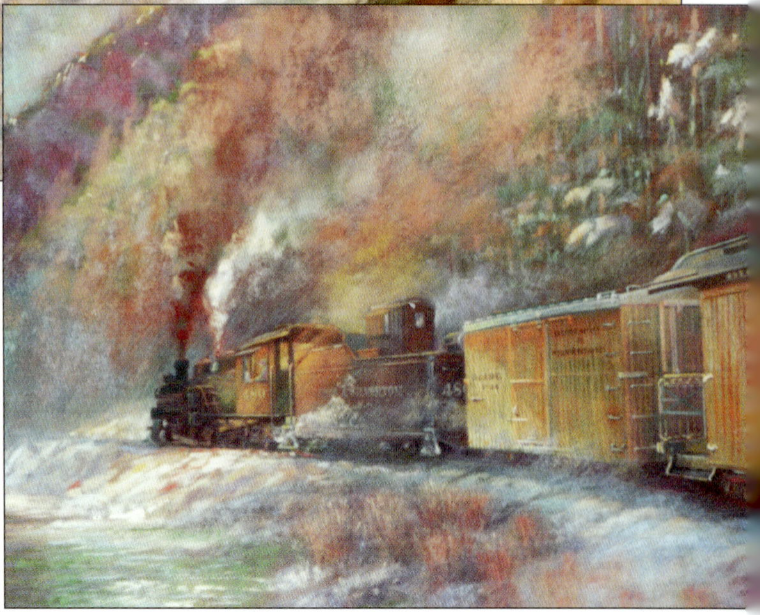

Chile and Colorado.

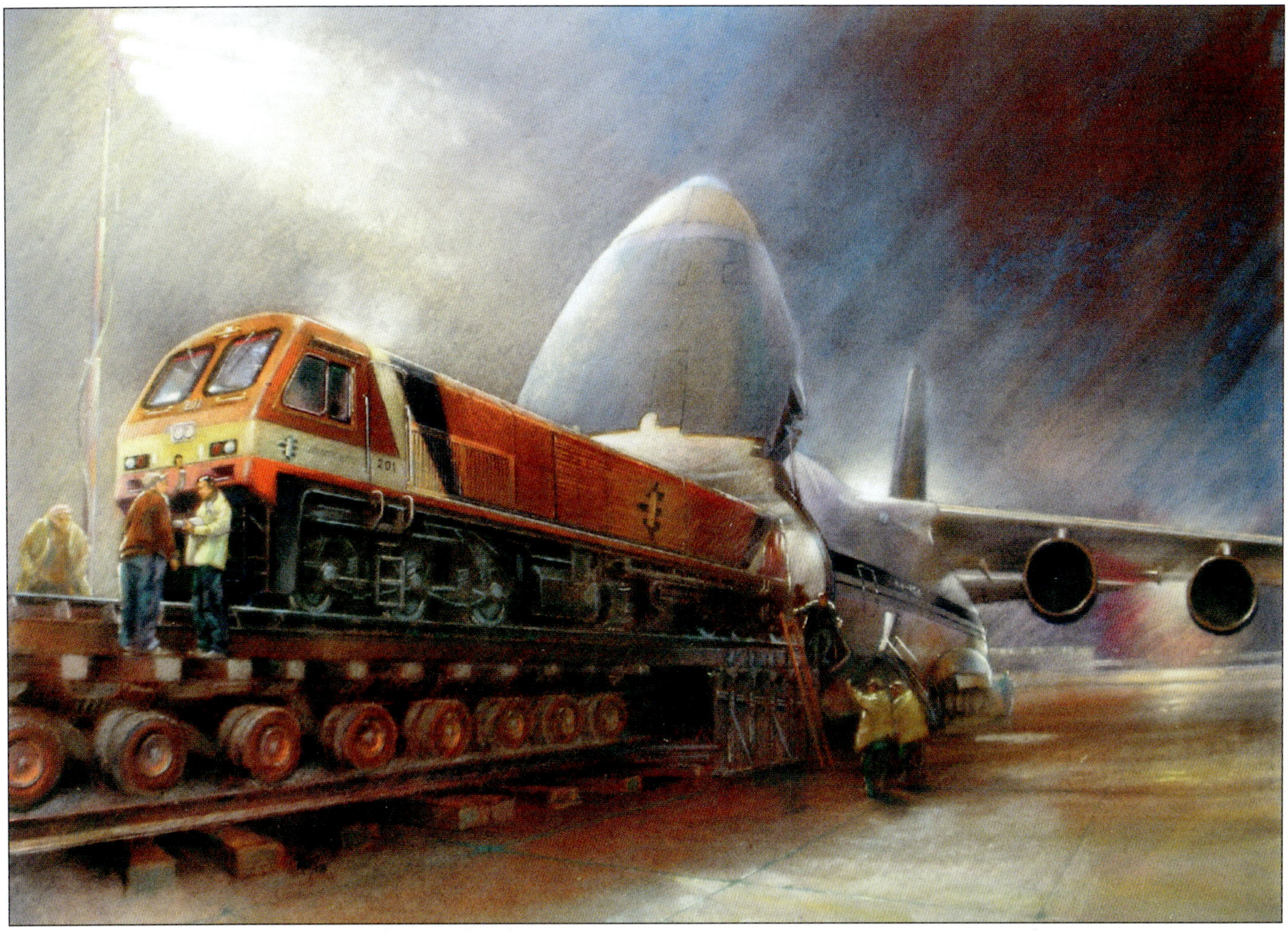

Delivery by air, Condor from Canada to Ireland.

Durango Silverton Railroad, Colorado, U.S.A.

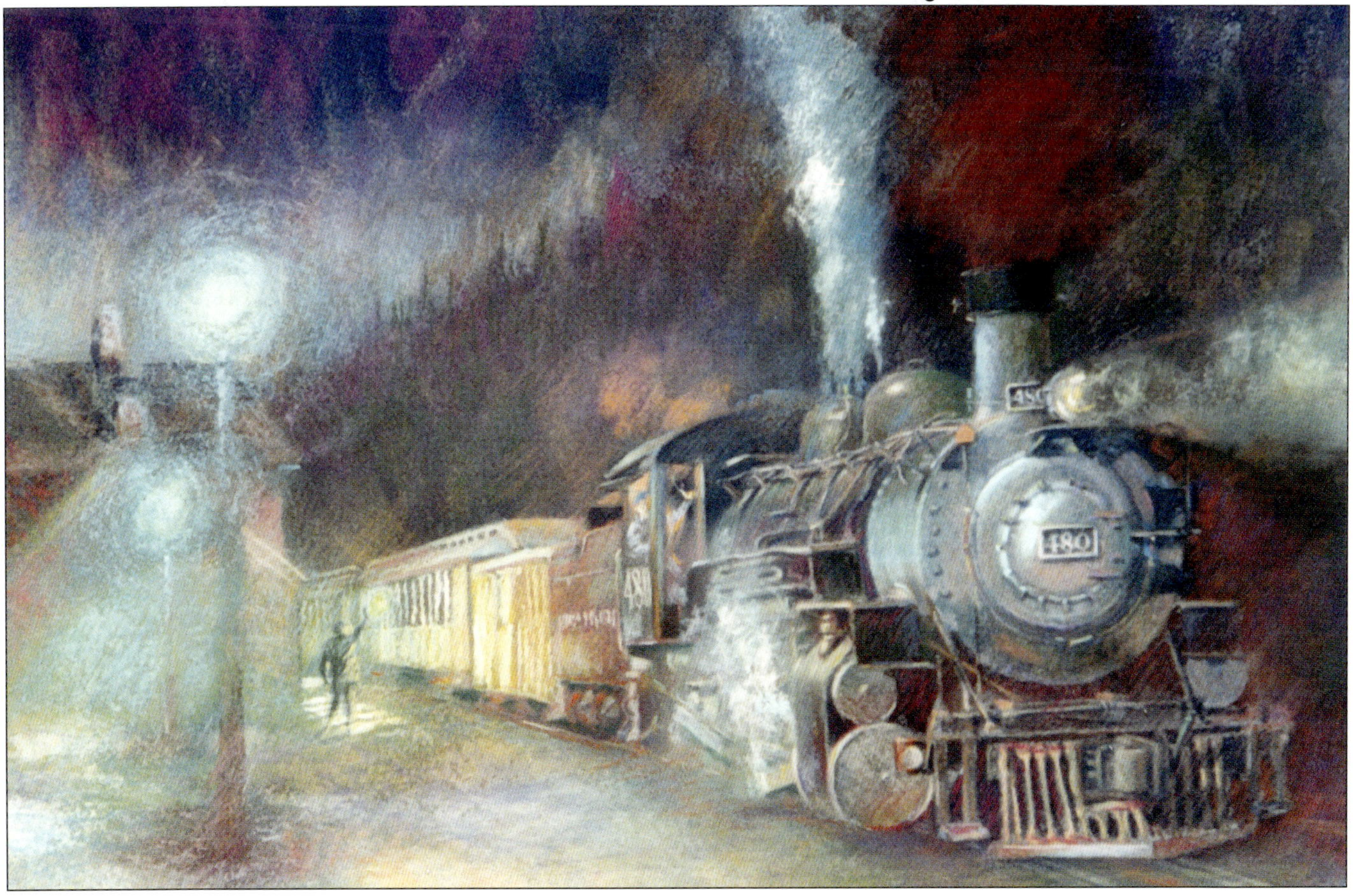

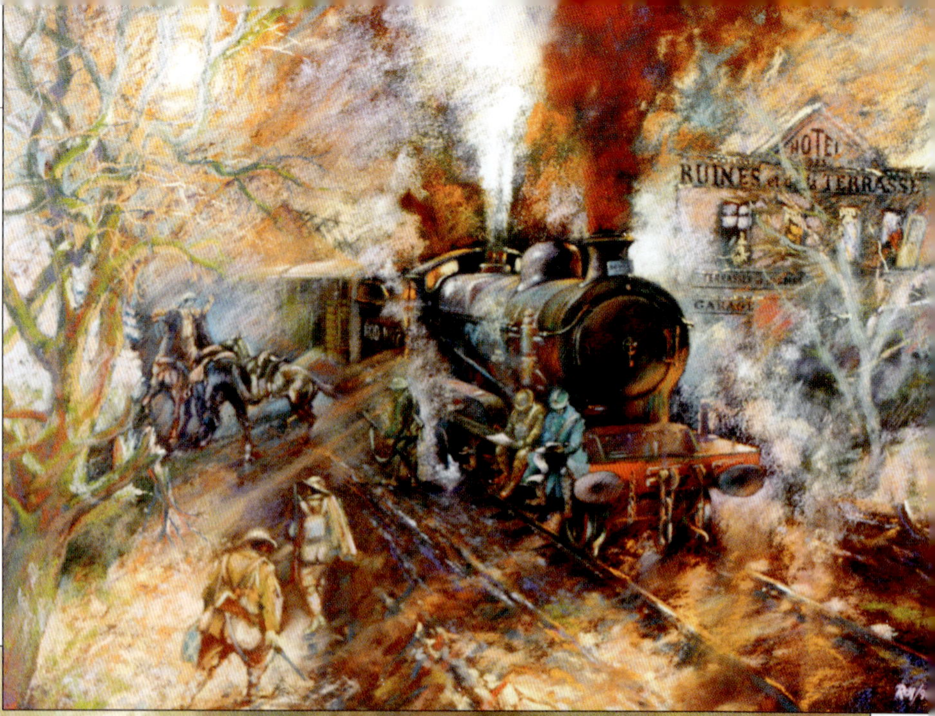

Robinson at war.

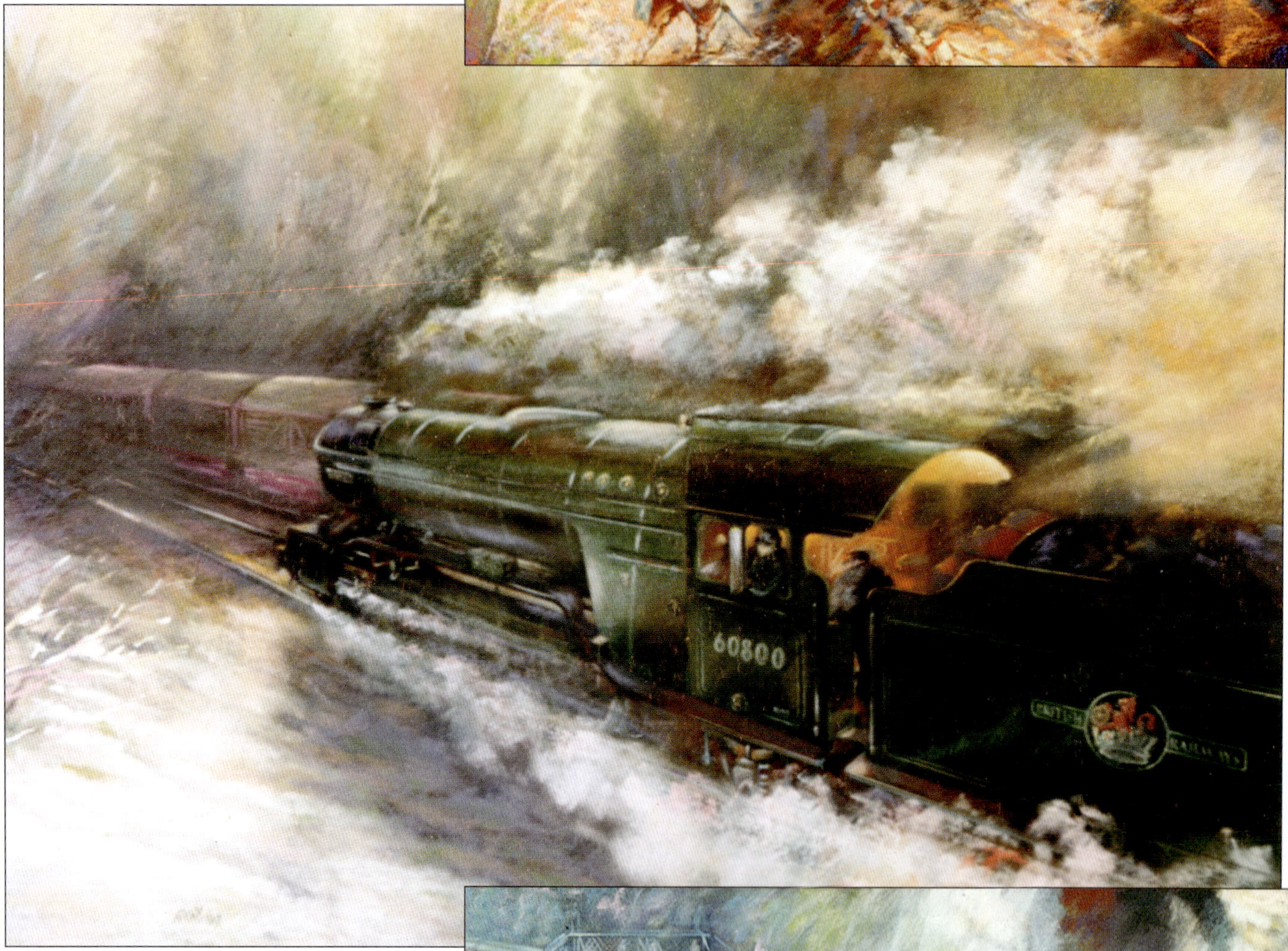

Green Arrow at speed.

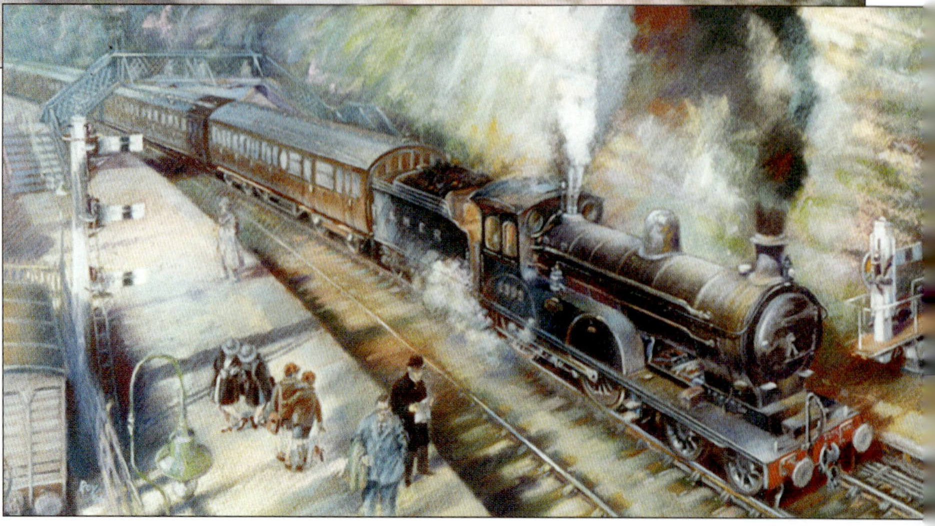

Wetherby Station.

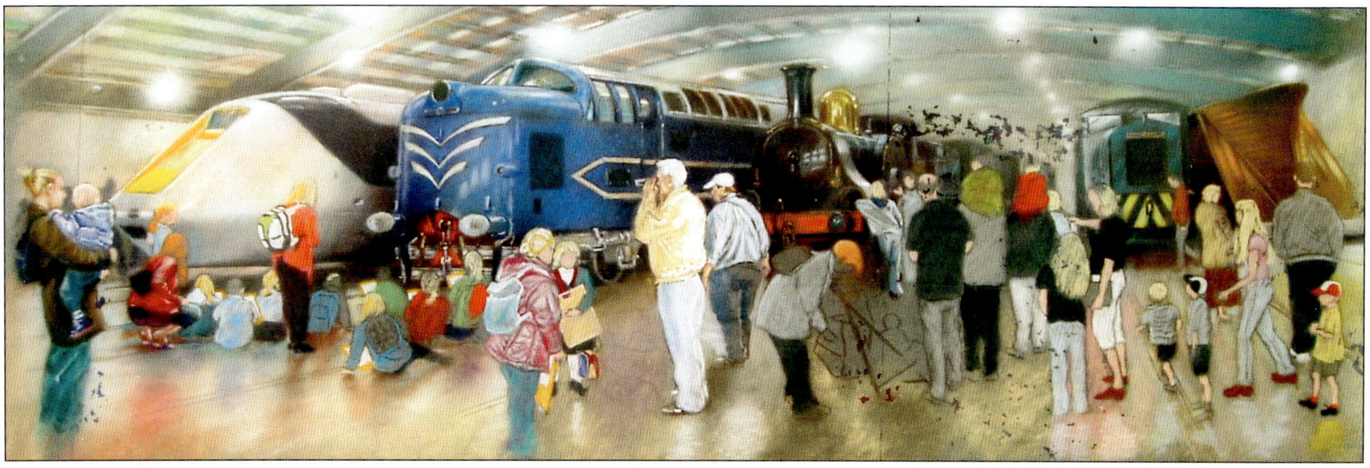

Visitors to the NRM.

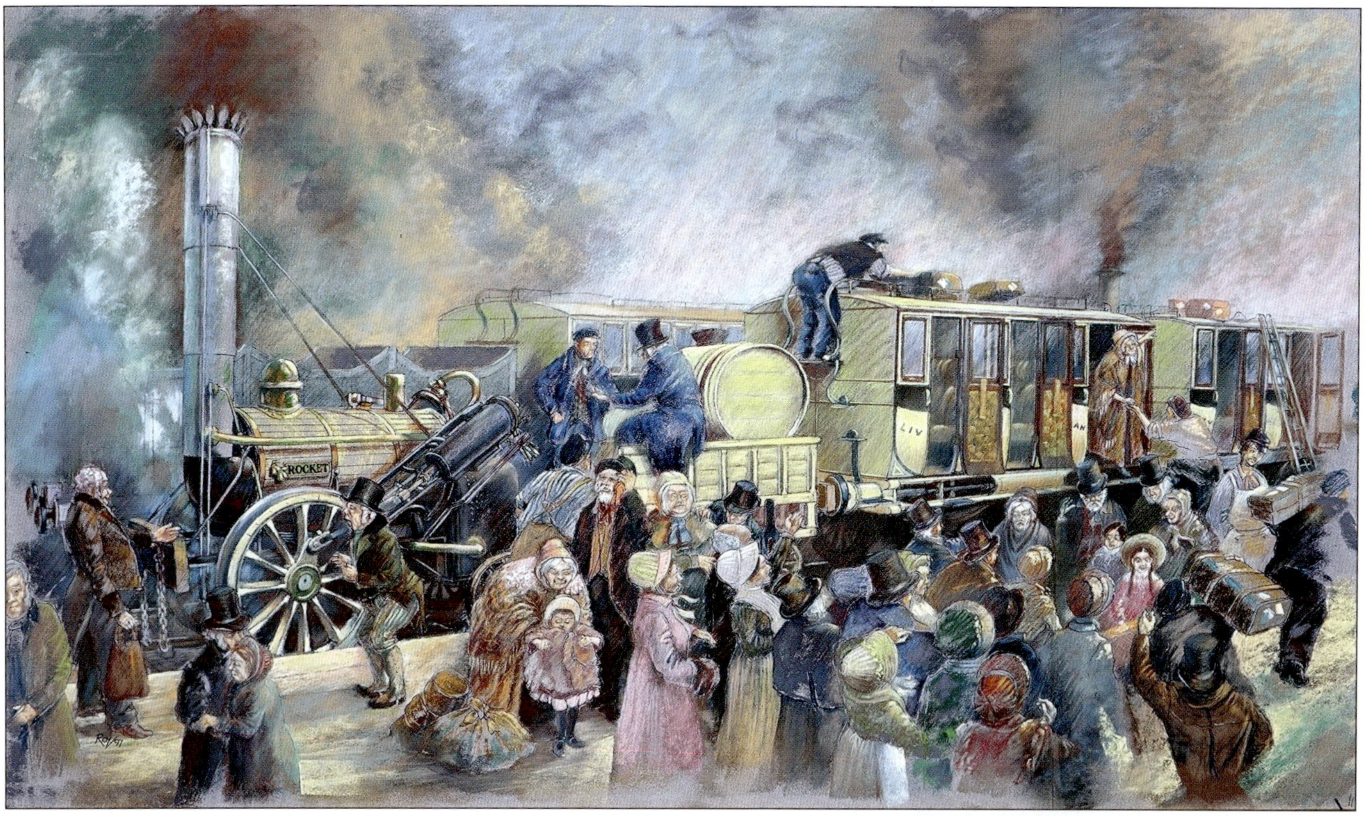

"Steam"... a new experience (Liverpool – Manchester) 1835.

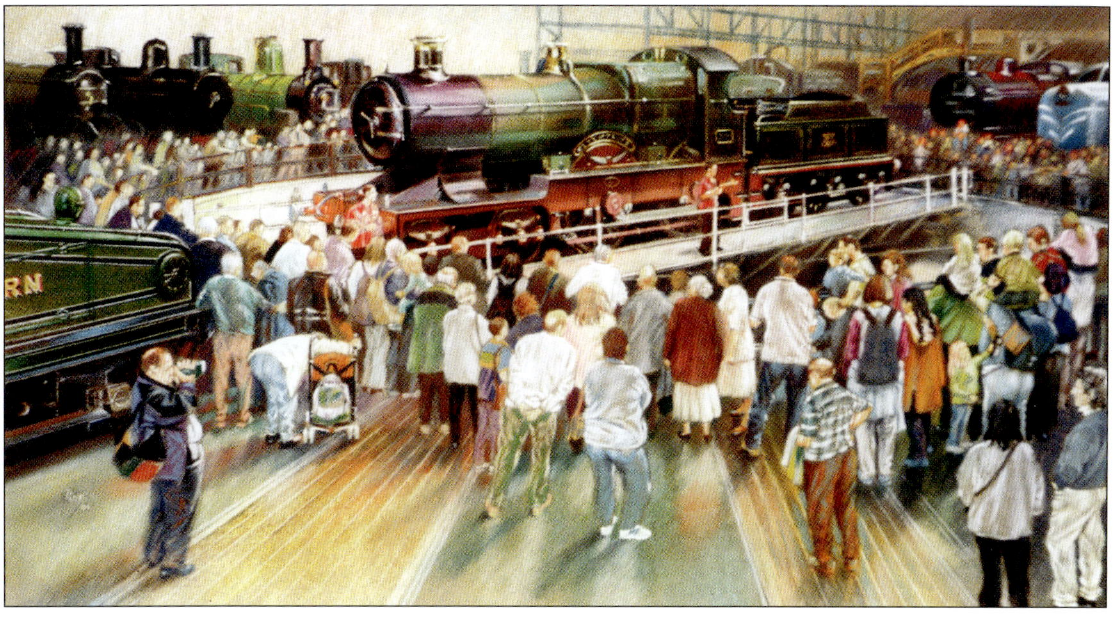

NRM "City of Truro" on the turntable.

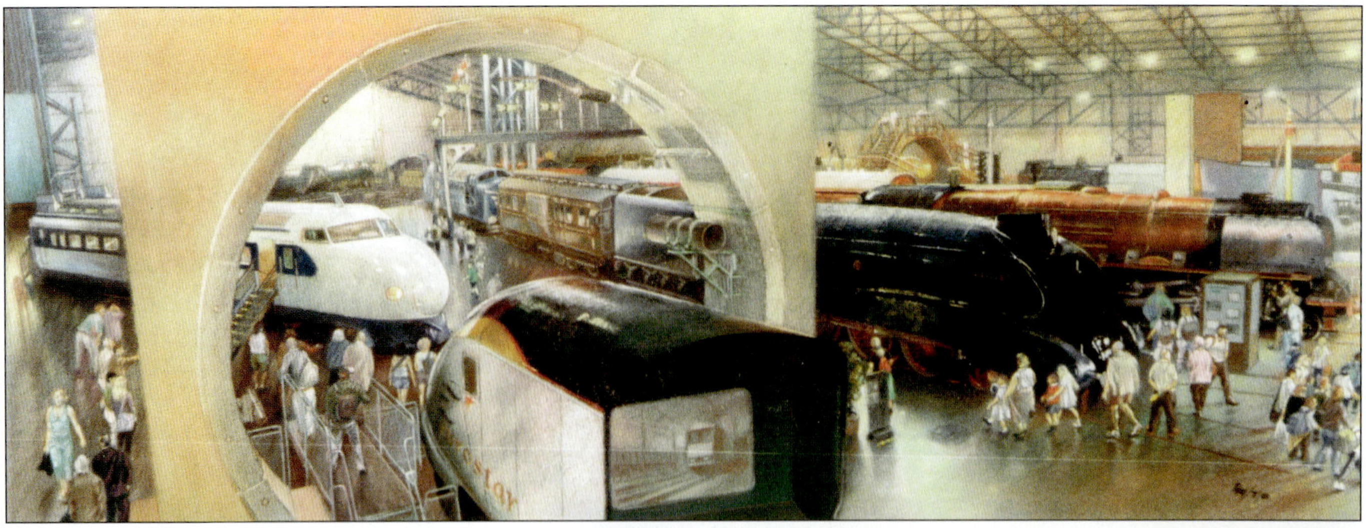

Welcome to Japan's Shinkansen – Bullet Train launch.

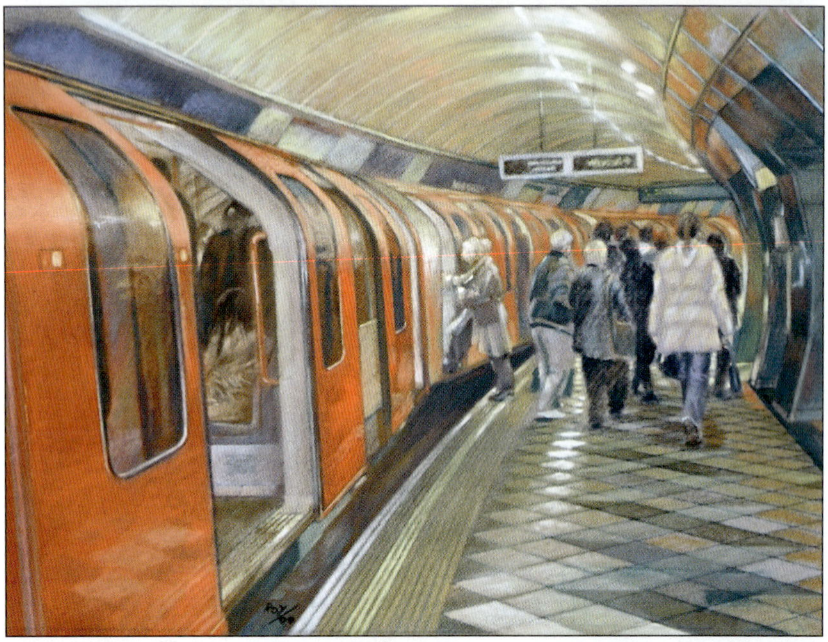

Mind the gap!

NRM the turntable.

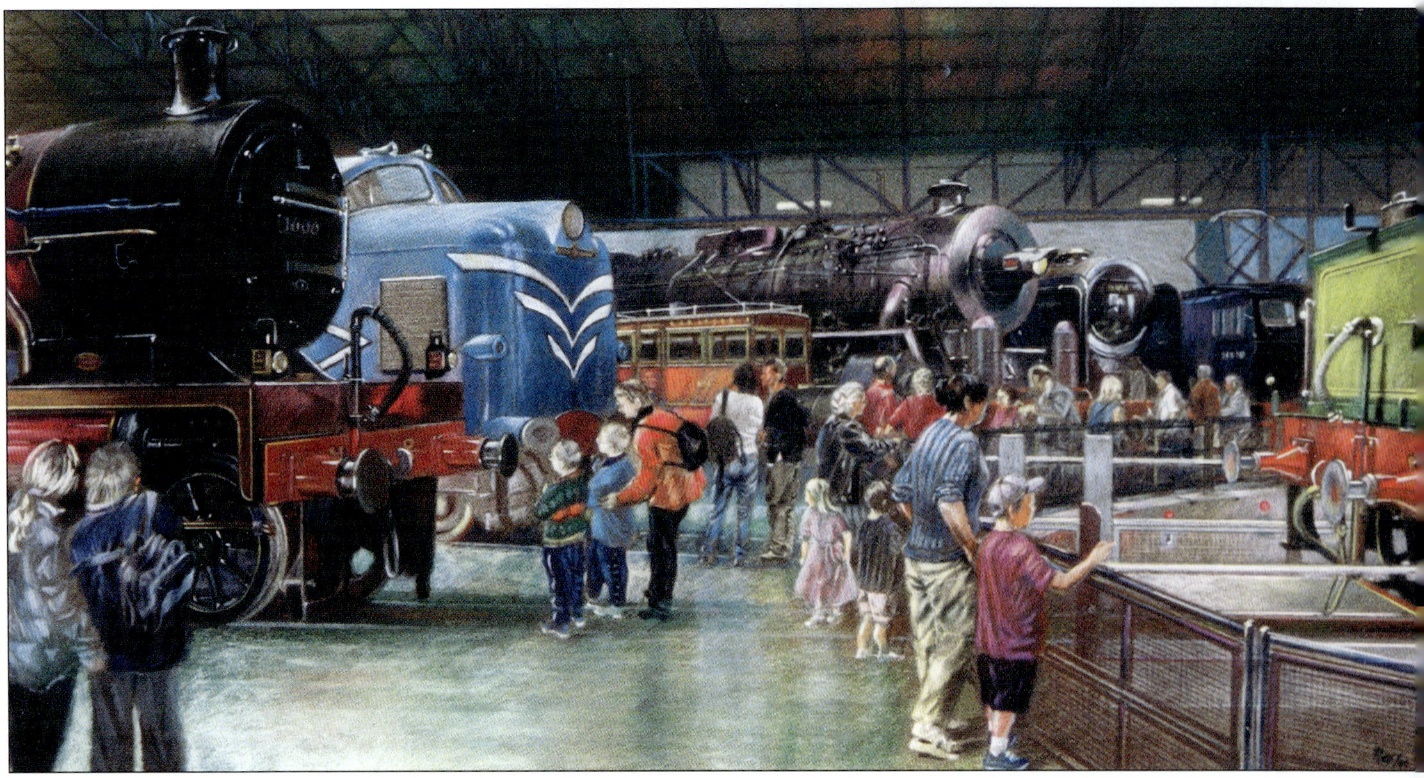

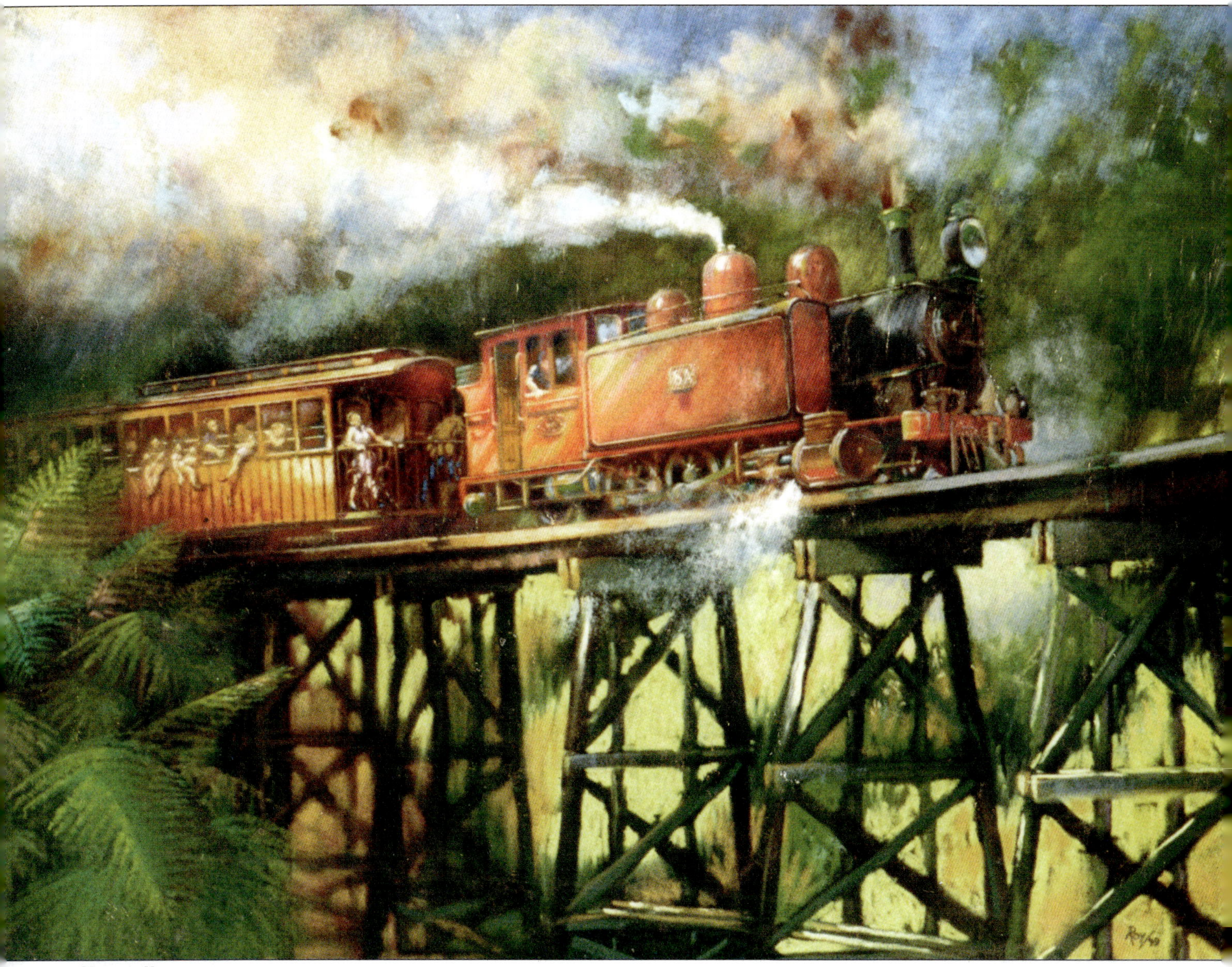

Puffing Billy.

Selection of locomotives at the NRM.

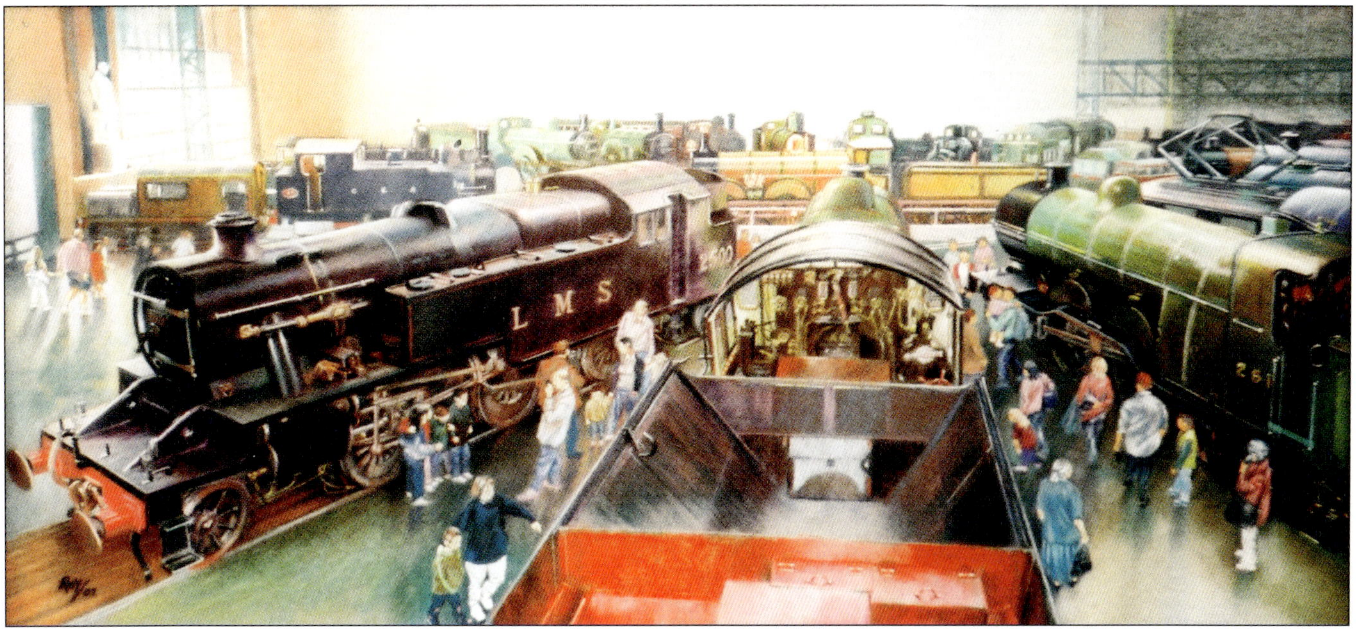

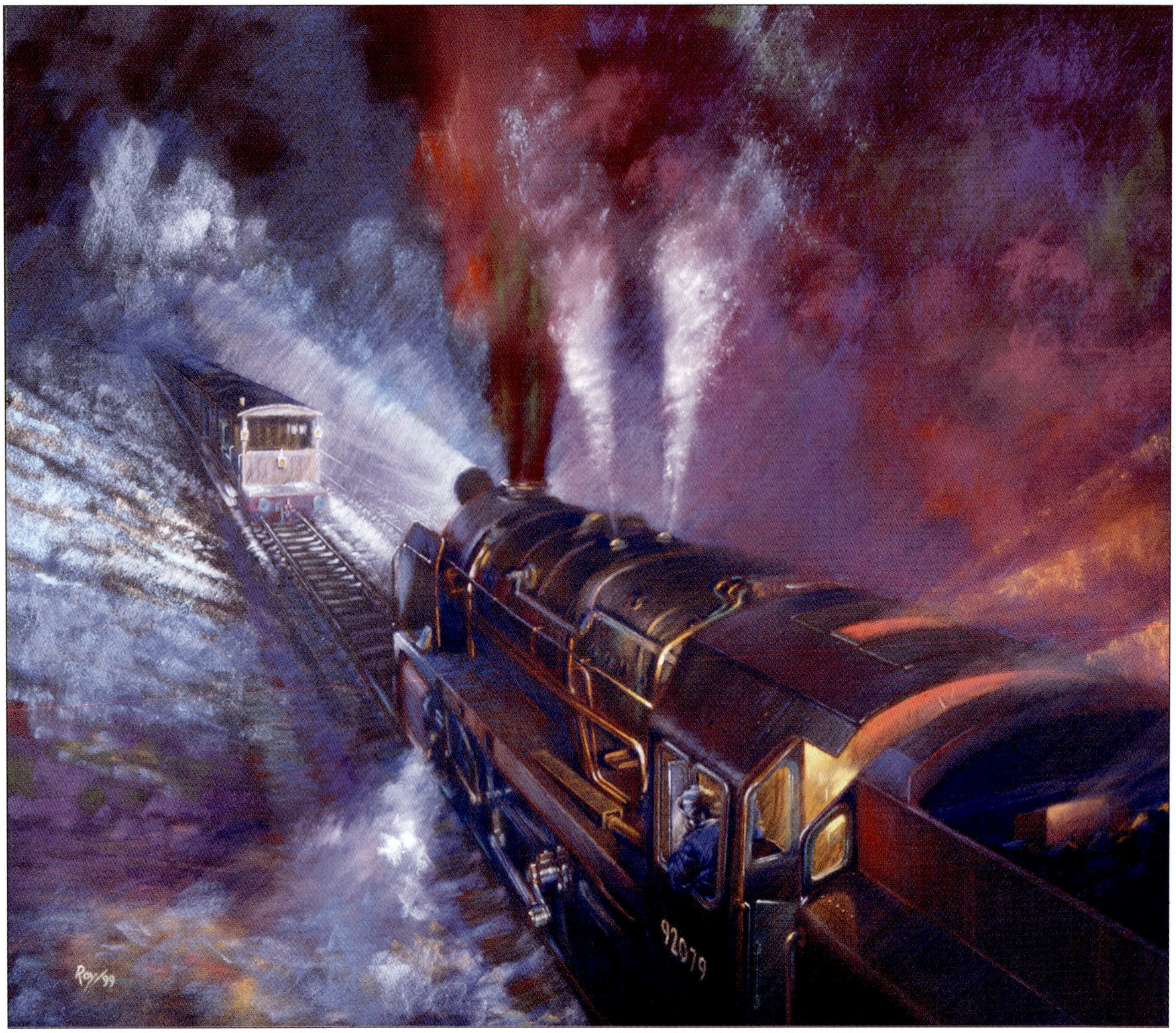

Banker – Big Bertha's successor.

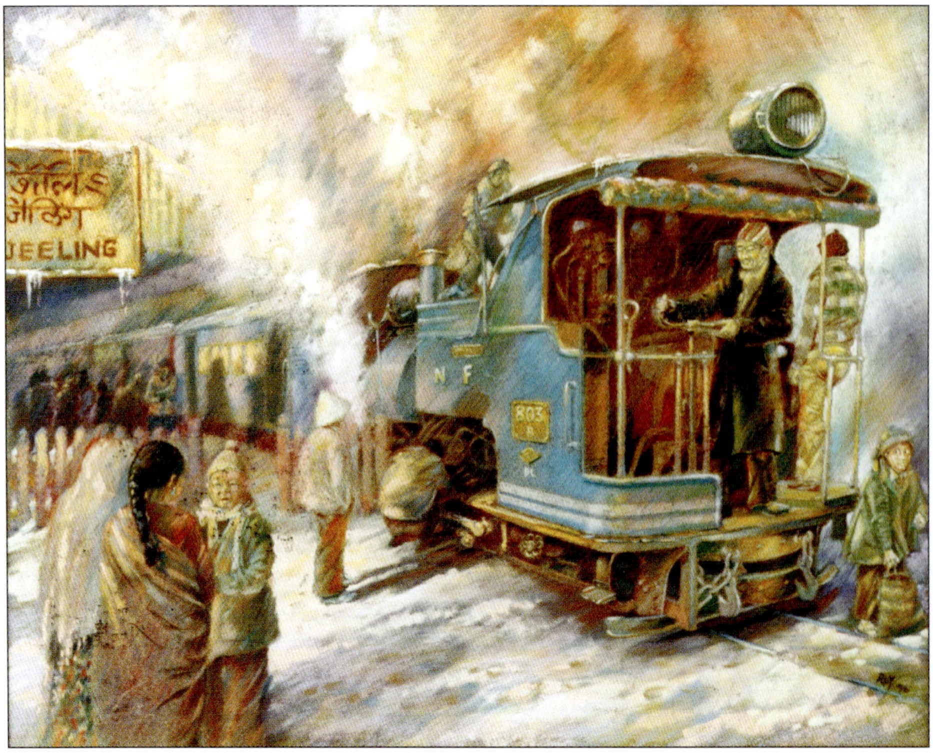

Himalayan.

CHAPTER SIX

Roy: "The Guild of Railway Artists" & "The Friends of the National Railway Museum"

Roy became an associate member of the Guild of Railway Artists (G.R.A.) in 1996 and was elected to a full member in 1999. He served as president from 2005 until he ceased to be active in 2015. For many years he was a member of the Friends of the National Railway Museum (F.N.R.M.) in York, again until he ceased to be active.

In 2003 the two organisations collaborated in the production of a book called "Along Artistic Lines".

The passage alongside is taken from that publication:

ACKNOWLEDGEMENT

The original idea for *Along Artistic Lines* – a joint venture between the Guild of Railway Artists and the National Railway Museum – came from Roy Wilson, without whose dedication this volume would not have been published.

Once the green light was given to proceed with the project by the GRA Council, Roy went into action, working as Co-ordinator. Name it, he did it, designing the book and the layout, yet finding time to create six paintings – all of which are reproduced in the book.

Another tireless worker on the project was Beverley Cole of the National Railway Museum. She like Roy had an unwavering enthusiasm resulting in the writing of an excellent text.

Thank you Roy and Beverley.

– Laurence Roche –

Laurence Roche
Past President,
Guild of Railway Artists

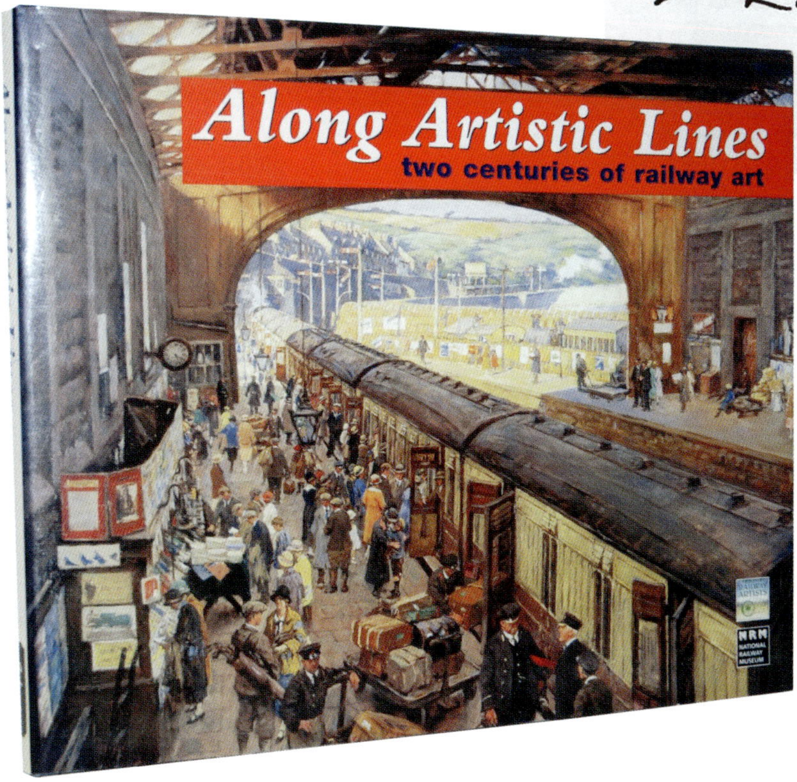

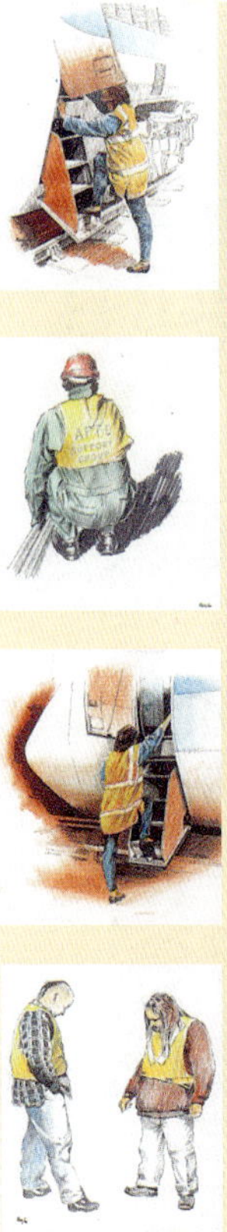

Preliminary figure studies incorporated in the APT-E painting.

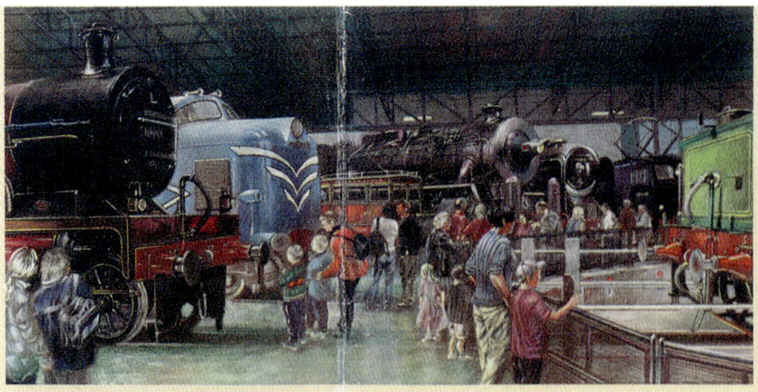

▲18 ▼23

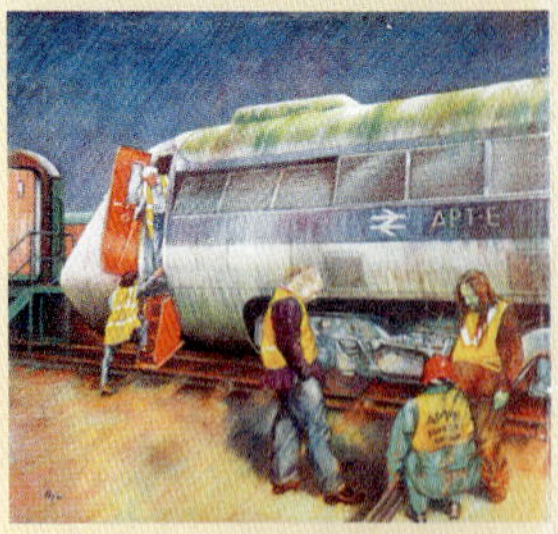

24. National Railway Museum, York. The Great Hall. Japan's Bullet Train viewed through the Channel Tunnel display and flanked by *"Mallard"* and *"Duchess of Hamilton"*.
35cm x 91cm Pastel (2001)

25. *"Big Bertha"*, Lickey Banker - 1919-1957.
49cm x 43cm Pastel (1997)

26. National Railway Museum, York. Great Hall the daily turntable demonstration featuring *"City of Truro"* (2001).
29cm x 50cm Pastel (2001)

27. Chinese 4-8-4 KF7 class in operation (Artist's impression).
49cm x 64cm Pastel (2001)

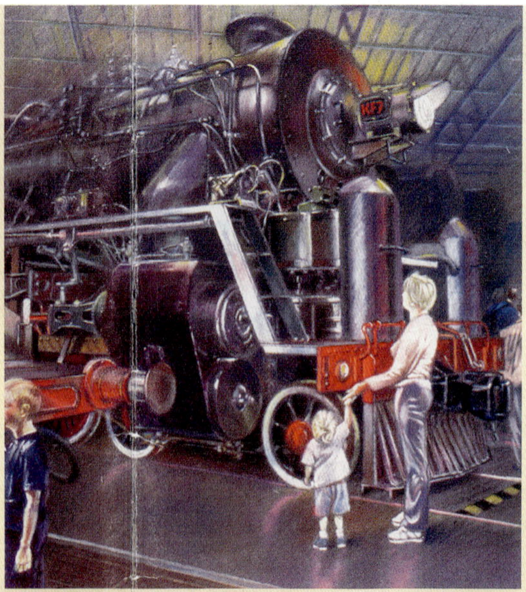

▲19 ▼27

NRM NATIONAL RAILWAY MUSEUM

Inspired - Roy Wilson's Railway Art 20 March - 30 June 2002

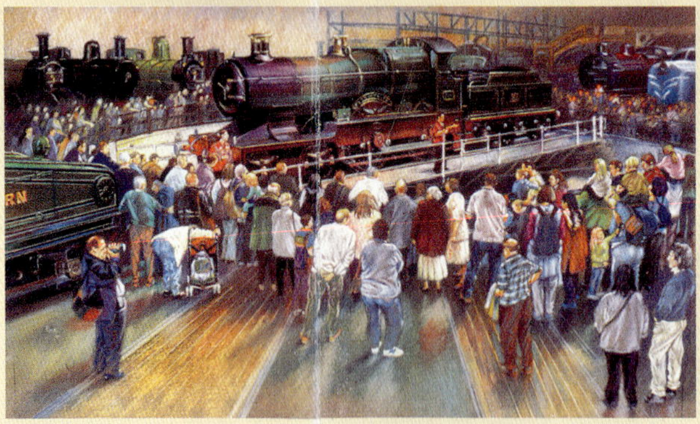

▲26

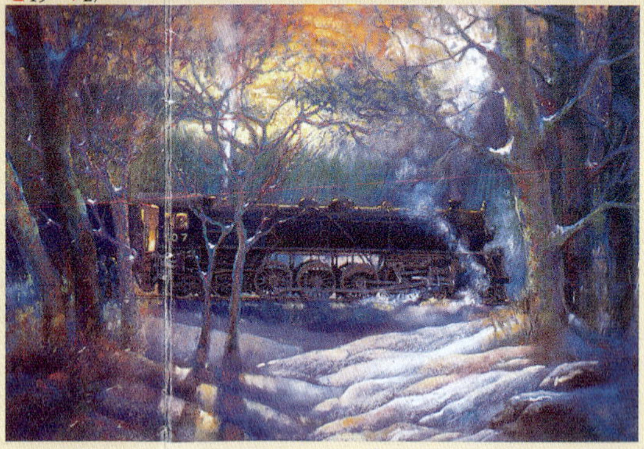

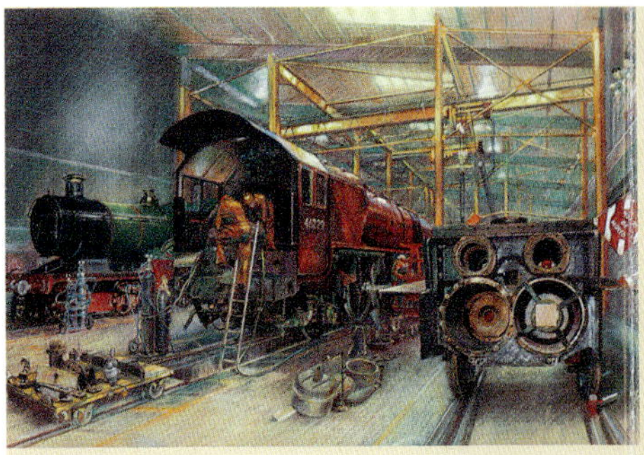

▲14 ▼20

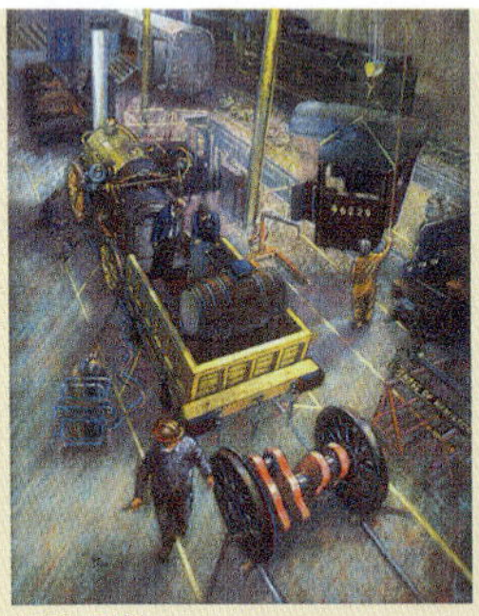

▲15 ▼21

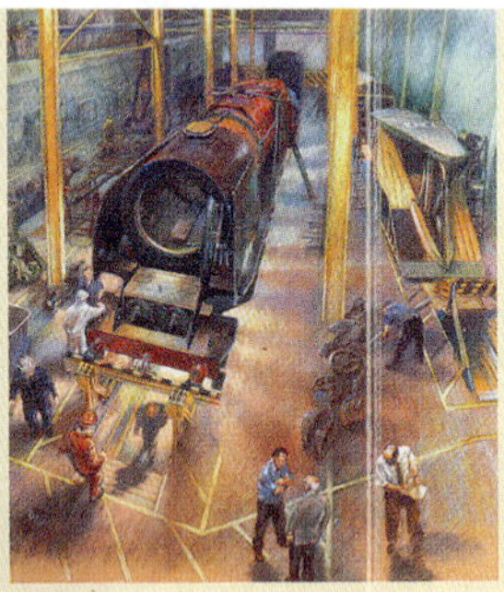

▲16

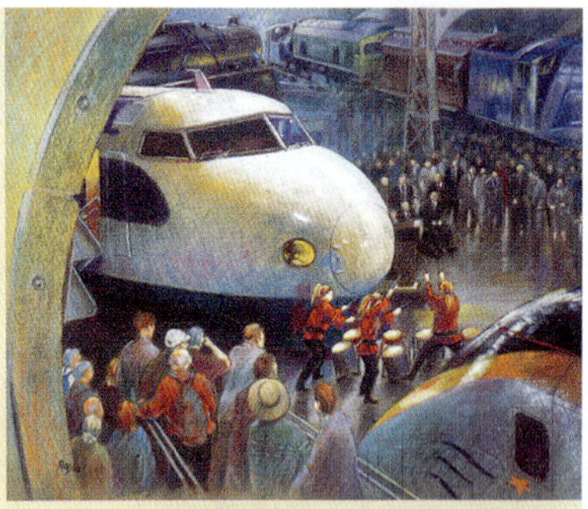

▲17 ▼22

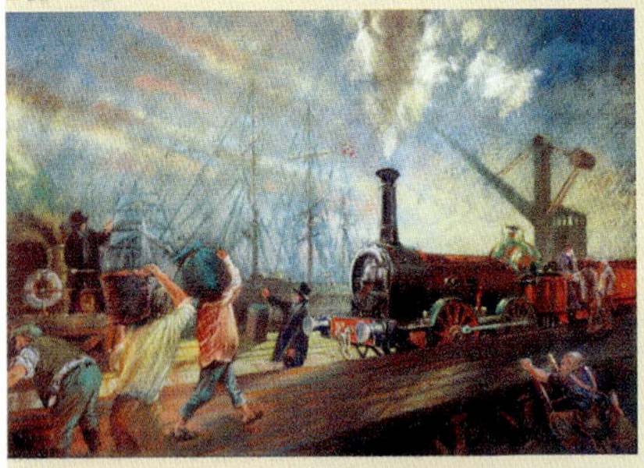

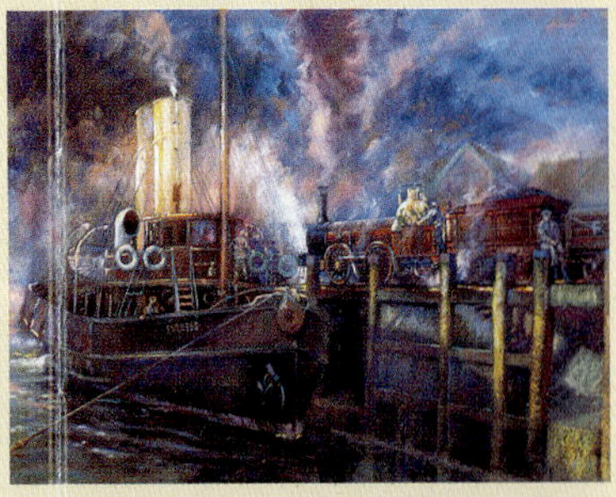

14. National Railway Museum, York. The New Workshop, first week of operation. *"City of Truro"*, *"Duchess of Hamilton"* and the LNWR *"Super-D"*.
40cm x 62cm Pastel (1999)

15. National Railway Museum, York. The New Workshop, restoration work on replica *"Rocket"*, *"Green Arrow"* and BR horsebox.
46cm x 39cm Pastel (2000)

16. National Railway Museum, York. The New Workshop, Restoration of *"Duchess of Hamilton"* and re-building of the NER 1891 Snowplough No12.
46cm x 36cm Pastel (2000)

17. *Welcome to Japan's Shinkansen* - Bullet Train launch 2001.
35cm x 45cm Pastel (2002)

18. National Railway Museum, York. The Turntable 2001.
31cm x 59cm Pastel (2001)

19. National Railway Museum, York. The Chinese 4-8-4 Class KFY (607) built by Vulcan 1935.
35cm x 28cm Pastel (1999)

20. Historic Composition *"Coppernob"*, Ramsden Dock, Barrow-in-Furness.
35cm x 48cm Pastel (2001)

21. Historic Composition *"Coppernob"*, Ramsden Dock, Barrow-in-Furness 1896.
46cm x 64cm Pastel (1996-1999)

22. *Chilean Transandine Railroad.* Kitson-Meyer adhesion rack locomotive, built Leeds 1909.
48cm x 64cm Pastel (2001)

23. National Railway Museum, York. APT-E Restoration survey. Britain's pioneering Advanced Experimental Passenger Train.
34cm x 37cm Pastel (2001)

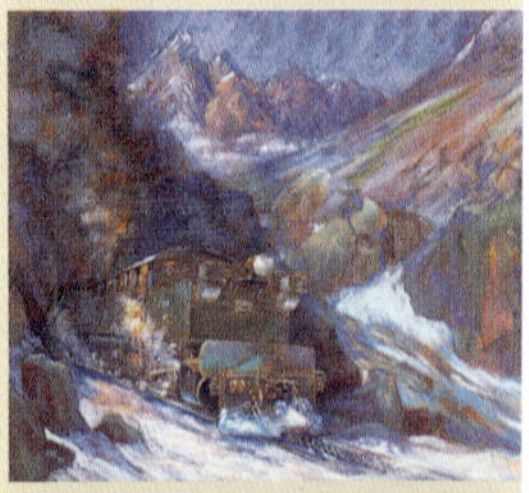

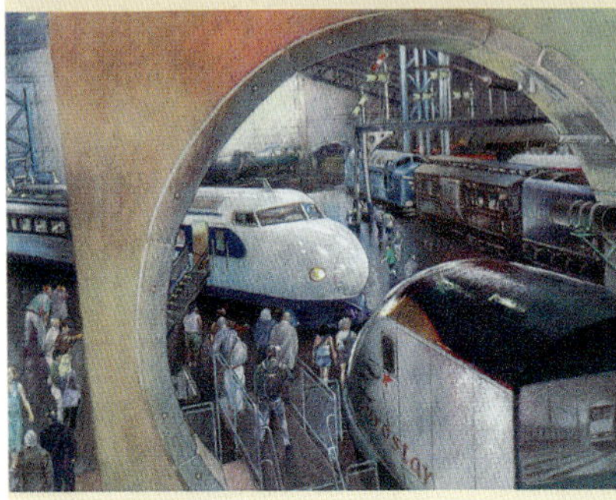

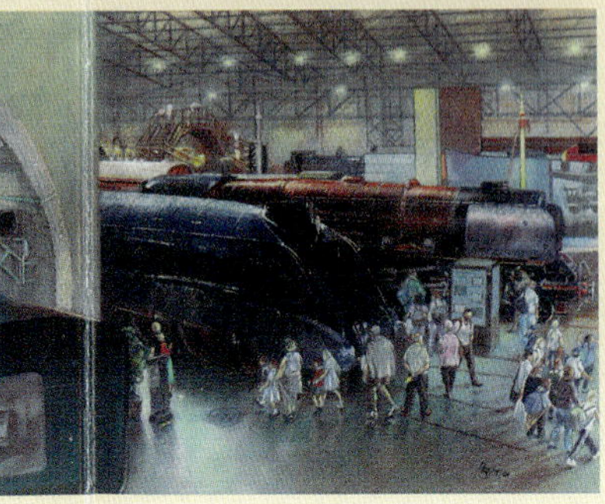

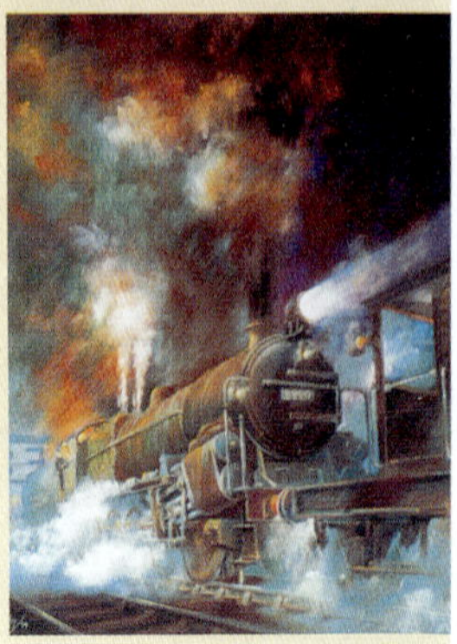

▲25

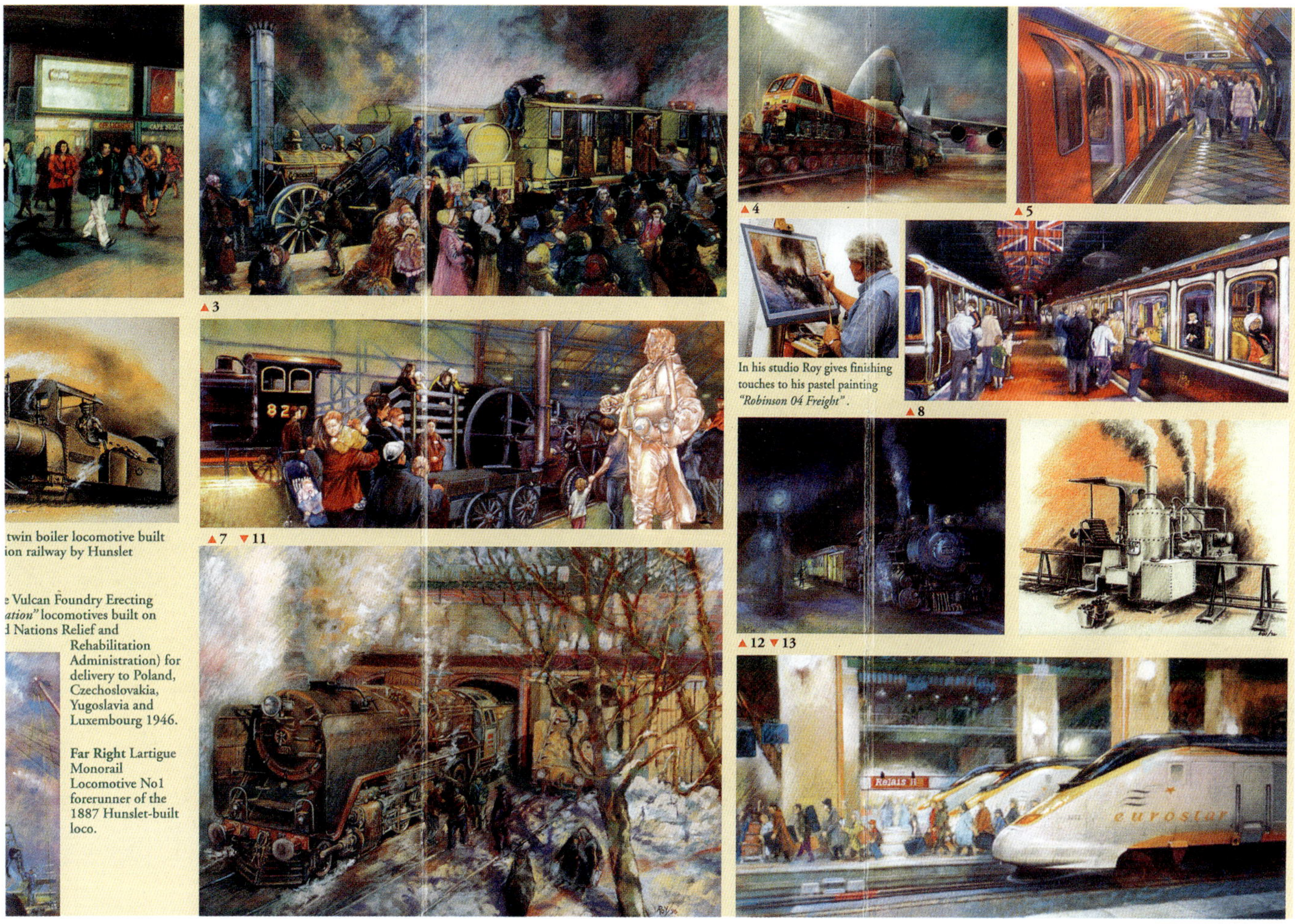

From 20th March to 30th June, 2002 Roy gave a "One-Man" exhibition at the NRM. The brochure (left and above) was published, by the NRM, to accompany that exhibition.

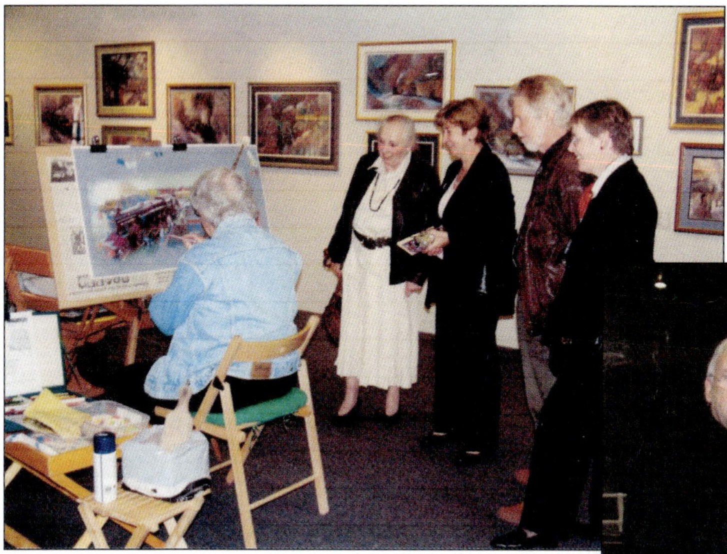

Roy was also "Artist in Residence" during the exhibition and the photograph (left) shows invited guests (including his wife, Dorothy on the left), observing the artist at work. His paintings are on display on the walls of the room.

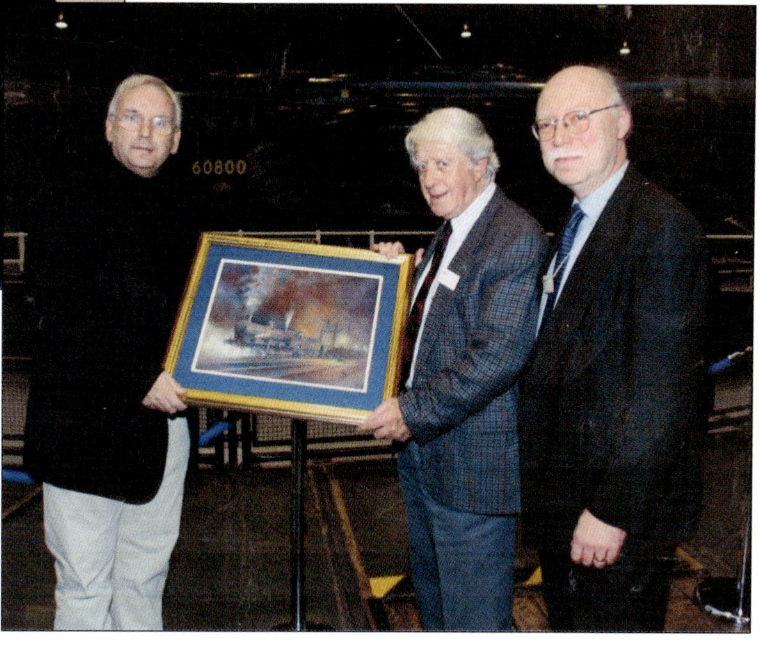

In 2009 Roy was commissioned by the NRM to produce a specific painting and present this to Pete Waterman for his services to the NRM. The painting is shown on page 100 and is entitled "Night goods." The locomotive illustrated was built at Crewe in June 1921, at a cost of £8,900, as LNWR number 485. Later it became LMS number 9395 before becoming 49395 under BR.

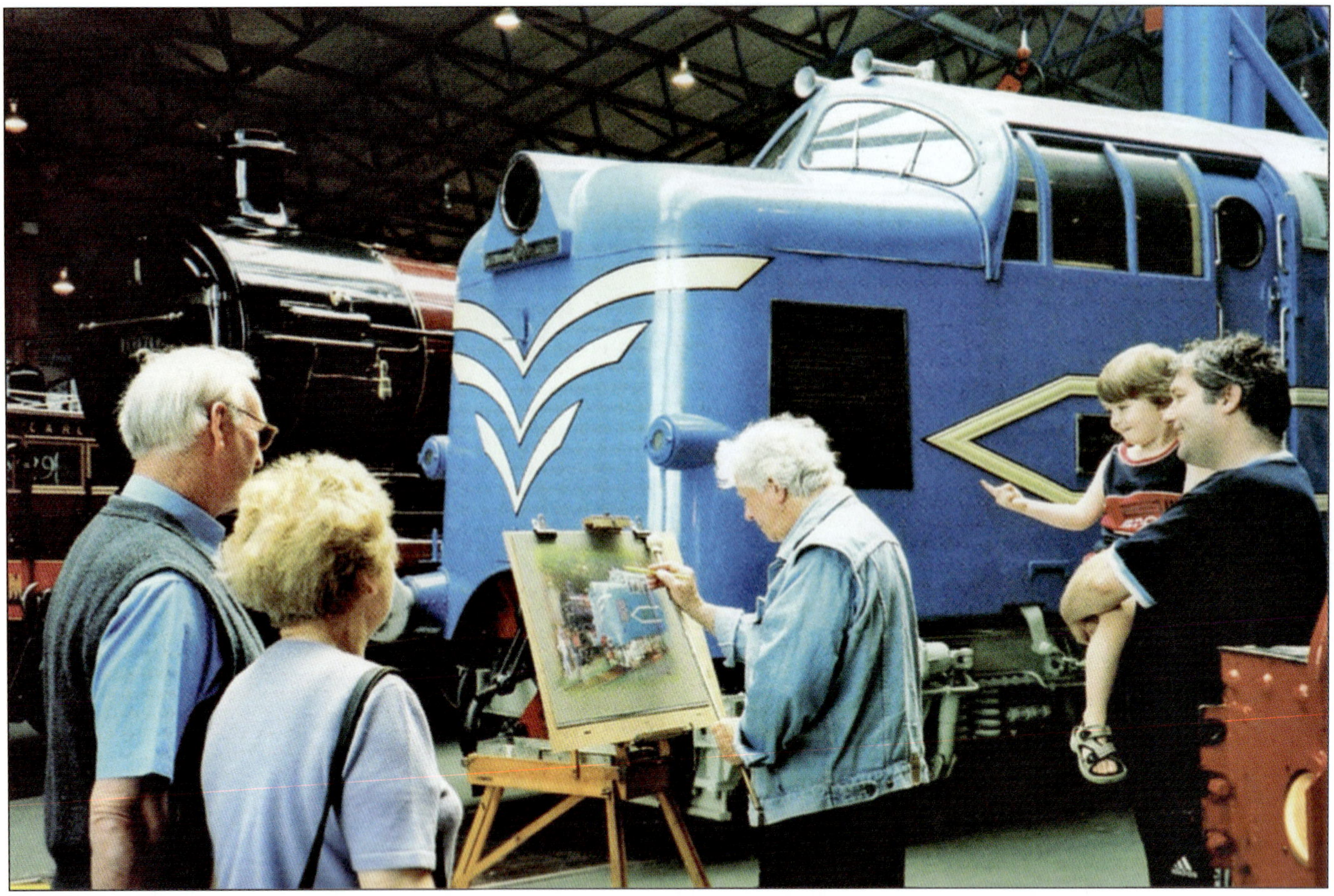

"Artist in Residence" at the National Railway Museum.

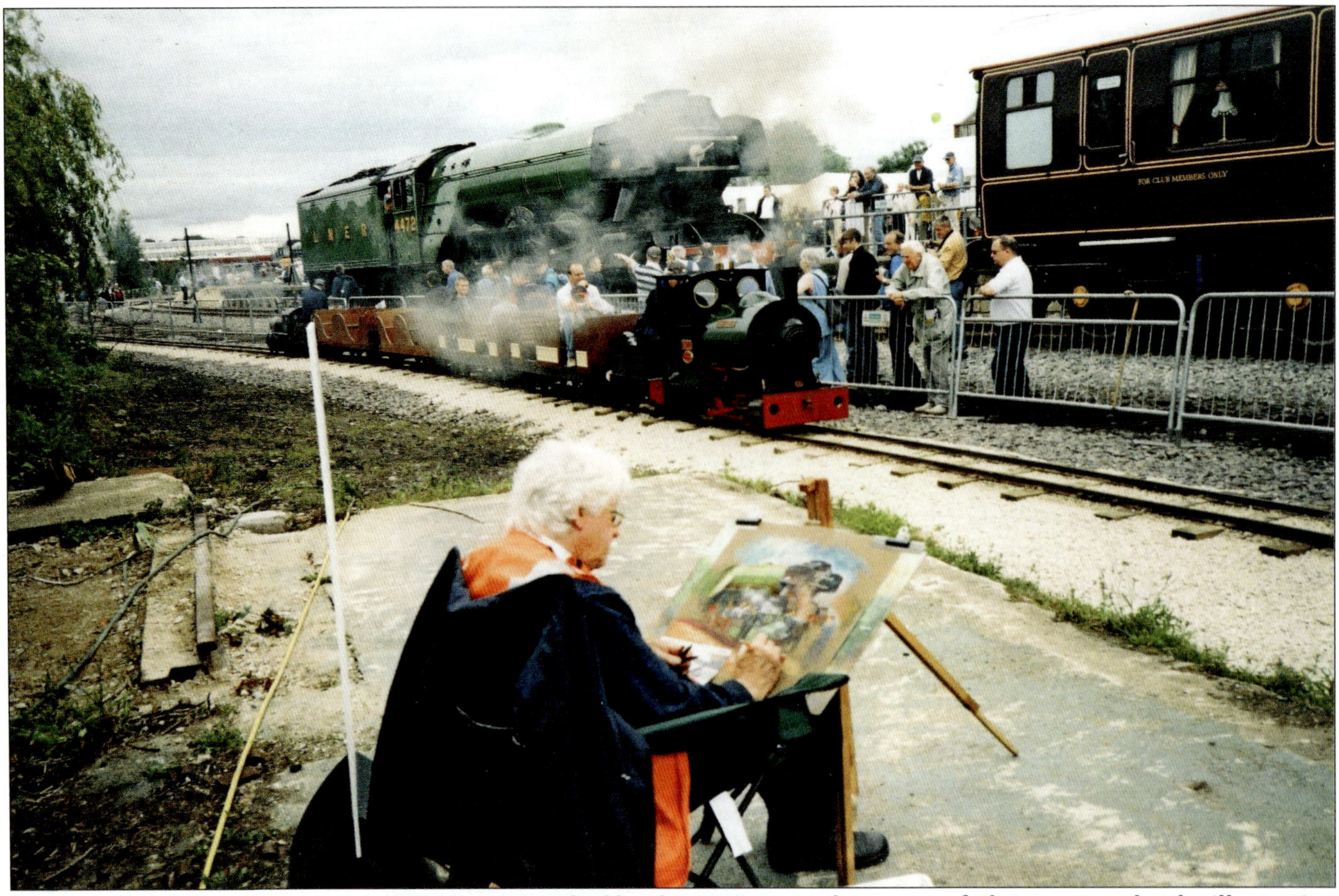

In 2002 Roy was asked by the NRM to produce a set of Christmas cards. The illustration (right) appeared on the back of the "NRM Review" for autumn of that year.

CHRISTMAS CARDS
Special Offer to Members

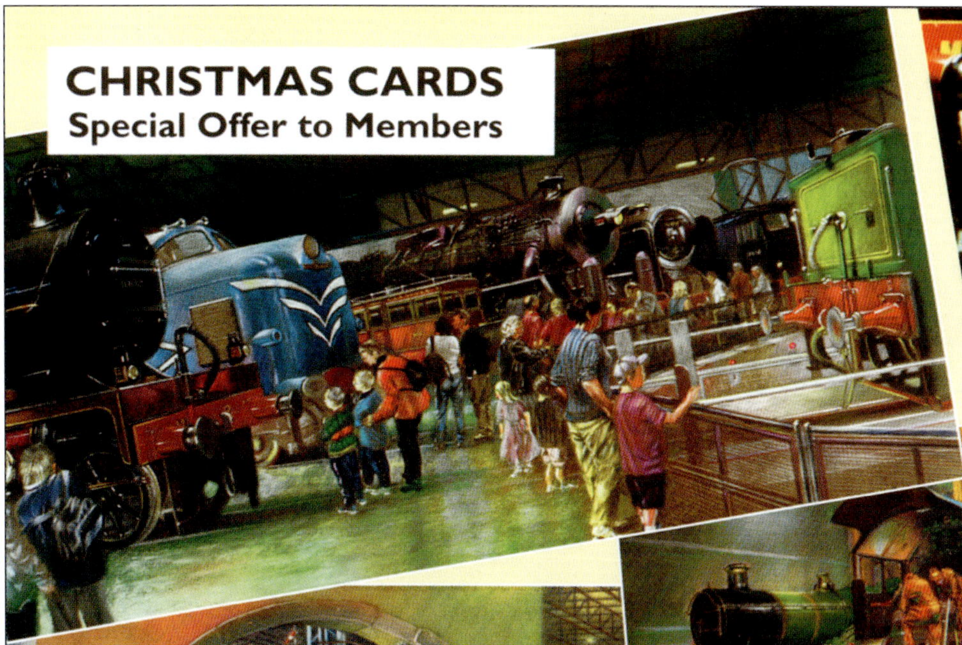

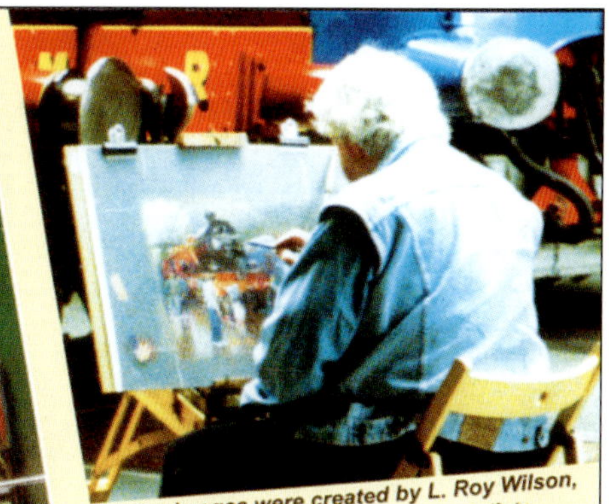

The images were created by L. Roy Wilson, Member of the Guild of Railway Artists.

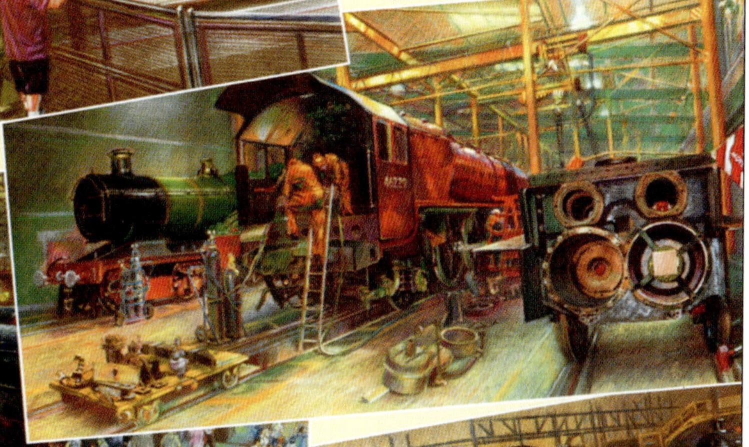

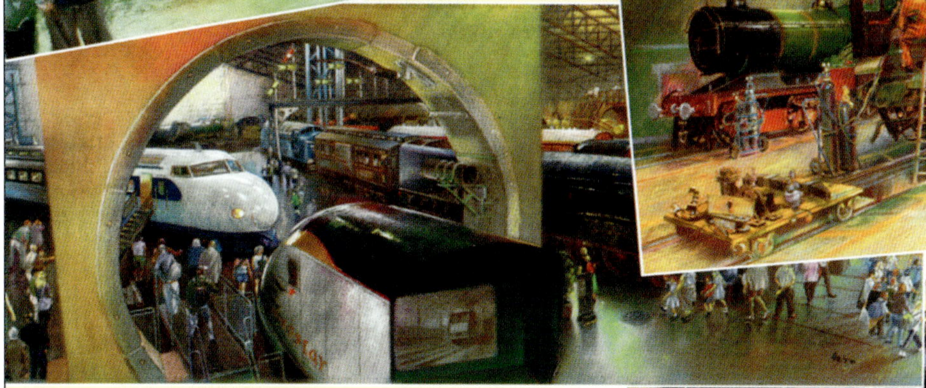

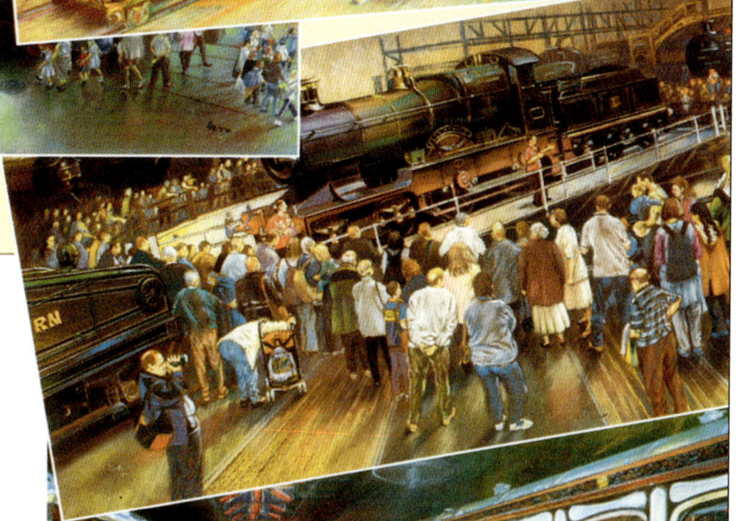

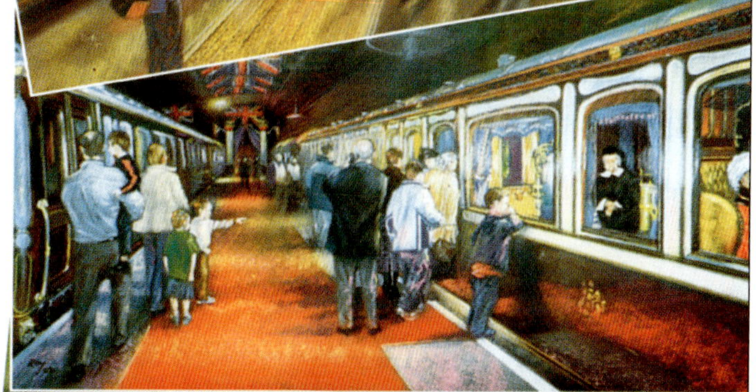

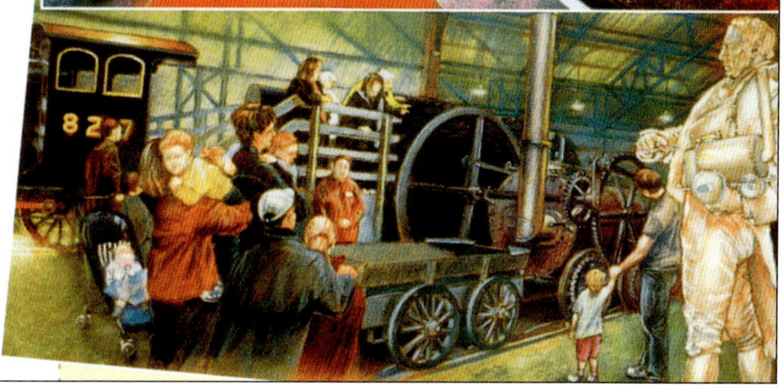

The cards measure 21cm x 10.5cm.

ORDER FORM

(Photocopy acceptable to avoid cutting this page).

To: Friends of the NRM Enterprises Ltd,
NRM, Leeman Road, York YO26 4XJ.

Please send me .... sets of Christmas Cards @ £2.40 per set of 6 including envelopes (postage free to Members)

Name: ....

Address: ....

....

....

Post Code: .... Tel: ....

*I enclose a cheque for £ ....
Made payable to FNRME.

*Please debit my credit card as follows
(VISA or MASTERCARD – please say which)

Expiry date | | | | |

*Complete as appropriate.

Signed: ....

Date : ....

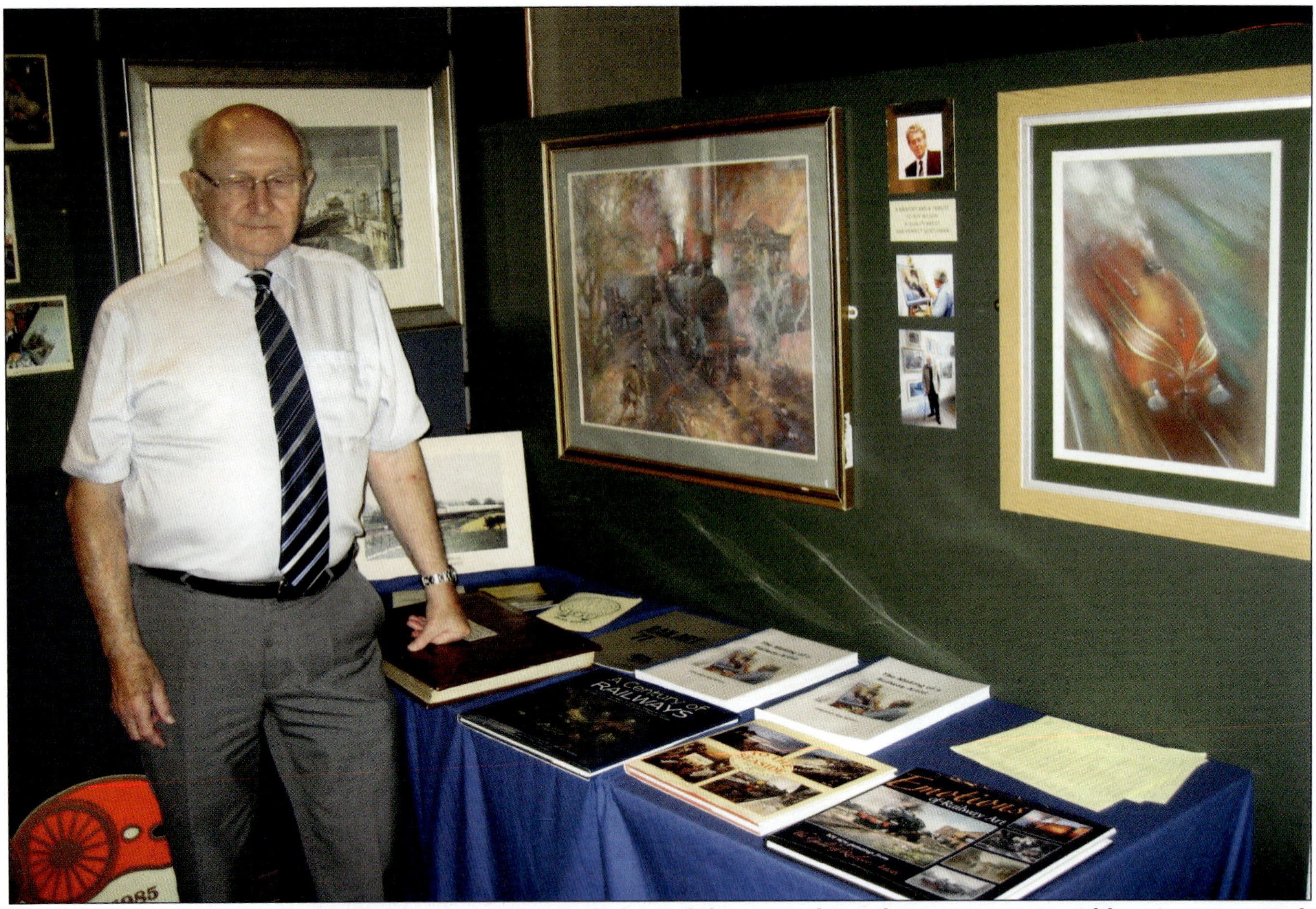

On 17th. August 2019 the Guild of Railway Artists unveiled an exhibition at the Railway Museum in Kidderminster to mark 40 years since their inauguration. This was an excellent exhibition with a very high standard of railway art. My wife Sylvia and I were invited to the opening ceremony which was officially opened by Lady Judy McAlpine, a Patron of the Guild.

Chairmen & Presidents of the Guild

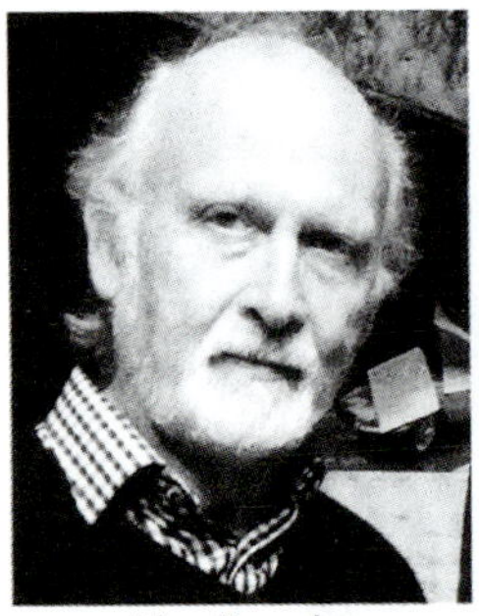

Alan Fearnley
1979-1984

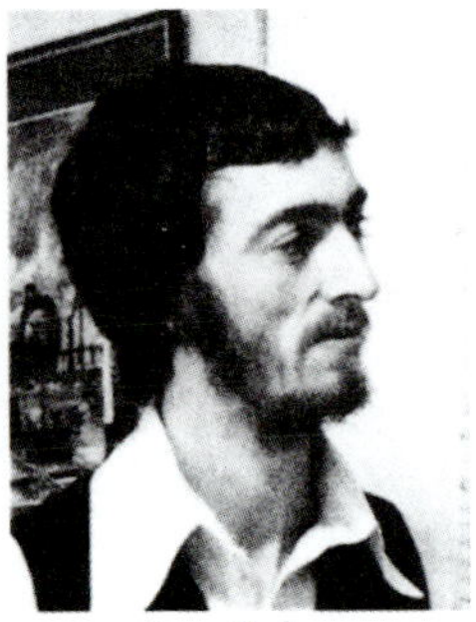

Sean Bolan
1984-1988

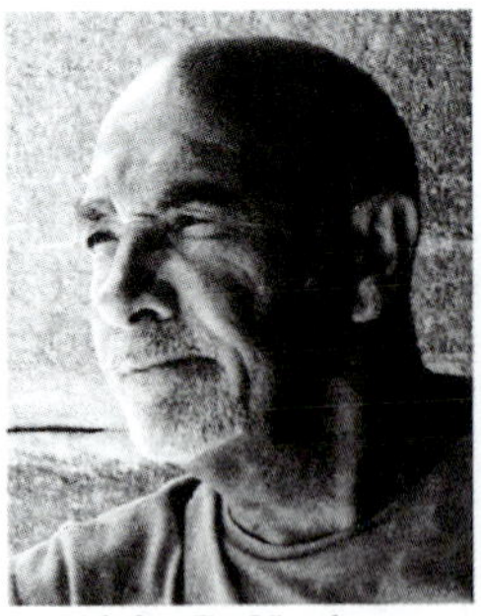

Philip D. Hawkins
1988-1998

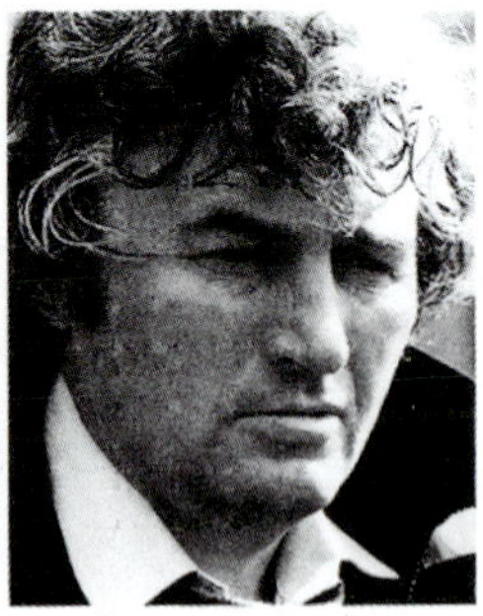

Lawrence Roche
1988 - 2002

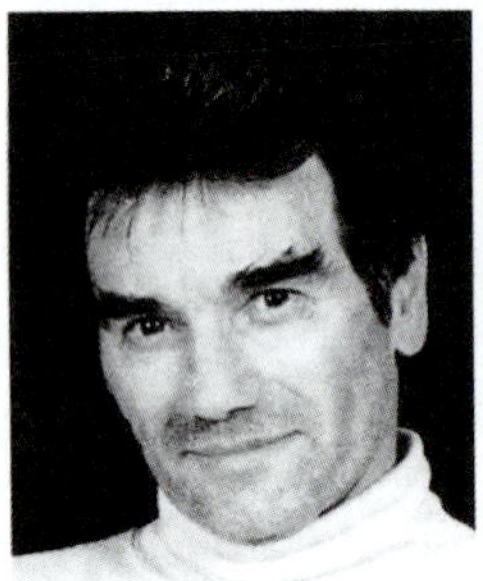

Mike Booth
2002-2005

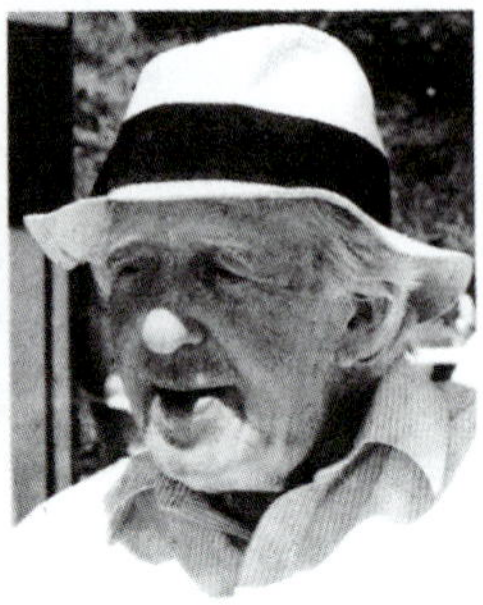

Roy Wilson
2005-2015

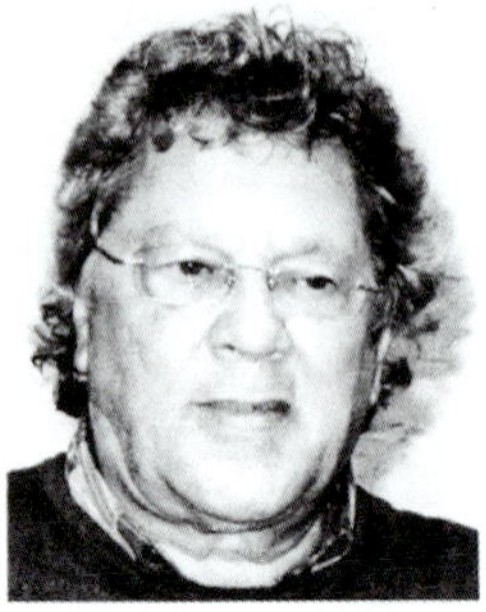

John Austin
2015-Present

The title of Chairman was changed to President in 1995

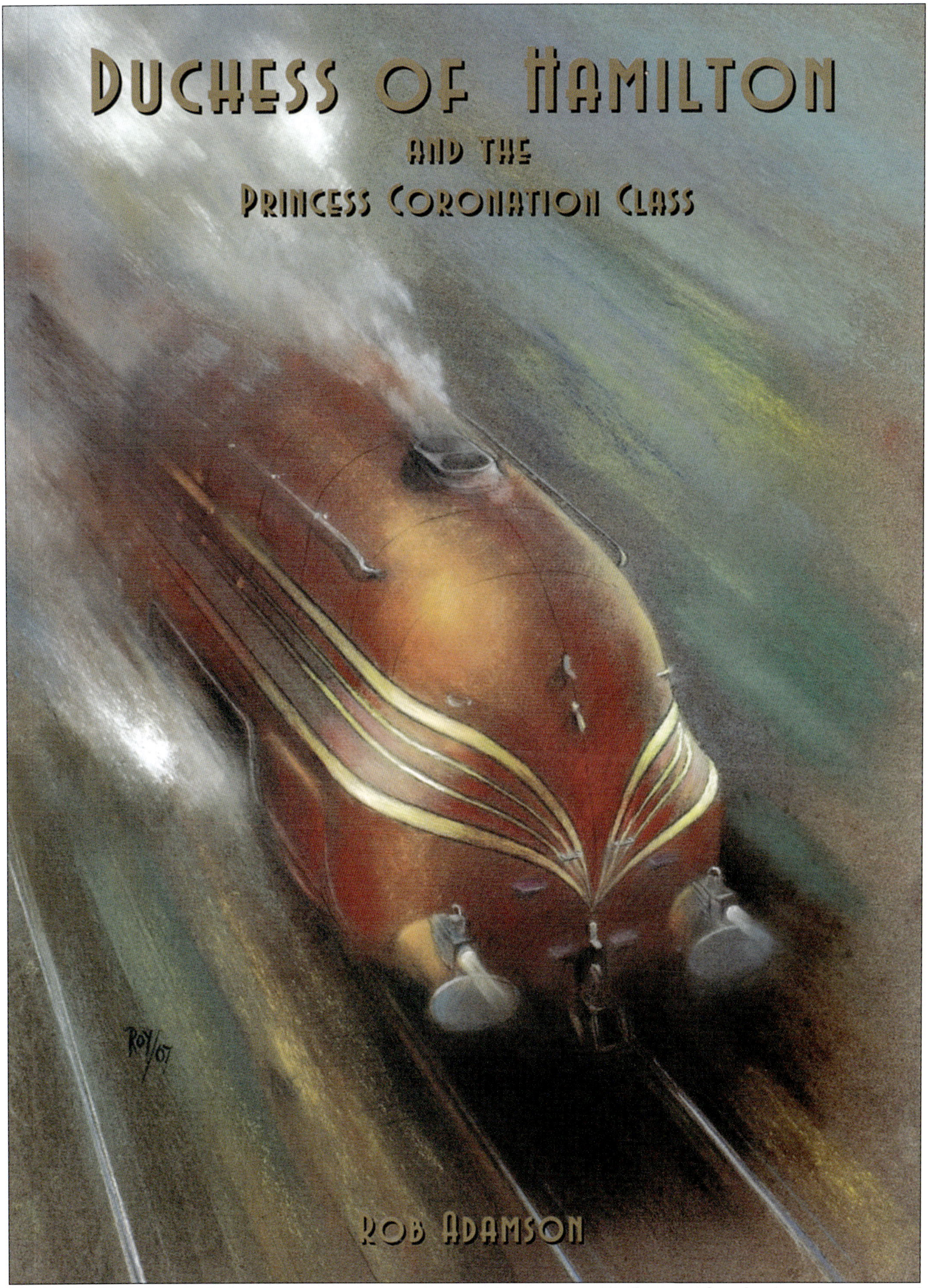

The painting in the top right hand of the display opposite and above was used as the cover for a book on the Duchess of Hamilton by Rob Adamson. This was published by "The Friends of the National Railway Museum Enterprises Ltd."

FNRM Christmas Card

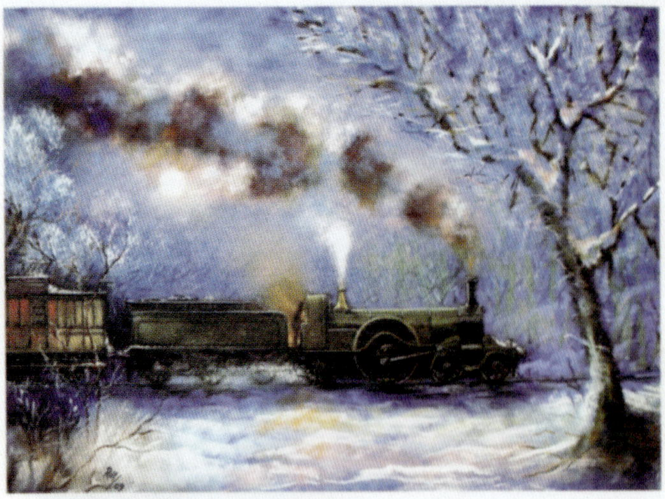

Specially painted for FNRM Enterprises by Roy Wilson,
President of the Guild of Railway Artists, the Christmas card, which is 160 mm square, depicts
Stirling 4-2-2 No 1 in a winter setting

Available now from the Friends' office or order on-line
at £5 for a pack of 10 including envelopes
Postage and packing is £1

Also from the on-line shop:

Buy railway publications and plaques
View the second-hand book list

All sales support National Railway Museum projects

FNRM ENTERPRISES LTD

In 2009 Roy was again asked to produce a Christmas card and this was advertised on the back of the "NRM Review for that year (see left).

Other organisations have also made use of his paintings.
"The Bromsgrove Society Local History Group,"for example, used two of his paintings. The first was his painting of "Big Bertha": used on cover of their society magazine (lower left).

The second example was undertaken as a commission by the society. They wished to feature an American locomotive that had been used on the "Lickey Incline" in the early eighteen hundreds and modified for use on an English railway by a local engineer called William Creuze. It had been manufactured by Norris of Philadelphia and the only example was a model produced 150 years ago and held by The Science Museum in London.

Roy worked from photographs to produce a couple of paintings (opposite page) and one was selected and used by the society as an illustration on the advertising literature for a forthcoming lecture on William Creuze (overleaf).

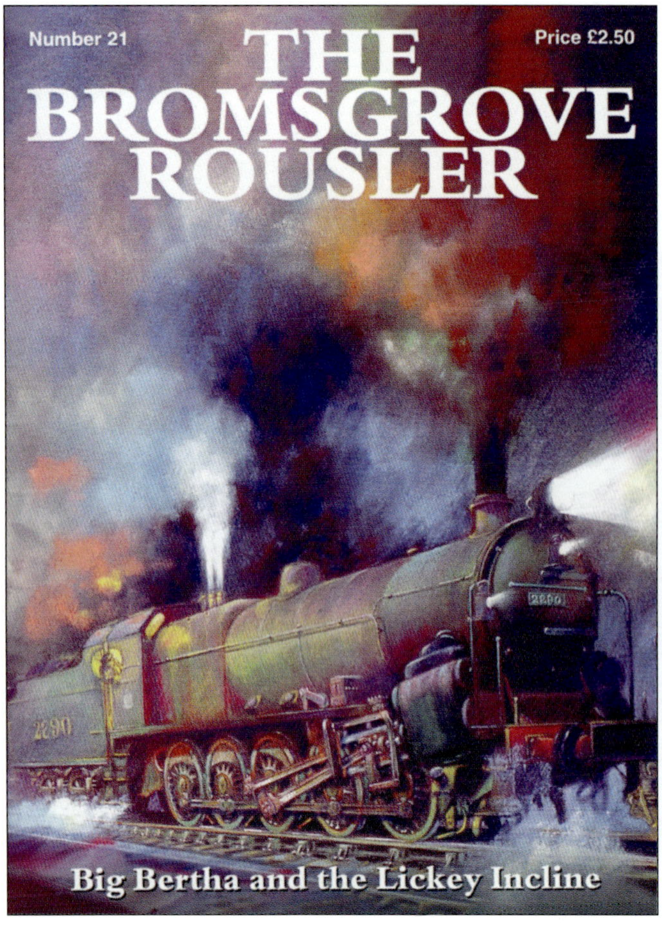

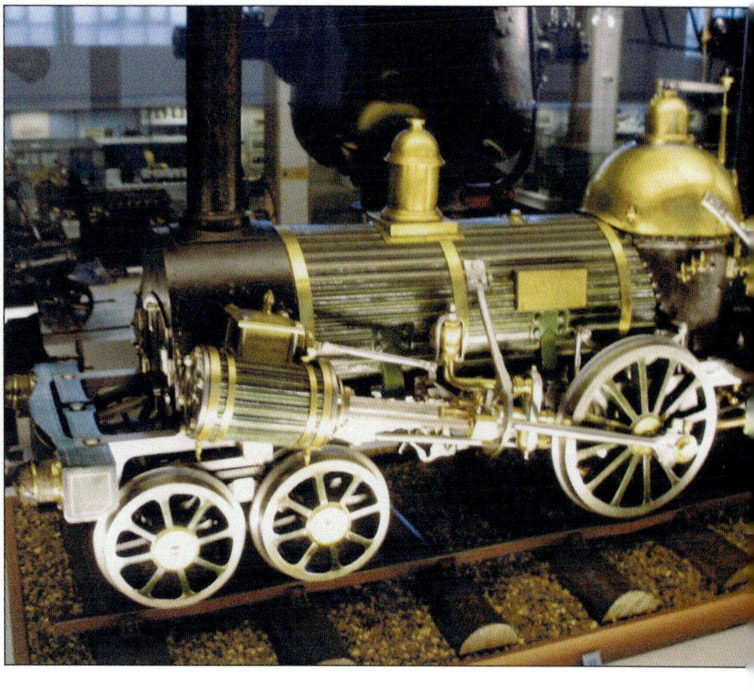

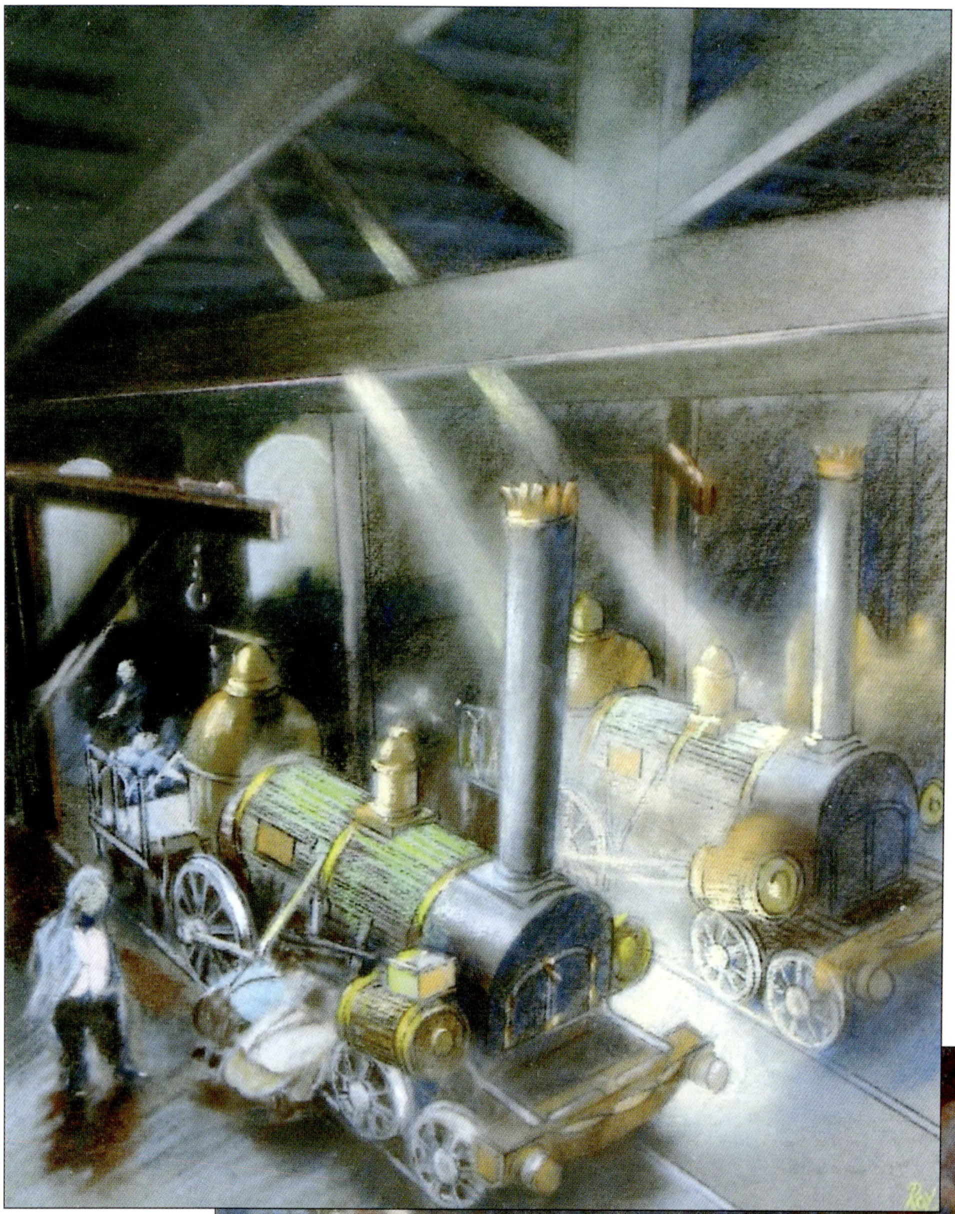

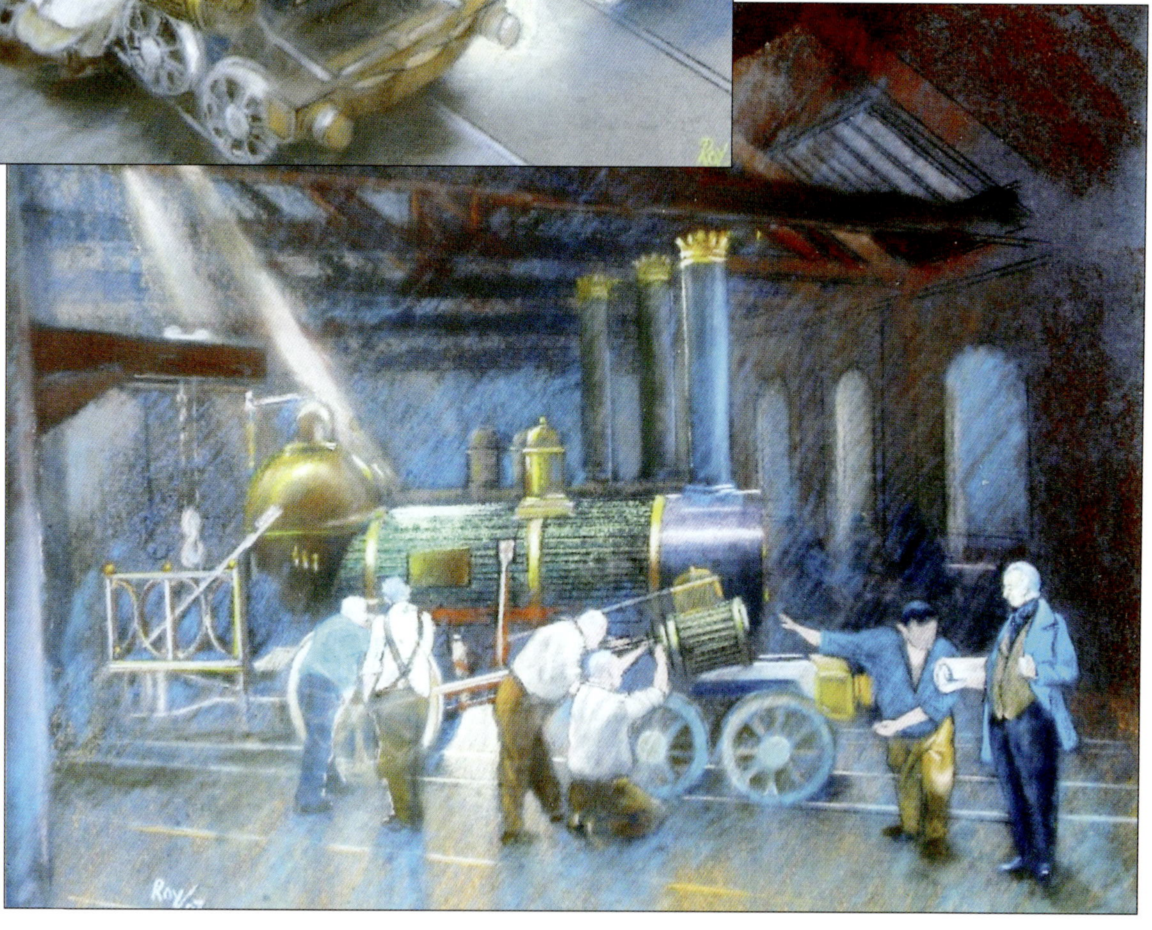

The Bromsgrove Society
Local History Group

Tuesday 12th January 2010

THE LIFE AND DEATH OF WILLIAM CREUZE BA

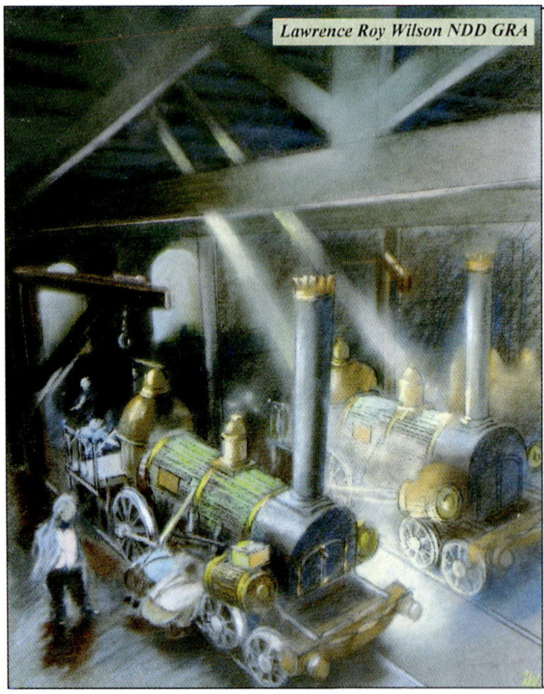

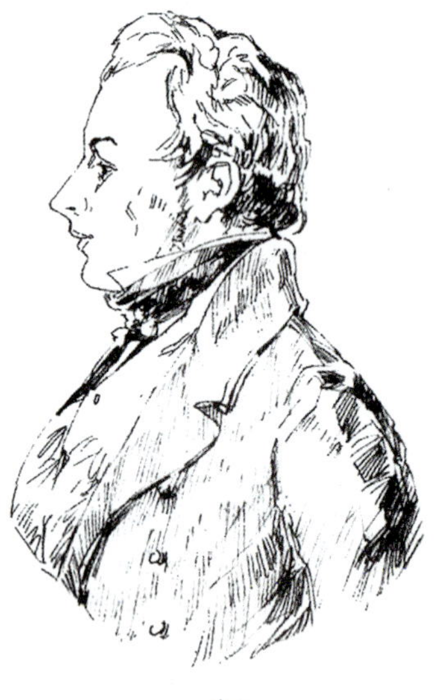

← 'Lickey Bankers' undergoing repairs 1841

An illustrated talk by Norman Hewer

Celebrating the bicentenary of William Creuze's birth, 10th January 1810 / 10th January 2010

This meeting will be held in the Methodist Centre, Stratford Road, Bromsgrove and commence at 7.45 p.m. For more information telephone 01527 575590.

Members £1.50 Non-members £2.00

The 2016 Exhibition

The year 2016 was significant for the Wilson family for one specific reason. Lawrence Roy Wilson reached 90 in June of that year. Roy (as he prefers to be known) is the Past President of the Guild of Railway Artists and has had a lifetime interest in steam locomotives in particular and railways in general. He chose pastels as his medium of painting and produced a prolific output of paintings in this genre.

The family decided that it would be a fitting birthday present to stage an exhibition of his work. His brother Brian approached John Adams, Director of the Carnforth Heritage Centre, with the idea and received an enthusiastic and positive response. He also approached Paul Atterbury, who is a Patron of the Guild as well as being a regular member of the Antiques Roadshow. He was also enthusiastic and agreed to officiate at the opening of the exhibition. This took place at 12 noon on Saturday, 2nd April and was attended by 30 members of the family as well as 13 friends who owned paintings by Roy. Twenty-five works were selected for display.

Refreshments were provided by the Carnforth Station Heritage Centre. John Adams and his staff were responsible for the hard work of hanging the exhibition in the Bateman Gallery and, following the opening, they transferred the exhibition to The Link Gallery where it remained until the end of June.

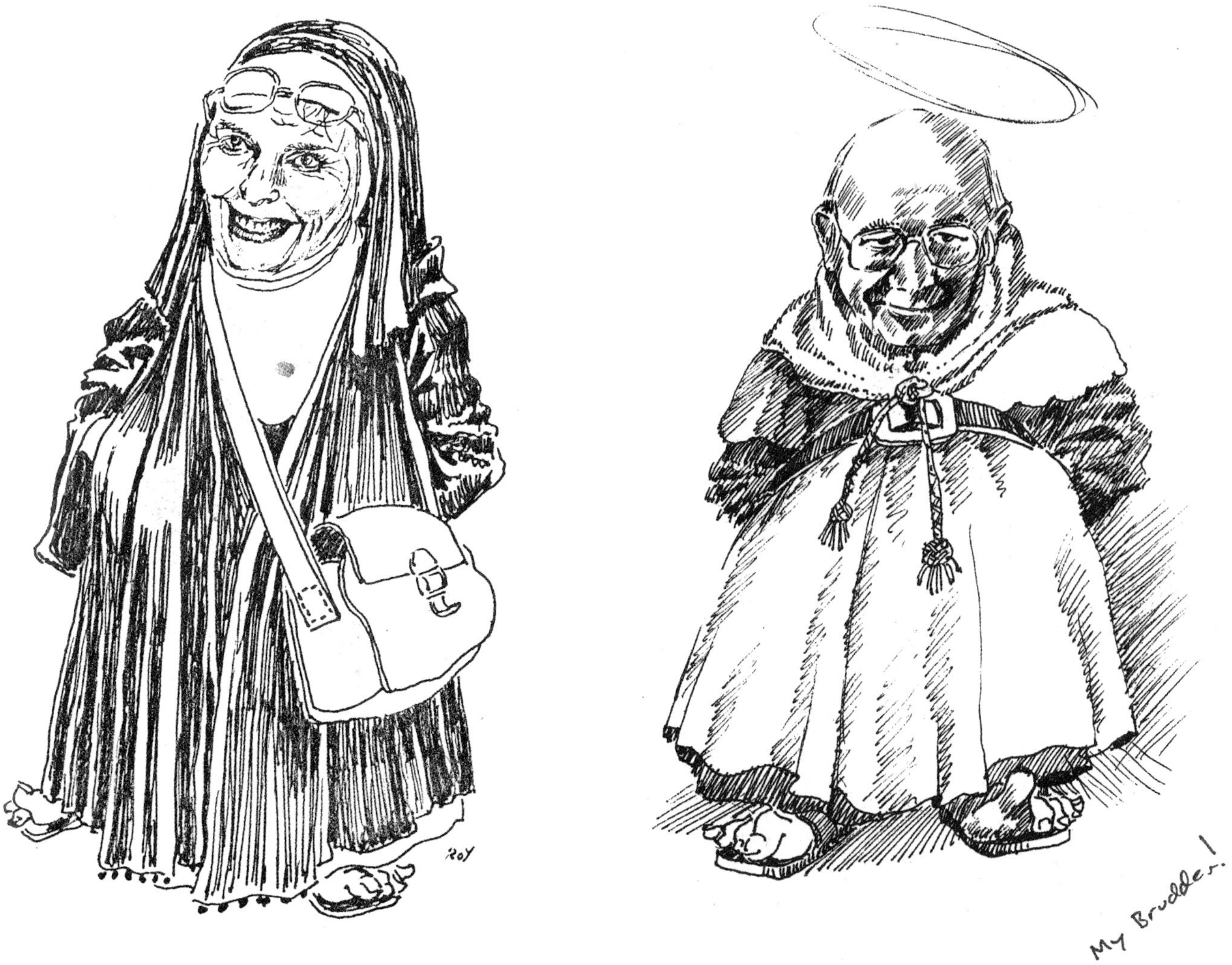

Sister Sylvia and Brother Brian

The Wilson Family as represented by Brother Roy

The Artist – Lawrence Roy Wilson

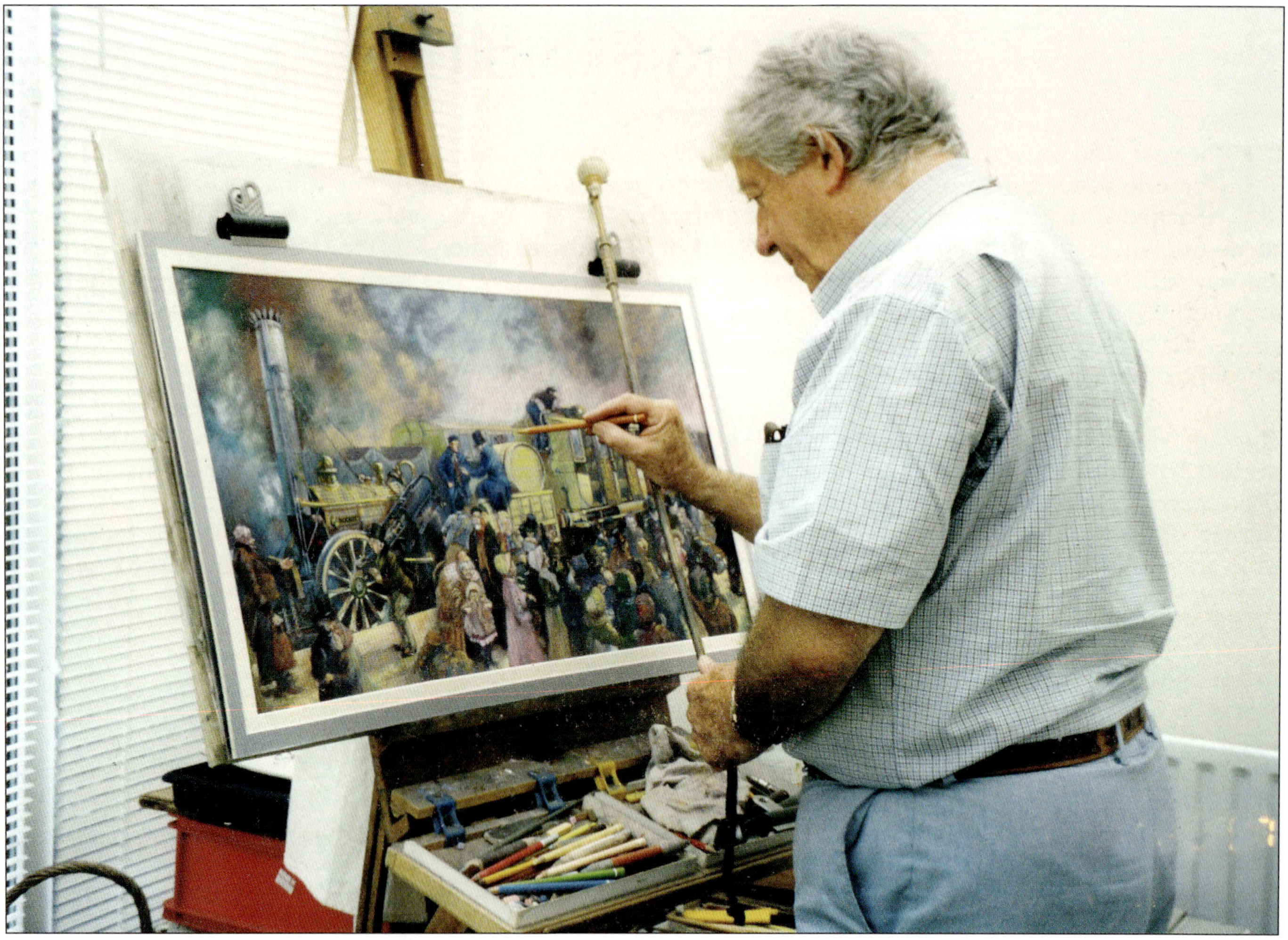

To Open the Exhibition – Dr Paul Atterbury

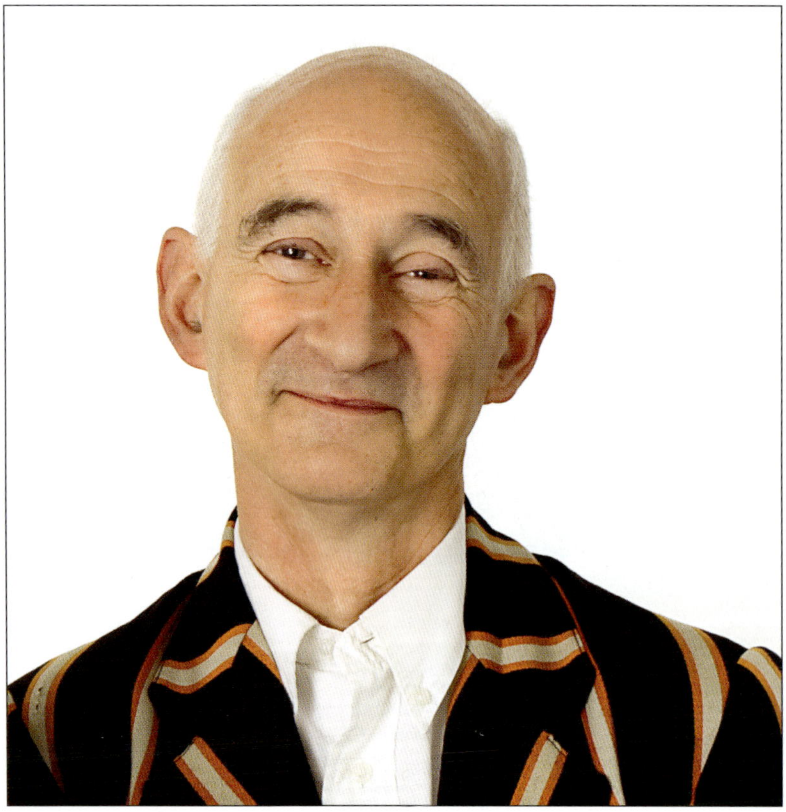

Dr Paul Atterbury is a patron of the Guild of Railway Artists, but is probably best known for his many appearances on the BBC programme, The Antiques Roadshow.

He initially worked for Sotheby Publications and Royal Doulton. Since 1981 he has been a freelance writer, broadcaster and lecturer. He has also been an Exhibition Curator for the Victoria and Albert Museum.

He has published around 30 books. These were mainly on ceramics and a variety of travel subjects. He has also published a number of railway-oriented books, his best-known being, "Branch Line Britain" and "Along Main Lines."

His last publication was for the Antiques Roadshow and published by BBC Books. It was entitled, "World War One in 100 Family Treasures."

The Day of the Opening

2ND OF APRIL 2016

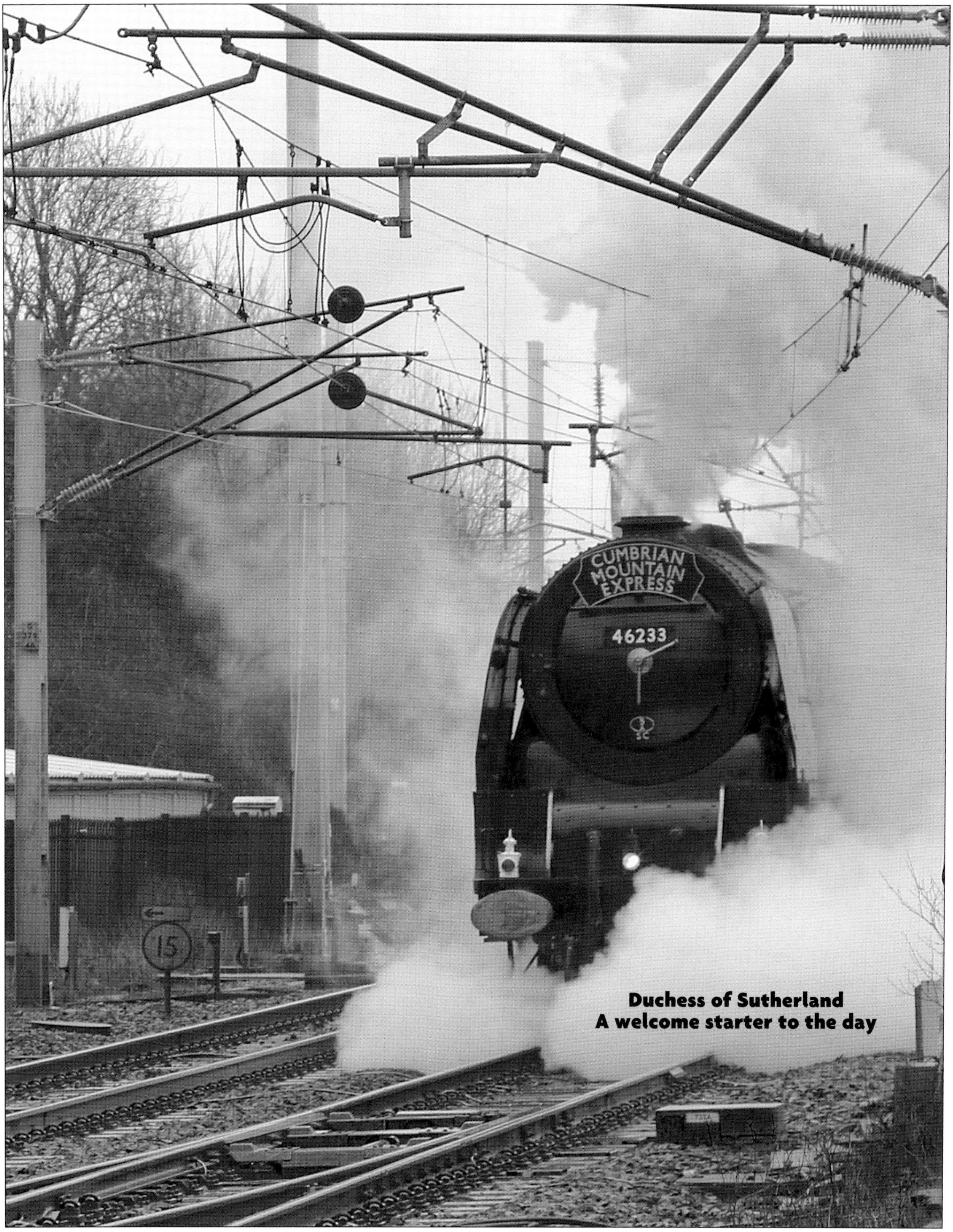

Duchess of Sutherland
A welcome starter to the day

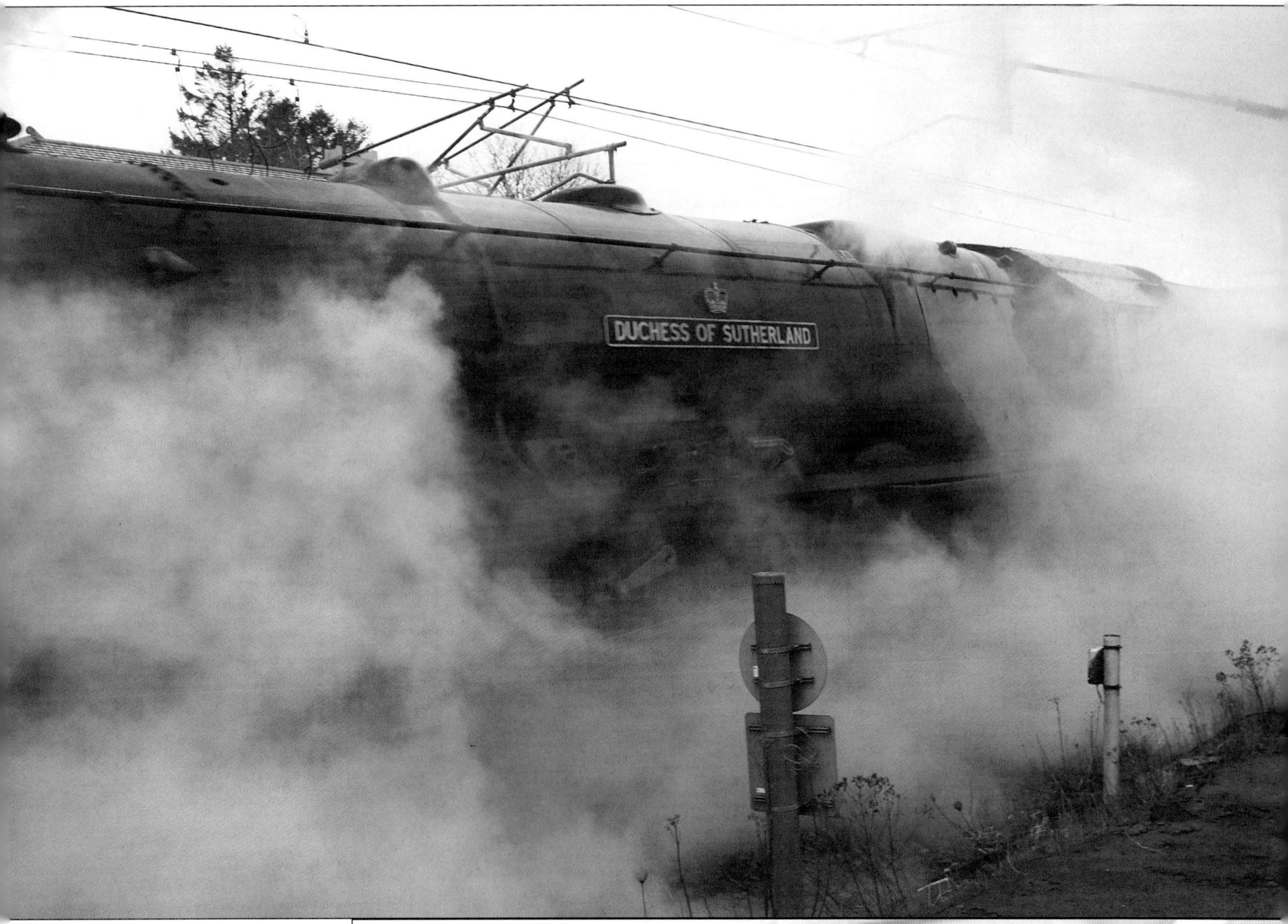

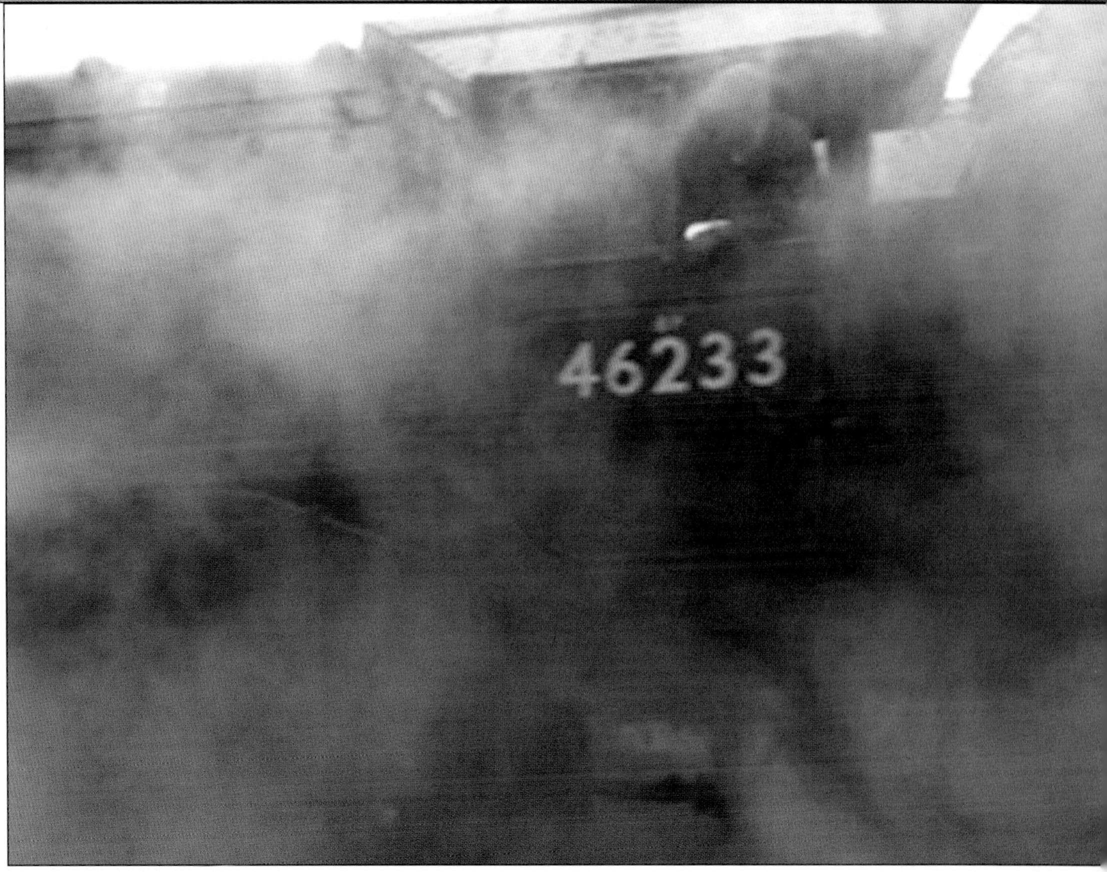

Duchess of Sutherland and the driver all steamed up!

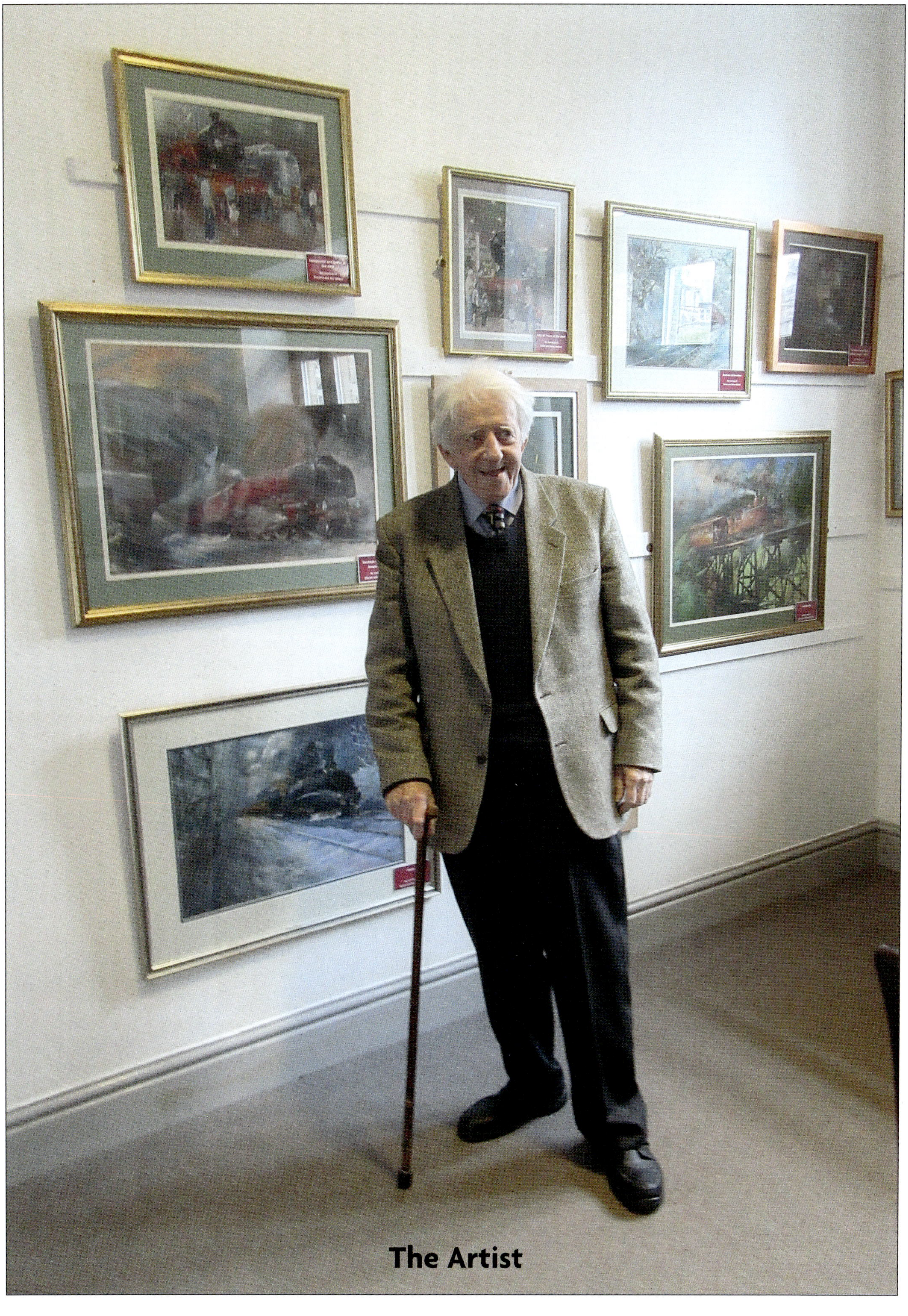

The Artist

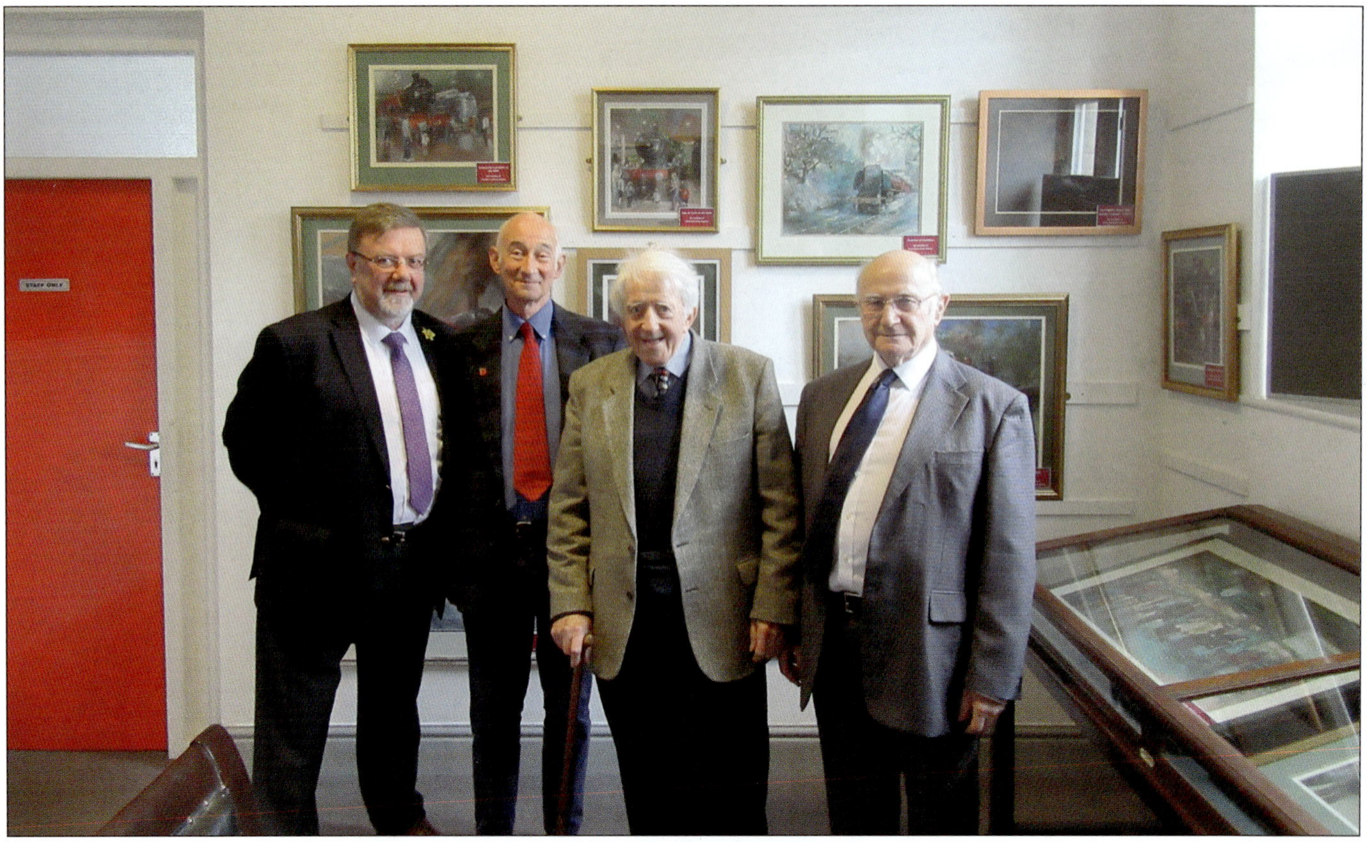

John Adams, Paul Atterbury, Roy Wilson, Brian Wilson (left to right)

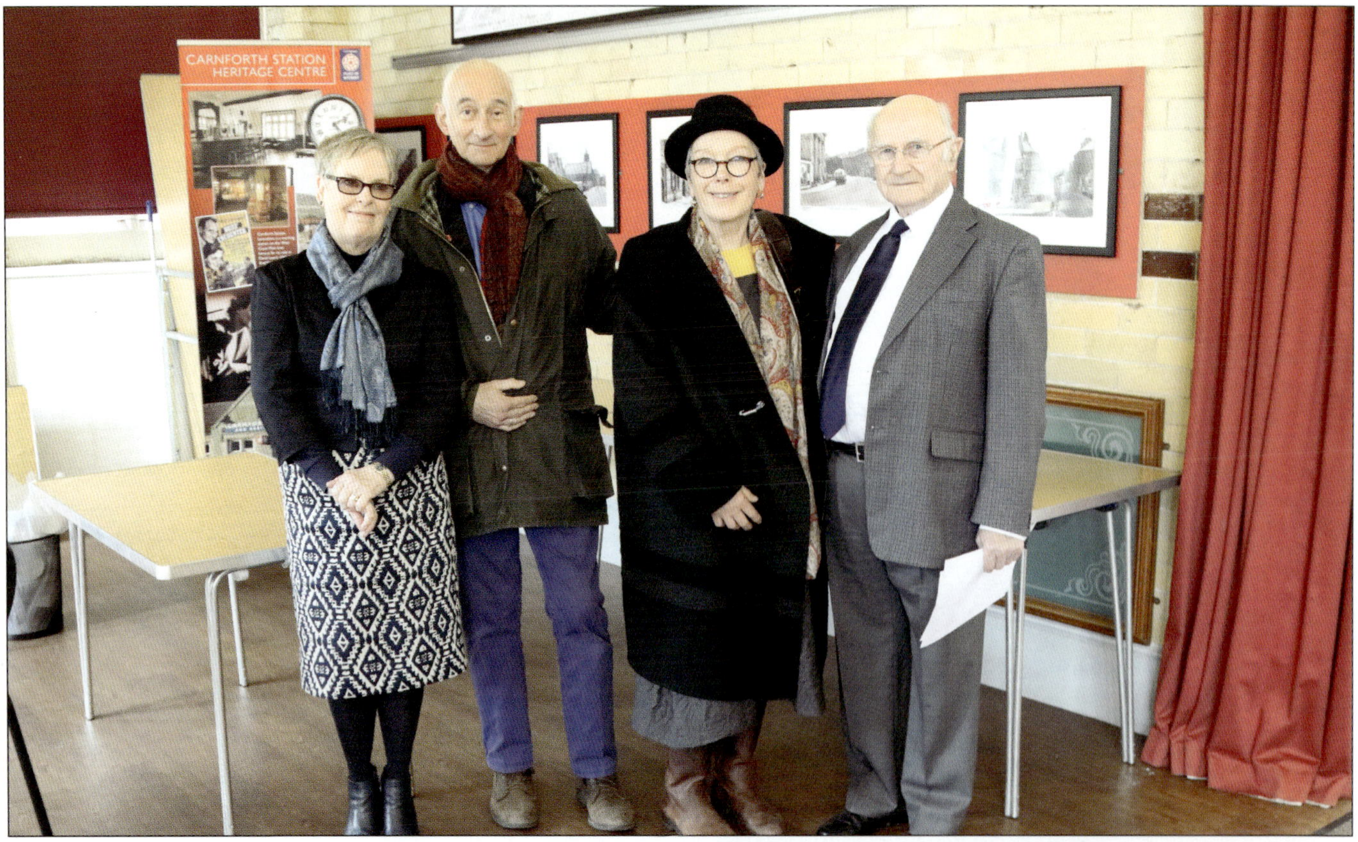

Sylvia Wilson, Paul Atterbury, Chrissie Atterbury, Brian Wilson (left to right)

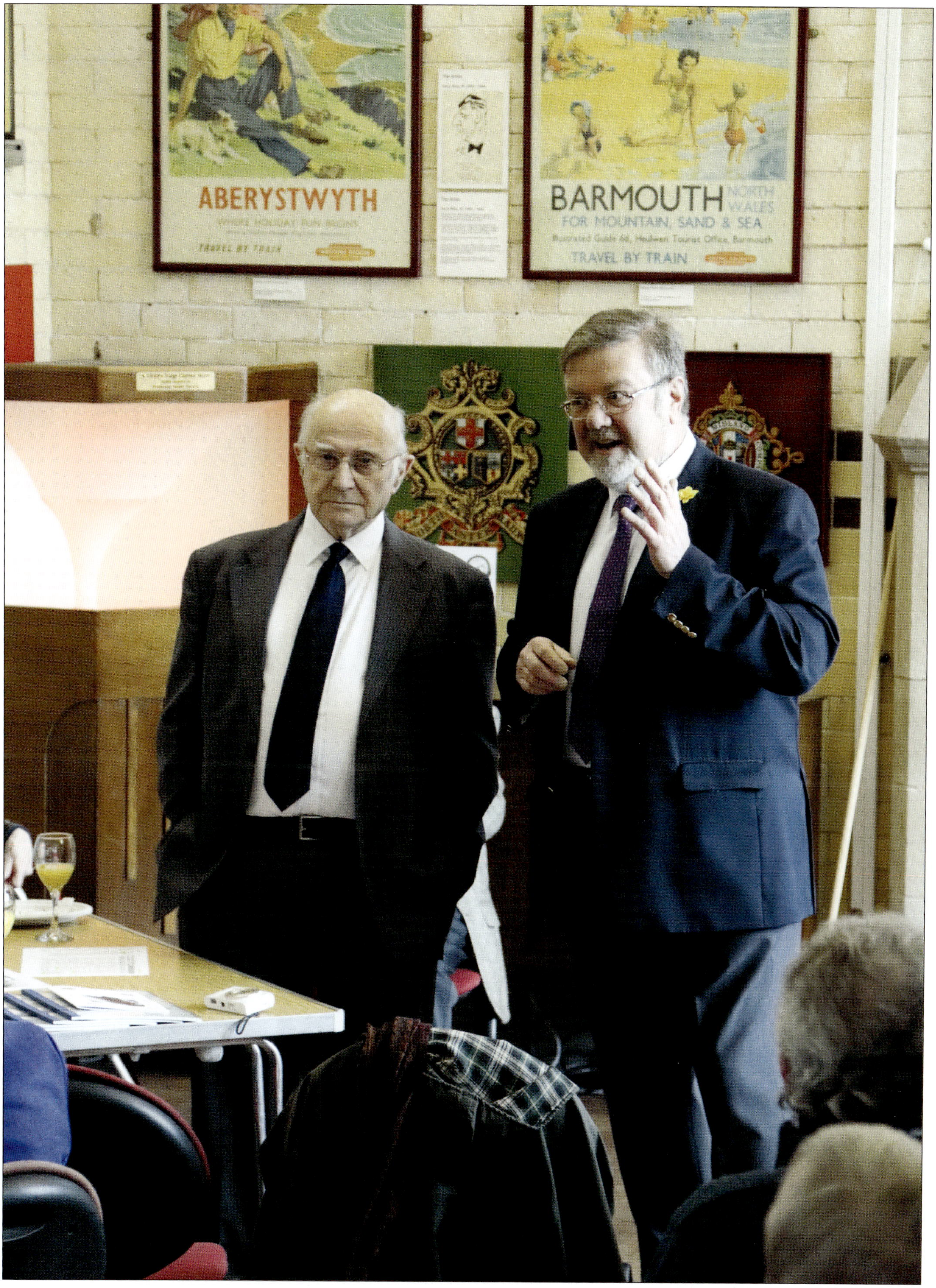

Introduction to The Heritage Centre by John Adams

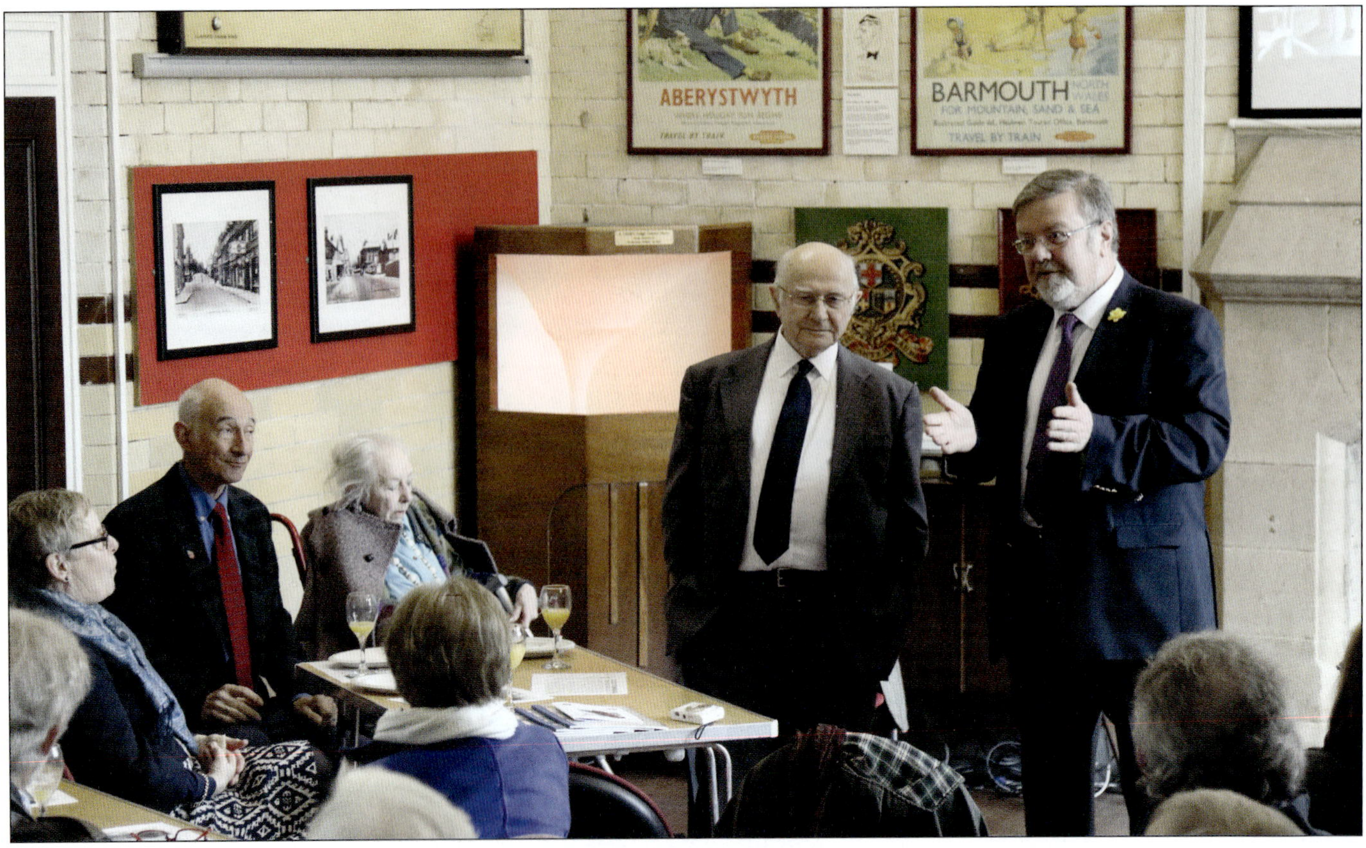
ABERYSTWYTH
TRAVEL BY TRAIN
BARMOUTH
FOR MOUNTAIN, SAND & SEA
TRAVEL BY TRAIN

The Welcome

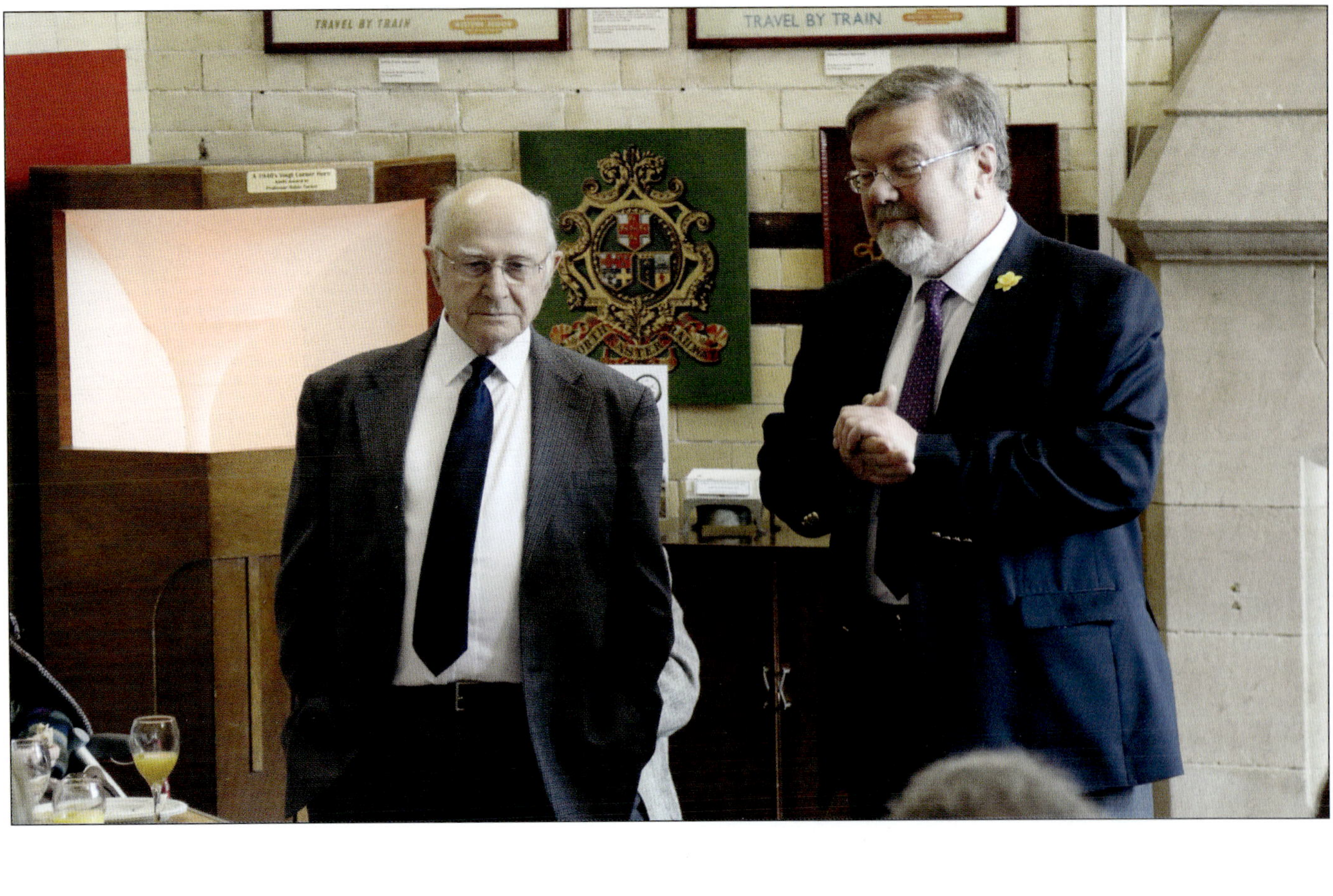
TRAVEL BY TRAIN
TRAVEL BY TRAIN

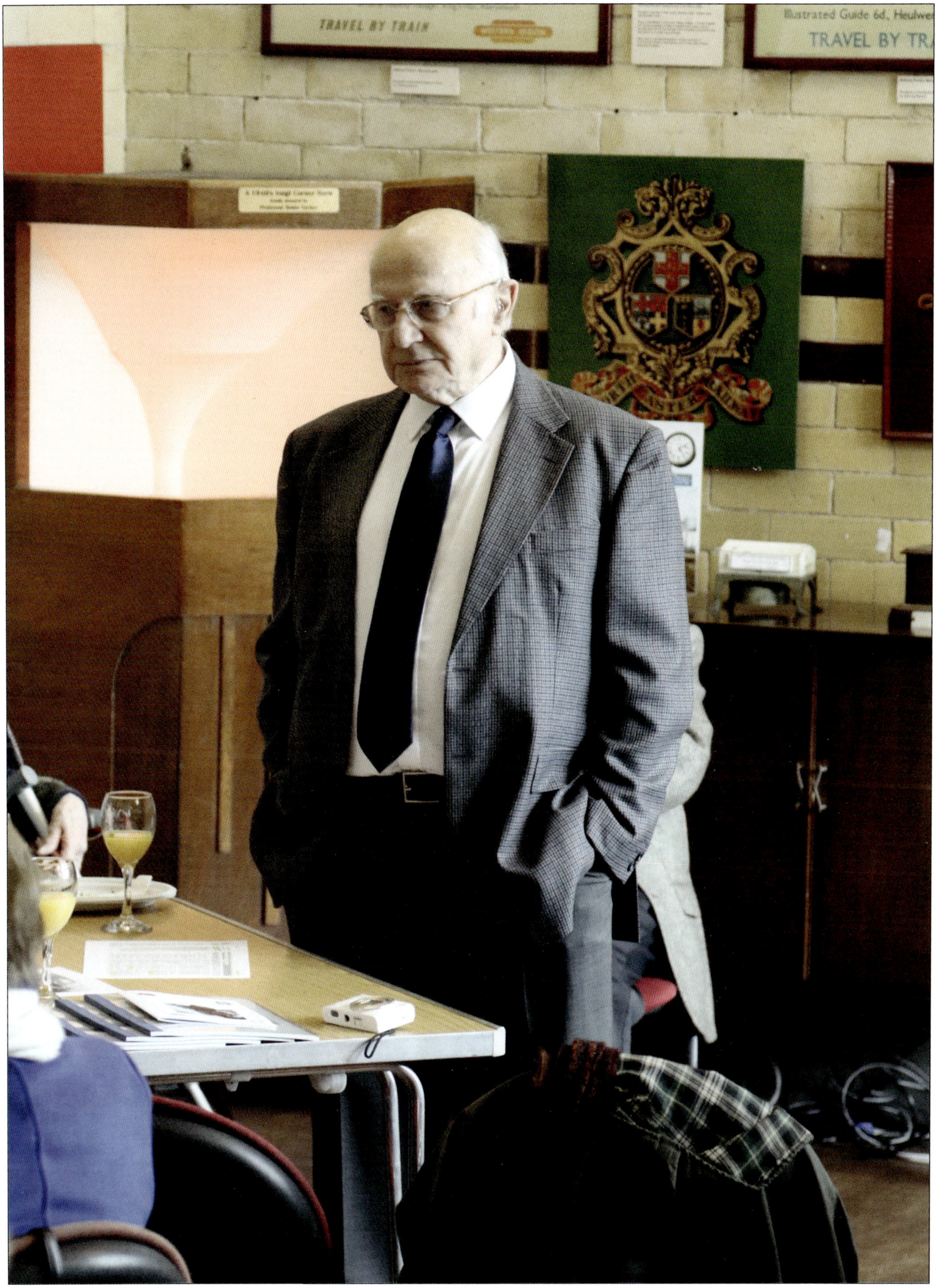

Thanks to all Contributors

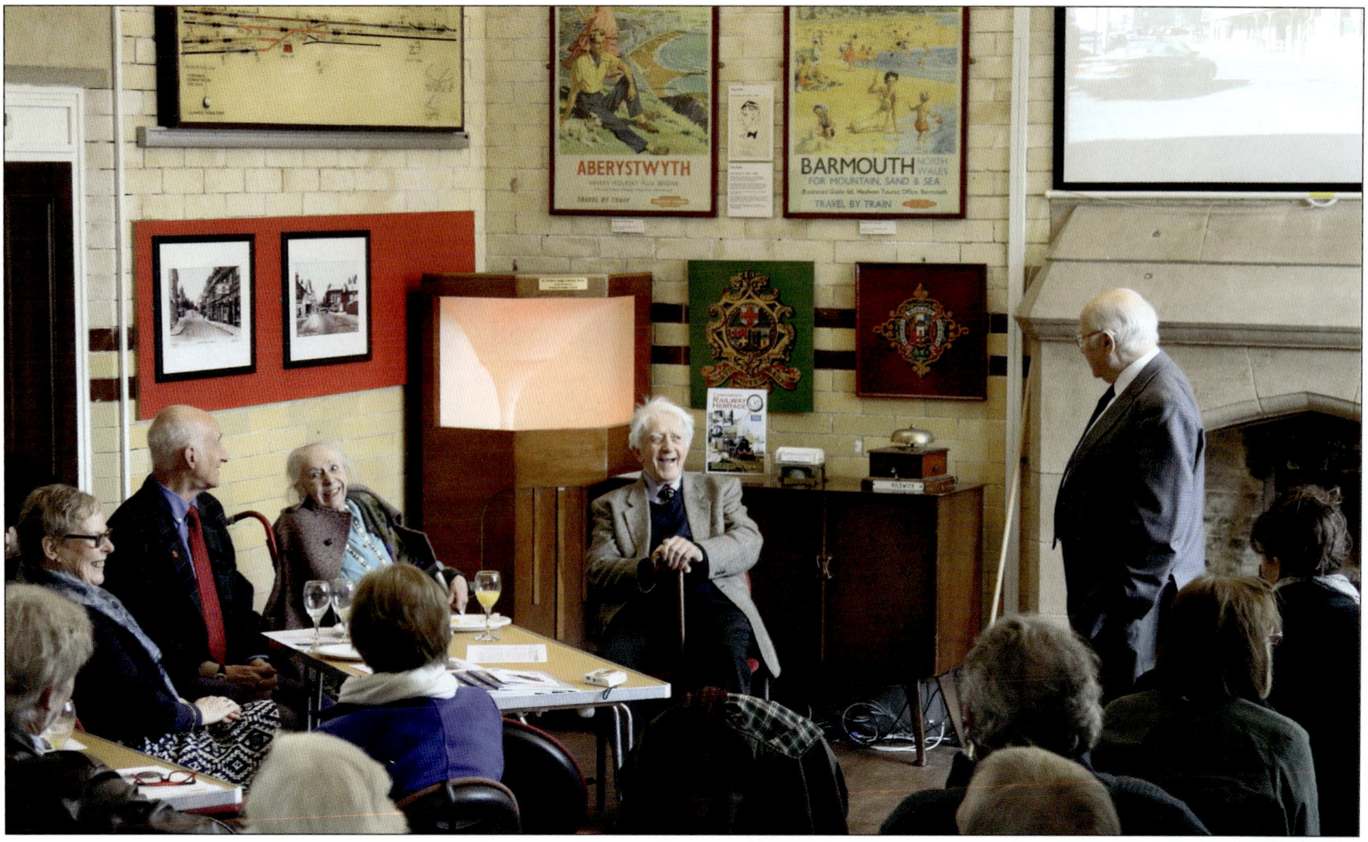

An Amusing Comment?

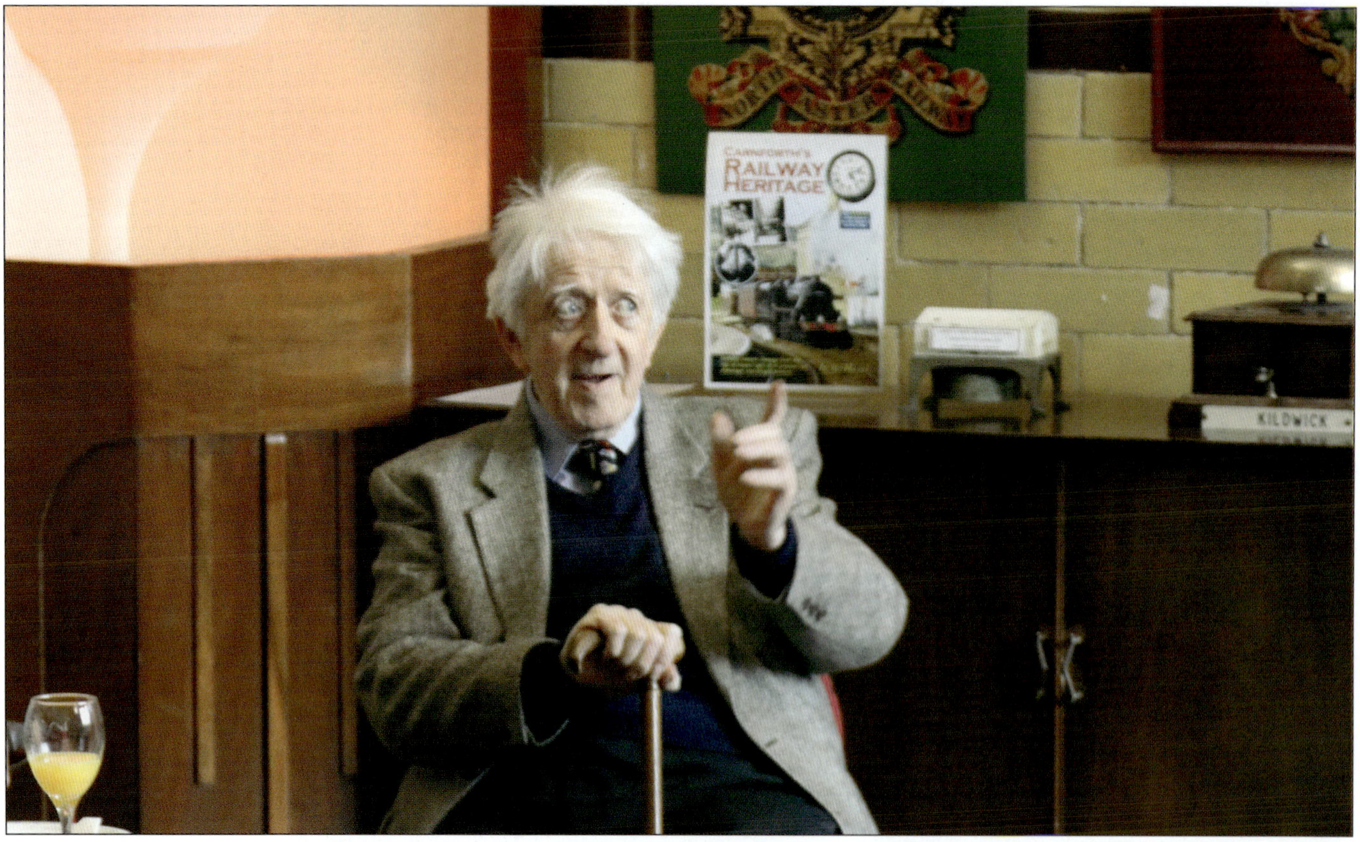

...and Reaction

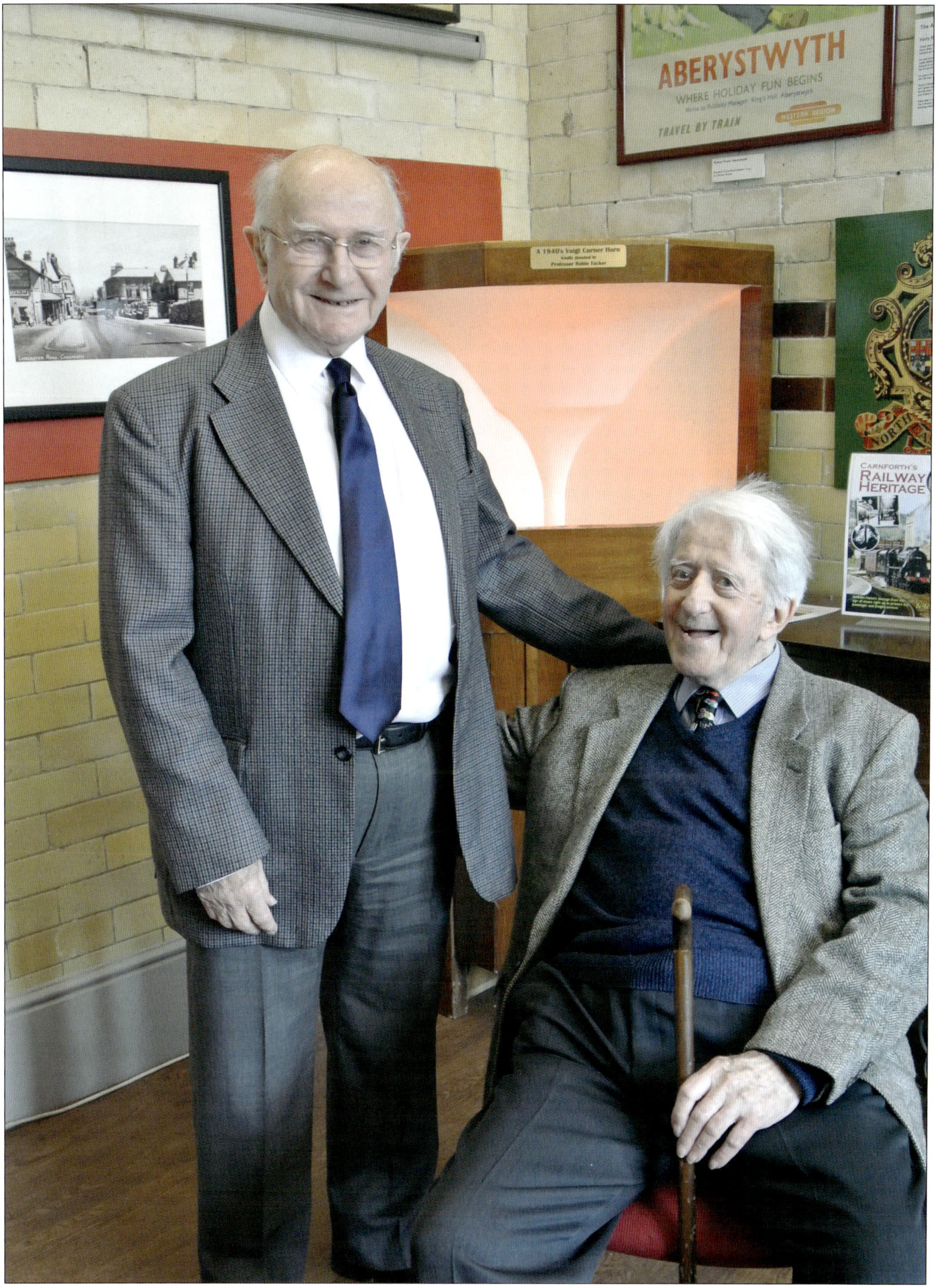

Still Friends

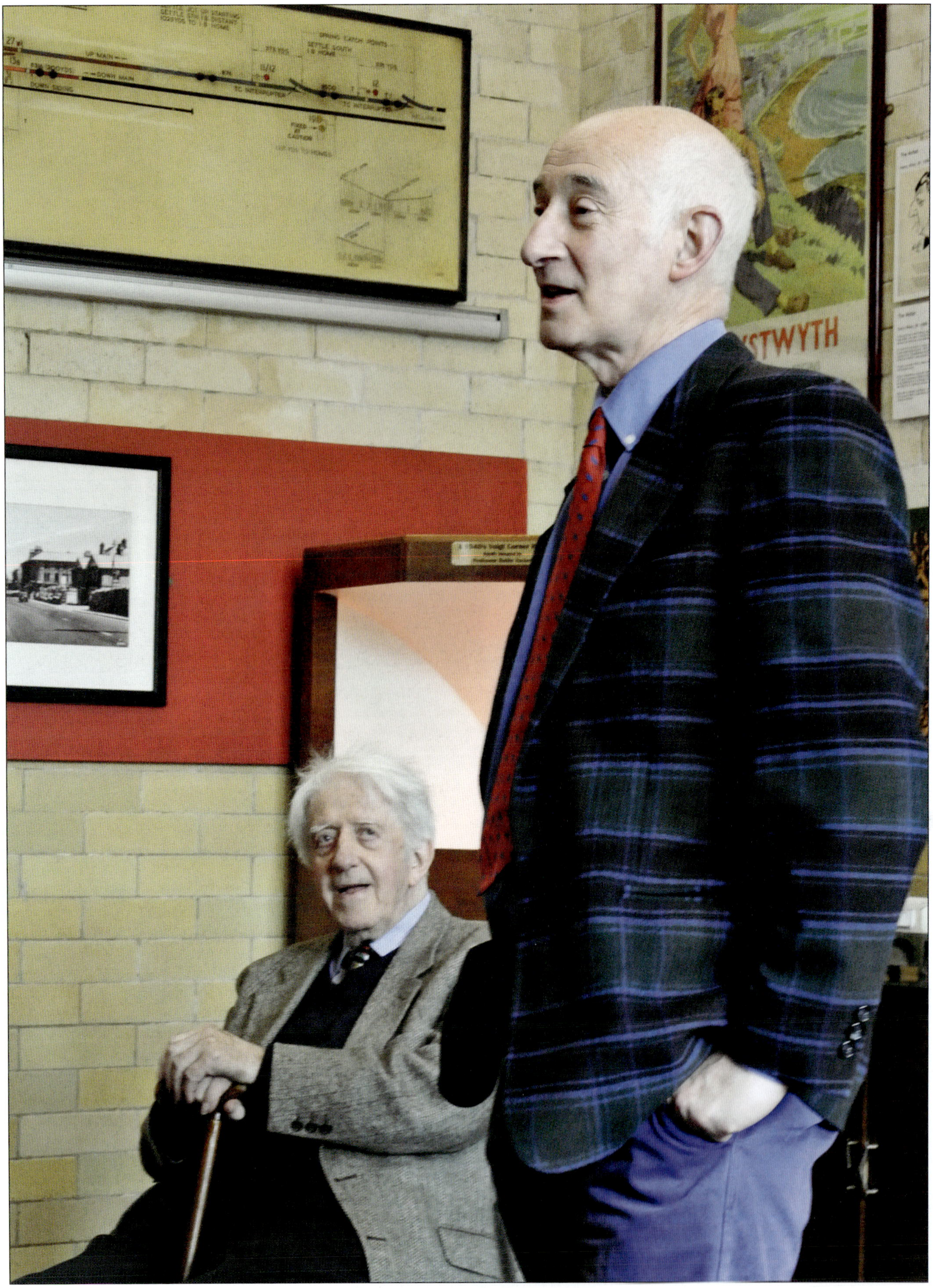

Opening Remarks

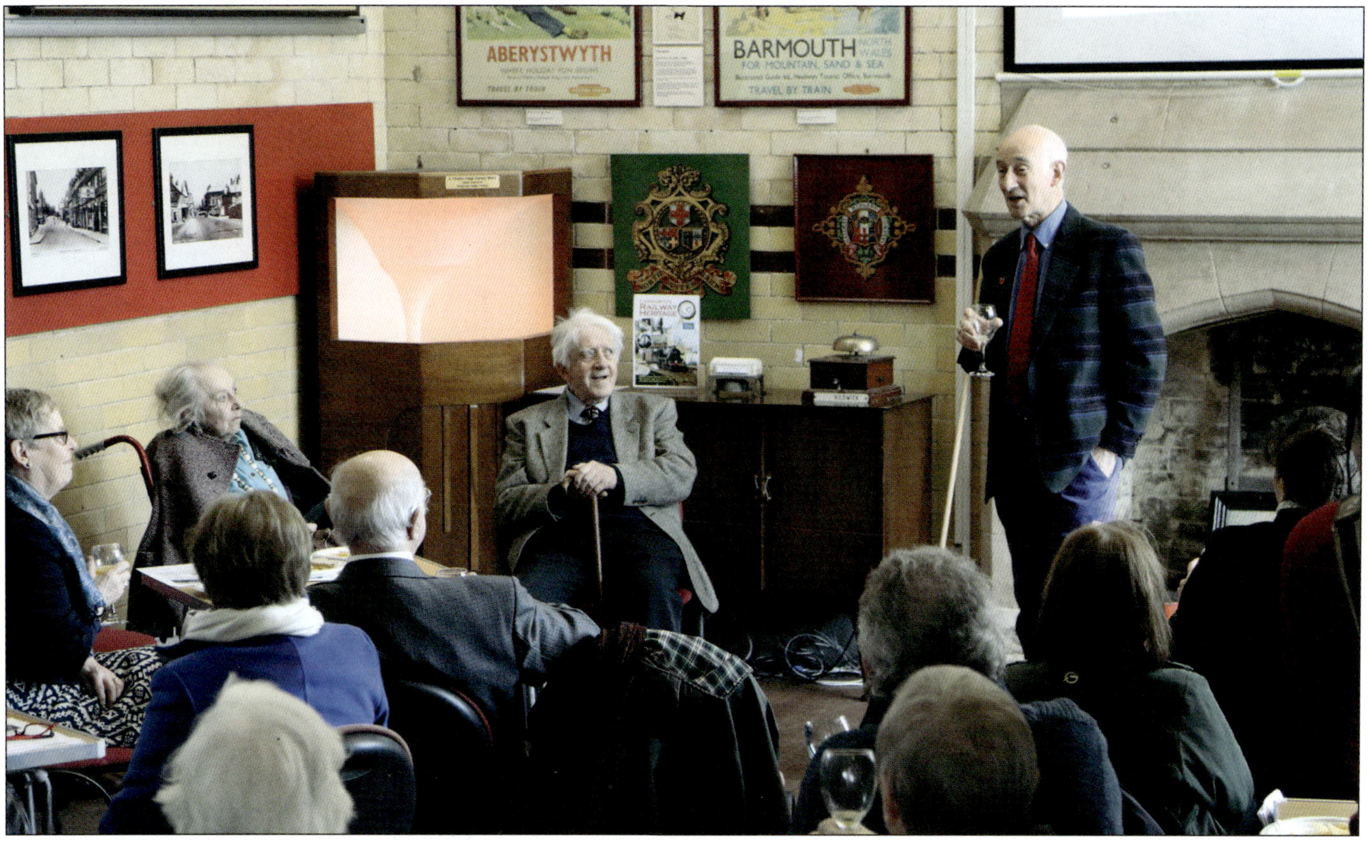
ABERYSTWYTH
BARMOUTH
FOR MOUNTAIN, SAND & SEA
TRAVEL BY TRAIN
RAILWAY HERITAGE

It's Open!

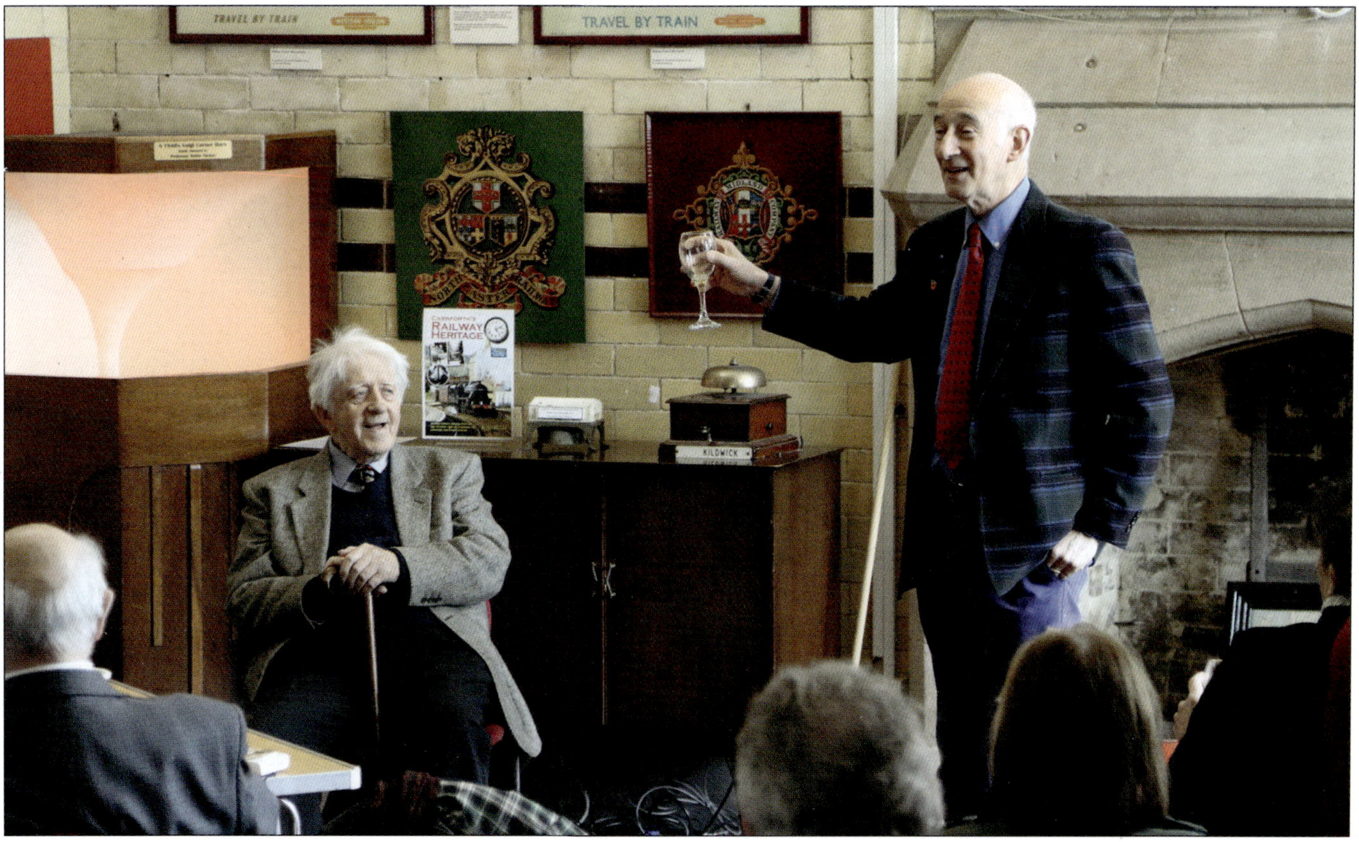
TRAVEL BY TRAIN
TRAVEL BY TRAIN
RAILWAY HERITAGE
KILDWICK

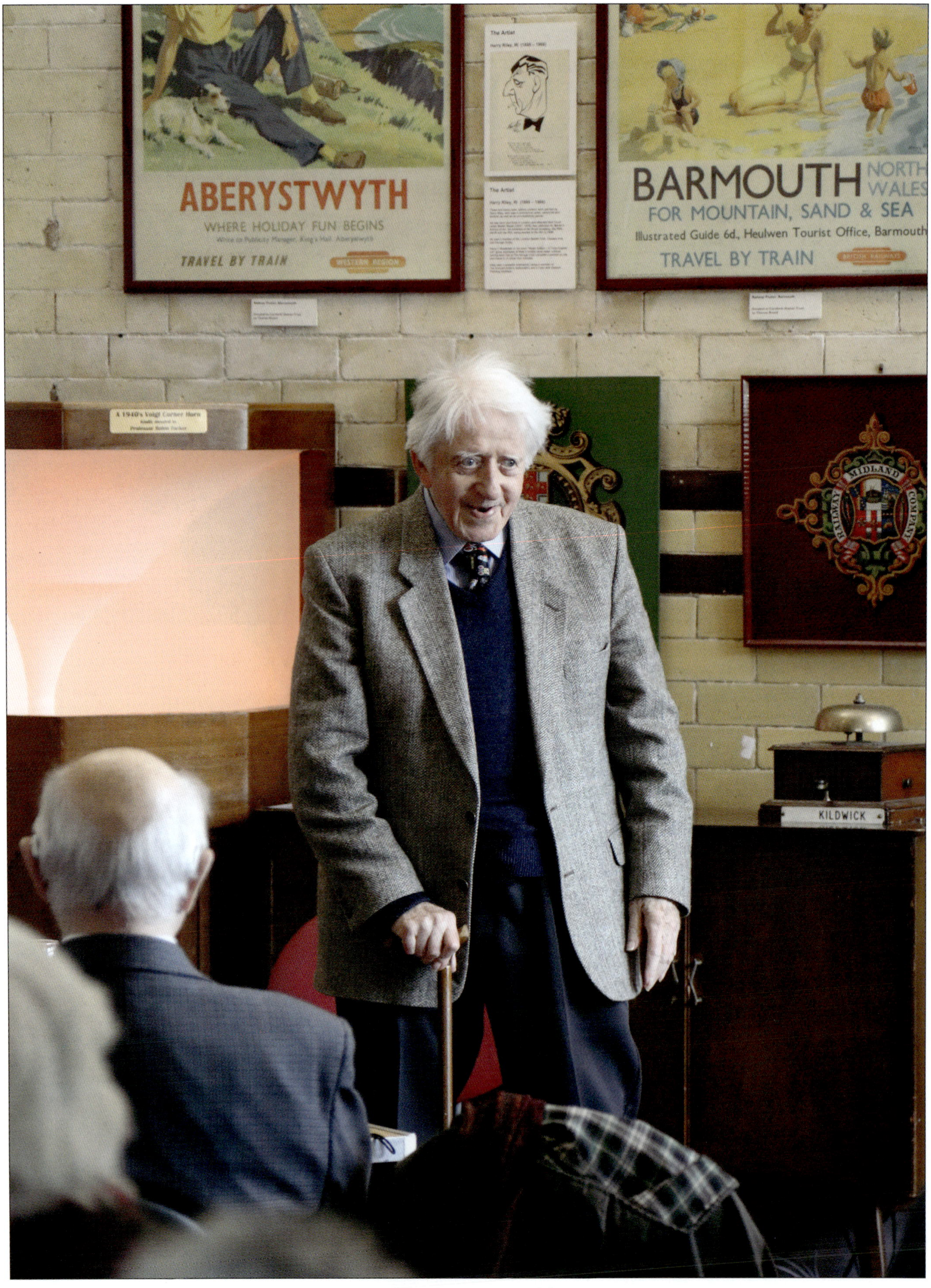

Thanks to All

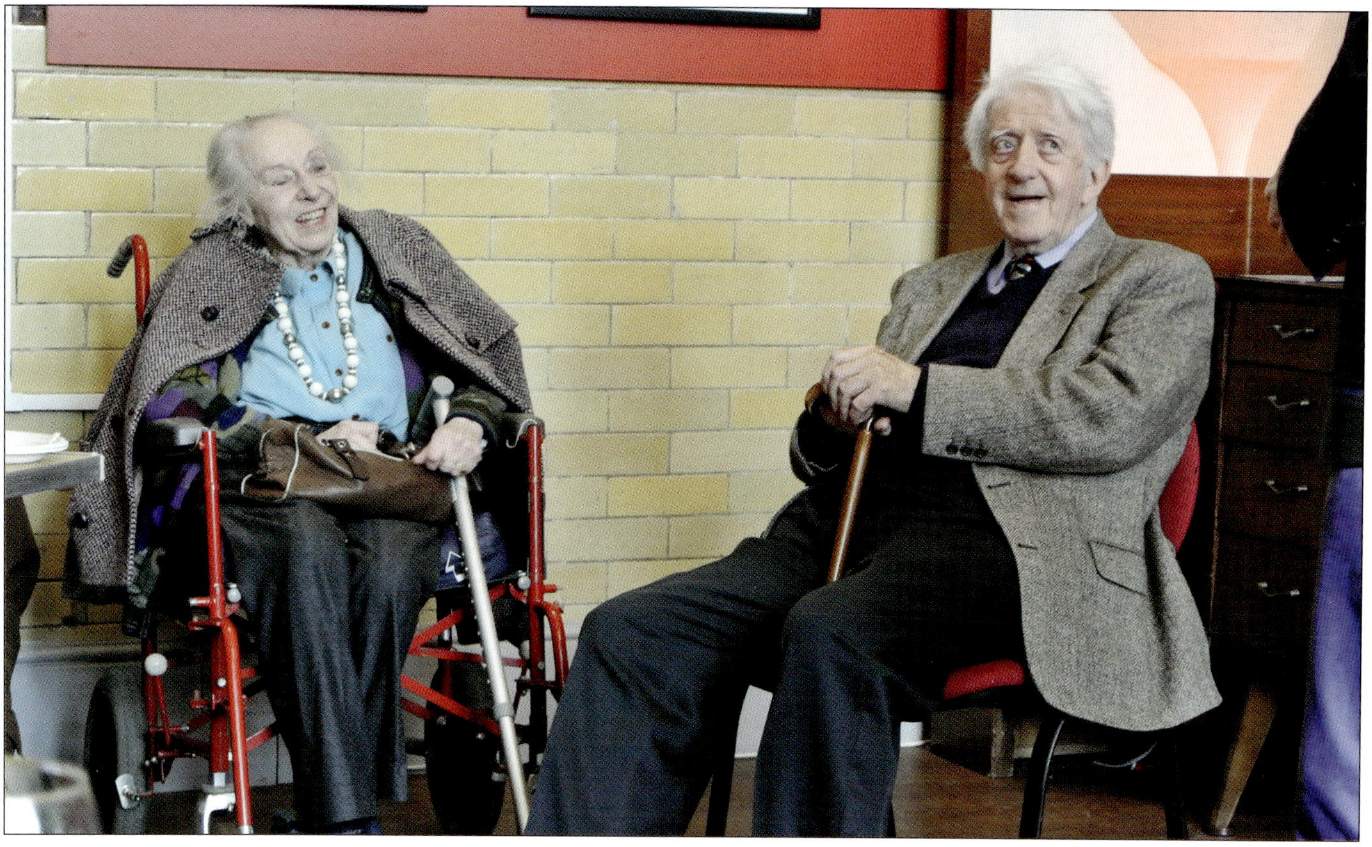

We Made It!
Dorothy and Roy Wilson

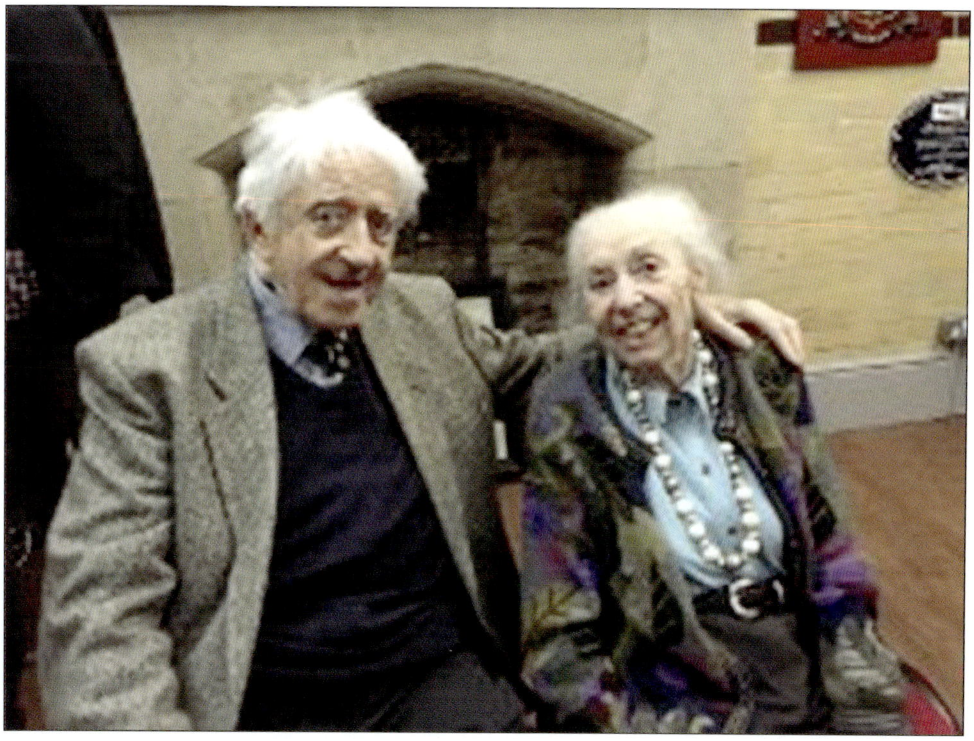

Acknowledgements

This book started out as a Christmas present for my brother Roy. As he was suffering from dementia by the time it was produced I did not expect him to read it. So I converted it to a PowerPoint presentation. This was a shortened version and I showed it to him on the television in his room at the care home.

He enjoyed the presentation, but he did not know that he was the artist. This reminded me that Roy's ability, as a railway artist, was also not well known and, certainly, not as well-known as he deserved to be, hence my desire to make his work available to a general market. I have received encouragement in this desire from a number of people. Not only from my family but from others, in particular The Friends of the National Railway Museum and The Guild of Railway Artists. I thank them all. I would like to express my thanks to Laurence Roche who wrote an appreciation of Roy in the book "Along Artistic Lines."

I would like to acknowledge the permission given by Aldon Fergusson of "The RAF Burtonwood Association" to publish the photographs related to the "Burtonwood Airbase" during the war. I am indebted to "Rail On-line" for permission to reproduce the photograph of "The Duchess steaming north" at Winwick Junction. I also wish to thank John Weston of the Bromsgrove Society for permission to include the cover for "The Bromsgrove Rousler" and the flier advertising the talk on William Creuze.

My thanks go to Alan Postlethwaite who accepted my proposal to produce this book and who pointed me in the direction of Trevor Preece and Judith Kirkham who have my thanks for doing an excellent job in progressing the design and production phases of the book. Alan also made the resources of Barrai Books available for the sales and distribution activity for which I am extremely grateful.

My thanks also go to Dr Paul Atterbury who produced the Foreword to the book and who also gave the opening remarks at Roy's last exhibition in 2016.

Finally I acknowledge the unending support I have had from my wife Sylvia for her proof reading and other helpful comments while I was working on the number of drafts. *Brian Wilson*

Postscript

Roy had started to show signs of Dementia towards the end of 2015.

He still recognised his wife, Dorothy and my family, but this knowledge gradually faded.

He had no family of his own.

This exhibition was the last occasion on which he remembered that he was the artist.

Towards the end he still knew who Dorothy, my wife Sylvia and I were, but he had lost the knowledge of the rest of my family.

For the last year he needed total care.

He was well looked after and highly regarded by the staff of the care home.

He died, peacefully, on the morning of February 4th 2019 in the company of some of the staff.

My family, who attended the opening of the exhibition, with Paul and Chrissie Atterbury.

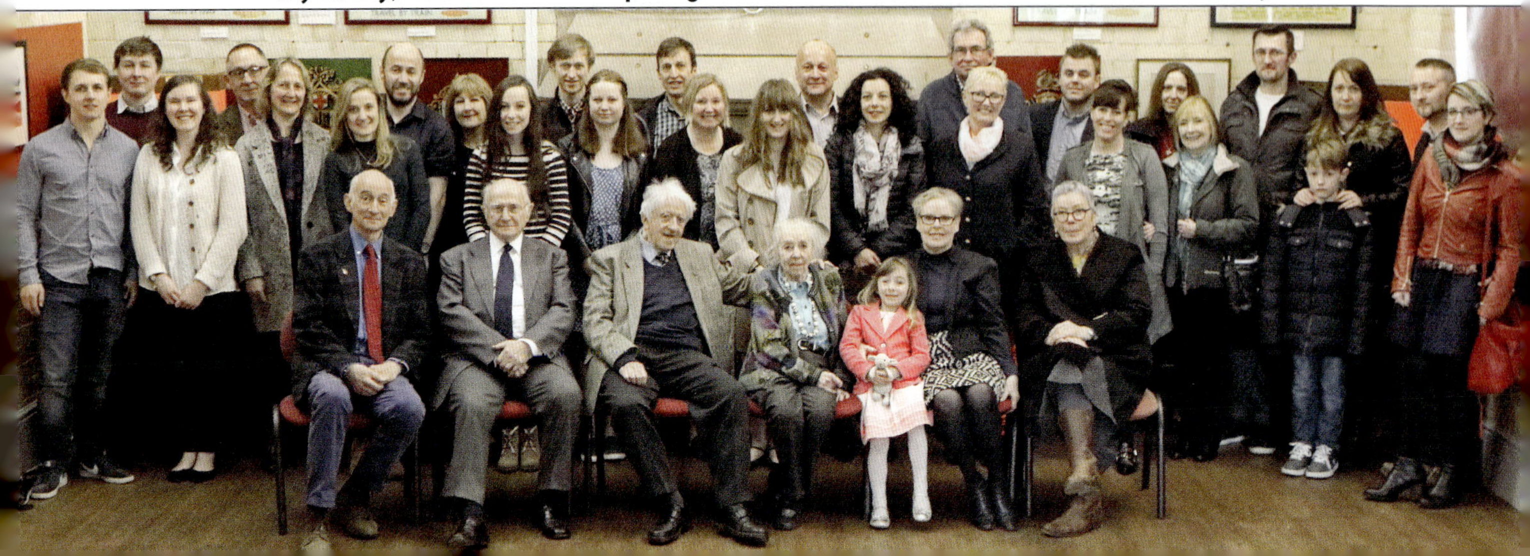